Oral Roberts

THE NEW TESTAMENT COMES ALIVE

A Personal New Testament Commentary

VOLUME ONE

MATTHEW, MARK, LUKE, JOHN

All Scripture quotations
are from the King James Version
of the Bible.

Printed by Parthenon Press
Nashville, Tenn.

BK 543

Introduction to the New Testament

Introduction to the New Testament

The Power of God's Word

The New Testament brings back great memories to me. When I was a child, my father read the Bible to me as I sat on his knee. I heard him preach the Bible. I grew up with the Bible.

But as a boy I left home, trying to run away from my family and from God. I didn't think I had a chance in life then. I had been born a stutterer. My parents, Ellis and Claudius Roberts, as loving as they were, had little education and very little money. I had big dreams. I wanted to be a lawyer. I wanted to be governor of Oklahoma someday. So I ran away, but I got tuberculosis and returned to my family a very sick youngster.

Mama and Papa read the Bible to me from time to time as I lay sick in bed for five months — and the power of God's Word began to take hold of my life again

I read the Bible hungrily during my conversion, healing, and call to the ministry. The words seemed to leap off the pages and God was in each of those words. I fell in love with the Bible. By the time I began the healing ministry in 1947, I had read the New Testament more than 100 times.

There was a special 30-day period in 1947 when God led me to read the four gospels and the book of Acts straight through while on my knees. Then I read them again and again with the rest of the New Testament until I had practically memorized them. I learned each event by memory, and I can tell you it marked my life as a Christian, a preacher, and an evangelist of the Word of God. My entire being is truly possessed by the Word of God.

As we share the living Word of God, I promise you through faith in His name that you will find faith in your heart. You will be closer to Christ, with a new and more intimate knowledge of Him. I predict that Christ will be the most real person in your life by the time we have read and studied the New Testament and you have meditated and prayed about it. You will be talking to Him where He really is — inside you, beside you, above you, beneath you, all around you, filling your whole world.

Spirit-Directed Writing

The Gospel of Matthew appears first in the New Testament although it was not written first. The Gospel of Mark and several other books, including most of Paul's writings, were written earlier. Matthew is placed first because of the sequence of events in the life of Jesus and because Matthew's genealogy or ancestry of our Lord is a perfect introduction.

Jesus wrote no books himself. The only time He wrote that we know about was when He stooped down and wrote in the sand with His finger. Those words are not recorded. It was left to others to write the books of the Bible, directed by the Spirit and under the inspiration of God himself.

You might ask, "Well, why didn't the Apostles and early Christians write more than they did? Why did they wait so long?"

Talking About Jesus

I think the reason they did not write any sooner than they did was that they expected Jesus to return any moment. They had witnessed or knew the story of His earthly life, the scene at the Cross, the dramatic event of the Resurrection of Jesus from the dead, and the outpouring of the Holy Spirit at the day of Pentecost. They did not write about it, they talked about it!

There were no books, no newspapers, no magazines, no television no popular press in those days. There was no public education and few people knew how to read. News traveled by word of mouth — and Jesus was news! They were talking about Jesus, telling His story, telling it out loud, retelling it over and over. There was reading of the older Scriptures in the Temple and in the synagogues, but what we know today as the New Testament was so new then that none of it had been written down.

In those days the Bible was not written or published for everyone to have a copy. It was written on papyrus and then cut into scrolls and laboriously copied by scribes from one generation to the next. A copy was used in the synagogue or in some functions of the Temple, to be read aloud and heard and then passed on to others to be memorized.

Finally, within the lifetimes of the early Christians and particularly of the Apostles, they realized the necessity to have a written, carefully documented, and systematically recorded life of our Lord Jesus Christ.

Table of Contents

The Gospel according to Matthew

The Gospel according to Matthew

There are four gospels: Matthew, Mark, Luke and John. Matthew wrote his gospel between A.D. 65 and A.D. 70. We believe it was before the destruction of Jerusalem and the Jewish Temple by the Roman general Titus. We are going to discuss Matthew and his remarkable ability to write the way he did, but first let us take a brief look at all the gospel writers and their work.

John stands alone. The gospel of John is concerned primarily with the last five months of Jesus' life. It deals more with His passion, His death, His resurrection, and the deep, eternal truths of what Jesus taught.

Matthew, Mark, and Luke are quite different from John. They are even called the "Synoptic Gospels" or the "three who saw the same."

They were covering generally the same events, but each from a different viewpoint. There is a similarity in Matthew, Mark, and Luke, and yet they are different. For example, Matthew writes as a Jew to Jews to prove that Jesus is the Messiah. He gives Jews concrete evidence upon which to base their faith to receive Jesus as the Messiah. Mark writes to the Roman world — the world of Gentiles who were concerned about power. So he opens his gospel with Jesus' healing, casting out demons, setting the people free. Mark's gospel is not as long as Matthew's or Luke's; however, it was written first. It is a book that both Matthew and Luke used to advantage when they wrote their gospels. Luke was interested more in the human side of Jesus than were the others because he was a doctor. He wanted to know certain events about the baby, the child, the mother. Luke gives the human side of Jesus. Matthew is writing primarily to the Jews, Mark to the Romans, Luke to the world, in the same way that John was writing to the world.

I want to point out that of these three, Matthew, Mark, and Luke, only Matthew knew Jesus personally. Mark was to be converted later, probably after the day of Pentecost. Luke probably was brought to the Lord by the Apostle Paul. Matthew alone, of the three, actually lived with Jesus and the Apostles.

As a young man, Mark may have seen Jesus but it was later that Mark was led to Christ. At first Mark traveled with his Uncle Barnabas and Paul. Later he traveled with Peter. So in one way, Mark was greatly affected by Peter, and his gospel reads somewhat like the writing of Peter.

Luke did not know Jesus personally as a human being. He arrived later as a practicing Greek physician who probably was led to Christ by Paul. At least we know that he became an important member of his family and then came back to trace the human side of Jesus in his gospel.

Prophecy Fulfilled

Matthew really knew Jesus on a day-by-day, minute-by-minute, event-by-event basis. He also knew the Bible; 16 times he says, "This was to fulfill what the Lord had written by the Prophets." He started with Jesus' Hebrew ancestry.

In this first chapter I discuss, there are 42 "begats." We have heard about the begats: so-and-so begat so-and-so. We have wondered, why are all these begats in there? Many years ago I was just wearied by it. I thought they were so dull. But there is something exciting about these begats. Matthew begins with them, laying the solid foundation for the entire faith of Jesus Christ. He wanted Jesus to be seen in direct connection with the old Hebrew tradition. Matthew traces Jesus to His original Hebrew history and tradition. But while Matthew starts with Jesus' ancestry, he ends his book in Chapter 28 with the Great Commission. He starts with the Jews and he ends with the world. He quotes Jesus as saying, "Go ye into all the world and preach the Gospel to every creature." He begins in a very narrow sense and then he opens up and takes in the whole world.

Matthew was an accountant. His job was collecting taxes. He was bitterly hated for this, because he was a Jew who had hired out to Roman overlords to collect their taxes from his Jewish people. He was thought of as a traitor. He had this job for one reason: he was a well-trained man. His mind was orderly and he had a business knowledge of shorthand to fully record Jesus' sayings and discourses. He had a mind for figures, and he tells us what Jesus says about money.

Matthew begins by arranging things in figures: 3's, 7's, 14's. He shows three messages to Joseph, three denials by Peter, three questions by Pilate, seven parables of the kingdom. In the genealogy of Jesus he arranges three groups of ancestors in 14's — 42 names in all. Yet, in the Hebrew, there are no figures as we use them, such as 1, 2, 3, and so forth. Why? In Hebrew, when figures are necessary, the letters of the alphabet stand for the figures. Also, in the English alphabet, we use vowels and consonants. In Hebrew there are no written vowels. Our vowels are A, E, I, O, U. There are no written vowels in the Hebrew language. For example, we spell the name of David D-A-V-I-D, David, but they use the letters D-W-D to stand for David. Each letter is taken as a figure and it adds up to 14. In another example, the D's stand for four and the W for six so it is 14 in all. That corresponds with his use of 14's in this first chapter, as he traces the genealogy of our Lord Jesus Christ.

You may wonder what this has to do with the New Testament and what you and I are to know about it. It is important because the Jewish people are very precise. God dealt with them in that manner. If you have read the Old Testament you know that. Therefore, in choosing a person to bring these things together, He chose Matthew so that through his orderly mind he could tell about the genealogy of Jesus in a way that the Jewish mind could accept. Without accepting His reality they could not have faith to believe He was the Son of God. Believe me, the Bible is not a scattered collection of sayings written at random by both somebodies and nobodies. The Bible is a carefully documented book, the most carefully documented book of all because it is God, inspiring people to speak by the Holy Spirit as He uses their abilities and talents to say precisely what God wants us to know about Him.

Christ's Ancestry Glorified

Above all, by knowing Jesus and seeing Jesus in the Bible, we can see what the Father is like and can know God better today.

The Messiah was expected by the people. They did not know when He would come, but they knew he would be the seed of David. This is why the genealogy traced to David and beyond was absolutely all-important to the Jewish mind. That was the reason for the 14's and the connection with David and Abraham.

Joseph was the foster father of Jesus, but it is he whom Matthew traced to David. Mary is placed at the end of these 42 names. In Luke, chapter three, her genealogy is traced to David because she also was of the seed of David. Then why did Matthew trace Jesus back through Joseph who was only his foster father? Because the royal line came through the male. The transmission of the throne rights from David to Jesus came through the male. That was a tracing of the royal line, but it was not the bloodline. Mary was placed at the end of the 42 names because of the bloodline. She also was traced to David. It was in her body that the Holy Spirit implanted that divine seed. It was her body that grew the physical body of the Lord Jesus Christ. In Joseph and Mary are both the royal line and the bloodline.

It is interesting five of the 42 are women: Tamar, Rahab, Bathsheba, Ruth, and finally Mary. Why do you suppose God would take three women such as Tamar, Rahab, and Bathsheba and list them as ancestresses of the human side of Jesus? Tamar was a seducer. Rahab had been a harlot. Bathsheba had committed adultery with David. Well, have you ever really thought about the mercy of God?

Rahab was a harlot in Jericho — a pivotal city. Joshua, the successor of Moses, sent two spies to find the best entrance to the Promised Land. Rahab understood that these two spies were of God and she began to believe God. She helped them and they remembered her when she put the scarlet thread out the window for them to see. When Israel overran the city, they rescued Rahab. She became an ancestress of our Lord Jesus Christ.

Bathsheba was the wife of Uriah the Hittite whom David had killed. Through David's confession of his sin, he was enabled to marry Bathsheba who gave him Solomon. You must understand these three women in the light of the mercy of God.

Barriers Broken!

Mary was the Virgin Mother who conceived Jesus, not by the seed of man but by the Holy Spirit having implanted the divine seed in her body. She speaks of obedience and faith.

These women illustrate a new relationship between men and women through Jesus Christ. Their social status was far below that of men in pre-Christian cultures. Jewish men traditionally prayed such prayers as, "I thank God he has not made me a Gentile, a woman, or a slave." Such male chauvinism degraded women as human beings. Jesus changed that. He wiped out the old contempt and elevated women to a status equal with men before God.

The different backgrounds of the women in Jesus' earthly genealogy show again that He broke down the barrier between saint and sinner so that both could come before God. There is a list of generations given by God in Genesis, but the list at the opening of the New Testament in Matthew is a roll call of ancestors of our Lord Jesus Christ. Matthew is saying, "This is who Jesus is. This is where He came from," because he knew the importance of ancestry to Jews.

The fourth woman was Ruth, a Moabite — Gentiles who hated the

Jews so much that God said that even to the 10th generation they would not be allowed to worship in the Temple. We need to know and understand that through Ruth, there was an infusion of Gentile blood into the bloodline of Jesus Christ himself. It is interesting that Ruth became the great-grandmother of David. Rahab was the great-great grandmother of David on the male side. All this certainly speaks of the grace of God for those who felt so unworthy, who were outside the Jewish people.

The Jews believed in purity of lineage. Without it, a person lost the right to be called a Jew or to be a member of the chosen people of God. There was to be no pollution of pedigree. Matthew knew the Jews were taught to memorize the genealogies of their ancestors, so in giving this genealogy, he was careful to point out Jesus' ancestors, name by name in three groups of 14, so that they could easily be memorized. Jews could know that there was a preciseness that God used in bringing forth His Son as the Messiah.

The Jews still place great emphasis upon genealogy. During World War II in the Holocaust, the Nazis would come into their synagogues, seize the genealogies, and destroy them. That is one of the haunting things about the Holocaust to the Jewish people to this very hour.

Jesus Knew His Origin

The opening of Matthew with Jesus' genealogy is great, because we all want to know who we are, where we came from, and where we are going. Matthew could list these "begats" because Jesus knew them. He knew who He was. He knew where He came from. He knew who His ancestors were, and Matthew knew that. He knew that was the most important thing in the world to use to start his book.

Whether we can trace our physical ancestry back hundreds or thousands of years or not, we can certainly know where we come from in the Lord. You are ready now to understand Matthew as you read. Remember that each name traces the ancestry of our Lord Jesus Christ, without whom we have no Redeemer. It is that important.

Matthew 1:1-17

> The book of the generation of Jesus Christ, the son of David, the son of Abraham. Abraham begat Isaac; and Isaac begat Jacob; and Jacob begat Judas and his brethren; and Judas begat Phares and Zara of Thamar; and Phares begat Esrom, and Esrom begat Aram; and Aram begat Aminadab; and Aminadab begat Naasson; and Naasson begat Salmon; And Salmon begat Booz of Rachab; and Booz begat Obed of Ruth; and Obed begat Jesse; and Jesse begat David the king; and David

the king begat Solomon of her that had been the wife of Urias; and Solomon begat Roboam; and Roboam begat Abia; and Abia begat Asa; and Asa begat Josaphat; and Josaphat begat Joram; and Joram begat Ozias; and Ozias begat Joatham; and Joatham begat Achaz; and Achaz begat Ezekias; and Ezekias begat Manasses; and Manasses begat Amon; and Amon begat Josias; and Josias begat Jechonias and his brethren, about the time they were carried away to Babylon: and after they were brought to Babylon, Jechonias begat Salathiel; and Salathiel begat Zorobabel; and Zorobabel begat Abiud; and Abiud begat Eliakim; and Eliakim begat Azor; and Azor begat Sadoc; and Sadoc begat Achim; and Achim begat Eliud; and Eliud begat Eleazar; and Eleazar begat Matthan; and Matthan begat Jacob; and Jacob begat Joseph the husband of Mary, of whom was born Jesus, who is called Christ.

So all the generations from Abraham to David are fourteen generations; and from David until the carrying away into Babylon are fourteen generations; and from the carrying away into Babylon unto Christ are fourteen generations.

God Has a Plan

The first of the three "fourteen generations" began with Abraham, the man who had the faith to believe that God was the most high God, possessor of heaven and earth and deliverer from all of our enemies. Abraham began to give tithes to the Lord. By his faith a promised son was born, Isaac. And then Isaac brought Jacob into the world and Jacob gave birth to the twelve sons of Jacob or Israel, called the Patriarchs. And from them came Israel.

And these first fourteen generations showed that God had a plan for a people, a destiny for them. Through those first fourteen generations God's plan came into fruition. He brought them into the land that he had promised Abraham, established them, and finally raised up David to be the King — the greatest king that Israel ever had. David united the people and ordered the building of the first temple. It was the high moment when the destiny of God's people was at a climax and the light of God was going to the ends of the earth.

God has a plan for your life and my life — a destiny for each of us and for all of us as a group. We can come to the climax of all our hopes and dreams in obedience to God as we believe and know that God is most high, that He is the source and possessor of all things. He is the deliverer of our lives from every destructive force and His power enables us to climb the highest mountain and stand there side by side with God and look into infinity and see that our destiny is fulfilled.

The second set of the fourteen generations ended with the captivity of these people. Nebuchadnezzar, the world dictator, came out of Babylon, tore down the walls of Jerusalem, destroyed the temple, and took into captivity the brightest of the people of Israel. They were taken to Babylon, captives to a heathen king because they had sinned. In disobedience of God they had walked away from God's plan and destiny for their lives. They had turned their backs upon what King David had done to unite the people and to send the light of Jehovah to the nations of the world.

The Seriousness of Sin

People don't talk about sin much anymore. The late Dr. Carl Menninger wrote a book, *Whatever Became of Sin?* This great psychiatrist reminded the world that sin is more than an aberration; it is a direct, knowing disobedience of God. It is a breaking of His covenants, a departure from His ways, and until we face up to sin in our lives and to ourselves as a people, sin is going to bring us into a captivity that will thrust us to the brink of destruction.

Israel was taken into captivity and during that awful period only a handful — a remnant — was able to hold on to their faith in God. We owe that remnant a lot.

The Hebrew people went away from the plan and purpose of God. In the third set of the fourteen generations they returned to Jerusalem and rebuilt it and the temple. They reestablished their worship, but they were never the same again because they never repented. A minority led the way back to God but the mass of the people never repented and it caused a great confusion. For those fourteen generations one word characterized them: confusion. Gone was the plan, gone was the purpose, gone was the destiny, and God was almost like a myth.

They began to rob God of tithes and offerings, to forsake His ways. He had said, "Return unto me and I will return unto you . . . bring you all the tithes and offerings into the storehouse and I will open the windows of heaven and pour you out a blessing where there is not room enough to contain it. And I will rebuke the devourer for your sake." Oh, the Jewish people knew the devourers! They knew they had shut up the windows of heaven because of their unrepented sin. Because the windows of heaven were closed upon the people of God, except for that remnant, and because they had robbed God in their giving, the devourers were eating them up and God said, "I will rebuke the devourers if you will only do what I tell you. If you will open your hearts, and begin giving of your love, and your finances, and your lives again."

During those fourteen generations, Malachi, the last prophet in the Old Testament, is heard. He ends it in chapter 4, verse 6, warning them to repent and return to God lest God smite the earth with a curse.

The Old Testament ended with the threat of a curse but when the fourteen generations were over, Jesus Christ was born with the promise of a blessing. "Ye shall call his name Jesus for he shall save his people from their sins."

When Jesus was born the plan was reestablished, the purpose was restated, and the destiny of a people was brought forth again. There was a flood of light and understanding through Jesus Christ who came into the world so that even you and I, all these years later, can know Him as our personal Savior, know His plan and purpose for our lives individually and as a group, and can stand so tall we feel as though our hands can touch the clouds above us.

Matthew 1:18-20

> Now the birth of Jesus Christ was on this wise: When as his mother Mary was espoused to Joseph, before they came together, she was found with child of the Holy Ghost. Then Joseph her husband, being a just man, and not willing to make her a public example, was minded to put her away privily. But while he thought on these things, behold, the angel of the Lord appeared unto him in a dream, saying, Joseph, thou son of David, fear not to take unto thee Mary thy wife: for that which is conceived in her is of the Holy Ghost.

A Divine Crisis

We begin to see now the unfolding of God's purpose in bringing His Divine Son to be born of a woman without the aid of a husband or the male seed.

At this time Matthew precisely points out the way Jesus was born. He did this by reminding the Jewish people of their own customs, that either their parents or the matchmaker would "betroth" the children to be married later in life. After the boy had had his bar mitzvah and become an adult and the girl had become an adult, the engagement became more formal and they were really betrothed. Because Joseph and Mary were betrothed to be married, for the next 12 months they would be considered husband and wife but without living with each other. The community would look upon them as husband and wife, although they knew there was no sexual contact between them. At the end of that 12 months they would have a beautiful and solemn wedding and would begin their family. As a matter of fact, that betrothal was considered so binding that the only way to get out of it that final 12 months before the real marriage was to have a divorce.

It was upon this background that Mary and Joseph were facing that one year before their marriage — their real marriage. Mary was discovered pregnant, and she was a virgin. It was something incredible. The virgin who had never had intercourse, who was betrothed to Joseph in such a binding way, was now pregnant, but not by him! Not knowing any more about it but being a decent man, he decided very privately to get this set aside so the girl could go off and have her baby.

You see, when Abraham began to believe God and the flow started, God was thinking of that flow that came all through the ancestors — the genealogy of Jesus, right down to Mary and to Joseph. Mary was visited by the Holy Spirit himself, the one who had been there to create the world, who had filled the prophets, who had given them promises of the coming Messiah, who had made them leaders of Israel to keep the people on the paths of righteousness. The Holy Spirit had moved upon this girl in a supernatural way and implanted the divine seed rather than the human male seed into her womb.

The body of that child began to grow. As her body swelled and her pregnancy was revealed, Joseph was faced with a dilemma, but the angels took charge. The same angels who had been working throughout the ages, who had been present among the people of Israel, who had done some of the mightiest of all deeds, appeared to Joseph. While he was dreaming, the angel said to him, "Don't be afraid to take Mary to be your wife, for the Holy Spirit has conceived His child in her."

Holy Spirit Action

Now remember the Jews always looked upon the Holy Spirit as the agent of creation, that the birth of this child was a creative act of God. They also believed in the recreation of the Holy Spirit as exemplified in Ezekiel 37 in the story of the reviving of the dry bones. So the Jews associated the Holy Spirit with creation and recreation. Although Joseph knew nothing about Pentecost and the Holy Spirit as a gift coming into those of us who are born-again believers, he, as a Hebrew, knew of the creative and recreative acts of the Holy Spirit.

Matthew 1:21-25

> And she shall bring forth a son, and thou shalt call his name JESUS; for he shall save his people from their sins. Now all this was done, that it might be fulfilled which was spoken of the Lord by the prophet, saying, Behold, a virgin shall be with child, and shall bring forth a son, and they shall call his name Emmanuel, which being interpreted is, God with us.

> Then Joseph being raised from sleep did as the angel of the Lord had bidden him, and took unto him his wife: And knew her not till she had brought forth her firstborn son: and he called his name JESUS.

God in Charge

God and His angels have always been in charge of this earth and human events. Here He has sent His angel to explain the unexplainable, to create that which cannot be done. The angel has spoken to Joseph; and Joseph, because of his faith, believes God through the angel. He senses the truth of the matter and decides to obey, and he called the child Jesus. Jesus is the Greek for the word Joshua, which means "God of salvation" or just "salvation." Joseph understood that the birth of this child would deal with the salvation of his people, "for he shall save his people from their sins."

The people were in sin. Sin had separated them from God. A Redeemer had come to save us from sin and to bring salvation. All this had been done because it had been prophesied. It had been planned of God from the very beginning. Isaiah 7:14 tells about the virgin who would bring forth a son, and His name would be called Immanuel, which means "God with us." Some people have said, "Why wasn't He named Immanuel rather than Jesus?" Well, the word Jesus or Joshua means "salvation," the God of salvation, and the term "Immanuel" speaks of the presence of God. Here he says, "Immanuel," God with us.

I'm told that when John Wesley was dying, his last words were the best of all: "God is with us."

When Joseph was raised from his sleep, he went to Mary and did not divorce her at all. He took her as his wife, but did not have sexual intercourse with her until after Jesus had been born. When the baby was born, Joseph said, "His name shall be called Jesus." From that moment Jesus was alive in the world.

Matthew 2:1-3

> Now when Jesus was born in Bethlehem of Judea in the days of Herod the king, behold, there came wise men from the east to Jerusalem, saying, Where is he that is born King of the Jews? for we have seen his star in the east, and are come to worship him. When Herod the king had heard these things, he was troubled, and all Jerusalem with him.

The Collision Course

King Herod, who was only half Jew, and a renegade Jew at that, was on a collision course with a new kind of king. Something in his bones, something in his ancestry, something in what someone had taught him as a child came pulsing up out of his being: "This may be the King of Kings and Lord of Lords. I am on a collision course with this new king. I am troubled."

In fact, the whole city of Jerusalem was troubled. What was happening? Change! God was surprising a world so sated by sin it was thought to be beyond surprise. But now God was invading the earth through His own Son, having him wrapped in human flesh. The moment that happened and the news spread about His birth, Herod got upset.

Matthew 2:4-12

> And when he had gathered all the chief priests and scribes of the people together, he demanded of them where Christ should be born. And they said unto him, In Bethlehem of Judaea: for thus it is written by the prophet. And thou Bethlehem, in the land of Juda, art not the least among the princes of Juda: for out of thee shall come a Governor, that shall rule my people Israel. Then Herod, when he had privily called the wise men, inquired of them diligently what time the star appeared. And he sent them to Bethlehem, and said, Go and search diligently for the young child; and when ye have found him, bring me word again, that I may come and worship him also.
>
> When they had heard the king, they departed; and lo, the star, which they saw in the east, went before them, till it came and stood over where the young child was. When they saw the star, they rejoiced with exceeding great joy. And when they were come into the house, they saw the young child with Mary his mother, and fell down, and worshipped him: and when they had opened their treasures, they presented unto him gifts; gold, and frankincense, and myrrh. And being warned of God in a dream that they should not return to Herod, they departed into their own country another way.

Matthew begins his gospel with the genealogy of Jesus in giving three groups of 14 of his ancestors. He tells precisely how it all began. These three groups had their own histories in accepting God's plan or rejecting it and then, at the end of the third group of 14, a baby is born, a marriage is interrupted, an angel visits the bridegroom, the marriage is not consummated because the Holy Spirit has impregnated the young virgin to be the host mother.

It was not an immaculate conception, so that Mary within herself would have all this. It was an implantation by the spirit of God, a creation, a creative act, a transmission of a seed from above to the earth, implanted in the young virgin — God in man, the incarnation. When that happened, the big change began to roll across the face of the earth. Herod the king got upset. Down deep he knew he was on a collision course with the King of Kings and Lord of Lords. He launched a search-and-destroy mission.

The King Star

Meanwhile, in the east, perhaps in the area of Persia, a group of wise men had been studying the stars, and a brilliant star appeared. History tells us that between 5 and 2 B.C. a brilliant star arose and the Egyptians had a name for it. It was the star signifying the birth of a king. This was a time when many people studied the stars, but there were special people who studied them with the wisdom of the ages in their hearts. There was a great expectation that the Jews would bring forth their king. Therefore, when this star arose so brilliantly and kept on shining, they could not describe it any other way than to say that it was the star of a king. Then God moved these wise men to take special gifts.

They went to see the baby, who had been moved from where he had been born in the stables and wrapped in swaddling clothes to a house where Joseph and Mary were living. This was possibly one or two months later.

The wise men looked up and saw that star again. Apparently it was moving, because it stood right over the house where the Holy Child lay.

They went inside with three kinds of gifts: gold, frankincense, and myrrh — gold for royalty, frankincense for priests, and myrrh for death. Gold was a gift for a king, frankincense was what the priests used in the worship, and myrrh was what was used to anoint the body of the dead. These gifts signified that Jesus would be a king, a priest, and a crucified Lord. After they had bowed before the new king and given their gifts, they had a dream from God that they were not to go back and report this event to King Herod, but to go home a different route — and they did.

The Importance of Gifts

There is so much bound up in this account that much could be said. However, I will be brief about the change in these men. They found someone to whom they could give their greatest gifts. The birth of Jesus began with God's gift to us and the wise men gave gifts to Him.

Giving is intertwined and interwoven with God and man. It is the very nature of God, and the very nature of those of us who worship God. When they had given their gifts, they had to change their course. They took a new way. That is what Christianity is all about. It gives us a new spirit and shows us a new way to live our lives.

Matthew 2:13-15

> And when they were departed, behold, the angel of the Lord appeareth to Joseph in a dream, saying, Arise, and take the young child and his mother, and flee into Egypt, and be thou there until I bring thee word: for Herod will seek the young child to destroy him. When he arose, he took the young child and his mother by night, and departed into Egypt: And was there until the death of Herod: that it might be fulfilled which was spoken of the Lord by the prophet, saying, Out of Egypt have I called my son.

The New Path

Apparently the wise men spent about a full day at the house with the newborn king, the Holy Child Jesus, to whom they presented their gifts of gold, frankincense, and myrrh. Then, being warned by God, they departed to their own country by a new way, the same as we do today when we meet Christ and are saved by His shed blood. We begin following a new path.

There were thousands of Jews in Egypt at that time. The political climate was good for them there, but bad in the Holy Land.

God's Sensible Gifts

You begin to understand now the first gift that the wise men brought, the gift of gold. God knew that this poor couple would not have the money for the trip to Egypt and to be sustained there and for the trip that they would have to take later to return to Galilee where they would raise the child. So he had gold brought to them. Here is God so intimately connected with the financial needs of His people that He put all the gold necessary in the hands of the Holy Family for the trip to Egypt. Let us not overlook the tremendous fact of God's constant concern for our living in a human body, on a human earth, and having human needs for transportation, for dwelling, for clothes, for food, and for all the things that we have to have to live our lives upon God's earth. So many people mistakenly think that God is a billion miles away when their financial needs arise or when their lives are interrupted like Joseph's. Well, I want to tell you that God is concerned about you in every way possible — spiritually, physically, emotionally, financially, and with the members of your family — with your safety and security. The gold is God's. Do not ever forget to whom the gold belongs. God said that the gold and silver of the earth are His. They do not belong to the devil. They belong to God and His people.

Recently I heard a man of God say that just prior to the second coming of Christ, the people of God would be gathering up the wealth of the world. Well, I do not know about that, but I do know if it is necessary, God will see to it that it is done. Therefore, we must keep an open mind and an expectant attitude at all times for our financial needs. If God is not concerned about your financial needs and will not hear your prayers that your financial needs will be met, then you have to ask yourself what kind of God He is, or what kind of understanding you have about Him.

Matthew the gospel writer says that they brought gold, and presented it to the Holy Child Jesus. He tells about this nighttime trip and of the needs that would be required for it. It is evident that the gold was given not only for the royalty of Jesus, for His kingship, but for His financial needs in this stressful period of His life. Would not it have been something for the Devil to have starved the Holy Child Jesus to death? God is not concerned about our starving; He is concerned about our eating, about our having the food we need, the clothes upon our backs, the transportation and the other things that are necessary — so accept that from the very beginning of the life of our Lord Jesus Christ.

Matthew 2:16-18

> Then Herod, when he saw that he was mocked of the wise men, was exceeding wroth, and sent forth, and slew all the children that were in Bethlehem, and in all the coasts thereof, from two years old and under, according to the time which he had diligently inquired of the wise men. Then was fulfilled that which was spoken by Jeremiah the prophet, saying, In Rama was there a voice heard, lamentation, and weeping, and great mourning, Rachel weeping for her children, and would not be comforted, because they are not.

The Devil Outwitted

Matthew here is stating that Rachel is viewed as the mother of the Jews. He connects this with Jeremiah 31:15 and says that it is the fulfillment of what was spoken by Jeremiah. This is one of the 16 times in Matthew's gospel that he says that something was fulfilled that was spoken by the prophet.

Herod was so angry because he knew he was on a collision course with the King of kings and the Lord of lords. He wanted to see that the baby was killed, so he extended the age up to two years in order that the child might not escape. But, you see, God outwitted the devil, as He always does. He had sent the angel to warn Joseph in a dream of what was coming and to take the child away at night. You can count on God outwitting the devil every time. You see, the devil is not omnipotent as is God. That is, he is not all-powerful. The devil is not omnipresent as is God. That is, he is not all-present or present everywhere at the same time. You can see that the devil is not omniscient as God is, which is all-wise. The devil is always behind, and so much less powerful. In no way can the devil even stand in the shadow of God. Therefore, let us take faith today in our God and know that God will outwit the devil in every situation and will make a way of escape when the trials and tribulations come against us.

Matthew 2:19-23

> But when Herod was dead, behold, an angel of the Lord appeareth in a dream to Joseph in Egypt, saying, Arise, and take the young child and his mother, and go into the land of Israel: for they are dead which sought the young child's life. And he arose, and took the young child and his mother, and came into the land of Israel. But when he heard that Archelaus did reign in Judaea in the room of his father Herod, he was afraid to go thither: not-withstanding, being warned of God in a dream, he turned aside into the parts of Galilee: And he came and dwelt in a city called Nazareth: that it might be fulfilled which was spoken by the prophets, He shall be called a Nazarene.

God's Busy Angels

God, in revelation knowledge, revealed to Joseph in Egypt that the hated enemy of the Holy Child Jesus, Herod, was killed. Matthew simply makes a terse statement that Herod was dead, but we are told by history, by Josephus particularly, how Herod died. He had terrible ulcers and convulsions. His genitals were putrified and his death was beyond description. God knew about his death, and the angel came directly again to Joseph at that time in Egypt. It is remarkable that the angel who talked to Joseph in Nazareth and then later in a house in Bethlehem then talked to him again in Egypt! You see, the angels of God are everywhere. In Hebrews 1:14 we are told that the angels are ministering spirits for those who believe God. The angels are so active today.

I have been in contact with angels on innumerable occasions, not because my name is Oral Roberts, but because my God is a God of His angels. The seraphim and cherubim are very active in our world, especially on behalf of those who have faith. Through revelation knowledge Joseph was told to rise, get up and go to, get the trip underway and return to the land of Israel, for they who were seeking His life were dead. But when he got into the land of Israel, apparently wanting to stay somewhere in the Jerusalem area, he learned that Archelaus, Herod's son, reigned there and being warned of God, he turned aside into Galilee.

God's Divine Pattern

Galilee is often called Galilee of the Gentiles. It had been greatly influenced by heathens. In 720 B.C. when the Assyrians took the 10 northern tribes called Israel into captivity, there came a group of people from all over into the land of Galilee. Many intermarried with some of the Jews who were left, so there was a tremendous heathen influence in Nazareth. But yet, it was here that God told Joseph to turn aside and to have the child raised, because the scripture had said in Isaiah 11:1: "He shall be called a Nazarene."

You see, God had a plan, a precise plan, and He carried it out precisely. Every event was in place like every piece of your clothing is in place upon your body. You can see that you are dealing with a God of authority, a God with a plan, a God who speaks by His prophets, a God who sees that every event takes place at its precise moment in history. You can know that your life is not an accident, that every event of your life is planned. The greatest security and safety you have is to slip your life into God's and to realize that you know God is going to follow His plan and enable you with your faith to follow it so that your life is an ordered life. It is not a life kicked to and fro like a wave upon the sea. It has a pattern, a divine pattern. Finally, you can come to know who you are and where you are going because you belong to God.

Matthew 3:1-2

> In those days came John the Baptist, preaching in the wilderness of Judaea, and saying, Repent ye: for the kingdom of heaven is at hand.

There were 400 so-called "silent years" between the end of the Old Testament and the final book of it called Malachi and the birth of Jesus Christ. During these silent years, there was no less activity of God, but there was no recognized prophet of God to speak to the people. However, there was a remnant that was passing the word of God from one family to another. This remnant of Jewish people clung to the promises of God. Nothing could stop them. They kept on releasing their faith, sending it up to God, holding steady in all trials and tribulations, also being quiet before God in the lonely hours of the night as they waited through those four centuries. People communicated from family to family the words of the Living God, and it was upon that scene that Jesus was born. It is very important that we notice and remember that while the Old Testament ends with a curse, the New Testament opens with a glad promise of life. Here we have John the Baptist, the forerunner of our Lord, coming with his ministry. His special word was, "Repent, for the kingdom of heaven is at hand." Why did he say that? Because God had not lost touch with His people. The promise had been dimmed. But then the cloud lifted, the dawn broke. The kingdom of heaven came down to kiss the earth, and people received a new hope, a new hope that they could have life and have it more abundantly. This, too, was a word of prophecy.

Matthew 3:3

> For this is he that was spoken of by the prophet Esaias, saying, The voice of one crying in the wilderness, Prepare ye the way of the Lord, make his paths straight.

God's Spokesman

Who was John the Baptist supposed to be? Who was he? He was a forerunner of Christ, a herald of His coming. He was one like those who preceeded the Oriental kings and proclaimed that the leader was coming. John was a forerunner in the sense of the word that he was saying, "The Messiah is coming."

John the Baptist was who and where he was supposed to be. Notice I said he was WHO he was supposed to be. Now he was WHERE he was supposed to be all right — in the wilderness, that particular area between Jerusalem and the Dead Sea down by the River Jordan. He was also what he was intended to be, and what was that? A voice crying in the wilderness, "Prepare ye the way of the Lord," a voice, not an echo. He was not just saying what somebody else had said, but was a voice speaking forth the living word of God for that particular moment in history, a voice crying, "Prepare ye the way because the Lord is coming and the kingdom of heaven is at hand."

At that time the Jewish people were very politically minded, living under the Roman overlords. Their belief was that the Messiah would come as the Lion of the Tribe of Judah and He would smite the Romans and restore the kingdom to Israel. But John the Baptist was speaking the words of God, not the words of the politically minded Jews. He was not saying that the Messiah was coming to restore the political kingdom of Israel, but He is coming to give the Kingdom of God, and therefore the Kingdom of Heaven is at hand. It is here in the now, John was saying.

A Great Inspiration

John the Baptist was there when he was supposed to be there. It is amazing to me that God works in such an absolute way — following His plan precisely so that at the exact moment in history the herald of Jesus would be raising his voice and like a trumpet sounding forth the word that the Son of God was coming, and that the power of the Spirit would identify Him. John later said that the Lord gave him a sign that when the Holy Spirit descended upon Jesus, that would be the sign by which he would recognize Him to be the Son of God. Therefore, John, in being who he was supposed to be, when he was supposed to be it, where he was supposed to be it, where he was supposed to act it out and to say what he was supposed to say, is an inspiration to you and me. You can be who you are supposed to be, and you can be what you are supposed to be where you are supposed to be and you can carry out the plan of God in your life that you are supposed to carry out.

Matthew 3:4,5

> And the same John had his raiment of camel's hair, and a leathern girdle about his loins; and his meat was locusts and wild honey. Then went out to him Jerusalem, and all Judaea, and all the region round about Jordan.

This may sound strange to us in this modern time of special foods and clothing, but it did not seem to matter particularly what John the Baptist wore or what he ate. It is true that that garment he wore was usually associated with that of a prophet. The main thing was, he had his mind on God, his source, and his eyes focused upon the coming of the Son of the living God.

How in the world do you think these people of Jerusalem, and throughout all Judea, including the area around the Jordan River, could have heard of this mysterious personality, this John the Baptist who was standing out there at the edge of the Jordan River and forecasting the coming of the Messiah? One reason is that there was a tremendous expectation at this time among the Jews for the Messiah. Can you imagine what the media would do today with a scene like this? There was no media to forecast that the Messiah was coming or what John the Baptist was doing by the River Jordan. There were no ads to describe where he was appearing. He simply appeared and began to lift up his voice and God took care of the rest. You see, we do not have to have everything in our favor. As far as this world is concerned, there does not seem to be any time that is especially right anyway. The important thing is that when John the Baptist was exactly who God wanted him to be, where God wanted him to be and doing what God told him to do, God did the rest. It is a divine-human reciprocity.

Without God I cannot — without me He will not.

It takes God and it takes you and me as we reciprocate or cooperate with God. Certainly word of mouth, "the grapevine," also carried the news.

Matthew 3:6-12

> And were baptized of him in Jordan, confessing their sins. But when he saw many of the Pharisees and Sadducees come to his baptism, he said unto them, O generation of vipers, who hath warned you to flee from the wrath to come? Bring forth therefore fruits meet for repentance: And think not to say within yourselves, We have Abraham to our father: for I say unto you, that God is able of these stones to raise up children unto Abraham. And now also the axe is laid unto the root of the trees: therefore every tree which bringeth not forth good fruit is hewn down, and cast into the fire. I indeed baptize you with water unto repentance: but he that cometh after me is mightier than I, whose shoes I am not worthy to bear: he shall baptize you with the Holy Ghost, and with fire: Whose fan is in his hand, and he will throughly purge his floor, and gather his wheat into the garner; but he will burn up the chaff with unquenchable fire.

John the Baptist had a ringing clear voice and sure knowledge of what God had told him to say. When he saw the Pharisees and the Sadducees come to him wanting to be baptized of him, he said, "Who warned you to flee the wrath of God?" He was referring to the burning of a field of stubble after the wheat had been harvested, and the snakes coming up out of it and fleeing. He considered those Sadducees, who were antisupernatural, anti-miracle, and those Pharisees, who had an outward show of righteousness but were inwardly hypocrites, as snakes who had fled just like snakes running away from a fire. And he told them, "I indeed baptize you to repentance," and he advised them to repent, but added that the One coming after him was mightier and confessed he was "not worthy to stoop down and tie up his shoelaces." John told them they would receive a new kind of baptism, a baptism "with the Holy Spirit and with fire."

The New Baptism

The word "spirit" in the Hebrew is "rock" which means "wind" (which means "breath"). In the Greek it means "wind," "breath," or "life." When Jesus comes He is going to be the baptizer — not John the Baptist, not man. But the Lord Jesus Christ is going to give a new kind of baptism. It will be by the Spirit of God. And that baptism is going to have a tremendous force to it that will just sweep the chaff, the unrealities of this world, along with the forces of the devil that come against us. That baptism will be absolutely unique and significant. We read about that baptism in the second chapter of Acts, and Peter's subsequent sermon in which he also said we should repent. When we repent, as in Acts 2:38, and are baptized into the name of Jesus, into the very essence of His name which is the fullness of the Godhead bodily, we shall receive the gift of the Holy Spirit. The very Spirit and the wind of the presence of God will fill our lives. Jesus said, "Ye shall be born again and you must be born again by the Spirit," by the breath and the wind of God which signifies the life of God coming into you. The life of God is overwhelming in its power against the forces of this world.

Another thing is important here. John the Baptist told the scribes and Pharisees they should not think too much of their ancestral relationship with Abraham. He told them, "God is able of these stones to raise up children unto Abraham." He warned them that their ancestral link to Abraham was absolutely nothing if that is all they stood on, for God is able to take the stones of the earth and transform them. Here he was speaking of the more valuable right relationship with God rather than with kinsmen, even if it was Abraham.

Here in America many claim that they are children of God either by their own right or because they were raised in a Christian home. That is very dangerous thinking. For I tell you that God is able to raise up Christians in ways we never dreamed. Our being connected with a Christian home is of value in the same way that those Jews were connected to Abraham. But that in itself will not stand alone in the presence of God, because God has no grandchildren. He just has sons and daughters. To be sons and daughters of God we must repent and believe, be filled with His Spirit and transformed into the image of His Son. We must receive our life directly from God, and for that there is no substitute. I praise God because you can be born again by the Spirit of God.

Matthew 3:13-15

> Then cometh Jesus from Galilee to Jordan unto John, to be baptized of him. But John forbad him, saying, I have need to be baptized of thee, and comest thou to me? And Jesus answering said unto him, Suffer it to be so now: for thus it becometh us to fulfil all righteousness. Then he suffered him.

Jesus and John

The Son of God knew His forerunner in the same way that the forerunner knew the Son of God. Jesus knew that John the Baptist was preaching repentance to the great multitudes and pointing to the coming of the Messiah. At that precise moment in history, Jesus walked up and there He stood. He came up out of the crowd, walked forward, and said to John, before John even recognized him, "Baptize me." And in that instant the revealing knowledge of God showed John that this was the Son of God. First John said, "Oh no! Don't come to be baptized of me. I need to come to You to be baptized. I need that baptism with the Holy Spirit. I need that."

The Sensing of Sin

The scripture says that John the Baptist was filled with the Holy Spirit before he was born, and yet he is saying that he needs the baptism of Jesus. He recognizes Jesus as the baptizer, but Jesus very carefully reminded John of the precise plan of God and that he should join with Him in carrying out those precise details. Remember that the Jews up to this time really had little to do with baptism. Baptism in water was not a continuing part of the Jewish way. They were baptized unto Moses in the Red Sea, but baptism in itself was not a natural part of the Hebrew faith. They did baptize proselytes to the Jewish faith; but at this point as John preached about repenting from sin, these Jews began to feel the sense of sin that the law of Moses made them feel. You see, they had not felt it in such a way before. They really had not paid any attention to their sinfulness. The fact of sin in their lives had been ignored. But when they heard the preaching of John the Baptist about the coming of this Messiah and that they must repent of their sins so He could come into their hearts, they were pricked in their hearts and they wanted to be baptized. They felt the need of it.

You are not going to want Jesus until you feel the sins in your life, the sense of sin in your being. That is what is going to cause you to want a Redeemer. That is what the law of Moses was all about: first, to the Jews their sense of sin, and second, that they couldn't save themselves from sin until they had the need of a Redeemer. Now the law was coming to pass. It was coming to its fulfillment. John the Baptist, who signaled the end of the Old Testament era and announced the new era of the coming of the kingdom of God, had begun to preach in such a way that the Jews felt the sense of sin and the need of a Redeemer. Water baptism, as presented by John, was an outward thing at that time. The inward sign was the preaching that took hold of their hearts to shake them up in their sinfulness and to reveal to them their absolute need of redemption by the Messiah.

Matthew 3:16-17

> And Jesus, when he was baptized, went up straightway out of the water: and lo, the heavens were opened unto him, and he saw the Spirit of God descending like a dove, and lighting upon him: And lo a voice from heaven, saying, This is my beloved Son, in whom I am well pleased.

The Trinity Revelation

These are only two short verses of description, but there is a world of events taking place here. Immediately upon His baptism, Jesus walked up out of the water. At that split second the heavens were opened. Can't you see it?

Jesus stood there with the heavens split asunder. He saw something. Yes, He saw Someone, the Spirit of God descending like a dove. During this spectacular manifestation of Almighty God, the Lord God of heaven and earth spoke from heaven, "This is my beloved Son. It is in Him that I am well pleased."

Here is the first revelation in our New Testament of the Father, the Son, and the Holy Spirit. Here the Father and the Holy Spirit are testifying and giving their witness that Jesus is the Christ, the Son of the Living God.

God had said to the Hebrews, "Oh Israel, the Lord thy God is one."

Our Jewish friends say today, "How then is God three?"

God is one, but He manifests himself in the dimensions of His fatherhood, of His spirit and of His Son, in ways that people can understand who He is.

When we Christians say Father, Son, and Holy Spirit, we are not speaking of three absolutely separate beings, separate from one another; we are speaking of one God with three powerful dimensions, without which we can never truly understand God.

Matthew 4:1,2

> Then was Jesus led up of the Spirit into the wilderness to be tempted of

> the devil. And when he had fasted forty days and forty nights, he was afterward an hungred.

Temptations

Here we are going to see Jesus operating in His faith and upon the Word of God. We are going to see Jesus tempted in every point the same as we are, as Hebrews, chapter six, later affirms that He was. We are going to see Jesus in His humanness. We are going to see Him on the side of His life that came up out of Mary's body, that human side of Jesus, the same kind of humanness that you and I have.

It is very important to notice that Jesus was led up of the Spirit into the wilderness to be tempted of the devil. Here is Jesus, Son of Man, Son of God, led up to be tempted, and He is led by the Spirit of God. We seem to have such a shock to our system when we are tempted, but we cannot be Christians unless we are tempted. The word "tempt" here really means to test, so that the Spirit led Jesus up into the wilderness to be tested of the devil.

Jesus did without food for 40 days and 40 nights in a fast. A fast is doing without food, but it is far more than that. People can do without food and that is not necessarily a fast of God. A fast is when the Spirit of God deals with you and me to do without food for so many meals so He can get deep inside our spirit. Our spirit then, as it is tested of the devil, rises up in harmony with God in a total dependence upon Him. That is to say, the weaker we are in our bodies, through the fast, the more our inner being is going to be dependent upon God. That is what fasting is all about, to learn how to be dependent upon God.

The Tempter

When the fast was over, the tempter came. The tempter always comes. Who is the tempter? The devil. The devil comes to tempt us even before we fast or while we fast, but particularly after we fast. He comes to tempt us at all times.

Matthew 4:3,4

> And when the tempter came to him, he said, If thou be the Son of God, command that these stones be made bread. But he answered and said, It is written, Man shall not live by bread alone, but by every word that proceedeth out of the mouth of God.

This is the first of three times that Christ says, "It is written." It showed that He depends upon knowing the Word of God and using His faith to apply it. You can make a very serious mistake here by saying, "Oh, that was Jesus and has nothing to do with me." It is written in the Bible because it has everything to do with you and me. It states clearly the three things that Christ used against temptation.

1) Knowing the Word of God accurately.
2) Being able to say specifically, "Devil, it is written in the Word of God."
3) Believing that Word will repulse the devil.

There is nothing that Jesus used that is not available to you and me as children of God every day, every hour, every moment of our lives. The Word of God which we read, study, believe, accept, and then use by our faith is always ours.

Matthew 4:4-6

> But he answered and said, It is written, Man shall not live by bread alone, but by every word that proceedeth out of the mouth of God. Then the devil taketh him up into the holy city, and setteth him on a pinnacle of the temple, and saith unto him, If thou be the Son of God, cast thyself down: for it is written, He shall give his angels charge concerning thee: and in their hands they shall bear thee up, lest at any time thou dash thy foot against a stone.

Satan Abuses Scripture

You see here, the devil can also quote scripture. The devil knows the scripture quite well, but he usually quotes it inaccurately. The devil is referring here to a scripture in Psalm 91:11-12, but he does not quote the scripture accurately. He added three words, "at any time," so that he made it read, "He shall give His angels charge concerning thee and in their hands they shall bear thee up lest at any time thou dash thy foot against a stone." "Lest at any time." Those three words, "at any time," are not in the original scripture. The scripture that said, "Lest thou dash thy foot against a stone," the devil makes it, "Lest at any time thou dash thy foot against a stone." What the devil is trying to say is that you can just do whatever you want to do; you don't have to follow the precise plan of God. But Jesus then spoke to the devil, "It is written again, Thou shalt not tempt the Lord thy God." (Matthew 4:7)

Know the Word of God

He is referring to Deuteronomy 6:16. You see, we have to know the Word of God in its context. We study the Bible, as Paul said to young Timothy, so that we can "rightly divide the word of truth" (II Timothy 2:15). It is not enough just to read the Word of God, though it is primary in our lives. We must study it by the anointing of the Holy Spirit so that we can understand it by revelation knowledge and then apply it in its accurate way.

Notice that here is a battle of two tremendous personalities who are both using the Word of God as a battleground! One is Jesus, who is quoting it accurately, and the other is the devil, who is quoting it inaccurately. Jesus said, "It is written," and the devil said, "It is written." But Jesus knew the scriptures in their context, in their proper application, better than the devil did, and so can you and I know the scriptures accurately.

Matthew 4:8-10

> Again, the devil taketh him up into an exceeding high mountain, and sheweth him all the kingdoms of the world, and the glory of them; And saith unto him, All these things will I give thee, if thou wilt fall down and worship me. Then saith Jesus unto him, Get thee hence, Satan: for it is written, Thou shalt worship the Lord thy God, and Him only shalt thou serve.

The Devil's Offer

The devil recognizes that Jesus is the Messiah and he accepts the fact that Jesus owns the world. He wants to barter him out of it. You can count on it that the devil knows who Jesus is. He doesn't doubt who Jesus is. He merely tries to make YOU doubt who Jesus is. The devil knew that although Jesus owned the world, the world itself had gone away from His ownership, rejected the ownership of God. The devil knew that Jesus Christ had come to redeem the world, to ransom it back, to save it. So the devil offered Jesus something that He wanted. The thing the devil offered Jesus that He wanted was to redeem the world back. Yes, the devil knew that it was Jesus', but the world — the human beings by their power of choice — had taken themselves away from God. Therefore, by their choice, they were in a world away from God, and Jesus wanted to save them. It's at the very point of Jesus' desire that the devil came to tempt Him. You see, there cannot be any temptation unless the devil comes to you at the point of something you want: Where your desire is. In James 1:14 we are told that we are only tempted when we are led away by our own lusts or desire. If you do not desire something, the devil could be there all day long and not have any effect in tempting you. He finds something you want and then comes at the point of your desire. It is not wrong to want something when it is in the will of God, and to want it with all your heart. God in His Word tells us He will give the righteous the desires of their hearts. So it is not wrong to desire what God has for you; God implanted that desire. However, when we desire it so much that we will do anything to keep it or to get it, we, in effect, fling wide the door to the devil. He marches in and begins pounding away at that point, magnifying that desire, talking to you about something that you want, telling you that you ought to have it no matter what the will of God is. Notice that in Verse 11 there is a definite change: "Then the devil leaveth him, and, behold, angels came and ministered unto him."

This is a reference to Hebrews 1:14 where the angels are sent to help us. As soon as Jesus had taken the Word of God to the devil and by His faith had said to the devil, "It is written and this is the way it is," the devil found nothing in Jesus.

Matthew 4:11

> Then the devil leaveth Him, and, behold, angels came and ministered unto Him.

New Force to Faith

Jesus had subordinated His desires to the will of the Heavenly Father to such an extent that the devil could not lay hands on any handle by which he could lead Jesus astray. You see, when we make up our minds that the Word of God is indeed God's Word, and that by our faith we can apply it, the devil has nothing in us either.

It is very important to understand that once we come through a temptation, we are in a weakened condition just as Jesus was. The Bible says here that the devil left Him and angels came and ministered unto Him. They brought Him food. He had been without it 40 days and nights. They brought Him encouragement in the Word of God, because that was what He had been quoting or reciting to the devil. They came to give new force to His faith, because it was that faith in God that Jesus had been using. When you stand up in your temptations against the devil, first by using the Word of God and then by applying your faith, the devil will leave you for a season just as he left Jesus, and the angels will come to you just as they came to Jesus and they will supply!

You may ask me, "How?" I do not know the how. I just have to know the Word of God, that when the devil left Him the angels came and ministered unto Him. And when Jesus said, "Take up your cross daily and follow Me," He also meant that scenes like this would take place in our lives, that after we had been tempted, the devil would leave us for that period, but the angels would come and minister to us. We should have a great expectation that the unseen powers of God will minister miraculously to our inner man. In fact, to our whole being.

Matthew 4:12-17

> Now when Jesus had heard that John was cast into prison, he departed into Galilee; And leaving Nazareth, he came and dwelt in Capernaum, which is upon the sea coast, in the borders of Zabulon and Nephthalim: That it might be fulfilled which was spoken by Esaias the prophet, saying, The land of Zabulon, and the land of Nephthalim, by the way of the sea, beyond Jordan, Galilee of the Gentiles; The people which sat in darkness saw great light; and to them which sat in the region and shadow of death light is sprung up. From that time Jesus began to preach, and to say, Repent: for the kingdom of heaven is at hand.

The Meaning of Repentance

John the Baptist had introduced repentance. Now Jesus takes it up. He simply follows precisely what He had given John the Baptist to say about His coming. He told people to repent, meaning, change your mind, turn around, go in the opposite direction. Why? Because, He said, "The kingdom of heaven is at hand." It is in the now. It is right here. In other words, everything that God is has come to us in the form of our Lord Jesus Christ. All the kingdom of God with its light, its salvation, its healing, deliverance, and provision for our lives is here, right now, for you and me, and every human being in the world. As Jesus came, heaven came down to kiss the earth and to bring a closeness between heaven and earth, that as we walk with Christ today we are members of both worlds. Our names are written both here on earth and in the Book of Life in Heaven. We are citizens of this world, but far more than that, we are citizens of the heavenly kingdom.

Matthew 4:18-20

> And Jesus, walking by the sea of Galilee, saw two brethren, Simon called Peter, and Andrew his brother, casting a net into the sea: for they were fishers. And He saith unto them, Follow Me, and I will make you fishers of men. And they straightway left their nets, and followed Him.

The Secret of Deliverance

How powerful are the words of Jesus Christ! He said to Peter and to his brother Andrew, "Brothers, fishermen, follow Me and I will make you, I will change you." Here, Jesus is speaking of the making power of God, the changing power of the Redeemer. He is revealing that there is something greater in this world than making a living, and it is to come into a life that has been created by God for us — a reborn life!

We are engaged in this world's pursuits and Christ crosses our path. What He is saying to us is the same thing: "Follow Me and I will make you, I will change you, I will transform your life. I will bring you into the kingdom of God." And do you know what they did? Straightway they left their nets and followed Him. Remember, the secret of deliverance is in instant obedience. I repeat, the secret of deliverance is in instant obedience.

Matthew 4:21-23

> And going on from thence, he saw other two brethren, James the son of Zebedee, and John his brother, in a ship with Zebedee their father, mending their nets; and He called them. And they immediately left the ship and their father, and followed Him. And Jesus went about all Galilee, teaching in their synagogues, and preaching the gospel of the kingdom, and healing all manner of sickness and all manner of disease among the people.

Teach, Preach, Heal

Matthew, Chapter 4, Verse 23 tells it all — that we are to teach, preach, and heal. He went about teaching, preaching, and then healing all manner of sickness and all manner of disease among the people. Notice the sequence in which His ministry went forth to touch the people. First, He taught. Second, He preached the Gospel that the kingdom of Heaven is at hand. Third, He healed. Teaching, preaching, and then healing. Why did the healing follow the teaching and the preaching? The teaching and preaching of the Word of God produces faith in your heart. It also produces faith in you when you are sick, at the very point of your need no matter what that need is. It does not matter what manner of disease it is. What matters is whether you are being taught. Are you receiving the preaching of the Word of God? You see, you can know through the teaching and preaching that your faith will come up out of your heart. In order to be like Jesus we teach, preach, and heal.

Be Like Jesus

In the spring of 1947 when I was a student in the university and also pastoring a small church, the Lord Jesus spoke in my heart and told me to be like Jesus and heal the people as He did. When I asked him how to be like Jesus, He told me to get down on my knees and to read consecutively, the four gospels and the Book of Acts, three times in 30 days, and He would show me Jesus. I remember when I got to Matthew 4:23 that this verse leaped up from the page and in effect said "Oral, be like Jesus. You must teach! You must preach! You must, heal! This is what Jesus did." This is the divine and the ageless formula for Christians today. This is the formula of Jesus himself. And when you and I have Christ in our heart, this is the formula we are to use.

Matthew 4:24,25

> And his fame went throughout all Syria: and they brought unto him all sick people that were taken with divers diseases and torments, and those which were possessed with devils, and those which were lunatick, and those that had the palsy: and he healed them. And there followed him great multitudes of people from Galilee, and from Decapolis, and from Jerusalem, and from Judaea, and from beyond Jordan.

Healing Power

It is important to understand that Jesus apparently did not heal everybody who was sick, but He healed every kind of disease. People who represented each disease came, and they were healed by the Lord. He wanted us to understand that there is no disease resistant to the healing power of Jesus Christ. I believe that. No, all people are not healed. All people apparently are not going to be healed, but we can be assured that every manner of disease IS being healed as we teach, preach, and heal in the name of Jesus.

Notice that He healed people who were taken with divers diseases and torments. Jesus healed people emotionally of their fears and stresses. He healed people of diseases such as palsy, which is in many instances a reference to a birth defect. He healed people of diseases and ailments of long-standing. He healed people who were mentally ill, described in Matthew as lunatic. He healed those who were possessed with devils, whose personalities were infected by an indwelling demon.

Jesus has placed in the chemicals of this earth many of the healing powers, but He has not left us without His own supernatural touch upon our lives. Because when Jesus healed, we are told, something went out of Him. He said, "I perceive that power has gone out of me." He has built healing into the very universe in which we live. He has added to that something coming out of Him as a person, His supernatural power. In addition, He has put healing properties and abilities within our own bodies, minds, and souls.

The Source of Healing

I say this to doctors. I say this to teachers, to preachers, to evangelists, to prophets, to lay people. I say it to everybody and to myself: *He is the Source of all health and healing.*

It is possible for us to be healed. That is the reality of it. We can stand upon the Word of God and upon our faith in Christ that wecan be healed from the crown of our heads to the soles of our feet. Jesus also is speaking of root causes of disease. He speaks of those who are tormented — that is to say, there is some inner "something" that is wrong, something wrong with their mental abilities. There is a torment there. He speaks also of diseases which have a terrific effect upon the mind.

Disease and the Mind

Doctors talk about psychosomatic diseases, of diseases coming up out of our own emotions. Well, let us turn that around and realize that diseases in our bodies also affect our emotions. I can tell you, having been a sick man, and having gone through some very terrible afflictions in my body, that it tore my emotions up. It brought great torment to me. Therefore, as we approach the healing of people through the power of medicine and through the power of prayer, we must understand the root of those diseases.

We are making a determined effort at the research tower of the City of Faith to find a root cure for a root cause. We know that God is with us, and we thank God for every partner who is standing with us in this gigantic effort to obey our God and find the root cause of disease. This may affect more people favorably than anything else that we have ever done to bring healing to the people, or that God has done through us to bring healing to humanity.

Sermon on the Mount

Chapter five begins the Beatitudes, or what we commonly call "the Sermon on the Mount" that our Lord Jesus Christ preached. A beatitude preached by our Lord Jesus Christ is a statement of a blessing of heaven, of an attitude of the spirit that is divine reality, that brings the greatest happiness to human beings even here on this earth. Matthew, in recording this sermon of Christ, probably did it over a period of time. He had heard Jesus wherever He gave all or part of this message, and from his notes Matthew was able to write the sermon in its entirety, verse by verse, word by word, so that you and I could read it in the same way. I have a real deep feeling about this sermon — not only because it is Jesus' message to us today,but because I have been at the traditional place where He preached it. I have been there several times. I have spoken the Word of God there to many people. I have sensed, in effect, the very presence of God on that piece of ground where Jesus sat and delivered this message.

Matthew 5:1-3

> And seeing the multitudes, he went up into a mountain: and when he was set, his disciples came unto him: and he opened his mouth, and taught them, saying, Blessed are the poor in spirit: for their's is the kingdom of heaven.

Poverty No Blessing

He did not say, blessed are those who are in poverty, because poverty is no blessing to anybody. If poverty is a blessing, then the billions on earth who are starving are blessed indeed. If poverty is a blessing to you, why don't you ask God for more? No, God wants to supply all our needs upon this earth. Here Jesus is speaking to us about how to be humble in our spirit. Remember, He said of himself, "For I am lowly in heart."

Matthew 5:4

> Blessed are they that mourn: for they shall be comforted.

Mourn is a reference to the compassion Jesus had for suffering people and that He wants us to have. He says when we have it, we are blessed of God. It means the same thing that we read in Matthew 14:14: When Jesus saw the multitude He was moved with compassion toward them and healed their sick.

Compassion is Supernatural

Compassion is not a human trait. Sympathy is a human trait.

Sympathy extended to people in need only creates self-pity, but compassion is supernatural. It is divine love. It is God's love going off inside us. It is feeling the way that God feels toward other people, particularly in their sufferings. So when He says, "Blessed are they that mourn, for they shall be comforted," He in effect is saying, "Blessed are they who are compassionate, for I will see to it that they receive compassion themselves."

Matthew 5:5

> Blessed are the meek: for they shall inherit the earth.

Meek Not Weak

Meekness is not equated with weakness. Christianity has become a stumbling block to many who think that being born again makes them doormats of society. But it means a lot like what my mother always said to me: "Oral, be little in your own eyes and obey God." What Mama was telling me was, don't be bigheaded. Don't think too highly of yourself, but see in the way that God sees. Love the way that He is, and obey what He tells you to do. Submit your will to His. Don't go around boasting except in Christ, and that His adequacy is complete for your inadequacies. We know Jesus was tender with children, but I will tell you He was strong against the money changers in the temple — driving them out as He upset their tables and telling them that they had made His Father's house a den of merchandise, instead of a house of prayer.

Moses is said to be the meekest man who ever lived, and yet he took on the wicked and violent Pharaoh in Egypt single-handedly. No, it does not mean that meekness is weakness. Jesus is saying that you are blessed when you submit your life to Him and let Him live His life through you, because He who owns the heaven and the earth will cause you to inherit the earth.

Matthew 5:6

> Blessed are they which do hunger and thirst after righteousness: for they shall be filled.

Here Jesus is speaking of the keen appetite and deep craving that we who are born again have when thinking His thoughts and doing things the way He does them, desiring above all else to have right relations with God in everything we do and everything we are — that deep desire to see God's righteous ways triumph in this world. Jesus' statement here is absolute. You shall have your hunger satisfied.

Matthew 5:7-9

> Blessed are the merciful: for they shall obtain mercy. Blessed are the pure in heart: for they shall see God. Blessed are the peacemakers: for they shall be called the children of God.

The Quality of Mercy

When Jesus speaks here of being merciful, I think we ought to remember Him on the cross as He prayed to the Father, "Father, forgive them for they know not what they do." To be merciful we have to take God's view rather than our own. God sees it in the scope of eternity and in the realm of divine love, which is the real reality of life. Love is the real reality of life. When Jesus speaks of the pure in heart, He is really talking about singleness of heart, that honesty that has no hidden motive or ulterior motive. He is speaking of not having a divided self, one that is trying to serve God and the world at the same time. We can possess the very nature of Jesus himself and because of that we shall see God.

Blessed Peacemakers

Then He says, "Blessed are the peacemakers, those who keep the peace." Remember, God says that He is the God of peace, and in the Bible, Christ is described as the Prince of Peace. The Bible speaks of that peace in our hearts that passes all understanding. Peace. Blessed are the peacemakers.

It is so easy to divide people, so easy to repeat tales, and to say things we hear other people say and run and tell it so that we tear people's hearts out of them. One of the things we will learn in Paul's writings is how to deal specifically with divisions among God's people. Jesus said, "There is great happiness in this," and I know it to be true. Then He adds that when you do that, you shall be called the children of God.

Matthew 5:10-12

> Blessed are they which are persecuted for righteousnes' sake; for their's is the kingdom of heaven. Blessed are ye, when men shall revile you and persecute you and shall say all manner of evil against you falsely, for my sake. Rejoice, and be exceeding glad: for great is your reward in heaven: for so persecuted they the prophets which were before you.

The Meaning of Persecution

Jesus described the treatment that you and I as born-again believers are going to experience in this world. As a matter of fact, we simply have to be open to the persecution that is inevitable. It is going to come simply because we are living for Christ. He is saying, Blessed are you when you allow yourself to be persecuted, when you do not flee from doing God's work just because the opposition rises against you. You know, friend, it is not at the edge of our Christian living that these persecutions strike us. They come when we are really doing the work of the Lord for His sake. I repeat, for his sake. We become so involved with Jesus Christ in life that what we do is for His sake. Jesus pronounces a blessing upon us when we take a stand for Him. We must stand as Paul says in Ephesians 6, "Having done all to stand, stand therefore."

I remember a man, converted in one of my crusades, who I later met again. He was facing extreme persecution through his testimony of Christ and he said to me, "Oral Roberts, you said to me that when I came to Christ, I would be blessed. I'm not as blessed now as I was before I was converted. Most people said nice things about me, but now they are coming at me from every side." I asked, "What are you doing?" "Well," he said, "I have begun reading my Bible. I've begun to try to practice the love of God, to be nice to people, to stand up for what's right in my community, and all of a sudden all hell has burst loose against me."

"Well," I said, "Jesus said that is one of His blessings. Blessed are you when you are reviled falsely for Jesus sake You are shining a light for the path of those who walk in the darkness of sin."

He said, "Hmmm, I'm going to have to think this over."

Well, I can speak for Oral Roberts. I have been thinking it over a long time, and in my own experience I have discovered that the closer I am to Christ and the more sincerely and openly I do His work, the more I am assured that I will be accused falsely for Jesus' sake. I also admit that sometimes I am persecuted for my own faults. I admit to you there is no joy in that. We suffer for our Lord when we know in our heart that our motive is right, that we are doing it because of the Word of God telling us to do it, and to follow in His footsteps.

But Jesus gives a wonderful word to us that we are blessed people.

Matthew 5:13

> Ye are the salt of the earth: but if the salt have lost his savour, wherewith shall it be salted? it is thenceforth good for nothing, but to be cast out, and to be trodden under foot of men.

"Salt" and Satan

Salt gives flavor. Salt preserves. It is at the very heart of much that we eat. Our Lord is saving that we who live for Him are the flavor. We are the flavor of this world because of His flavor. The flavor of His own divine nature has filled our lives. In flavoring our lives, and preserving our lives, we, in turn, give a beautiful flavor to this world and are the preservers of this world.

Did you know that if people were taken out of this world today, all the forces of the Antichrist would immediately be manifested? The devil would take over and make mankind so completely godless that there would be no flavor of life. There would be nothing to hold people together. We, as believers, should know that we can live an effective life for Jesus Christ in the same way that salt is an effective flavor and preservative. Now, hear that. You are the salt of the earth, and God is complimenting you by calling you the salt of the earth.

Matthew 5:14-16

> Ye are the light of the world. A city that is set on an hill cannot be hid. Neither do men light a candle, and put it under a bushel, but on a candlestick; and it giveth light unto all that are in the house. Let your light so shine before men, that they may see your good works, and glorify your Father which is in heaven.

Light Up Life

When we are in Christ, we do not conceal ourselves. He says, "You are light. Let it shine. Let it shine."

Our Lord is grieved by all those people who say they are Christians but declare it is a "private" matter and it is their own business and nobody else's business. If you are a closet Christian, all your light is in the closet. It is in nobody's house; it is not in your everyday relationships.

Light is light. You can enter a room that is absolutely dark and strike a match, and the light will penetrate the total darkness of that room. Jesus is so thrilled about our being the light of the world that He wants us to accept the fact that we are light and let it shine!

Matthew 5:17,18

> Think not that I am come to destroy the law, or the prophets: I am not come to destroy, but to fulfill. For verily I say unto you, Till heaven and earth pass, one jot or one tittle shall in no way pass from the law, till all be fulfilled.

Jesus and the Law

This is the first time that Matthew quotes Jesus saying, "Verily I say unto you," or "Truly I say unto you." Jesus speaks of His divine authority, the authority that is above all authority. He speaks as the great law giver himself, "Verily I say unto you."

He is speaking to Jewish believers and unbelievers alike, people who are bound up in keeping the law of Moses. Their whole lives are concerned with it, and Jesus is speaking of His own personal relationship to the law of Moses.

To those who were fearful Jesus would not have proper reverence for the authority and principles of the Old Testament or who hoped He would become a religious revolutionary concerning it, Jesus issued a categorical statement:

"I came not to annul or abrogate the Old Testament, the old covenant. I came not to do away with the laws that My Father gave Moses. I came to fulfill the purpose for which that law was given by keeping it perfectly in spirit and embodying the principle of it in myself in living for and by paying the full penalty of the law's demands against sin by becoming the Redeemer for sin." That is what Jesus was saying. And at that point He said, "Truly I say unto you," and then indicated that He would not change even a jot or a tittle.

In speaking of the jot and the tittle Jesus referred to, the jot is the smallest Hebrew letter, like an apostrophe. The tittle is a stroke which distinguishes some Hebrew letters from others. As He said, not the smallest letter or stroke will pass from the law of Moses until all is fulfilled. Jesus is clearly speaking of the unerring accuracy of the Word of God.

Matthew 5:19,20

> Whosoever therefore shall break one of these least commandments, and shall teach men so, he shall be called the least in the kingdom of heaven: but whosoever shall do and teach them, the same shall be called great in the kingdom of heaven. For I say unto you, That except your righteousness shall exceed the righteousness of the scribes and Pharisees, ye shall in no case enter into the kingdom of heaven.

Scribes and Pharisees

I want to emphasize again the preciseness with which our God works. Jesus is saying there was an absolute reason for the giving of the law, for the commandments to be lived out by men. Although

He has come as the Messiah to fulfill them, he is saying that if any of us break even the tiniest part of those commandments and teach other men to break them, we are actually the smallest of the least people in the kingdom of heaven. But if we do them and teach them, we will be great in the kingdom of God. Therefore He says, "Except your righteousness shall exceed that of the scribes and Pharisees, you will not enter into the kingdom of God."

Jesus was always surrounded by the scribes and Pharisees who, on the one hand, were doing some wonderful things; on the other hand, they were so motivated by ulterior motives that they were far, far from the kingdom of God.

A scribe was a highly trained person, skilled in the Word of God, and capable of reproducing it in writing so precisely that every t was crossed and every i was dotted.

The scribes would carry that over to the commandments of God — keeping the letter of them, keeping the outward form of them, seeing that every t was crossed and every i was dotted, but leaving out their inner and real meaning.

The Pharisees were a group of Jewish people who were zealous for the law of Moses, and in that they were correct. They began a revival among a backslidden people to get them to return, to keep the commandments of God. By the time Jesus arrived, they had become so degenerated in spirit that they were merely legalistic. They had placed their main emphasis upon the outward observance of that law.

For example, in the law of Moses the sabbath day was to be kept holy and no work done during that day. But the Pharisees overemphasized what God had in mind, and before they got through they had about 100 books of definitions of what you could or could not do on the sabbath day. They defined the kinds of work. When Jesus arrived they declared He could not even heal on the sabbath! They criticized Him for healing the sick on the sabbath.

That is not what God had in mind in keeping the sabbath day holy. The sabbath, to be kept holy, had to begin in your heart. The sabbath was made for man, not man for the sabbath. What Jesus was doing was showing them that the spirit of the law runs deeper than the outward observance of the law, and therefore He said, "Unless your righteousness goes beyond that of the scribes and Pharisees, you cannot enter into the kingdom of God." He meant the kind of righteousness rather than the degree of it. We see several examples that Jesus gives of this starting in Verse 21.

Matthew 5:21-24

Ye have heard that it was said by them of old time, Thou shalt not kill;

and whosoever shall kill shall be in danger of the judgment: but I say unto you, That whosoever is angry with his brother without a cause shall be in danger of the judgment: and whosoever shall say to his brother, Raca, shall be in danger of the council: but whosoever shall say, Thou fool, shall be in danger of hell fire. Therefore if thou bring thy gift to the altar, and there rememberest that thy brother hath ought against thee; leave there thy gift before the altar, and go thy way; first be reconciled to thy brother, and then come and offer thy gift.

The Meaning of "Kill"

Jesus starts here with the sixth commandment: Thou shalt not kill, which in its true rendering is murder. Thou shalt not murder. Therefore God, in giving this commandment, Thou shalt not murder, neither forbade His people to go to war or to have capital punishment. He is saying first that whoever murders will have to answer to the court.

Second, if murder is in your heart continuously, if it is there long enough festering inside you, that means you are going to murder. It is as if you have already done the deed. You are a murderer because you're living murder in your heart, and you are in danger with the court that cannot be seen, the court of Almighty God.

Then He used the term "Raca," or being brainless or empty-headed, really giving vent to a violent passion and to fierce name-calling. He says that they are going to jerk you up and judge you for that. Then He comes right to the heart of the matter, that when you go to the temple or the synagogue with a gift, seeking forgiveness, and remember that you have wronged someone who has a just complaint against you, you must remove that stumbling block before you make your offering to God. When we take our gifts to God, we must look inside our hearts and know that our hearts are reaching out toward God, and toward doing good in this world. It goes far beyond the giving of money, but it includes money. We just simply have to remember that our Lord is talking about the spirit of it as much as He is talking about the giving of it.

Matthew 5:25-28

Agree with thine adversary quickly, whiles thou art in the way with him; lest at any time the adversary deliver thee to the judge, and the judge deliver thee to the officer, and thou be cast into prison. Verily I say unto thee, Thou shalt by no means come out thence, till thou hast paid the uttermost farthing. Ye have heard that it was said by them of old time, thou shalt not commit adultery: but I say unto you, That whosoever looketh on a woman to lust after her hath committed adultery with her already in his heart.

The Sin of Lust

When the creditor is trying to do you a favor and make it possible for you to pay your debts, pay up what you owe. Be very careful; be flexible. Assure him that you are going to start on it, that you are going to be making payments, or he is going to deliver you up to the court of law. Jesus used that example as a springboard to talk about the seventh commandment: Thou shalt not commit adultery. The audience listening to Him knew exactly what He meant, because they knew that commandment by heart. But Jesus is saying something about it that was in the original meaning when God gave the seventh commandment among the ten to Moses. He is saying that the immoral act begins in an immoral desire. He calls it the sin of lust. Jesus explains the immoral desire to commit the overt act of adultery. Anyone who looks at a man or a woman with a persistent desire and keeps on thinking, "If I was with that man or with that woman I would commit this deed," soon reaches a point with that lust that the thought becomes the sin of adultery just as much as the act. The desire and the act are different, I realize that, but as far as sin is concerned, Jesus is saying the sin is already committed.

Someone may ask, "How can I handle life then, because bad thoughts are always coming into my mind!" Lust is not a passing thought in your mind. Lust is not a bad dream in which you are with someone, and you wake up so glad the dream is not so. That is not lust. Jesus is realistic. He understands our humanity, and He, in effect, is telling us we don't have to live with this lust. He says He has given us the very spirit of himself, the spirit of purity, so we do not have any deep desire to commit adultery. There is a way out. Jesus' sermon continues in verse 29 . . .

Matthew 5:29,30

> And if thy right eye offend thee, pluck it out, and cast it from thee: for it is profitable for thee that one of thy members should perish, and not that thy whole body should be cast into hell. And if thy right hand offend thee, cut it off, and cast it from thee: for it is profitable for thee that one of thy members should perish, and not that thy whole body should be cast into hell.

The Power of Choice

Jesus is not saying that we are literally, physically to pluck the eye out of our head or sever our right hand from our wrist. He is not talking about physical mutilation. If that is all He were talking about, taking your eye out or cutting your hand off would solve it all. He is dealing with things in your heart. And if you took all your legs and arms off and cut your eyes out — severed them from your body — and it was still in your heart, you would not have gained a thing. Just as any member of your body with gangrene that cannot be cured is amputated, so He is saying, "Amputate from your being that thought, that idea, that lust, that thing that's pulling you down."

And now you say, "Well, how do I do it?" Jesus has so made you and me that we have the power of choice. When someone says, I don't have any will power, he is lying and you know he is lying. You and I do have will power. We can choose. God made us different from all the animals of the earth. We have the power of choice.

Jesus handled it in a much more extreme circumstance when He said, "Not My will but thine be done. I surrender My will to the heavenly Father's will. I do that." God is not going to come down and take Oral Roberts' will and twist it around to do what he wants it to do. Oral Roberts is going to have to exercise that will. How do you do it? This way:

He has given us His holy Word, the Bible. The Word of God is a two-edged sword. It divides evil from righteousness. It divides doubt from faith. It divides hate from love. It divides untruth from truth. The Word of God is even more powerful than a two-edged sword, we are told in the book of Hebrews. We have the opportunity of going to church as often as possible. I am in church myself through my own ministry. But when I am not ministering, I am in the house of God.

What I am saying in those two illustrations of the Word and of going to the house of God is to say that there is a way. God makes a way. What you feel that you cannot eliminate from your life, you actually can: first, by the exercise of your choice — using your will power — and then by your faith — believing God is going to supernaturally help you. Believe me, He is a supernatural God. Second, you cut off whatsoever tends to stimulate unholy passions in your life.

There are times when you just turn your television set off because of the type of program that is on it, or you refuse to read certain magazines and books because of the unsavory material. As I said, you can do it.

Matthew 5:31,32

> It hath been said, Whosoever shall put away his wife, let him give her a writing of divorcement: but I say unto you, That whosoever shall put away his wife, saving for the cause of fornication, causeth her to commit adultery: and whosoever shall marry her that is divorced

committeth adultery.

The Suffering of Divorce

This statement by Jesus is still being argued about today. But friend, Jesus is speaking of what God originally had in mind — the ideal — and that is that marriage is totally sacred. Because of its sacredness, it produces something that's almost indescribable, a oneness where the two flesh become one. More than that, the two spirits become one. Now, anyone who breaks up that relationship is going to be judged severely.

In that day that Jesus was talking about, marriage had become so loosely carried on that the man could divorce his wife for practically anything. If he did not like the way she salted his food, he would walk up and say, "I divorce you; I divorce you; I divorce you," and get a piece of paper and say that he was divorced.

Jesus really had a hidden meaning here, that the woman had rights just as the man did. But He was also holding up the ideal. He did not say that divorce is blaspheming the Holy Spirit. He carefully put limits around the marriage and called divorce an intrusion, a breakage of that relationship that let in all kinds of suffering. The important thing for you to carry in your heart, in what Jesus said here, is that He was going beyond the letter of the law to the spirit. And we must be careful in being judgmental toward divorced persons, just because of the letter of the law. There are hundreds of thousands of Christian men and women suffering because of divorce right now who are being condemned out of hand for this and who are being condemned out of hand because they got divorced without knowing the spirit of the matter, without knowing the background of it. This is a serious matter here and in due time you and I are going to face it — face to face in the Word of God.

Matthew 5:33-37

Again, ye have heard that it hath been said by them of old time, Thou shalt not forswear thyself, but shalt perform unto the Lord thine oaths: but I say unto you, Swear not at all; neither by heaven; for it is God's throne: nor by the earth; for it is his footstool: neither by Jerusalem; for it is the city of the great King. Neither shalt thou swear by thy head, because thou canst not make one hair white or black.

But let your communication be, Yea, yea; Nay, nay; for whatsoever is more than these cometh of evil.

Christian Motive

Jesus is going beyond the saying of words or making of vows. He is saying that He is listening to every word we say. He is looking at our heart, which is behind everything that we say and every vow that we make. He is saying there are some things we cannot do. We can't change our hair white or black. Therefore, we ought to be straightforward so that when we say yea, or yes, we mean yes. When we say no, we mean no. We should not have something hidden inside us that conceals our true motives. In other words, our motive is to be centered in Christ — simple, sincere, and motivated in our hearts by him.

Matthew 5:38-41

> Ye have heard that it hath been said, An eye for an eye, and a tooth for a tooth: but I say unto you, That ye resist not evil: but whosoever shall smite thee on thy right cheek, turn to him the other also. And if any man will sue thee at the law, and take away thy coat, let him have thy cloak also. And whosoever shall compel thee to go a mile, go with him twain.

Jesus is referring here to the occupying army of the Romans and the laws they made against the Jewish people. For example, if a Roman came along carrying a heavy load and he met a Jew, he could compel him to carry it up to a mile. Then the Jew could hand it back and the Roman could not do anything about it according to Roman law. But Jesus was saying, "When you have carried it a mile, and the man wants you to carry it even a second mile, do not get mad and spit in his face and throw it off your shoulder. Just say to him, 'Sir, I'll carry it a second mile.' "

Jesus is saying that it is not the letter of the law that counts, it is the spirit which is love that counts. In effect, He is saying, "Plant a seed of faith."

Matthew 5:42-48

> Give to him that asketh thee, and from him that would borrow of thee turn not thou away. Ye have heard that it hath been said, Thou shalt love thy neighbour, and hate thine enemy. But I say unto you, Love your enemies, bless them that curse you, do good to them that hate you, and pray for them which despitefully use you, and persecute you; that ye may be the children of your Father which is in heaven: for he maketh his sun to rise on the evil and on the good, and sendeth rain on the just and on the unjust. For if ye love them which love you, what reward have ye? do not even the publicans the same? And

> if ye salute your brethren only, what do ye more than others? do not even the publicans so? Be ye therefore perfect even as your Father which is in heaven is perfect.

Jesus is getting right down on our level and telling us that circumstances hit every one of us, and they keep on coming at us. He is saying, "Don't deal with those from a legalistic standpoint or just from the letter or from the outward part but deal with them from your spirit, which is the way God made you." Your mind is limited in its ability to cope with that circumstance. Your body is limited in its ability to handle it, but your spirit is not limited, especially when you are born of the Holy Spirit. When the Holy You can manifest that spirit toward these circumstances. I believe Jesus is right. I encourage you and me and everyone else to live by His Spirit.

Matthew 6:1-8

> Take heed that ye do not your alms before men, to be seen of them: otherwise ye have no reward of your Father which is in heaven. Therefore when thou doest thine alms, do not sound a trumpet before thee, as the hypocrites do in the synagogues and in the streets, that they may have glory of men. Verily I say unto you, They have their reward. But when thou doest alms, let not thy left hand know what thy right hand doeth: that thine alms may be in secret: and thy Father which seeth in secret himself shall reward thee openly. And when thou prayest, thou shalt not be as the hypocrites are: for they love to pray standing in the synagogues and in the corners of the streets that they may be seen of men. Verily i say unto you, They have their reward. But thou, when thou prayest, enter into thy closet, and when thou hast shut thy door, pray to thy Father which is in secret; and thy Father, which seeth in secret shall reward thee openly. But when ye pray, use not vain repetitions, as the heathen do: for they think that they shall be heard for their much speaking. Be not ye therefore like unto them: for your Father knoweth what things ye have need of, before ye ask him.

In dealing with prayer and giving, Jesus is taking us back to the very Spirit of God which motivates our prayer and giving in the first place. He contrasts it with the manner in which any of the Jewish people did their praying and their giving in a "showy" way, so they would be praised of people. For example, when they brought their gifts to the synagogue or to the temple, there were chests that were trumpet-shaped. When they dropped their large coins into them, they made a big sound, heralding the giver. People would turn and say, "Look, isn't that something?" So they got their reward from men.

When many of them prayed they would raise their hands with palms outward, lift their voices high, and pray in such a way that when people saw them they would turn and say, "Oh what a praying person! Did you ever hear such a prayer in your life?" Jesus is saying, "Folks, you got it all wrong. When you pray, just make a closet in your heart and let your heart take charge of your praying. Whether it is loud or whether it is quiet, whether it is public or whether it is private, just let your heart do the praying. When you give, don't let people around you dictate what you give. Let your heart do the giving. When your heart does the giving, your Father is going to see your giving, and He is going to reward you openly just as He does in rewarding you openly when you pray with your heart."

One of the many reasons I love God is that He has made it possible for us to pray in the spirit, to pray in tongues where we can actually pray under our breath. We can pray quietly in our private devotions. We can pray as we walk, as we sit, as we drive our car, as we work — when nobody else is even listening. We do not have to be concerned with how long the prayer is or how loud. We can pray in the spirit and then through interpretation of our tongue back to our mind, we can pray with our understanding. We are going to talk a lot about that in I Corinthians 14.

Jesus is not telling you that you are not ever to pray in public or to give in public. He is not excluding your praying and giving from the sight or the hearing of other human beings. He is talking about the spirit in which you and I do it. If we do it only to impress other people, then our reward is from those people, and what a sorry reward that is. Because when the going gets rough, people cannot do much for you. When push comes to shove, it is God who counts. This is the backdrop for Jesus teaching us how to pray in what we commonly call the Lord's Prayer.

Matthew 6:9-13

> After this manner therefore pray ye: Our Father which art in heaven, Hallowed be thy name. Thy kingdom come. Thy will be done in earth, as it is in heaven. Give us this day our daily bread. And forgive us our debts, as we forgive our debtors. And lead us not into temptation, but deliver us from evil: For thine is the kingdom, and the power, and the glory, for ever. Amen.

The Believer's Prayer

We call this the Lord's Prayer, but it is really the believer's prayer, for Jesus told us to pray in this manner. It is always good to say this prayer and to use the very same words, but it is even better to take the spirit of what He said here and use that as the basis for all our prayers to our heavenly Father. God is our source. It is from God that we receive everything. Therefore, our prayers are to be directly to Him, and our expectations are to be directly from Him. He mentions the kingdom coming and God's will being done on this earth as it is in heaven, that heaven and earth are not divided. They are made by the same creator, and that we really want what is happening in heaven to be happening here on the earth, and we are to make that come to pass. Then, Jesus is very careful to let us know He cares about our food, shelter, and raiment. Give us this day our daily bread. As one lady said, "Life is so daily." Yes, that's the way it's supposed to be. It is daily. But thank God, God is daily. God is in every moment of our existence. In fact, the only unit of time He recognizes is the now. All the eternal past and all our tomorrows are wrapped up in this special moment right now. When Jesus tells us that we are to forgive and we are to pray that we are not led into temptation, He is speaking again of our hearts, that we are to have a forgiving spirit because we are going to be wronged. Yes, there will be some temporary losses, even financially. But He is telling us that in our prayers we should cover such events and forgive, because it is in our forgiveness that we receive the forgiveness of God.

God is not going to lead us into temptation. He is telling us to pray that we will not enter into temptations that are too great for us. We are to ask for deliverance from the evil of this world, because the kingdom is God's, and the power and the glory, and it is forever. You and I live in time, but we also live in eternity. There is an eternity in our now and there is now in our eternity. Our Father is telling us that He is God. He is source; He is everything. As we wrap our daily lives around Him, He is going to take care of us.

Matthew 6:14-18

> For if ye forgive men their trespasses, your heavenly Father will also forgive you: but if ye forgive not men their trespasses, neither will your Father forgive your trespasses. Moreover when ye fast, be not, as the hypocrites, of a sad countenance: for they disfigure their faces, that they may appear unto men to fast. Verily I say unto you, They have their reward. But thou, when thou fastest, anoint thine head, and wash thy face; that thou appear not unto men to fast, but unto thy Father which is in secret: and thy Father, which seeth in secret, shall reward thee openly.

The Humble Fast

Again Jesus Christ is appealing to us to live in the spirit, to know that our heart is right with God, to speak from a forgiving heart and from a heart that is reaching up to do the will of the Father. We are not to make any public display of our spirituality for the sake of that display. Our attention is to be fully upon God, for why do we fast? We fast because we feel a need in our lives — a need to be closer to God, to be better able to release our faith in God, to have the ability to stand against all temptation and persecution, to resist evil. Therefore, our fast should be in the most humble way, with our entire attention upon our heavenly Father to give us strength, inner strength to stand against everything.

Matthew 6:19-34

Lay not up for yourselves treasures upon earth, where moth and rust doth corrupt, and where thieves break through and steal: but lay up for yourselves treasures in heaven, where neither moth nor rust doth corrupt, and where thieves do not break through nor steal: for where your treasure is, there will your heart be also. The light of the body is the eye: if therefore thine eye be single, thy whole body shall be full of light. But if thine eye be evil, thy whole body shall be full of darkness. If therefore the light that is in thee be darkness, how great is that darkness! No man can serve two masters; for either he will hate the one, and love the other; or else he will hold to the one, and despise the other. Ye cannot serve God and mammon.

Therefore I say unto you, Take no thought for your life, what ye shall eat, or what ye shall drink; nor yet for your body, what ye shall put on. Is not the life more than meat, and the body than raiment? Behold the fowls of the air; for they sow not, neither do they reap, nor gather into barns; yet your heavenly Father feedeth them. Are ye not much better than they? Which of you by taking thought can add one cubit unto his stature? And why take ye thought for raiment? Consider the lilies of the field, how they grow; they toil not, neither do they spin; and yet I say unto you, That even Solomon in all his glory was not arrayed like one of these.

Wherefore, if God so clothe the grass of the field, which today is, and tomorrow is cast into the oven, shall he not much more clothe you, O ye of little faith? Therefore take no thought, saying, What shall we eat? or, What shall we drink? or, Wherewithal shall we be clothed? (For after all these things do the Gentiles seek.) For your heavenly Father knoweth that ye have need of all these things. But seek ye first the kingdom of God, and his righteousness; and all these things shall be added unto you. Take therefore no thought for the morrow; for the morrow shall take thought for the things of itself. Sufficient unto the day is the evil thereof.

Possessions and Priorities

The sweep of history is involved here, that when it is all said and done, what counts is our relationship with our heavenly Father. That is what Jesus is saying. In no way does He tell us that we are not to eat, to have clothes, houses, automobiles, land — the things of this world that are necessary for both our existence and our progress. Jesus does not frown upon the things of His earth. He is not against us having "things." He simply says, "Get your priorities straight." For example, He sums it all up in Verse 33 . . .

> "But seek ye first the kingdom of God, and his righteousness; and all these things shall be added unto you."

Notice that they are to be added. How are they to be added? They are to be added through the Lord as we seek Him, as we put Him first in our lives, in our giving, in our believing, in our living, and in our receiving. Therefore, whatever we need of both heaven and earth will be ours, providing we seek the Lord with our whole heart and put Him first in our lives.

Matthew 7:1-6

> Judge not, that ye be not judged. For with what judgment ye judge, ye shall be judged: and with what measure ye mete, it shall be measured to you again. And why beholdest thou the mote that is in thy brother's eye, but considerest not the beam that is in thine own eye? Or how wilt thou say to thy brother, Let me pull the mote out of thine eye; and behold, a beam is in thine own eye?
>
> Thou hypocrite, first cast out the beam out of thine own eye; and then shalt thou see clearly to cast out the mote out of thy brother's eye. Give not that which is holy unto the dogs, neither cast ye your pearls before swine, lest they trample them under their feet, and turn again and rend you.

Again Jesus Christ is appealing to us in the inner man. We are to look inside and to see how we are serving the Lord. To me Jesus is telling us to be wise, and if we will be wise, He will put us on the right path.

Matthew 7:7-11

Ask, and it shall be given you; seek, and ye shall find; knock, and it shall be opened unto you: for every one that asketh receiveth; and he that seeketh findeth; and to him that knocketh it shall be opened. Or what man is there of you, whom if his son ask bread, will he give him a stone? Or if he ask a fish, will he give him a serpent? If ye then, being evil, know how to give good gifts unto your children, how much more shall your Father which is in heaven give good things to them that ask him?

Good God

He begins by saying, "Ask, seek, knock." It is a fact if we do not ask, we'll never receive. If we do not seek, we will not find. If we do not knock, the doors will not be opened. Therefore, we have to be aggressive in the spirit of asking, of reaching out. I believe the thrust of what Jesus is saying to you and me in the now, through this passage, is that God is a good God. And we are to view Him above the goodness of men. If we can accept the fact that at times people are good, surely we can expect to believe that God is good all the time. God is a good God and God will always be a good God.

Matthew 7:12-14

Therefore all things whatsoever ye would that men should do to you, do ye even so to them: for this is the law and the prophets. Enter ye in at the strait gate: for wide is the gate, and broad is the way, that leadeth to destruction, and many there be which go in thereat: because strait is the gate, and narrow is the way, which leadeth unto life, and few there be that find it.

Jesus is not speaking here of a narrow, physical road, but He is saying that in this world, which is on its way to hell because its whole system is unlike God, and is against men's present and future welfare, there is a better way. But it is a way that requires living by the Word of God, releasing our faith to God, and making up our minds. I am going to follow Christ, and friend, He says what he means and means what He says.

Matthew 7:15-27

Beware of false prophets, which come to you in sheep's clothing, but inwardly they are ravening wolves. Ye shall know them by their fruits. Do men gather grapes of thorns, or figs of thistles? Even so every good tree bringeth forth good fruit; but a corrupt tree bringeth forth evil fruit. A good tree cannot bring forth evil fruit, neither can a corrupt tree bring forth good fruit. Every tree that bringeth not forth good fruit is hewn down, and cast into the fire. Wherefore by their fruits ye shall know them.

Not every one that saith unto me, Lord, Lord, shall enter into the kingdom of heaven; but he that doeth the will of my Father which is in heaven. Many will say to me in that day, Lord, Lord, have we not prophesied in thy name? and in thy name have cast out devils? and in thy name done many wonderful works? And then will I profess unto them, I never knew you: depart from me, ye that work iniquity. Therefore whosoever heareth these sayings of mine, and doeth them, I will liken him unto a wise man, which built his house upon a rock: and the rain descended, and the floods came, and the winds blew, and beat upon that house; and it fell not: for it was founded upon a rock.

And every one that heareth these sayings of mine, and doeth them not, shall be likened unto a foolish man, which built his house upon the sand. And the rain descended, and the floods came, and the winds blew, and beat upon that house; and it fell: and great was the fall of it.

Jesus is warning us against outward professions, against unwarranted public displays. Again He is appealing to our inner man. He is saying His spirit is within us and that all of our deeds are to emanate and originate from within, not from without. For example, He says that at the judgment there will be people coming to Him and calling Him by His name, Lord, and claiming that they have done many miracles. I want you to notice He does not agree with that. He simply says, "I never knew you. Depart from Me because you have been living in your sins."

Jesus is telling us that we are to build our lives upon Christ; when we do, we are on the rock. When we are on the rock rather than the sands, our lives will endure, not only now but forever and ever.

Matthew 7:28,29

And it came to pass, when Jesus had ended these sayings, the people were astonished at his doctrine: for he taught them as one having authority, and not as the scribes.

There is authority in the Word of God, in the life of our Savior Jesus Christ, and in our Christian experience today. We do not go around apologizing for our Christian life or for doing good deeds or for seeing miracles happen through the name of Christ. But we are to do what we do with authority, knowing in our hearts that God is our God and we are His children.

Matthew 8:1-4

When he was come down from the mountain, great multitudes followed him. And, behold, there came a leper and worshipped him, saying, Lord, if thou wilt, thou canst make me clean. And Jesus put forth his hand, and touched him, saying, I will; be thou clean. And immediately his leprosy was cleansed. And Jesus saith unto him, See thou tell no man; but go thy way, shew thyself to the priest, and offer the gift that Moses commanded, for a testimony unto them.

God's Healing Power

The great question that the sick have, even today, is the same one that the leper had in Jesus' time. They say, "If it be the will of God." But Jesus put that question down. He took care of it forever. He said, "I will . . . be thou clean." I believe without the shadow of a doubt that it is God's will to heal. Now, I believe He heals through medicine, I believe he heals through prayer, I believe He heals through love, I believe he heals through climate — often He heals through all these things since He is the source of healing. But He wants us well.

Notice that He told the leper to tell no man about his healing. Some people think they are not to tell about their own healing because of this particular verse of scripture. There may be an isolated instance when God sovereignly might not want us to relate a healing incident in our lives, but generally speaking, He wants us to tell it because others are waiting to hear it. When they hear it, their faith is going to rise and many of them, too, will be delivered.

Matthew 8:5-13

And when Jesus was entered into Capernaum, there came unto him a centurion, beseeching him, and saying, Lord, my servant lieth at home sick of the palsy, grievously tormented. And Jesus saith unto him, I will come and heal him. The centurion answered and said, Lord, I am not worthy that thou shouldest come under my roof: but speak the word only, and my servant shall be healed. For I am a man under authority, having soldiers under me: and I say to this man, Go, and he goeth; and to another, Come, and he cometh; and to my servant, Do this, and he doeth it. When Jesus heard it, he marvelled, and said to them that followed, Verily I say unto you, I have not found so great faith, no, not in Israel. And I say unto you, That many shall come from the east and west, and shall sit down with Abraham, and Isaac, and Jacob, in the kingdom of heaven. But the children of the kingdom shall be cast out into outer darkness: there shall be weeping

and gnashing of teeth. And Jesus said unto the centurion, Go thy way; and as thou hast believed, so be it done unto thee. And his servant was healed in the selfsame hour.

The Power of Contact

In my view, the eighth chapter of Matthew's gospel is the most powerful healing chapter in the Word of God. This healing of the Roman army captain's servant, his simple faith which Christ called "great faith," may be the most perfect healing for us to study, for it contains in it the essential elements for us to base our faith on for our healing in the now. Notice that when the centurion came to Christ and told Him about his suffering servant, Jesus said, "I will come and heal him." Jesus has come. And He has come to heal. "I will come and heal him." That is what was uppermost in Christ's mind — the deliverance of lost and suffering humanity. That is what He thinks about today. He is touched by the feelings of our infirmities. When we hurt, He feels our hurt and He has come.

The servant was lying at a distance, and the Roman captain said, "It is not necessary for you to come, Lord. I'm not a man worthy of your coming in my house. But I'm a man under authority; I know what authority is. When I tell a soldier to do a certain thing, he does it without questioning me, because he knows that I speak in the authority of Caesar, the emperor of the Roman Empire — the mightiest force in the world. But Jesus, I know that you are a man under authority. You have the authority of heaven and earth. I have the authority of Caesar. But you have the total authority. Speak in the authority of your own being . . . just say the word and tell the disease to leave my servant's body. When you tell the disease to leave, it will submit to your authority and my servant shall be healed."

Jesus was so elated, he turned to the audience and said, "Look at this man! I've been searching for faith like his all over Israel and not found it. This is what great faith is."

This is encouraging to you and me because we do not have to be somebody special in order to have great faith. Jesus turned to this Roman army captain and said, "You just go on home. I've spoken the word." And, as he went, the servant was healed. One of the important things to point out here is a point of contact.

The captain said, "If you will just say the word." That is like going over there and turning on a light switch which is connected to the light company. The moment you flip the switch, the current flows through. The switch is the point of contact with the source of light power. So when you use a point of contact such as this captain did,

"Speak the word only," or you have the laying on of hands, or any similar thing, you have a point of contact with the power of God. It is good to have a point of contact, because it helps you set the time and put your faith directly in line with God himself.

We need to read this passage over and over and learn that we, as believers, must center our faith upon the authority of our Lord. It means in the now that we have faith no matter how small it is, the authority of our Lord. When we release that faith, He is going to tell us the wonderful good news that we are being healed.

Matthew 8:14,15

> And when Jesus was come into Peter's house, he saw his wife's mother laid, and sick of a fever. And he touched her hand, and the fever left her: and she arose, and ministered unto them.

Peter's wife's mother was feverishly ill. She was in bed. Peter was a married man and his mother-in-law lived with them, but this must have been a very loving woman, and they had great love for her. When Jesus went home with Peter, He saw Peter's mother-in-law, and He touched her hand. Can't you see that? He touched her hand, and the touch of the Master caused the fever to leave her. She just got out of bed, dressed, and immediately began to cook for them.

Matthew 8:16,17

> When even was come, they brought unto Him many that were possessed with devils: and He cast out the spirits with his word, and healed all that were sick: that it might be fulfilled which was spoken by Esaias the prophet, saying, Himself took our infirmities, and bare our sicknesses.

The Meaning of Sin

He is referring here to Isaiah 53:4. Jesus used Isaiah's word when He met those who were possessed with demons, He spoke the word, and He also healed their sick. We have been asked, "Who is a demon? What is a demon?" Demons are fallen angels. Somewhere in the dateless past there was war in heaven. We are told of this in Isaiah, and in Ezekiel, that Lucifer, the bright shining archangel of God, who was the nearest to God, rose up in open rebellion and committed high treason against the Creator. When Lucifer said, "I will ascend above God," "I will" became sin.

We sin with our will. Sin is no light thing. Sin is not a mistake that we make. Sin is not something we do when we do not know better. Sin is a willful thing. It is when we know and then we "will" to do wrong. This is what Lucifer did. He knew that God was God, but in his heart he willed to rise above God, to set God aside, and to become God himself. A great portion of the angels followed him in this rebellion and God said, "There is sin in your heart and I will cast you out to the earth."

There was a cataclysmic event that took place in history when Lucifer, who then became the devil, or tormentor, was cast out of heaven to this earth. When Lucifer fell, along with the other angels, they lost their celestial bodies. It is a very important thing to understand that there are bodiless spirits in this world which Jesus called demons or devils and that they seek to enter human beings. They seek to set aside the blood of Christ and their same purpose is to will against God, to fight God. The only way they really have to strike against God is to embody themselves in some human being or in human beings en masse so that they can lead a man, or woman, or a mass of people, against whatever God stands for.

People wonder why there are wars and destructions on this earth. They often say, "If there is a God, why does He permit wars?" Others blame the church and blame God for what is going wrong in the world. That is exactly what the devil wants us to do. The devil is a liar and the father of lies. Jesus said that himself. He is a destroyer. He is the one who comes to steal and kill and destroy. He is the one who inspires wars between individuals, among families, between nations, and the nations of the world. Because we have opened ourselves to sin, demons have greater liberty in the world. I thank God that when we believe in Jesus Christ and His blood is applied to our hearts, the devil can never cross the blood line. No demon can ever enter a child of God as long as that child of God lives under the shed blood of Jesus Christ.

I once was afraid of demons and of people who were possessed by demons — of what they might do to me as I prayed for them. But God took that fear away, and I have been without fear for all these years. I have seen Jesus Christ's power manifested to destroy the works of Satan — to cast out devils. Many, many times I have seen people freed of demons and heard them say, "I'm free! I'm free! Jesus has set me free!" Oh, I praise God that Jesus is the Son of God and that He is master over demons. Let us read Matthew 8:17 again and follow it with a prayer.

Matthew 8:17

> That it might be fulfilled which was spoken by Esaias the prophet, saying, Himself took our infirmities, and bare our sicknesses.

Dear friend, he is talking about you and me, our infirmities, our sicknesses, the things of disharmony and disunity in our lives. I am a man, Oral Roberts, called of God to take His healing power to my generation. When I read this verse my soul is stirred. I feel compassion flowing through me, and I want to join with you in prayer.

Would you please touch yourself or touch someone there with you, and let us pray together that Matthew 8:17 will actually come to pass in your life. Let us pray.

> *Father, in my own spirit I hear our Lord saying that He himself took our infirmities and bore our sicknesses. I thank you because You have borne them and we do not have to carry them any longer. Now, friend, through Jesus Christ of Nazareth I pray for you to be healed. Be healed from the crown of your head to the soles of your feet. I come against this sickness and affliction. I come against this hurting, this pain. I come against this financial need. I come against this problem that is tearing you apart. I come against this family situation that is not pleasing to God. I come against this lack of peace. Yes, I come against sin through the power of Jesus' name — himself who took your infirmities and bore your sicknesses — I ask God to heal you, to deliver you, to set you free, and now be healed. Be made whole. Through Jesus Christ I believe and I receive it with you. Amen and amen.*

Matthew 8:18-20

> Now when Jesus saw great multitudes about him, he gave commandment to depart unto the other side. And a certain scribe came, and said unto him, Master, I will follow thee whithersoever thou goest. And Jesus saith unto him, The foxes have holes, and the birds of the air have nests; but the Son of man hath not where to lay his head.

There may have been times when Jesus did not have a house or a bed to lay His head upon, though that certainly would not have been often. This message is much deeper than that. He is saying that human society had no place for Him, that no matter what He did or where He went, people as a rule were not ready to accept God. Society ruled him out. We need to think about that when we are not accepted, when it is apparent that certain groups in this world are not going to have anything to do with us as true Christians. We need to look back and understand that we are no better than our Lord. Yet we know that we can have what we need to have in this world.

Matthew 8:21,22

> And another of his disciples said unto him, Lord, suffer me first to go and bury my father. But Jesus said unto him, Follow me; and let the dead bury their dead.

We are not to take this quite as literally as it sounds. It does not mean that we are not to be there in the burial of a loved one, such as a father or a mother. It means that Jesus is using the extreme figure of speech to show us that obeying Him is the number-one thing in our lives.

Matthew 8:23-27

> And when he was entered into a ship, his disciples followed him. And, behold, there arose a great tempest in the sea, insomuch that the ship was covered with the waves: but he was asleep. And his disciples came to him, and awoke him, saying, Lord, save us: we perish. And he saith unto them, Why are ye fearful, O ye of little faith? Then he arose, and rebuked the winds and the sea; and there was a great calm. But the men marvelled, saying, What manner of man is this, that even the winds and the sea obey him!

Faith is the Key

In the very boat from which Jesus had been preaching a little earlier, He now calls His disciples to go across the Sea of Galilee. Because it is not a large body of water — some 14 miles long and 7 or 8 miles wide — you might think that that was not a very important trip. Certainly, not a dangerous one. But you see, the Sea of Galilee is situated several hundred feet below sea level. It is rimmed by high mountains and it is subject to violent tropical storms that often strike without any notice. Within minutes the winds can churn the sea with such violence that no ship of the type made at that time could survive that storm. Jesus knew all about this and so did the fishermen. When He called them into the boat to go across the Sea of Galilee, at this time, He was on His way to heal the demoniac of Gadarene. Doubtless the prince of the powers of the air, the devil, knew all about this great miracle that Jesus would do on this demon-possessed person. Suddenly the storm struck and the disciples went to pieces.

I think Matthew included this great episode in the life of the disciples and Jesus to show us the kind of world that we live in. We are so situated with this world that the most violent storms can strike without notice, not only physical storms, but storms that strike at the very roots of our existence and of our relationship with God. But Jesus was in that boat and He did not tell them to take that particular boat and that particular trip just to go under. He knew He was going over and He went to sleep. There is something about God we ought to think about, and that is what He knows. He knows what we are going to come up against and what is coming against us. He knows that He is with us. He knows that He has put a lot of faith in us. In the midst of it, when the disciples cried for Him to save them and He did rebuke the winds and the sea and every violent force and brought them across safely, He then asked these questions: "Why were you so afraid and why did you have such little faith? Oh, you of little faith!" It is amazing how many miracles he has placed within our faith. He has actually put inside you and me what it takes, if we will exercise it, to get through the storms. My family has undergone about every kind of storm you can imagine. But I can tell you, every time we faced these terrible things and began to use our faith, we got through them and we are still getting through them. The only times we do not is when we do not use the power of the faith that God has put in us.

When Jesus brought them safely to the other side, the disciples were overwhelmed. You see, they had not yet quite understood the incarnation, that He truly was the Son of God, and that is one of our problems today. Many Christians do not really understand who Jesus is, that He is the Son of God, that He has all power, that He can rebuke the forces that destroy us. I think sometimes we come into the Christian experience and do not go on into it sufficiently to learn the power of our faith and the power of the Christ who lives within us. Bear in mind that Jesus says you have all the faith necessary. Start learning how to use it — to release it and send it to God. Then watch God do His stuff!

Matthew 8:28-34

> And when he was come to the other side into the country of the Gergesenes, there met him two possessed with devils, coming out of the tombs, exceeding fierce, so that no man might pass by that way. And, behold, they cried out, saying, What have we to do with thee, Jesus, thou Son of God? art thou come hither to torment us before the time?
>
> And there was a good way off from them an herd of many swine feeding. So the devils besought him, saying, If thou cast us out, suffer us to go away into the herd of swine. And he said unto them, Go. And when they were come out, they went into the herd of swine: and, behold, the whole herd of swine ran violently down a steep place into the sea, and perished in the waters. And they that kept them fled, and

went their ways into the city, and told everything, and what was befallen to the possessed of the devils. And, behold, the whole city came out to meet Jesus: and when they saw him, they besought him that he would depart out of their coasts.

Jesus' Special Power

Here is Jesus of Nazareth having a confrontation with demon spirits who have possessed two men and have made them so violent in their behavior that they were a menace to society. In that time such individuals were cast out of the city and were made to live alone. Where they lived at this time was so dangerous that people did not even dare to pass that way. Jesus did, however, because He always goes where the hurting, bound, tormented people are, and the devils knew Him. When we get to the book of James we will see how the devils believe and tremble. That does not mean they are saved, but they understand who God is, because devils or demons are the spirits of fallen angels who followed Lucifer, the great archangel, in his rebellion against the Heavenly Father and were cast out with him to the earth and lost their heavenly bodies. Now they are spirits without bodies and therefore are powerless, unless they have human embodiment. We see them here embodied in two human beings who were so violent that people were scared to death of them but Jesus was not. He met them and they knew him. They knew the time was coming when they would be cast into the pit. They were frightened that Jesus was going to send them out of the earth into hell already, and so the devils, aware of a great herd of hogs (some 2,000 of them feeding nearby), and fearing that Jesus would cast them out of the bodies of these men, wanted embodiment so much that they besought Him, if He cast them out, to let them enter into those swine. When that happened and they entered the swine, those hogs went mad. They ran violently down the side of the mountain and into the waters and were drowned. The herdsmen were afraid. They ran into the town, told the story of what had happened to those who had been possessed with devils — and it scared the city to death. The people rushed out and besought Him that He would leave their coasts. They were not comfortable with these violent men but they were more comfortable with them than they were with Jesus who made them free men.

It is a pretty good picture of the world we live in. People are so frightened of Jesus, and their real fear is because of His power to clean people up and to free them from the power of the devil, of demons, of sickness and disease, of sin, of fear. Keep in mind that there is a confrontation going on all the time between Jesus and the demon powers of this world. As we trust Him, Jesus is going to give us the victory.

Matthew 9:1-8

> And he entered into a ship, and passed over, and came into his own city. And, behold, they brought to him a man sick of the palsy, lying on a bed: and Jesus, seeing their faith said unto the sick of the palsy; Son, be of good cheer; thy sins be forgiven thee. And, behold, certain of the scribes said within themselves, This man blasphemeth. And Jesus knowing their thoughts said, Wherefore think ye evil in your hearts? For whether is easier, to say, thy sins be forgiven thee; or to say, Arise, and walk? But that ye may know that the Son of Man hath power on earth to forgive sins (then saith he to the sick of the palsy,) Arise, take up thy bed, and go unto thine house. And he arose, and departed to his house. But when the multitudes saw it, they marvelled, and glorified God, which had given such power unto men. And as Jesus passed forth from thence, He saw a man, named Matthew, sitting at the receipt of custom; and he said unto him, Follow me and he arose, and followed Him.

God Sees Faith

Jesus was very concerned about the root cause, not only about the sickness of the body but about the sins of the man. The same Greek root word for saved is also the word for heal, and Jesus was coming in the power of His own human and divine nature to forgive and to heal, to set people free in soul and body.

Naturally, He began by telling this man who had come by faith, "Son, be of good cheer, your sins are forgiven you." And He was demonstrating the almightiness of God that was being manifested in His Son Jesus Christ to both save and heal, which is the very reason why He came to this world.

We could ask the question, "Why did He do both of these to this one particular sick person?" He did it partly because of those who brought Him, dear friends, who believed with all their hearts, and Jesus saw their faith. Faith is something God sees. Faith has in it the implied power to produce miracles, and faith set Jesus off, set Him into motion. They brought the sick man, and Jesus did not move toward him until He saw their faith. Jesus was "turned on" by the faith of the man, because He knew He had put the miracles in our faith, and the faith of the man was released. Jesus did the rest while the Jews were carried away with their ideas that the man was blaspheming. The crowd just raised their hands and shouted for joy, because they saw God walking among them and another person saved and healed.

Matthew 9:9

> And as Jesus passed forth from thence, he saw a man, named Matthew, sitting at the receipt of custom: and he saith unto him, Follow me. And he arose, and followed him.

This refers to a man who was called a publican, and in other terms, a sinner. At that time, the Roman Empire ruled over the world. They were in control of the Holy Land. They sent their tax gatherers from Rome, and these people then hired Jewish people who would work under them. These people would bear down unjustly upon the Jewish people, collecting taxes far beyond the norm. They were the most despised group in Israel. But when Jesus passed by one of these men whose name was Matthew (who later wrote this gospel), He saw a man. That's right. In Verse 9 it says He saw a man. He saw within Matthew a man who was despised because of the rude and wicked way he had dominated his fellow Jews. Jesus saw in that person, the man, someone He could release into the fullness of humanity. He said to him two brief words: "Follow Me." Evidently Matthew had seen Jesus, for this is a scene in Jesus' hometown, Capernaum. He had seen His mighty miracles, heard His powerful messages, listened to Him say that the kingdom of heaven was at hand. Matthew was really abhorring what he had done. He was ready. God always comes to us when we are ready. It is like a piece of fruit ripening upon a tree. When it is green you have to pull it, but when it is ripe and you touch it, it falls off in your hand. Matthew was ripe and ready. All Christ had to say with power was, "Follow Me." This man rose up, left his tax collecting, broke with the Roman empire, and in the face of all he had done in the past, which was evil, took up a new path and began to follow the gentle and pure Galilean.

Matthew 9:10

> And it came to pass, as Jesus sat at meat in the house, behold, many publicans and sinners came and sat down with him and his disciples.

This is a direct result of Matthew's conversion. When the other publicans and sinners saw that Jesus was not too good to stop and talk to a sinner, they flocked to Him. They saw in Jesus a man who hated their sin but loved them as sinners, who hated the way they collected taxes, but loved them as publicans, and they responded. Jesus sat down with them to eat. This is one of the missing elements in the

Christian faith. So many times we are too scared of our Christian peers, scared to go where there are sinners, or to associate with people in their sinful condition with the desire to lead them to Christ. One of the reasons that the Church takes such a stand against this is that when some Christians associate with sinners they soon become like them. But we are not to let the failures of a few keep us from going to sinners, because Christ came into this world to save sinners.

In my own ministry, the largest number of people who respond to me are those who do not know God. I want to tell you it is the joy of my heart to reach these people with the glorious gospel of deliverance through Jesus Christ our Lord.

Matthew 9:11-13

> And when the Pharisees saw it, they said unto his disciples, Why eateth your Master with publicans and sinners? But when Jesus heard that, he said unto them, They that be whole need not a physician, but they that are sick. But go ye and learn what that meaneth, I will have mercy, and not sacrifice: for I am not come to call the righteous, but sinners to repentance.

Church or Club

The Pharisees by now had lost their original inspiration to restore the fullness to the old covenant and to stand up for the kingdom of God and its power among men. They now have an outward form of godliness, but they deny the power of God. When they see Jesus sitting there with sinners and publicans, they draw themselves aside in their so-called superiority, and they say to His disciples, "Why is your Master eating with these kinds of people?"

You see, we can almost inadvertently make the church an exclusive club. We can congregate together — so separate from our fellow men that we actually withdraw from their human existence and their daily experiences, not entering into compassion for them. We develop a feeling that, well, we are better than you are. Well, we are sinners saved by grace. We were just like they are, but Jesus saved us. Therefore, we ought to have the deepest love for people who are like we once were. In order for that to happen, we must be among them. We must encourage them to come to the house of God or to come hear us preach wherever we are, or to become friends with us so that we might live out the Christian life in their presence.

Matthew 9:14,15

> Then came to him the disciples of John, saying, Why do we and the

> Pharisees fast oft, but thy disciples fast not? And Jesus said unto them, Can the children of the bridechamber mourn, as long as the bridegroom is with them? but the days will come, when the bridegroom shall be taken from them, and then shall they fast.

What Fasting Means

This is a reference to what fasting really is. The scribes and Pharisees fasted openly that others might admire them and say how holy they were. Jesus said, "As long as I am present — I, the bridegroom, am here on earth — there is no way that My disciples can fast." They might do without food, but doing without food in itself is not fasting. It is more than doing without food. It is when we are not enough aware of Christ's presence. It is when we need more of God. It is when it is necessary for the presence of God to dwell in us, and that we know it dwells in us, or when we have burdens too great to bear, or loved ones we are not able to reach, and we feel so inadequate. It is at such times that we may take a meal and dedicate it to God by not eating a bite of it and taking that same period of time in prayer, in dedicating our thoughts to God, calling upon Him. The moment we experience His presence to any measurable degree, we start eating again, because there is no virtue in just leaving off food. The virtue is in recapturing the spirit and the presence of God. The fast is of the spirit, and the doing without food is the submission of the body to the spirit, but it is the spirit of ourselves that is wholly dependent upon God that makes the fast worthwhile.

Matthew 9:16-19a

> No man putteth a piece of new cloth unto an old garment, for that which is put in to fill it up taketh from the garment, and the rent is made worse. Neither do men put new wine into old bottles: else the bottles break, and the wine runneth out, and the bottles perish: but they put new wine into new bottles, and both are preserved.
>
> While he spake these things unto them, behold, there came a certain ruler, and worshipped him, saying, My daughter is even now dead: but come and lay thy hand upon her, and she shall live. And Jesus arose.

Jesus arose. Apparently He was sitting. He was taking care of business — of His work. But the moment that a man with a sick child came to Him, He arose.

Matthew 9:19-22

> And Jesus arose, and followed him, and so did his disciples. And, behold, a woman, which was diseased with an issue of blood twelve years, came behind him, and touched the hem of his garment: for she said within herself, If I may but touch his garment, I shall be whole. But Jesus turned him about, and when he saw her, he said, Daughter, be of good comfort; thy faith hath made thee whole. And the woman was made whole from that hour.

The Whole Person

Because of the nature of this woman's disease which made her unclean, the Jewish law was that she could not get near other people. In fact, if she touched someone she made him unclean. When she came close to Jesus, saying within herself, "If I could only touch His clothes, I should be healed," she, according to Jewish law, made Him unclean. But Jesus paid no attention to such laws, for He turned to her and said, "Daughter, be of good comfort, thy faith hath made thee whole."

You see, He placed the miracle-working power of God in our faith. When she came up with that unclean disease, touching Him, and everybody was saying that she would make Him unclean, he knew that the moment did not even exist but something greater existed. The miracle-working power of her released faith would come pouring out of the Lord into her being, and she not only would be healed of just that particular affliction, but her whole person would be healed. Jesus used the word whole, w-h-o-l-e, whole-person healing. There is a lot of talk about holistic healing, and I have nothing against that, but I like whole, w-h-o-l-e, whole-person healing much better. That is what we are trying to do in this ministry, particularly at the City of Faith Health Care Center where we are merging prayer and medicine and reaching out for the wholeness of the person.

Matthew 9:23-31

> And when Jesus came into the ruler's house, and saw the minstrels and the people making a noise, he said unto them, Give place: for the maid is not dead, but sleepeth. And they laughed him to scorn. But when the people were put forth, he went in, and took her by the hand, and the maid arose. And the fame hereof went abroad into all that land. And when Jesus departed thence, two blind men followed him, crying, and saying, Thou son of David, have mercy on us. And when he was come into the house, the blind men came to him: and Jesus

said unto them, Believe ye that I am able to do this? They said unto him, Yea, Lord. Then touched he their eyes, saying, According to your faith be it unto you. And their eyes were opened; and Jesus straitly charged them, saying, See that no man know it. But they, when they were departed, spread abroad his fame in all that country.

Exercising Faith

When He touched their eyes, He said something very special to them: "According to your faith be it unto you." At Jesus' touch, the eyesight had not come. Do you understand that? The eyesight had not come merely because Jesus touched their eyes. Faith, on their part, was to be involved. They believed that He was the Son of David. He wanted them to believe that He was in the now. He was there. He was able and willing. So He said, "According to your faith be it unto you."

Someone said to me many years ago, "Oral, never doubt the power of your own faith in God." Now here are two blind men who had not seen Jesus in the flesh, even as He touched their eyes, did not bring eyesight. He caused their faith to come forth, and when their faith went into action, their eyes opened. So we are not to doubt the power of our own faith.

Matthew 9:32-34

As they went out, behold, they brought to him a dumb man possessed with a devil. But when the devil was cast out, the dumb spake: and the multitudes marvelled, saying, It was never so seen in Israel. But the Pharisees said, He casteth out devils through the prince of the devils.

Believe, Don't "Play"

It is said that this man who could not speak was possessed with the devil. Now, that did not mean then that all people who could not speak had a devil, nor does it mean that today. It does mean there is a particular kind of demon who is a dumb demon — that is, he cannot speak. When he enters a human being, he takes away the power of speech. When that devil came out, the man's speech returned, and the multitude was amazed, saying, "It was never so seen in Israel." I want to make a point here that there is a central place for miracles in the kingdom of God. In the gospel of Jesus Christ, in the Christian church today, how often do we see such scenes as this? Is it not true that too many churches frown upon even the belief in devils? Or that Jesus came to cast out devils? Or that we who believe are to use our faith to cast out devils and to help these poor benighted people? It is worth saying today again, that it is time the Church quit playing church. It is time that Christians quit playing at their Christian experience. It is time that Christians begin believing their own faith. It is time that people see suffering people, especially people who are tormented by demons, and realize that through the name of Jesus we have power. We are able to help these people. The time is now. Believe me, when people see it, they will say, "We have never seen anything like this."

That is what this whole world needs. Its appetite is sated. People feel that they have seen and heard and experienced everything. But my friend, they have not seen or heard or experienced the mighty delivering power of Jesus Christ, the Son of the living God. Never was there such a bright hour as now for us to use our faith and to produce these miracles through faith in Jesus Christ, to stir the imagination of lost and suffering people so that multitudes of them will come to Christ.

Matthew 9:35-38

> And Jesus went about all the cities and villages, teaching in their synagogues, and preaching the gospel of the kingdom, and healing every sickness and every disease among the people. But when he saw the multitudes, he was moved with compassion on them, because they fainted, and were scattered abroad, as sheep having no shepherd. Then saith he unto his disciples, The harvest truly is plenteous, but the labourers are few; pray ye therefore the Lord of the harvest, that he will send forth labourers into his harvest.

This ends the ninth chapter of Matthew's gospel, but it ends with a powerful statement about the life-style of Jesus Christ. He went about the cities and the towns teaching, preaching, and healing. This was always His method: to teach, to preach, and to heal. In my own heart, I am crying out for us, the Christians, to examine the way of our own life-style. Are we teaching the gospel? If we say yes, fine. Are we preaching the gospel? If we say yes, fine. Are we healing the sick through faith? If we say yes, fine. But if we are only doing one or two of these, then we are leaving the whole out.

Matthew 10:1

> And when he had called unto him his twelve disciples, he gave them power against unclean spirits, to cast them out, and to heal all manner of sickness and all manner of disease.

This is a singular statement of Jesus Christ. It is a trademark of His ministry and of the Christian faith. He stated very clearly that He gave them power. It was a given power, not an inherited power, not a learned power: it was a power as a gift of God. It was a power against something. What was it against? Unclean spirits or what we call devils or demons. Then He added, "to heal all manner of sickness and all manner of disease." It's very noteworthy to point out that He did not give His disciples power to heal all sickness and heal all disease, but all manner or all types of sicknesses and all types of diseases.

In my own ministry of the Christian faith of winning souls and bringing healing to the sick, I have seen many, many types of sicknesses and diseases healed, but I have never seen all sickness healed and all disease healed. It says that there is no sickness that can resist our Lord. No type of disease can withstand His healing power. But it does not mean that all sicknesses and diseases are going to be healed here in this world.

When we who follow Christ die, and the resurrection day comes, Christ raises us from the dead. Then, if there is any sickness or any disease that was in our bodies when we died, all of that sickness and disease will be removed once and forever. Many times we are healed here, but we will all be healed — and totally healed — in the resurrection.

Matthew 10:2-15

Now the names of the twelve apostles are these; The first, Simon, who is called Peter, and Andrew his brother; James the son of Zebedee, and John his brother; Philip, and Bartholomew; Thomas, and Matthew the publican; James the son of Alphaeus, and Lebbaeus, whose surname was Thaddaeus; Simon the Canaanite, and Judas Iscariot, who also betrayed Him.

These twelve Jesus sent forth, and commanded them, saying, Go not into the way of the Gentiles, and into any city of the Samaritans enter ye not. But go rather to the lost sheep of the house of Israel.

And as ye go, preach, saying, The kingdom of heaven is at hand.

Heal the sick, cleanse the lepers, raise the dead, cast out devils: freely ye have received, freely give. Provide neither gold, nor silver, nor brass in your purses, nor scrip for your journey, neither two coats, neither shoes, nor yet staves: for the workman is worthy of his meat. And into whatsoever city or town ye shall enter, enquire who in it is worthy; and there abide till ye go thence. And when ye come into an house, salute it. And if the house be worthy, let your peace come upon it: but if it be not worthy, let your peace return to you. And whosoever shall not receive you, nor hear your words, when ye depart out of that house or city, shake off the dust of your feet. Verily I say unto you, It shall be more tolerable for the land of Sodom and Gomorrha in the day of judgment, than for that city.

I pray that we of the Christian faith, of the Church of Jesus Christ of Nazareth, will realize what we have. The kingdom of heaven is in us. And as we teach and preach, we are to bring healing to people.

You and I have tremendous responsibility. At the same time, we are not to be offended by people who do not receive us. Even if we shake the dust off our shoes and go to some other place, we remain with a loving spirit toward them, for in the end, it is love that wins out.

Matthew 10:16

Behold, I send you forth as sheep in the midst of wolves: be ye therefore wise as serpents, and harmless as doves.

That world out there that does not regard God or man, follows the devil and has much Satanic wisdom. While we live amidst it, we are to be very wise, harmless, without malice. It is better to be harmed than to harm someone else. Verse 17 says . . .

Matthew 10:17

But beware of men . . .

Jesus is speaking of man in his unsaved humanity, man who follows the devil rather than God. Beware of this present wicked world. And then He continues in Verse 17 . . .

Matthew 10:17-20

. . . for they will deliver you up to the councils, and they will scourge you in their synagogues; and ye shall be brought before governors and kings for my sake, for a testimony against them and the Gentiles. But when they deliver you up, take no thought how or what ye shall speak: for it shall be given you in that same hour what you shall speak. For it is not ye that speak, but the Spirit of your Father which speaketh in you.

He says that we will be opposed. We will even be brought into judgment or trial. There will be occasions when we will be imprisoned, ushered into court. The accusers will be coming at us from every side. Jesus never exempted us from trials and tribulations. He did not say we would not be imprisoned or thrown into court. This present wicked world is not a friend of God. Therefore, we must not depend upon our own human wisdom and knowledge; we are to have a childlike trust in God's Holy Spirit who dwells within us, that He will give us the words to say. Once we have said those words, we are to stop and trust that God our source will do what must be done.

Matthew 10:21,22

> And the brother shall deliver up the brother to death, and the father the child: and the children shall rise up against their parents, and cause them to be put to death. And ye shall be hated of all men for my name's sake: but he that endureth to the end shall be saved.

Spirit of Persistence

This 22nd verse of Matthew 10 is one of the foundation stones of our Christian faith. "He that endureth to the end shall be saved." It refers back to Daniel 12:12 which speaks of persistence. The Christian faith is one of persistence. It is not simply that first act of conversion, though that is the entrance into the kingdom of God. It does not merely consist of our going to church and reading our Bible and saying our prayers and going about our work the best way we know how. It is the spirit of persistence. We endure anything that is thrown at us. We never give up. We know we are going to make it. We have the spirit of persistence in our heart. We just simply will not lie down and let the devil destroy us, nor will we become discouraged because of the opposition of men. We will not allow circumstances to discourage us to the point we throw up our hands and say, "Oh, what's the use?" and then quit. You get up and push on. You keep on believing. You keep on teaching. You keep on witnessing. You keep on healing. You keep on living a good life. You keep on loving. He is the one who is going to make it. What a joy it is going to be when we shall have made it and the Lord says, "Come, my faithful servants and enter into the joy of your Lord." Those are going to be the sweetest words we will ever hear.

Matthew 10:23-28

> But when they persecute you in this city, flee ye into another: for verily I say unto you, Ye shall not have gone over the cities of Israel, till the Son of man be come. The disciple is not above his master, nor the servant above his lord. It is enough for the disciple that he be as his Master, and the servant as his Lord. If they have called the Master of the house Beelzebub, how much more shall they call them of his household? Fear them not therefore: for there is nothing covered, that shall not be revealed; and hid, that shall not be known.

> What I tell you in darkness, that speak ye in light: and what ye hear in the ear, that preach ye upon the housetops. And fear not them which kill the body, but are not able to kill the soul: but rather fear him which is able to destroy both soul and body in hell.

Jesus tells us when we are persecuted to simply go to another place, for we shall not have done all of our work until the power of our Lord Jesus Christ comes. He says that in the midst of the worst trials and tribulations, we are not above Him. We read about Him and it is so difficult to relate to what He went through as far as facing the devil is concerned. But it does help us relate to Him when we go through some of these things ourselves. However, we can take comfort in knowing that there is nothing coming against us that has not already come against Him, and that He has met and conquered.

Matthew 10:29-31

> Are not two sparrows sold for a farthing? and one of them shall not fall on the ground without your Father. But the very hairs of your head are all numbered. Fear ye not therefore, ye are of more value than many sparrows.

We Are Somebody!

In that time a sparrow was worth maybe a couple of pennies, and yet when one fell, the Heavenly Father who created it, saw it. Christ says that God is so careful in His love for us that He has numbered the hairs on our head. Therefore, we are not to be afraid because our value is beyond all calculation. We are of more value than all the sparrows in the world put together. We need a good self image as a child of God. We do not realize how valuable we are. We are the most valuable creatures that God ever made. We are His masterpiece. Yes, we are God's masterpiece. We're God's through creation; we are His through redemption; we are His through faith and our choice; we are His because He is our Lord. We are His property. We are somebody!

Matthew 10:32,33

> Whosoever therefore shall confess me before men, him will I confess also before my Father which is in heaven. But whosoever shall deny me before men, him will I also deny before my Father which is in heaven.

While we are not running around screaming at the top of our

voice that we are Christians, we are to have the unshakeable conviction that we belong to God and that we confess Him as our Lord and Savior. There is no place in our hearts for secret denial or for public denial. We belong to God.

Matthew 10:34-39

> Think not that I am come to send peace on earth: I came not to send peace, but a sword. For I am come to set a man at variance against his father, and the daughter against her mother, and the daughter-in-law against her mother-in-law. And a man's foes shall be they of his own household. He that loveth father or mother more than me is not worthy of me: and he that loveth son or daughter more than me is not worthy of me. And he that taketh not his cross, and followeth after me is not worthy of me. He that findeth his life shall lose it: and he that loseth his life for my sake shall find it.

Our Lord Jesus Christ is telling us that the coming of the gospel into the world is going to be against all Satanic forces. Because the devil is in the world and against God, against all His people, and against all good, Jesus comes against the Satanic world with a sword, not to give it peace in its sins. Those who reject the gospel are not at peace. They do not like to have their sins revealed. They do not enjoy seeing the sweep of the purpose of God on this earth.

In many worldly homes loved ones turn against one another. There are times, in our own families, that little things like offering thanks for the food can cause an uproar. But the point is that when we live our Christian lives, there is going to be much turmoil and most of it is going to be created by those who really do not want Christ.

In Verse 39 Jesus sums it up by saying that he who hangs onto his own life, apart from God, is ultimately going to lose his life, but he who gives God his life is going to save it.

Matthew 10:40-42

> He that receiveth you receiveth me, and he that receiveth me receiveth him that sent me. He that receiveth a prophet in the name of a prophet shall receive a prophet's reward; and he that receiveth a righteous man in the name of a righteous man shall receive a righteous man's reward. And whosoever shall give to drink unto one of these little ones a cup of cold water only in the name of a disciple, verily I say unto you, he shall in no wise lose his reward.

Giving is Rewarding

Note the word "cold" in reference to water. A cup of "cold" water.

Why did he say "cold" water? Because that is going out of your way. That is going the extra mile — doing something special. It is not just saying, "Oh here, have some water." If it is hot it means cooling the water. If it is cold, it means heating the water. It is doing something from the heart, not just outwardly, but from the inner spirit.

Christ is telling us that we are going to be rewarded. We Christians should understand that Christ comes with rewards, and that our giving carries its own reward, because the other end of giving is an act of receiving — giving and receiving. That is the key of the Christian faith.

Matthew 11:1-6

> And it came to pass, when Jesus had made an end of commanding his twelve disciples, he departed thence to teach and to preach in their cities. Now when John had heard in the prison the works of Christ, he sent two of his disciples, and said unto him, Art thou he that should come, or do we look for another? Jesus answered and said unto them, Go and shew John again those things which ye do hear and see: the blind receive their sight, and the lame walk, the lepers are cleansed, and the deaf hear, the dead are raised up, and the poor have the gospel preached to them. And blessed is he, whosoever shall not be offended in me.

Keep the Faith

John the Baptist, after his introduction of Jesus Christ as the Son of God, seemed to fade into the background. Actually, he was still active, even though by this time he had been thrust into prison, where doubts assailed him. The walk as a believer, a disciple of Christ, is sometimes a lonely one. Here on earth we are never rid of our humanity. There are experiences in which we are ecstatic in our faith. And then there are times when the bottom seems to drop out. Maybe we do not sleep well or we hear things that we should not hear. We let people and circumstances get to us, or perhaps someone is doing a greater work than we are doing and that has a negative effect upon us. Whatever it was, John the Baptist wanted to know if Jesus was really the Messiah. Jesus did not rebuke John the Baptist for his apparent doubts. Instead He said, "You go tell John that the poor are responding to the gospel spiritually, physically, financially, emotionally. They are responding to God and are becoming strong in their faith. And tell him of the mighty miracles." He was sending a subtle message to John and to all others who might have doubts: Do not be offended. Keep the faith.

Matthew 11:7-11

And as they departed, Jesus began to say unto the multitudes concerning John, What went ye out into the wilderness to see? A reed shaken with the wind? But what went ye out for to see? A man clothed in soft raiment? behold, they that wear soft clothing are in kings' houses. But what went ye out for to see? A prophet? yea, I say unto you, and more than a prophet. For this is he, of whom it is written, Behold, I send my messenger before thy face, which shall prepare thy way before thee.

Verily I say unto you, Among them that are born of women there hath not risen a greater than John the Baptist: notwithstanding he that is least in the kingdom of heaven is greater than he.

Special Privilege

Jesus Christ was putting His full approval upon John the Baptist, stating emphatically that no one born of women had been greater.

Then He adds one of the most powerful and moving statements in the entire Word of God: "He that is least in the kingdom of heaven is greater than he."

You see, John the Baptist was operating under the old covenant. The Church of Jesus Christ had not yet been established. Our Lord had not been to the cross to shed His blood for a new covenant, fulfilling the old and bringing forth the new which is a greater covenant because it is based upon greater promises. Here in this Christian age, Christ is our Savior, the Son of the living God who has brought the kingdom of God into the now of our lives. That kingdom is so great that even the least of us, Christ says, is greater than John the Baptist.

Oh, what a privilege it is to be a child of God today and to know that however great they were before Christ, those who believe in Christ today live with Him and sit with Him in heavenly places! They are citizens of the new kingdom.

Matthew 11:12

And from the days of John the Baptist until now the kingdom of heaven suffereth violence, and the violent take it by force.

There is an aggressiveness in the kingdom of God. We see it in Jesus Christ assaulting the citadels of the devil, coming against sin, disease, demons, fear, poverty, everything that was unlike God. He is telling us we have to be aggressive, not with some physical violence, but with a spirit of aggressiveness to follow our Lord with deep love and to do the things that must be done. Things have to be made to happen. Christ is telling us that is what it is all about. Be aggressive with our faith. Stand against sin, disease, demons, fear, poverty, all negative forces. Stand up for the deliverance of God. Believe that we can do what we are called to do and nothing shall be able to stop us.

Matthew 11:13-19

For all the prophets and the law prophesied until John. And if ye will receive it, this is Elias, (Or Elijah) which was for to come. He that hath ears to hear, let him hear. But whereunto shall I liken this generation?

It is like unto children sitting in the markets, and calling unto their fellows, and saying, We have piped unto you, and ye have not danced; we have mourned unto you, and ye have not lamented. For John came neither eating nor drinking, and they say, He hath a devil. The Son of man came eating and drinking, and they say, Behold a man gluttonous, and a winebibber, a friend of publicans and sinners. But wisdom is justified of her children.

Please God First

Our Lord is talking about the ways of people. They seem unable to find satisfaction. They say, "We have done this and you did not respond," and, "We have done something else and you did not respond." In other words, He is telling us, we can't please people. We have to please God. Our uppermost thought must be to follow our Lord Jesus Christ and let the chips fall where they will.

Matthew 11:20-26

Then began he to upbraid the cities wherein most of his mighty works were done, because they repented not: Woe unto thee, Chorazin! woe unto thee, Bethsaida! for if the mighty works, which were done in you, had been done in Tyre and Sidon, they would have repented long ago in sackcloth and ashes. But I say unto you, It shall be more tolerable for Tyre and Sidon at the day of judgment, than for you.

And thou, Capernaum, which art exalted unto heaven, shall be brought down to hell: for if the mighty works, which have been done in thee, had been done in Sodom, it would have remained until this day. But I say unto you, That it shall be more tolerable for the land of Sodom in the day of judgment, than for thee.

> At that time Jesus answered and said, I thank thee, O Father, Lord of heaven and earth, because thou hast hid these things from the wise and prudent, and hast revealed them unto babes. Even so, Father: for so it seemed good in thy sight.

Christ Cherishes Repentance

Here is a city of people who had exalted themselves to heaven, but Christ said that because of their unbelief, they would be brought down to hell.

The more we see of God's goodness and the more we experience His love, and then fail to repent and turn our lives away from the devil, the more difficult it will be for us. Jesus thanked God for those humble ones who had received Him, who, when they saw the glory of the Lord through miracles and the goodness of God, repented, turned to Him, gave their lives to Him, and followed Him. He thanked God that these things had been revealed to babes — to people who were not learned in the philosophies and the so-called "great things" of the world, but who had the simple faith of a child to follow Jesus Christ.

Matthew 11:27-30

> All things are delivered unto me of my Father: and no man knoweth the son, but the Father; neither knoweth any man the Father, save the Son, and he to whomsoever the Son will reveal him.
>
> Come unto me, all ye that labour and are heavy laden, and I will give you rest. Take my yoke upon you, and learn of me; for I am meek and lowly in heart: and ye shall find rest unto your souls. For my yoke is easy, and my burden is light.

Learn of God

This is one of the great statements of Jesus because it shows Him relating to you and me. When I grew up and thought about God, it seemed that He was so far away. He was ancient, a God of judgment who might slap me into hell for the slightest misstep, and I was able finally to virtually push Him out of my mind.

But when I was flat on my back with tuberculosis, much of which I had brought upon myself by the way I had lived, these words were very precious to me. It was as though Christ was saying, "Oral, come unto Me with your labour, and because you are heavy laden, I will give you the rest you have sought. Oral, you need My yoke upon you; you need My discipline, My authority. Learn of me. You have such a hungry, thirsting mind; you want to learn." And that is true, I did. He said, "Learn of Me. Start all your learning with Me, for I am meek and lowly in heart and you will find rest unto your soul. And Oral, My yoke is easy, My burden is light."

Yes, there is a yoke and there is a burden for those of us who follow Jesus Christ. But it is easy and it is light. It is a feeling of peace, an inner joy, a knowing that you know, that you know, that God is real!

Matthew 12:1-8

At that time Jesus went on the sabbath day through the corn; and his disciples were an hungred, and began to pluck the ears of corn, and to eat. But when the Pharisees saw it, they said unto him, Behold, thy disciples do that which is not lawful to do upon the sabbath day. But he said unto them, Have ye not read what David did, when he was an hungred, and they that were with him; how he entered into the house of God, and did eat the shewbread, which was not lawful for him to eat, neither for them which were with him, but only for the priests?

Or have ye not read in the law, how that on the sabbath days the priests in the temple profane the sabbath, and are blameless? But I say unto you, That in this place is one greater than the temple. But if ye had known what this meaneth, I will have mercy, and not sacrifice, ye would not have condemned the guiltless. For the Son of man is Lord even of the sabbath day.

The sabbath day was given as a day of rest. The sabbath was made for man, not man for the sabbath. When we hold up a day above other days to the extent that that day becomes more important than human beings or the needs of our lives, our sacrifices to God are worthless. He is calling upon us to be merciful, humane people.

Matthew 12:9-21

And when he was departed thence, he went into their synagogue: and, behold, there was a man which had his hand withered. And they asked him, saying, Is it lawful to heal on the sabbath days? that they might accuse him. And he said unto them, What man shall there be among you, that shall have one sheep, and if it fall into a pit on the sabbath day, will he not lay hold on it, and lift it out? How much then is a man better than a sheep? Wherefore it is lawful to do well on the sabbath days.

Then saith he to the man, Stretch forth thine hand. And he stretched it forth; and it was restored whole, like as the other. Then the Pharisees went out, and held a council against him, how they might destroy him. But when Jesus knew it, he withdrew himself from thence: and great multitudes followed him, and he healed them all; and charged them that they should not make him known: that it might be fulfilled which was spoken by Esaias the prophet, saying, Behold my servant, whom I have chosen; my beloved, in whom my soul is well pleased: I will put my spirit upon him, and he shall shew judgment to the Gentiles. He shall not strive, nor cry; neither shall any man hear his voice in the streets. A bruised reed shall he not break, and smoking flax shall he not quench, till he send forth judgment unto victory. And in his name shall the Gentiles trust.

Faith with Force

What is the thrust Jesus is making here? First, when He is in the synagogue, He encounters a man with a withered hand. Before He could do anything to heal him, the enemies of the gospel ask Him, "Is it right to heal on the sabbath day?"

Jesus said, "If one of you have a sheep and it falls into a pit on the sabbath day, you go out and lift it up in order to save its life. And don't you realize that a man is so much better than a sheep? Do you not understand it is lawful to do well on the sabbath day?"

Next, ignoring the critics, He turned His full attention upon the man with the withered hand and said, "Stretch forth thine hand." Now what did the man do? He could have said, "But Lord, stretch it forth for me. Speak and just cause my arm automatically to lengthen and to fill in with flesh." No, Jesus told him he had to do something. And that is always true. There is something we have to do. Things have to be made to happen. That is why God gave us faith. If things did not have to be made to happen, God would not have given us faith.

Faith is the striking force of the power of God in your life. Faith is what storms the forts of the devil and invades the world of demon power, sickness and disease, and sin. Faith released to God releases the lightning-like power of God to deliver us. When Jesus said, "Stretch forth thine hand," the man went into motion. With all the strength and faith he had, he began to move. He might have been able to move that withered arm very slightly, at least at first.

So very often when I am praying for people who are paralyzed or who are in wheelchairs, unable to walk for a long time, I say to them, "When I speak the word of faith to you in the name of Christ, if you can only move a foot, move it, or a toe or a finger, move it. Do something. Get the thing going. Start your faith coming up out of your heart. Say to your faith, 'Faith, go up to God! Faith, go up to God!'" In effect, that is what this man did. As he made the effort physically and spiritually to stretch forth his arm, his hand, the whole of his hand and arm were made whole like the other. That made the Pharisees so mad, they set up a plan to kill Jesus. When Jesus knew it, He withdrew. But the multitudes did not join in that criticism and that plot to kill Christ. They followed Him and He healed them all.

Matthew 12:22-32

Then was brought unto him one possessed with a devil, blind, and dumb: and he healed him, insomuch that the blind and dumb both spake and saw. And all the people were amazed, and said, Is not this the son of David?

But when the Pharisees heard it, they said, This fellow doth not cast out devils, but by Beelzebub the prince of the devils. And Jesus knew their thoughts, and said unto them, Every kingdom divided against itself is brought to desolation; and every city or house divided against itself shall not stand: and if Satan cast out Satan, he is divided against himself; how shall then his kingdom stand? And if I by Beelzebub cast out devils, by whom do your children cast them out? therefore they shall be your judges.

But if I cast out devils by the Spirit of God, then the kingdom of God is come unto you. Or else how can one enter into a strong man's house, and spoil his goods, except he first bind the strong man? and then he will spoil his house. He that is not with me is against me; and he that gathereth not with me scattereth abroad.

Wherefore I say unto you, All manner of sin and blasphemy shall be forgiven unto men: but the blasphemy against the Holy Ghost shall not be forgiven unto men. And whosoever speaketh a word against the Son of man, it shall be forgiven him: but whosoever speaketh against the Holy Ghost, it shall not be forgiven him, neither in this world, neither in the world to come.

The Unforgiveable Sin

The question is, What is blaspheming the Holy Spirit? What is the sin that can never be forgiven? What Jesus is saying is that the Spirit of God, the Holy Spirit, is the agent through whom all the work of God is done in human life. It is like the Holy Spirit being the gate through which you pass, or the door by which you enter into a house. The Holy Spirit is the one without whom no one can come to God. And if the Holy Spirit is blasphemed, that is, set aside as a profane thing, then all avenues to God are closed. Therefore, Jesus said, "If you say anything against the Son of Man or blaspheme something else, that can be forgiven you, but if you come against the sole agency that can bring you to God and you blaspheme and profane that, setting it aside in your heart eternally, then you have no way to God. There is no possibility of your ever being forgiven."

Now some may ask, Have I committed the sin of blaspheming the Holy Spirit because I have said something against the Holy Spirit, or against the Church, or against God? Not necessarily. Many times we, in our sin, say things that we should not say. But the very fact that you asked the question "Have I committed the unpardonable sin?" probably means you have not. However, if you finally come to the point that you do not want the Holy Spirit to deal with your heart, and you make an eternal choice within you that you are not going to listen to the Holy Spirit and if instead you are saying, "That thing — the Holy Spirit — is of the devil; I will have nothing to do with it," you have committed the unpardonable sin — that is the sin that is unpardonable. Because then you place yourself forever beyond the reach of forgiveness, repentance, and salvation. So let us be careful that we honor the Holy Spirit and that we welcome Him in our heart.

Matthew 12:33-37

> Either make the tree good, and his fruit good; or else make the tree corrupt, and his fruit corrupt: for the tree is known by his fruit. O generation of vipers, how can ye, being evil, speak good things? for out of the abundance of the heart the mouth speaketh. A good man out of the good treasure of the heart bringeth forth good things: and an evil man out of the evil treasure bringeth forth evil things.
>
> But I say unto you, That every idle word that men shall speak, they shall give account thereof in the day of judgment. For by thy words thou shalt be justified, and by thy words thou shalt be condemned.

Jesus says we should speak out of the abundance of our hearts. Even then, Jesus warns us of idle words, of just talking to hear our heads rattle. That has no redeeming value. Conversely, He is speaking positively toward us, encouraging us that when we believe right with our hearts we should speak forth with our mouths so that we make things happen. We cause things to come into being, and reality takes hold of our lives.

Matthew 12:38-41

> Then certain of the scribes and of the Pharisees answered, saying, Master, we would see a sign from thee. But he answered and said

> unto them, An evil and adulterous generation seeketh after a sign; and there shall no sign be given to it, but the sign of the prophet Jonas: for as Jonas was three days and three nights in the whale's belly; so shall the Son of man be three days and three nights in the heart of the earth. The men of Nineveh shall rise in judgment with this generation, and shall condemn it: because they repented at the preaching of Jonas; and, behold, a greater than Jonas is here.

The Greatest Sign

Jesus said He would give an adulterous and wicked generation only one sign and that was the sign of Jonah the prophet. You may recall in the book of Jonah, in the Old Testament, that God called this prophet to go to Nineveh and preach: "Yet forty days and Nineveh shall be overthrown."

Jonah rebelled and took passage on a ship to Tarshish, in the opposite direction. While he was on the boat, God created a great storm to bring the prophet to his senses. Finally Jonah told the captain to throw him overboard. The Bible says God had prepared a great fish to swallow Jonah. It was while in the belly of this great fish that something extraordinary happened. A sign took place, the sign of the resurrection. The story of Jonah is really the story of the resurrection of Jesus Christ from the dead.

Here is a man who is swallowed by a great fish and for days he lives in the belly of that fish. Many Bible scholars believe Jonah actually died and when it came time for God's purpose, the great fish vomited Jonah out upon the shore and new life came into his being. Rising up with resurrection life, Jonah went to Nineveh and began to preach and almost instantly the word carried throughout a city that took 3 days to cross, and that city of tens of thousands of people repented before God and God spared it.

Jesus was saying that the greatest sign would be when He went to the cross and was killed and then buried, and God would raise Him from the dead. My friend, the heart of the gospel is the resurrection. You know, the resurrection is something that is in your heart every day. It is that power that causes you to believe that you are never going to die. You will not die the second death. You will not go into hell. And neither on this earth will you be defeated. Oh, they may stop you (they think). And they may slow you down (they think). But when you believe in the resurrection you are sowing the seeds of life and nothing is going to defeat you. Men may think you are defeated. But in the eyes of God, you win. My friend, you win.

Matthew 12:42-45

The queen of the south shall rise up in the judgment with this generation, and shall condemn it: for she came from the uttermost parts of the earth to hear the wisdom of Solomon; and, behold, a greater than Solomon is here.

When the unclean spirit is gone out of a man, he walketh through dry places, seeking rest, and findeth none. Then he saith, I will return into my house from whence I came out; and when he is come, he findeth it empty, swept, and garnished.

Then goeth he, and taketh with himself seven other spirits more wicked than himself, and they enter in and dwell there: and the last state of that man is worse than the first. Even so shall it be also unto this wicked generation.

Spiritual Vacancy Dangerous

Here we have a scene in which an unclean spirit has been cast out, but the person did not go ahead and follow Jesus Christ. For example, we are told that when the unclean spirit is cast out of a person that this unclean spirit begins roving about in the old habitations, that is, in places where he does not possess human beings, dry places, seeking satisfaction and finding none. So he says, "I'll go back to this person out of whom I've been cast." But he realizes that he cannot reenter alone, so he secures the cooperation of seven other demons who are more powerful than he is and they arrive.

Here is this person who has been freed; the demons are gone. He is cleaned up but Christ through His spirit has not filled him up. There is nothing to keep these demons from entering. There are even more of them and they are more powerful. They make his last state worse than when he only had one demon.

When I deal with the demon-possessed and through the name of Jesus bring deliverance so that they are set free from demon power, I never stop with that.

First, through the name of Jesus, I bind the demons from reentering. Next I work with the person to be sure that he turns his life over to Jesus Christ and begins to be filled with the Holy Spirit. Rather than being filled with an evil spirit, he is filled or she is filled with the Holy Spirit. If the Holy Spirit fills us up, there is no way that a negative force such as a demon can enter in, no matter how many demons come our way. The Spirit of God is greater than the devil that is in the world. Greater is He that is in you than he that is in the world.

Jesus went through this particular scene, but He applied it to the last days, to this wicked generation, to the people to whom He had come with the message of deliverance. He was anointed to set them free. But freedom is not enough. One must do something with his freedom. One must follow on after God, or something worse takes place.

Matthew 12:46-50

> While he yet talked to the people, behold, his mother and his brethren stood without, desiring to speak with him. Then one said unto him, Behold, thy mother and thy brethren stand without, desiring to speak with thee. But he answered and said unto him that told him, Who is my mother? and who are my brethren? And he stretched forth his hand toward his disciples and said, Behold my mother and my brethren! For whosoever shall do the will of my Father which is in heaven, the same is my brother, and sister, and mother.

Jesus' Larger Family

It was a very human thing for Mary His mother and His brothers to come to where He was ministering and desire to spend some time with Him. But Jesus by then was engulfed in the total call of God upon His life. He was involved with humanity. He was bringing the kingdom of heaven at hand. And when He was told that His mother and brothers wanted to talk to Him, He said, "Who? Who is my mother? Who is my brother? My sister? Whoever does the will of My Father which is in heaven, that one is My mother, My brother, My sister."

Matthew 13:1-23

> The same day went Jesus out of the house, and sat by the sea side. And great multitudes were gathered together unto him, so that he went into a ship, and sat; and the whole multitude stood on the shore.
>
> And he spake many things unto them in parables, saying, Behold, a sower went forth to sow; and when he sowed, some seeds fell by the way side, and the fowls came and devoured them up: some fell upon stony places, where they had not much earth: and forthwith they sprung up, because they had no deepness of earth: and when the sun was up, they were scorched; and because they had no root, they withered away.
>
> And some fell among thorns; and the thorns sprung up, and choked them; but other fell into good ground, and brought forth fruit, some an hundredfold, some sixtyfold, some thirtyfold. Who hath ears to

hear, let him hear.

And the disciples came, and said unto him, Why speakest thou unto them in parables? He answered and said unto them, Because it is given unto you to know the mysteries of the kingdom of heaven, but to them it is not given. For whosoever hath, to him shall be given, and he shall have more abundance: but whosoever hath not, from him shall be taken away even that he hath. Therefore speak I to them in parables: because they seeing see not; and hearing they hear not, neither do they understand. And in them is fulfilled the prophecy of Esaias, which saith, By hearing ye shall hear, and shall not understand; and seeing ye shall see, and shall not perceive: for this people's heart is waxed gross, and their ears are dull of hearing, and their eyes they have closed; lest at any time they should see with their eyes, and hear with their ears, and should understand with their heart, and should be converted, and I should heal them.

But blessed are your eyes, for they see: and your ears, for they hear. For verily I say unto you, That many prophets and righteous men have desired to see those things which ye see, and have not seen them; and to hear those things which ye hear, and have not heard them.

Hear ye therefore the parable of the sower. When any one heareth the word of the kingdom, and understandeth it not, then cometh the wicked one, and catcheth away that which was sown in his heart. This is he which received seed by the way side. But he that received the seed into stony places, the same is he that heareth the word, and anon with joy receiveth it; yet hath he not root in himself, but dureth for a while: for when tribulation or persecution ariseth because of the word, by and by he is offended.

He also that received seed among the thorns is he that heareth the word; and the care of this world, and the deceitfulness of riches, choke the word, and he becometh unfruitful.

But he that received seed into the good ground is he that heareth the word, and understandeth it; which also beareth fruit, and bringeth forth, some an hundredfold, some sixty, some thirty.

Seed-Faith Foundation

Jesus has explained very well what He was saying here. I would like to call to your attention two things. One is that you have to put the seed in, and in putting in the seed, it should always be put in good soil. In your giving, in what you do for the Lord and what you give to God's work, you should select the best soil, because if you do not, the seed will be scattered. There will be nothing to cause it to multiply. The second thing is that when you sow seed in good soil the way God has said to sow it, God will multiply it, and the measure that He multiplies to you is one-hundredfold, sixtyfold, thirtyfold.

Now let me encourage you in your receiving. Many Christians feel guilty when they give expecting God to bless them. Well, if we give to people, expecting them to do something for us, then we should feel guilty, because we are not to do it that way. When we help people, we are to give with a glad heart, expecting nothing in return. But if we never receive anything in return, we will finally have given away what we have and we will be diminished. God never intended for you and me to be diminished because of our giving to Him. In other words, He does not penalize you and me for giving. He rewards us for our giving. But, just as you have to be in a giving attitude, you must be in a receiving attitude. As your giving is an action (it is something you do), receiving is also an action (it is something you do). They go hand in hand. One cannot exist without the other. One supports the other. One completes the other. We give and we receive. Giving and receiving. Sowing and reaping. Planting and harvesting.

Christ is telling us what we have we are to invest, and through investing it, through our faith, we make things happen. When we make things happen, then we will be recipients of the blessings of God. We are to be enlarged in our lives. We are to receive for our health, our spiritual growth, our mental stimulation, our emotional health. Yes, we are even to be blessed in our families. We are to receive because we have given to God. The Lord multiplies our seed sown a hundred times, sixty times, thirty times, and one of those should be ours. We should stand up for it.

Our God will not disappoint us. Any time we are disappointed in our receiving, it is because we have not given or sown in good soil, and have not expected to receive. We have not acted in a spirit of receiving; we have not put forth our hand to receive what God is giving us. So I praise God that this is one of the most positive statements of Christ in the Bible. It is His divine principle of sowing and reaping. It is the very foundation of our seed-faith, of making whatever we do a seed that we sow and then expecting our God to multiply it back. It is seed-faith unto God and then back to us.

Matthew 13:24-30

> Another parable put he forth unto them, saying, The kingdom of heaven is likened unto a man which sowed good seed in his field: but while men slept, his enemy came and sowed tares among the wheat, and went his way. But when the blade was sprung up, and

brought forth fruit, then appeared the tares also. So the servants of the householder came and said unto him, Sir, didst not thou sow good seed in thy field? From whence then hath it tares? He said unto them, An enemy hath done this. The servants said unto him, Wilt thou then that we go and gather them up?

But he said, Nay; lest while ye gather up the tares, ye root up also the wheat with them. Let both grow together until the harvest: and in the time of harvest I will say to the reapers, Gather ye together first the tares, and bind them in bundles to burn them: but gather the wheat into my barn.

Trusting God's Judgment

Many times we in the kingdom of God look about us and see so much hypocrisy. We say, "Well, there are too many hypocrites in the church: therefore, I'm not going to take part." But if God were to come down and arbitrarily remove everybody who is insincere from going to church or trying to be part of the body of Christ, He would do much damage. We are not going to have a perfect group while on this earth.

We are the church militant but we are not yet the Church triumphant. We are militant, aggressive in our witness for Christ, but we are not yet resurrected. We have not been brought into that divine excellence in the triumph of Jesus Christ over the death of our bodies through the resurrection of the dead, or the catching away of the bride in his second coming. Right now, we are all imperfect in some way. Some are closer to God than others. Some are growing up to be saints of God. Others are turning out to be hypocrites. But there is a judgment day coming and our Father, who sees all, will judge righteously. Our own judgment might be faulty. But His will be perfect.

Matthew 13:31-51

Another parable put he forth unto them, saying, The kingdom of heaven is like to a grain of mustard seed, which a man took, and sowed in his field: which indeed is the least of all seeds: but when it is grown, it is the greatest among herbs, and becometh a tree, so that the birds of the air come and lodge in the branches thereof.

Another parable spake he unto them; The kingdom of heaven is like unto leaven, which a woman took, and hid in three measures of meal, till the whole was leavened. All these things spake Jesus unto the multitude in parables; and without a parable spake he not unto them: that it might be fulfilled which was spoken by the prophet, saying, I will open my mouth in parables; I will utter things which have been kept secret from the foundation of the world.

Then Jesus sent the multitude away, and went into the house: and his disciples came unto him, saying, Declare unto us the parable of the tares of the field. He answered and said unto them, He that soweth the good seed is the Son of man; the field is the world; the good seed are the children of the kingdom; but the tares are the children of the wicked one; the enemy that sowed them is the devil; the harvest is the end of the world; and the reapers are the angels.

As therefore the tares are gathered and burned in the fire; so shall it be in the end of this world. The Son of man shall send forth his angels, and they shall gather out of his kingdom all things that offend, and them which do iniquity; and shall cast them into a furnace of fire: there shall be wailing and gnashing of teeth. Then shall the righteous shine forth as the sun in the kingdom of their Father. Who hath ears to hear, let him hear.

Again, the kingdom of heaven is like unto treasure hid in a field; the which when a man hath found, he hideth, and for joy thereof goeth and selleth all that he hath, and buyeth that field.

Again, the kingdom of heaven is like unto a merchant man, seeking goodly pearls: who, when he had found one pearl of great price, went and sold all that he had, and bought it.

Again, the kingdom of heaven is like unto a net, that was cast into the sea, and gathered of every kind: which, when it was full, they drew to shore, and sat down, and gathered the good into vessels, but cast the bad away.

So shall it be at the end of the world: the angels shall come forth, and sever the wicked from among the just, and shall cast them into the furnace of fire: there shall be wailing and gnashing of teeth. Jesus saith unto them, Have ye understood all these things? They say unto him, Yea, Lord.

Parables Explained

Jesus used parables or stories from everyday life. Jesus wanted to communicate. He was not talking about the meaning of something and letting it stand in its own right; He applied the parables to whomever He was talking to. For example, He talked about the seed, the tiny mustard seed that when planted just takes off and grows and grows and grows, and He was referring to the tremendous resurgent power of the gospel. When you accept Jesus with the tiniest amount of faith, it takes off and God's power begins to be poured into you. You grow and you grow and you grow.

Then He talked about leaven. Leaven made the bread light and fluffy, every woman understood that. Unleavened bread was heavy and almost tasteless and every woman understood that. Jesus knew that the Jews looked upon leaven as a bad thing, as reference to something evil. But He took that and turned it around to show that leaven, when used properly, reveals the transforming power of God that can enter life — enter any life without value, a life without seasoning, a life without promise, and turn that life around and make something of that man, woman, or child. I glory in that, because when I look back where I was when Jesus found my poor little life, I lift up my heart in praise for every good thing He brings forth through me today and thank Him for His transforming power. Also, Jesus knew the customs of the Bedoin tribes. They were nomads in those days of no banks, and they usually hid their treasures in the ground. They knew where the treasures were hidden. But here is a person who discovers a treasure in the ground, and when he sees it he hides it in the ground again. The field is not his so he rushes to buy the whole field.

Jesus said that is like the kingdom of God. For when you discover the kingdom of God, you discover the greatest of treasures. You make it the whole of your life. Jesus compares himself with a pearl of great price so that suddenly, the top priority in our lives is to find Jesus Christ, to give ourselves to Him unreservedly, because we have not only the greatest, but the loveliest of all the gifts of life.

Many times Jesus had watched the fishermen cast their nets into the sea of Galilee and catch many fish. They would separate the fish, the good from the bad. Jesus said that is like the kingdom of God, too; we throw out the net of the gospel and it reaches everybody. We do not go just for one kind of fish, or one kind of human being — we go for all men and women to bring them into the kingdom of God.

Being human, we cannot judge with the ability of God and His angels. Jesus says that when the end comes, He will send His angels and will sever those who are truly right with God and those who are not. It is our business to cast the net, to give the gospel, to love our fellow man and be witnesses of His love and let God do the judging.

Matthew 13:52-58

> Then said he unto them, Therefore every scribe which is instructed unto the kingdom of heaven is like unto a man that is an householder, which bringeth forth out of his treasure things new and old. And it came to pass, that when Jesus had finished these parables, he departed thence.

> And when he was come into his own country, he taught them in their synagogue, insomuch that they were astonished, and said, Whence hath this man this wisdom, and these mighty works? Is not this the carpenter's son? is not his mother called Mary? and his brethren, James and Joses, and Simon, and Judas? And his sisters, are they not all with us? Whence then hath this man all these things?
>
> And they were offended in him. But Jesus said unto them, A prophet is not without honor, save in his own country, and in his own house. And he did not many mighty works there because of their unbelief.

Free Will Permitted

They simply did not know Jesus' true identity. You can imagine the astonishment of the people of that little city where He had grown up and who did not understand the spiritual import of His background, of His birth, of His life, of His ministry, and of His mission in the world. When they looked at Him, they saw Him through the eyes of His brothers and sisters, that is, His half brothers and half sisters, and His mother, Mary, who is an ordinary person, and His foster father, Joseph. So of course they were upset. Jesus said, "A prophet is not without honor, except in his own country, and in his own house."

The bottom line is that in that town, He could do no mighty miracles because they simply would not believe. Notice that God does not force himself upon people.

People say, "Why doesn't God stop all the wars? Why doesn't God force all people to be good? Why did God let that man murder somebody or rape this girl? Why did God let all these bad things happen?" It is ridiculous to have such thoughts, because God honors the will of man. He created man in His own image and gave him a will, the freedom of choice. Surely, He could have gone into Nazareth, His hometown, and wiped them all out. But what purpose would that have served? He honored their will. He endured their scorn, ridicule, and unbelief. He simply did not remain long where He was not appreciated. He went where people would believe. Jesus did His work among believing believers.

In my own home city of Tulsa, there are people who are truly friends of mine. They believe in me. They trust me, and they do anything to help. But there are some who, simply because I am Oral Roberts, living in Tulsa, Oklahoma, would not cross the street to hear me preach and would oppose me on anything that I do. So I understand and I fully appreciate what Jesus went through. As a matter of fact, He is my role model, and He is yours, too.

Matthew 14:1-13

At that time Herod the tetrarch heard of the fame of Jesus, and said unto his servants, This is John the Baptist; he is risen from the dead; and therefore mighty works do shew forth themselves in him. For Herod had laid hold on John, and bound him, and put him in prison for Herodias' sake, his brother Philip's wife. For John said unto him, It is not lawful for thee to have her. And when he would have put him to death, he feared the multitude, because they counted him as a prophet. But when Herod's birthday was kept, the daughter of Herodias danced before them, and pleased Herod. Whereupon he promised with an oath to give her whatsoever she would ask. And she, being before instructed of her mother, said, Give me here John Baptist's head in a charger.

And the king was sorry: nevertheless for the oath's sake, and them which sat with him at meat, he commanded it to be given her. And he sent, and beheaded John in the prison. And his head was brought in a charger, and given to the damsel: and she brought it to her mother. And his disciples came, and took up the body, and buried, it and went and told Jesus. When Jesus heard of it, he departed thence by ship into a desert place apart: and when the people had heard thereof, they followed him on foot out of the cities.

Mission Unlimited

John the Baptist, the forerunner of Christ, after having done his greatest of great works, now is harmed. Bad things begin to happen to him. He is thrown into prison. But he remains true to God in prison. While there, he has an opportunity to witness for God. It is always glorious to remember that wherever we are, we have a place of witness. Our mission field is where we are. We do not always have to go to Africa or Asia or some other foreign place in order to be a missionary. Our mission field can be where we are. That makes it possible for those who are especially called to go to the uttermost bounds of the earth and do their work for God. It also makes it possible for those who are not called to go to a mission field far away to witness in their own local mission field, to go into the world of those about them.

If a person is a musician or a singer, then he goes into the world of those who care for music and singing. If a person is a carpenter, then that can be his mission field. If a person is a merchant, that is his mission field. If a person is a physician or a dentist or another health professional, wherever he or she works, that is their mission field. The point is that we are all witnesses of Christ.

Matthew 14:14

And Jesus went forth, and saw a great multitude, and was moved with compassion toward them, and he healed their sick.

The Meaning of Compassion

Jesus did not stop the work of the kingdom because one of the servants of God had given his life. God's work goes on. Jesus is a man of action. He is always in movement, making things happen. He went forth and saw a great multitude. Most people would have just seen a crowd. There were thousands of people. But Jesus saw something different. He saw something in them that most people would never see. What He saw moved His inner spirit. He was moved with compassion toward them.

I remember when I began this ministry in 1947, I had read through consecutively, three times in 30 days, the four gospels and the Book of Acts — on my knees. And when I finished reading, Jesus revealed himself to me. He let me see people. He let me see people as He sees them. And what I saw almost took my breath away. By the Spirit I saw that everybody in the world is sick in some way. I heard their groans, cries, and sighs. Friend, it broke my heart. I never knew Jesus so well as I did that day, for He let me see and hear people. What I saw moved me with compassion, and the very next week I began this healing ministry.

What is a good explanation of compassion? Here is what I have discovered. Compassion is when you feel an almost irresistible urge to touch people, to help rid them of the things that are destroying them. Compassion is divine love. It is God at work inside you. It is God caring for man whom He created, hurting with him, wanting to restore him to HOLINESS and to WHOLENESS at the same time!

We are not going to bring healing to the sick until we are moved with compassion. As long as we feel sorry for them, we will do what we can, but not with divine love, not with that irresistible urge to touch them and to help rid them of the things that are destroying them. Compassion is love in action — God's love working through us and acting itself out in the prayer of faith, in the word of faith, in the touch of faith, in the giving of ourselves, even as the Lord Jesus Christ gave himself to the people.

Matthew 14:15-21

And when it was evening, his disciples came to him, saying, This is a desert place, and the time is now past; send the multitude away, that they may go into the villages, and buy themselves victuals. But

Jesus said unto them, They need not depart; give ye them to eat. And they say unto Him, We have here but five loaves, and two fishes. He said, Bring them hither to me. And He commanded the multitude to sit down on the grass, and took the five loaves, and the two fishes, and looking up to heaven, he blessed, and brake, and gave the loaves to his disciples, and the disciples to the multitude. And they did all eat, and were filled: and they took up of the fragments that remained twelve baskets full. And they that had eaten were about 5,000 men, beside women and children.

Embryo of Miracles

This is a reference to the feeding of the 5,000 which is described in great detail in John's gospel. However, there is something special here in this brief mention of it by Matthew. He says that when Jesus saw the tremendous multitude who had followed Him and hung on to His teachings until they had literally run out of anything to eat and had no money to buy, Jesus simply turned to his disciples and said, "Give ye them to eat."

They were confused by this command because they could only find five loaves and two fish, yet Jesus still said, "Give ye them to eat."

Jesus recognizes a faith in us that we do not recognize in ourselves. He also knows what faith is. He knows that faith has the miracle-working power of God in it and that if we could dissect faith or tear it apart, look at it, see the inside of it the way God does, we would see an embryo miracle. When He said, "Give ye them to eat," He was not beside himself. He was not trying to confuse them, nor was He asking them to do something impossible. They could do it. Later, He was to say in the gospel of John that "greater things than these shall ye do, because I go to my Father." It is a very encouraging word to us, because there are virtually impossible situations all around us — situations that we can handle because Jesus says we can.

Matthew 14:22-33

And straightway Jesus constrained his disciples to get into a ship, and to go before him unto the other side, while he sent the multitudes away. And when he had sent the multitudes away, he went up into a mountain apart to pray: and when the evening was come, he was there alone. But the ship was now in the midst of the sea, tossed with waves: for the wind was contrary.

And in the fourth watch of the night Jesus went unto them, walking on the sea. And when the disciples saw him walking on the sea, they were troubled, saying, It is a spirit; and they cried out for fear. But straightway Jesus spake unto them, saying, Be of good cheer; it is I; be not afraid.

And Peter answered him and said, Lord, if it be thou, bid me come unto thee on the water. And he said, Come. And when Peter was come down out of the ship, he walked on the water, to go to Jesus. But when he saw the wind boisterous, he was afraid; and beginning to sink, he cried, saying, Lord, save me. And immediately Jesus stretched forth his hand and caught him, and said unto him, O thou of little faith, wherefore didst thou doubt?

And when they were come into the ship, the wind ceased. Then they that were in the ship came and worshipped him, saying, Of a truth thou art the Son of God.

Jesus Is Helper

At this time in our Lord's life, He felt a very urgent need to spend more time in prayer. I would like for you to visualize Him there in the night hours, praying. I would like for you to see also His disciples in the ship which was in the Sea of Galilee going to the other side, at Jesus' orders. Suddenly His disciples were about to be destroyed. What will Christ do? He is praying. He is putting prayer first in His life. But the Bible tells us how He saw them. In the next scene, Jesus has come down to help them, but He has no boat. That does not hinder Him.

He simply starts walking upon the water which becomes like a glassy pavement under His feet. In the terror of that stormy night, as the lightning flashed and illumined His face, He was like a divine silhouette upon the dark waters. The disciples saw Him but did not recognize Him. The fear of the storm blotted Him out. They saw something and cried, "It is a ghost. It is a spirit."

But across the waves came the strong commanding voice of the Master, "It is I, don't be afraid."

Peter, that impetuous man, that man of faith, said, "Okay, Lord, if it is You, if it is really You, bid me come unto You. Enable me to walk on the water."

Oh, I love Peter at this point, because Peter was recognizing that while the storms of life come, we are not to allow them to destroy us. We are supposed to come through the storm. He knew that much about Jesus. Jesus said, "Come." That means Jesus wants us to come through the storm. It also means He wants us to walk in His steps — and Peter did.

The Bible says that Peter went toward Jesus, walking on the water. Do not forget that Peter actually walked on water. Walking on the water through faith is a symbol of walking on the storms that come against our lives. No matter what form those storms take, our faith is triumphant. We do walk on the water. We do come through our failures, our mistakes, our opposition, and all the devil's wrath. Peter walked on the water. But the moment he took his eyes off Jesus, he had no source left. You see, God is the source of our total supply, not man. Jesus was the one who enabled him to walk on water. Jesus was the source of the infinite power Peter grasped and used to subdue the waves the same way Jesus did. When Peter took his eyes off the Lord and lost his source, fear entered his heart. Fear is the reverse form of faith. Faith is believing God; that is, believing right. Fear is the product of believing wrong, the product of not believing God. When you believe God with your whole heart, it is impossible for you to be afraid. Fear can only enter a vacuum. It can only come in when we are no longer using our faith and trusting God as the source of our total supply. Fear did to Peter what it does to us. It began to sink him. And as he was going down he said three words in prayer: "Lord, save me." Someone has said that if he had said more, he would have drowned. Then was no time for a long prayer. It was time to get the words of action out and to call upon the Lord. The Word tells us that Jesus took him by the hand, lifted him up, and said, "Oh, you of little faith." Then He lifted him up and then the ship arrived. The majesty of our Savior, His majesty over all things, was never better displayed than then — or now in our lives.

Matthew 14:34-36

> And when they were gone over, they came into the land of Gennesaret. And when the men of that place had knowledge of him, they sent out into all that country round about, and brought unto him all that were diseased; and besought him that they might only touch the hem of his garment: and as many as touched were made perfectly whole.

Wherever Jesus was, and the sick found out about Him, they flocked to Him. I think that is one of the greatest things in the Bible! Our God is a healing God.

Matthew 15:1-9

> Then came to Jesus scribes and Pharisees, which were of Jerusalem, saying, Why do thy disciples transgress the tradition of the elders? for they wash not their hands when they eat bread. But He answered and said unto them, Why do ye also transgress the commandment of God by your tradition? For God commanded, saying, Honour thy father and mother: and, He that curseth father or mother, let him die the death. But ye say, Whosoever shall say to his father or his mother, It is a gift, by whatsoever thou mightest be profited by me; And honour

not his father or his mother, he shall be free. Thus have ye made the commandment of God of none effect by your tradition.

Ye hypocrites, well did Esaias prophesy of you, saying, This people draweth nigh unto me with their mouth, and honoureth me with their lips; but their heart is far from me. But in vain they do worship me, teaching for doctrines the commandments of men.

God's Word Supreme

The scribes and Pharisees believed that the elders of the people of Israel could add to the words of the prophets, and that whatever they added as interpretation was even greater than what the original prophets had said. When Jesus was sure of this, He struck out at it, because He would not abide people who would add to or take away from the Word of God. Jesus said, "You are a bunch of hypocrites. Well did the prophet Esaias prophesy of you that you say it with your lips, but your heart is far from God."

This is a real word to you and me today. We should value the Word of God above everything that man says. My words are the best words I know how to say as I am inspired of God, based upon my study, meditation, and prayer. But God's word is always above Oral Roberts' word or above anybody else's word. The number-one thing is that we serve Him with our hearts and not merely with our lips.

Matthew 15:10-20

And he called the multitude, and said unto them, Hear, and understand: Not that which goeth into the mouth defileth a man; but that which cometh out of the mouth, this defileth a man. Then came his disciples, and said unto him, Knowest thou that the Pharisees were offended, after they heard this saying? But he answered and said, Every plant, which my heavenly Father hath not planted, shall be rooted up. Let them alone: they be blind leaders of the blind. And if the blind lead the blind, both shall fall into the ditch.

Then answered Peter and said unto him, Declare unto us this parable. And Jesus said, Are ye also yet without understanding? Do not ye yet understand, that whatsoever entereth in at the mouth goeth into the belly, and is cast out into the draught? But those things which proceed out of the mouth come forth from the heart; and they defile the man.

For out of the heart proceed evil thoughts, murders, adulteries, fornications, thefts, false witness, blasphemies: These are the things which defile a man: but to eat with unwashen hands defileth not a man.

Again and again, Jesus was striking at the tradition of the elders which they had put above the Word of God itself. Jesus emphasized that what is in our heart is what counts.

Matthew 15:21-28

> Then Jesus went thence, and departed into the coasts of Tyre and Sidon. And, behold, a woman of Canaan came out of the same coasts and cried unto him, saying, Have mercy on me, O Lord, thou son of David; my daughter is grievously vexed with a devil. But he answered her not a word. And His disciples came and besought him, saying, Send her away; for she crieth after us.
>
> But he answered and said, I am not sent but unto the lost sheep of the house of Israel. Then came she and worshipped him, saying, Lord, help me.
>
> But he answered and said, It is not meet to take the children's bread, and to cast it to dogs. And she said, Truth, Lord: yet the dogs eat of the crumbs which fall from their masters' table. Then Jesus answered and said unto her, O woman, great is thy faith: be it unto thee even as thou wilt. And her daughter was made whole from that very hour.

Faith Produces Results

One of the most remarkable things about the Lord Jesus Christ is that although there were people in His time who were not of the covenant of Abraham, who were not descendants of Abraham as the children of Israel were, even though they were supposedly outside, He had mercy on them.

Yet, He always tested them to see if their faith was genuine. For example, here is a mother with a demon-possessed daughter. She cries unto the Lord for help, and the Bible says He answered her not a word. Then she turned to His disciples, and they were so upset they said, "Master, send her away, for she even cries after us."

So many ministers today take offense when the sick and afflicted or the demon-possessed are brought to them for prayer. They simply do not want to have anything to do with them.

But Jesus said, "I am not sent but to the lost sheep of the house of Israel."

The mother said, "Lord, help me."

Right in the face of what Christ had said, she persisted. Then He said something that seemed so cruel.

"Woman, it is not right to take the children's bread and to give it to the dogs." The term "children" referred to the children of Israel who were the first children of God. Dogs referred to the Gentiles because that is what the Jewish people called the Gentiles. From the Jewish standpoint they were a cruel, rapacious people who did not want to have anything to do with God.

Then she said, "Truth, Lord. You are right. Yet, Master, remember this about dogs. The children of Israel, when they eat, take their little puppies into their laps. And while they do not give them a whole loaf, they give them the crumbs that fall from the table. Yes, I am a member of the Gentile race. We are but dogs in that we have not followed God, and we are a cruel people. But Master, if I can't have a loaf, may I have a crumb?"

She had that much faith. And even that kind of faith produced results. In other words, if we do not have everything we would like to have, if we come with an honest and believing heart, and we hold on, Jesus will never turn us away.

Matthew 15:29-32

> And Jesus departed from thence, and came nigh unto the sea of Galilee; and went up into a mountain, and sat down there. And great multitudes came unto him, having with them those that were lame, blind, dumb, maimed, and many others, and cast them down at Jesus' feet; and he healed them. Insomuch that the multitude wondered, when they saw the dumb to speak, the maimed to be whole, the lame to walk, and the blind to see: and they glorified the God of Israel.
>
> Then Jesus called his disciples unto him, and said, I have compassion on the multitude, because they continue with me now three days, and have nothing to eat: and I will not send them away fasting, lest they faint in the way.

The Healing Ministry

Notice that the people who brought the lame, the blind, the dumb, the maimed, and many others, cast them down at Jesus' feet. They had been such a burden upon those who cared for them, that they just carried them and cast them down and there they lay at Jesus' feet. He healed them.

Have we ever gotten a true picture of Jesus? Do we understand that He is the healing Christ? This is the thing that we are recapturing in the Christian faith today through the charismatic outpouring of the Holy Spirit — the healing ministry. The healing ministry is so powerful, not only through people like Oral Roberts, or Richard Roberts, or others, but also through any believing child of God. And now a great multitude has gathered around Him.

Matthew 15:33-39

And his disciples say unto him, Whence should we have so much bread in the wilderness, as to fill so great a multitude? And Jesus saith unto them, How many loaves have ye? And they said, Seven, and a few little fishes. And he commanded the multitude to sit down on the ground. And he took the seven loaves and the fishes, and gave thanks, and brake them, and gave to his disciples, and the disciples to the multitude.

And they did all eat, and were filled: and they took up of the broken meat that was left seven baskets full. And they that did eat were 4,000 men, beside women and children. And He sent away the multitude, and took ship, and came into the coasts of Magdala.

Faith is Continuous

This is another scene where Jesus feeds a multitude, except it is 4,000 men rather than 5,000 men. Also, it is 6 months later, and a Gentile area. The other feeding of the 5,000 was primarily for Jewish people who had their baskets in which they carried their kosher food, but here the people have hampers. These are primarily Gentile people, probably with a sprinkling of Jews. But the main thing that Jesus is pointing out to His disciples is that His work is a continuing work.

Faith does not work just one time and stop. Wherever there is human need and we exercise our faith by releasing it to God, we can expect God to multiply our sown seed, our faith released, and we can continue bringing deliverance to people.

The disciples probably thought the feeding of the 5,000 was just something Jesus did. He had told them to give the people something to eat, and the disciples had not grasped that. They still had not understood, but Jesus was talking about the ongoing power of our Christian faith. We continue to be Christians, Christians who bring deliverance to people.

We help people, and we do it on a continuous basis.

Matthew 16:1

The Pharisees also with the Sadducees came, and tempting desired him that he would shew them a sign from heaven.

Old and New Sadducees

The Sadducees were people in Israel then who did not believe in miracles, or in the resurrection of the dead. That says something to us about the millions of people in the church today who give lip service to the Bible and the kingdom of God, but who do not believe in immortality, or life after death, or the resurrection, or the miracles of God for now. The Sadducees denied them in the past and they deny them now. These Sadducees tempted Christ by asking Him for a sign from heaven.

Matthew 16:2-11

He answered and said unto them, When it is evening, ye say, It will be fair weather: for the sky is red. And in the morning, It will be foul weather to day: for the sky is red and lowring. O ye hypocrites, ye can discern the face of the sky; but can ye not discern the signs of the times? A wicked and adulterous generation seeketh after a sign; and there shall no sign be given unto it, but the sign of the prophet Jonas. And he left them, and departed. And when his disciples were come to the other side, they had forgotten to take bread.

Then Jesus said unto them, Take heed and beware of the leaven of the Pharisees and of the Sadducees. And they reasoned among themselves, saying, It is because we have taken no bread. Which when Jesus perceived, he said unto them, O ye of little faith, why reason ye among yourselves, because ye have brought no bread? Do ye not yet understand, neither remember the five loaves of the 5,000, and how many baskets ye took up? Neither the seven loaves of the 4,000, and how many baskets ye took up? How is it that ye do not understand that I spake it not to you concerning bread, that ye should beware of the leaven of the Pharisees and of the Sadducees?

Jesus was constantly striking at the teaching of the Pharisees, scribes, and Sadducees, people whose hearts were not right with God, but who were outwardly religious and claimed to be spiritual leaders. He was telling His disciples to keep their minds on God, to remember His mighty miracles, such as the feeding of the 5,000 and the feeding of the 4,000, and also to remember the baskets full of food that were taken up extra as a result of those miracles.

Matthew 16:12-19

Then understood they how that he bade them not beware of the leaven of bread, but of the doctrine of the Pharisees and of the Sadducees. When Jesus came into the coasts of Caesarea Philippi, he asked his disciples saying, Whom do men say that I the Son of man am? And they said, Some say that thou art John the Baptist: some, Elias; and others, Jeremias, or one of the prophets.

He saith unto them, But whom say ye that I am?

And Simon Peter answered and said, Thou art the Christ, the Son of the living God.

And Jesus answered and said unto him, Blessed art thou, Simon Barjona: for flesh and blood hath not revealed it unto thee, but my Father which is in heaven. And I say also unto thee, That thou art Peter, and upon this rock I will build my church; and the gates of hell shall not prevail against it. And I will give unto thee the keys of the kingdom of heaven: and whatsoever thou shalt bind on earth shall be bound in heaven: and whatsoever thou shalt loose on earth shall be loosed in heaven.

Christ Gives Power

Great power is given to those whose confession of faith is that Jesus Christ is the Son of God. He is not speaking of a mere man here, followed by some other man in each generation, but He is speaking of those who truly believe that Christ is the Son of God, and who make that confession. They are the ones who have the keys of the kingdom of heaven.

Matthew 16:20

Then charged he his disciples that they should tell no man that he was Jesus the Christ.

This was a very precarious time, because many of the followers of Jesus were wrongfully thinking that He was to be the warrior king, that is, He would throw off Roman rule, declare himself to be the king of Israel, and restore the kingdom to Israel. This was a very hot political issue then, and Jesus told them not to reveal the experience they had just shared.

Matthew 16:21-23

From that time forth began Jesus to shew unto his disciples, how that he must go unto Jerusalem, and suffer many things of the elders and chief priests and scribes, and be killed, and be raised again the third day. Then Peter took him, and began to rebuke him, saying, Be it far from thee, Lord: this shall not be unto thee. But He turned, and said unto Peter, Get thee behind me, Satan: thou art an offence unto me: for thou savourest not the things that be of God, but those that be of men.

"Kingdom" Misunderstood

Shortly after Peter had said that Jesus Christ was the Son of the

Living God, he became indignant at Jesus for breaking his dreams. We believe that even Peter was caught up in the idea that Jesus would become a warrior king and restore the kingdom of Israel. Right after his tremendous confession of faith (which seemed to go to his head), Peter rebuked Christ. The language is so strong, saying, "Peter took Him," that he may have taken Him by the shoulders and shook Him, and said, "This shall not be unto you, Lord." Oh, Peter was vehement! He did not understand, but the Lord understood. He knew that the words from Peter's mouth were the words of the devil. And he said, "Peter, you devil, you get behind Me. You are an offense unto Me."

Jesus Christ will not compromise, not even with the so-called leader, Peter, who led the other disciples into calling Jesus the Son of God. Jesus would have nothing to do with His kingdom being an earthly kingdom for that day. He knew it was the kingdom of God. Entrance into it would be through the heart, not through the head.

He knew that without His death, there would be no resurrection, and with no resurrection, there would be no Christian faith or Christian church. Without a Christian church, there would be no light sent to the ends of the earth. There would be no salvation for the sons of men.

Matthew 16:24-27

> Then said Jesus unto his disciples, If any man will come after me, let him deny himself, and take up his cross, and follow me. For whosoever will save his life shall lose it: and whosoever will lose his life for my sake shall find it.
>
> For what is a man profited, if he shall gain the whole world and lose his own soul? or what shall a man give in exchange for his soul? For the Son of man shall come in the glory of his Father with his angels; and then he shall reward every man according to his works.

The Seed of Faith

Jesus Christ made the statement that those who would follow Him should take up their crosses and follow Him by denying themselves. He was at this time on His way to the cross of Calvary. He knew what it meant to give up all rights to himself, but to submit His own will to the heavenly Father's will.

That strikes against human nature. Human beings want their own will. We see that in babies, in little children. They want their own way. They want all attention given to them. Jesus, in dealing with us as His children, knows our nature. And He says that if we really want to follow Him, we are to deny ourselves, that is to say, give up all rights to ourselves in line with the will of God. That does not mean that we renounce ourselves as human beings. It does not mean that we have no rights at all. But it means that God's rights are greater than our rights. It means that if we can have the faith and the courage to submit ourselves to our heavenly Father, by taking up our cross and following His Son Jesus Christ, we are going to come into power, authority, joy, and fullness of living such as we never dreamed.

Jesus says to us that if we cling to ourselves and demand to have our own way and therefore, try to save our lives, that in that very act, we will lose our lives. We will not have the rights of the heavenly Father conferred upon us. We will not be able to exercise His authority over sin, sickness, disease, demons, fear, poverty, and the other things that are against God.

This is one of the most beautiful and powerful examples of seed-faith in the entire Word of God. We plant our lives as a seed of our faith. And when we do, God will multiply that seed. He will restore and reward our lives. This is a very powerful, positive statement of Christ about living the fullness of life, that in giving ourselves as a seed of our faith, He will multiply us, and we will live lives to the fullest.

Matthew 16:27-17:9

> For the Son of man shall come in the glory of his Father with his angels; and then he shall reward every man according to his works. Verily I say unto you, There be some standing here, which shall not taste of death, till they see the Son of man coming in his kingdom.
>
> And after six days Jesus taketh Peter, James, and John his brother, and bringeth them up into an high mountain apart, and was transfigured before them: and his face did shine as the sun, and his raiment was white as the light. And, behold, there appeared unto them Moses and Elias talking with him.
>
> Then answered Peter, and said unto Jesus, Lord, it is good for us to be here: if thou wilt, let us make here three tabernacles; one for thee, and one for Moses, and one for Elias. While he yet spake, behold, a bright cloud overshadowed them: and behold a voice out of the cloud, which said, This is my beloved Son, in whom I am well pleased; hear ye him.
>
> And when the disciples heard it, they fell on their face, and were sore afraid. And Jesus came and touched them, and said, Arise, and be not afraid. And when they had lifted up their eyes, they saw no man, save Jesus only. And as they came down from the mountain, Jesus charged them, saying, Tell the vision to no man, until the Son

of man be risen again from the dead.

Hearing God's Voice

In this powerful scene on the highest mountain in Palestine, probably Mount Hermon in the north, where Jesus' outward physical appearance was so dramatically changed until His face shone like the sun, there was a very special touch of God. An inner shining came from within His flesh, going through His flesh, and revealing itself in His face. During this, two men appeared. One was Moses, the other, Elijah. Moses had been dead 1,700 years. He was the one, you remember, whom God had buried. No one knew where. The other was Elijah, who had been translated 1,000 years earlier. Both of these men had been with God — one through death, and the other through translation. They have returned in their spiritual state and are recognizable. This is one of the greatest proofs in the Bible of immortality, of the resurrection, of life after death.

They talked with Jesus. What do you suppose they talked about? Doubtless they talked about the coming death at Calvary, about Christ's own resurrection, and the building of the Church. It was a tremendous scene. The three disciples wanted to stay on the mountain. A bright cloud overshadowed them. They heard the voice of God: "This is my beloved Son in whom I am well pleased. Hear ye him. Put your priorities straight. Do not get your minds upon men, even as great as Moses or Elijah."

Moses was the first great lawgiver, and Elijah was the first great prophet in Israel. They represented the sum total of the mighty presence of God among His people Israel. But even in that, God was saying, "You listen to Me."

Today, God still speaks. When He told me to build Him a university, to build it on the Holy Spirit and His authority, He said, "Raise up your students to hear My voice." God was telling me that while our voices are important, and while our teaching of these students is indispensable in this world, we are to bear in mind that the most important thing is what they hear from God. So many students of Oral Roberts University tell me that their most important experience at ORU, with their academic and spiritual education, is that they finally do hear God's voice, God speaking in their inner man. I am so glad that God does speak to people in these last days, and that it is His voice that is more precious than all other voices put together.

Matthew 17:10-21

And his disciples asked him, saying, Why then say the scribes that

Elias must first come? And Jesus answered and said unto them, Elias truly shall first come, and restore all things. But I say unto you, That Elias is come already, and they knew him not, but have done unto him whatsoever they listed. Likewise shall also the Son of man suffer of them. Then the disciples understood that he spake unto them of John the Baptist. And when they were come to the multitude, there came to him a certain man, kneeling down to him, and saying, Lord, have mercy on my son: for he is a lunatick, and sore vexed: for ofttimes he falleth into the fire, and oft into the water. And I brought him to thy disciples, and they could not cure him. Then Jesus answered and said, O faithless and perverse generation, how long shall I be with you? how long shall I suffer you? bring him hither to me. And Jesus rebuked the devil; and he departed out of him: and the child was cured from that very hour.

Then came the disciples to Jesus apart, and said, Why could not we cast him out? And Jesus said unto them, Because of your unbelief: for verily I say unto you, If ye have faith as a grain of mustard seed, ye shall say unto this mountain, Remove hence to yonder place; and it shall remove; and nothing shall be impossible unto you. Howbeit this kind goeth not out but by prayer and fasting.

Discerning Spirits

The glory of God that had come upon them while they were on the mountaintop was now to be tested. It had been given for the purpose that they could better meet the needs of humanity. Whenever you and I are especially blessed, it is always for a greater purpose than ourselves. It is to further prepare us to help somebody. Therefore, when Jesus and His disciples came down the mountain, a whole crowd of desperately needy people was waiting. One of them came with a little child, whom many would call epileptic today. It was a child who had fits and fell into water, into fire. He really was demon-possessed. Not all epilepsy is caused by demons. However, there is a type of epilepsy that is caused expressly by a demon. This was that case.

In order for us to know the difference, we have to have the DISCERNING of spirits. When they brought the child to the disciples, they could not do a thing. That is a terrible thing to say about so many of the believers today, including ministers, that they simply do not recognize that through the gifts of the spirit there is the power of DISCERNMENT against demons.

Seed-Faith Scripture

Then Jesus almost lost His temper. He said, "You people without faith. How long do you think I am going to be with you in the flesh like this? When will you undersand that you are to use your own faith?" Then Jesus rebuked the devil, and when He rebuked this devil, calling him out of the person, the child was cured from that very hour.

Matthew 17:20 is one of the most powerful seed-faith scriptures in the Word of God. It tells us that our faith has to happen. It must go into action. Jesus compared it with the planting of a seed, even the smallest seed. When that seed is planted it changes its nature, that is, it is transformed from a seed into a growing plant. As it grows up, nothing can stand in its place. Jesus says our faith is like that. First, we are to believe with our heart, and that is a seed of our faith. And second, we are to actually call the thing out. Remember that Jesus rebuked the devil. He called him out. He commanded the devil to loose that little boy. And the devil came out. It is terribly important to speak forth the Word of God, to speak in the name of God, to speak through the power of our faith. Jesus said that when our seed-faith is fully acted upon, then these mountains of need will be removed. As we stand there, nothing will be impossible unto us. How powerful we believers are!

Matthew 17:22,23

> And while they abode in Galilee, Jesus said unto them, The Son of man shall be betrayed into the hands of men. And they shall kill him, and the third day he shall be raised again, and they were exceeding sorry.

How we need to hear what Jesus is saying! He never says something about death unless He covers it with life and resurrection.

Matthew 17:24-27

> And when they were come to Capernaum, they that received tribute money came to Peter and said, Doth not your master pay tribute? He saith, Yes. And when he was come into the house, Jesus prevented him, saying, What thinkest thou, Simon? of whom do the kings of the earth take custom or tribute? of their own children or of strangers? Peter saith unto him, Of strangers. Jesus saith unto him, Then are the children free. Notwithstanding, lest we should offend them, go thou to the sea, and cast an hook, and take up the fish that first cometh up: and when thou hast opened his mouth, thou shalt find a piece of money: that take, and give unto them for me and thee.

Christ Paid Taxes

Many people wonder about paying taxes, being subject to the laws of the land. Well, our Lord lived under an occupying army: the Romans. And He paid His taxes. But the second thing that people are concerned about is how Jesus did this miracle, or was it really a miracle? Did it happen?

Let us talk about this fish that had money in its mouth. First, it is a miracle if this fish did have money in its mouth. Second, it is a miracle that Peter could locate that fish out of all the millions of fish in the sea. Third, it is a miracle if it did not have money in its mouth when Peter started fishing, but swam out and located the money and got it in its mouth. Yes, I believe that. I believe that God is concerned so much that He can do material things like that by showing us where they are, revealing their location, and then we honor Him. The money was used to pay His taxes and Peter's.

Matthew 18:1-7

> At the same time came the disciples unto Jesus, saying, Who is the greatest in the kingdom of heaven? And Jesus called a little child unto him, and set him in the midst of them, and said, Verily I say unto you, Except ye be converted, and become as little children, ye shall not enter into the kingdom of heaven. Whosoever therefore shall humble himself as this little child, the same is greatest in the kingdom of heaven. And whoso shall receive one such little child in my name receiveth me. But whoso shall offend one of these little ones which believe in me, it were better for him that a millstone were hanged about his neck, and that he were drowned in the depth of the sea. Woe unto the world because of offences! for it must needs be that offences come; but woe to that man by whom the offence cometh!

Jesus was always concerned about status seekers, people who wanted attention called to themselves for attention's sake. He wanted all of us in the kingdom of God to be like little children, to be humble, not to take the high place, but to sit back and wait for God to bring us forth. This is the Christian way.

Matthew 18:8,9

> Wherefore if thy hand or thy foot offend thee, cut them off and cast them from thee: it is better for thee to enter into life halt or maimed, rather than having two hands or two feet to be cast into everlasting fire. And if thine eye offend thee, pluck it out, and cast it from thee: it is better for thee to enter into life with one eye, rather than having two eyes to be cast into hell fire.

Jesus is not referring to us physically mutilating our bodies. Here, He is simply saying that when we do something to offend God, stop it. Get it out of our spirit. And we can.

Matthew 18:10

> Take heed that ye despise not one of these little ones; for I say unto you, That in heaven their angels do always behold the face of my Father which is in heaven.

Guardian Angels

This is the first reference in Matthew to this type of angel, the angels that belong to each child of God. Yes, we do have guardian angels. God assigns angels to us. In Hebrews, Chapter one, we are told that these angels are sent to minister for us. Not to us, but for us. They are to work on our behalf.

Matthew 18:11-14

> For the Son of man is come to save that which was lost. How think ye? if a man have 100 sheep and one of them be gone astray, doth he not leave the ninety and nine, and goeth into the mountains, and seeketh that which is gone astray? And if so be that he find it, verily I say unto you, he rejoiceth more of that sheep, than of the ninety and nine which went not astray. Even so it is not the will of your Father which is in heaven, that one of these little ones should perish.

Here we see the ultimate desire of God is for those dear ones who have gone astray. He never gives up, does He? His love is everlasting. How He rejoices and all those in heaven rejoice when one lost person comes to his senses and returns to God. We should hold on and hold on and hold on, letting our love reach out, reach out, reach out.

Matthew 18:15-17

> Moreover if thy brother shall trespass against thee, go and tell him his fault between thee and him alone: if he shall hear thee, thou hast gained thy brother. But if he will not hear thee, then take with thee one or two more, that in the mouth of two or three witnesses every word may be established. And if he shall neglect to hear them, tell it unto the church: but if he neglect to hear the church, let him be unto thee as an heathen man and a publican.

I think the important thing is that the burden is upon those of us who have been wronged, who have been trespassed against. God gives us a course to take. Even if they spit in our face when we try to make things right, we are to hold onto our peace and our love.

Matthew 18:18-20

> Verily I say unto you, Whatsoever ye shall bind on earth shall be bound in heaven: and whatsoever ye shall loose on earth shall be loosed in heaven.
>
> Again I say unto you, That if two of you shall agree on earth as touching anything that they shall ask, it shall be done for them of my Father which is in heaven. For where two or three are gathered together in my name, there am I in the midst of them.

Unity in Faith

Where two or three are gathered in Christ's name, they constitute a local church, whether they be two or three or two or three hundred, or two or three thousand or even more. The main thing is unity in the faith, agreement on the name of Jesus Christ, and the releasing of our faith. I thank God that even when two or three of us agree on anything on this earth that we shall ask, it shall be done for us of our Father which is in heaven.

I have this agreement with the partners of my ministry. Time and time again, I see God working miracles in their behalf, in my behalf, and in our behalf together.

God works this way with any two or three who meet together in the name of Christ and ask. It is important to ask. It is important to agree. And it is important to release our faith and let God use the keys of the kingdom on our behalf.

Matthew 18:21-22

> Then came Peter to him, and said, Lord, how oft shall my brother sin against me, and I forgive him? till seven times? Jesus saith unto him, I say not unto thee, Until seven times: but Until seventy times seven.

In other words, keep on forgiving. There is never a point where one stops forgiving. For it is in our forgiving of others that God forgives us. If you or if I have anything in our hearts unforgiven, then we should forgive others that God may forgive that in us. It is in sweet forgiveness that we have deliverance from God.

Matthew 18:23-35

> Therefore is the kingdom of heaven likened unto a certain king, which would take account of his servants. And when he had begun to reckon,

one was brought unto him, which owed him ten thousand talents. But forasmuch as he had not to pay, his lord commanded him to be sold, and his wife, and children, and all that he had, and payment to be made. The servant therefore fell down and worshipped him, saying, Lord, have patience with me, and I will pay thee all.

Then the lord of that servant was moved with compassion and loosed him and forgave him the debt.

But the same servant went out, and found one of his fellowservants, which owed him an hundred pence. And he laid hands on him, and took him by the throat, saying, Pay me that thou owest. And his fellowservant fell down at his feet, and besought him, saying, Have patience with me, and I will pay thee all. And he would not: but went and cast him into prison, till he should pay the debt.

So when his fellowservants saw what was done, they were very sorry, and came and told unto their lord all that was done.

Then his lord, after that he had called him, said unto him, O thou wicked servant, I forgave thee all that debt, because thou desiredst me. Shouldest not thou also have had compassion on thy fellowservant, even as I had pity on thee?

And his lord was wroth, and delivered him to the tormentors till he should pay all that was due unto him. So likewise shall my heavenly Father do also unto you, if ye from your hearts forgive not every one his brother their trespasses.

Always Forgive

Notice again the ultimate love of God, how compassionate He is. So willing to forgive, and yet He is stung at our unforgiving spirit. We want the world, and yet we will not even give the time of day to someone we dislike. We are not to jump on other people.

Think . . . think of what you owe God — when God has forgiven your sins. When God has given you breath to breathe, when God has been with you and taken care of you, and yet you turn around and will not even forgive some slight little defect in a fellow brother or sister. I praise God because the Christian faith is full of love.

Matthew 19:1-12

And it came to pass, that when Jesus had finished these sayings, he departed from Galilee and came into the coasts of Judaea beyond Jordan. And great multitudes followed him and he healed them there. The Pharisees also came unto him, tempting him and saying unto him, Is it lawful for a man to put away his wife for every cause?

And he answered and said unto them, Have ye not read that he which made them at the beginning made them male and female, and said, For this cause shall a man leave father and mother and shall cleave to his wife and they twain shall be one flesh? Wherefore they are no more twain, but one flesh. What therefore God hath joined together, let not man put asunder.

He saith unto them, Why did Moses then command to give a writing of divorcement and to put her away?

He saith unto them, Moses, because of the hardness of your hearts, suffered you to put away your wives. But from the beginning, it was not so. And I say unto you, Whosoever shall put away his wife, except it be for fornication, and shall marry another, committeth adultery. And whosoever marrieth her which is put away doth commit adultery.

His disciples said unto him, If the case of the man be so with his wife, it is not good to marry.

But he said unto them, All men cannot receive this saying, save they to whom it is given. For there are some eunuchs which were so born from their mother's womb. And there are some eunuchs which were made eunuchs of men. And there be eunuchs which have made themselves eunuchs for the kingdom of heaven's sake. He that is able to receive it, let him receive it.

God's "Life-styles"

God created man to be male and female. Because of that, a man will leave his father and mother and cleave to his wife and they will be one flesh. Therefore, man should not put them asunder. God made them male and female.

Today people are talking about "alternate lifestyles," as if God made male and male, and then He made female and female. You see how impossible that is? Not only is it not relevant, and not godly, it is impossible. For God made mankind male and female. No one is going to unmake the male or unmake the female.

A male may take up habitation with another male or even try to enter into what they call a male marriage. A female may take up with a female in lesbianism and even try to have a so-called marriage, calling it an "alternate life-style."

First, they were not created for that purpose.

Second, it is impossible for them to be one flesh.

Third, there can be no children born.

Fourth, the human race would die out, and it would not be long until there would not be a human being on the face of this earth. Now, if we are going to follow the devil and the way he perverts God's creation, we can talk about alternate life-styles. But I am not interested in that, and no born-again believer who believes the Bible is going to buy any of that stuff. If this so-called "alternate life-style" invades the Church, the handwriting is on the wall. I predict there will be an uprising from coast to coast and from church to church. The uprising will begin with God, and if God has to start a whole new movement, God will do it, because His Church is to be pure. I just want to say that I am on the side of the Lord and the side of the way He created us as male and female. I am for the family. I am for the home.

Matthew 19:13-26

Then were there brought unto him little children, that he should put his hands on them, and pray; and the disciples rebuked them. But Jesus said, Suffer little children, and forbid them not, to come unto me; for of such is the kingdom of heaven.

And he laid his hands on them, and departed thence. And, behold, one came and said unto him, Good Master, what good thing shall I do, that I may have eternal life?

And he said unto him, why callest thou me good? there is none good but one, that is, God: but if thou wilt enter into life, keep the commandments.

He saith unto him, Which? Jesus said, Thou shalt do no murder, Thou shalt not commit adultery, Thou shalt not steal, Thou shalt not bear false witness, Honour thy father and thy mother; and, Thou shalt love thy neighbour as thyself.

The young man saith unto him, All these things have I kept from my youth up: what lack I yet?

Jesus said unto him, If thou wilt be perfect, go and sell that thou hast and give to the poor and thou shalt have treasure in heaven and come and follow me.

But when the young man heard that saying he went away sorrowful: for he had great possessions.

Then said Jesus unto his disciples, Verily I say unto you, That a rich man shall hardly enter into the kingdom of heaven. And again I say unto you, It is easier for a camel to go through the eye of a needle, than for a rich man to enter into the kingdom of God.

When his disciples heard it, they were exceedingly amazed, saying, Who then can be saved? But Jesus beheld them, and said unto them, With men this is impossible; but with God all things are possible.

Simple Faith

Jesus spoke about little children and of allowing them to come to Him, for of such is the kingdom of God. He wanted to make a point to a group of people who were concerned with the law of Moses to the extent that they probably had something like 100,000 commandments that they had added to the original commandments God gave Moses. They made it so big it was impossible to carry out. But they really did not know about the simple faith that a little child has in Jesus Christ.

He knew that they could go all their lives and never learn all those oral traditions of the law that had been passed down, but a little child, so fresh from God, so simple in its faith toward God, would have childlike faith and God would accept that. But, all these people going through these thousands and thousands of extra commandments added to the law of Moses could reach a place that even though they thought they kept the law and were wealthy, they had not even understood the two basic tenets of the law of Moses.

First, it was given to create a sense of sin, and second, because of the sense of sin, they could not save themselves. They needed a Redeemer and should therefore look for the promised Messiah. That is what they really missed. A little child had that simple faith. We do not have to overindulge in trying to understand every little thing that comes along, but one thing is important — that is simple faith in God.

Matthew 19:27-20:16

Then answered Peter and said unto him, Behold, we have forsaken all, and followed thee. What shall we have therefore?

And Jesus said unto them, Verily I say unto you, That ye which have followed me, in the regeneration when the Son of man shall sit in the throne of his glory, ye also shall sit upon twelve thrones, judging the twelve tribes of Israel.

And everyone that hath forsaken houses, or brethren, or sisters, or father, or mother, or wife, or children, or lands, for my name's sake, shall receive an hundredfold, and shall inherit everlasting life.

But many that are first shall be last; and the last shall be first.

For the kingdom of heaven is like unto a man that is an householder, which went out early in the morning to hire labourers into his vineyard. And when he had agreed with the labourers for a penny a day, he sent them into his vineyard. And he went out about the third hour, and saw others standing idle in the Marketplace, and said unto them; Go ye also into the vineyard, and whatsoever is right I will give you. And they went their way. Again he went out about the sixth and ninth hour, and did likewise. And about the eleventh hour he went out, and found others standing idle, and saith unto them, Why stand ye here all the day idle? They say unto him, Because no man hath hired us. He saith unto them, Go ye also into the vineyard; and whatsoever is right, that shall ye receive.

So when even was come, the lord of the vineyard saith unto his steward, Call the labourers, and give them their hire, beginning from the last unto the first. And when they came that were hired about the eleventh hour they received every man a penny. But when the first came, they supposed that they should have received more; and they likewise received every man a penny.

And when they had received it, they murmured against the goodman of the house, saying, These last have wrought but one hour, and thou hast made them equal unto us, which have borne the burden and heat of the day.

But he answered one of them, and said, Friend, I do thee no wrong. Didst not thou agree with me for a penny? Take that thine is, and go thy way: I will give unto this last, even as unto thee. Is it not lawful for me to do what I will with mine own? Is thine eye evil, because I am good?

So the last shall be first, and the first last; for many be called, but few chosen.

I think the Lord is trying to tell us that He is seeking laborers. Some are ready almost instantly. Others are ready a little later. Then there are those who postpone until the message comes to them again and again and finally, those who eventually hear God calling them and come in with a whole heart.

The lord of the vineyard is showing his gratitude, his generosity, not his unfairness. Some workers thought he was unfair, but he was simply being generous for the work that was done.

Jesus said that many are called, but few chosen. Everybody In the world is called of God. God's voice is going to the ends of the earth. And people are hearing, but all are not distinguishing the words.

All are called, but few are chosen. That means that while all are called, only a few choose their calling. They choose their calling. If now you feel the call of God in your heart to serve Him, it is up to you to choose. Few choose their calling. Will you be one?

Matthew 20:17-19

And Jesus, going up to Jerusalem, took the twelve disciples apart in the way, and said unto them, Behold, we go up to Jerusalem; and the Son of man shall be betrayed unto the chief priests and unto the scribes, and they shall condemn him to death, and shall deliver him to the Gentiles to mock, and to scourge, and to crucify him. And the third day he shall rise again.

Resurrection Victory!

Jesus knew in advance that He would be betrayed. He would be condemned. He would be delivered up to the Gentiles who would mock Him, scourge Him, and crucify Him. He knew also the joy, that on the third day He would rise again from the dead.

It is one thing to know in your spirit that many sufferings are coming, but the greatest thing to know is that through the power of the resurrection, God is going to bring you forth in victory.

Matthew 20:20-28

> Then came to him the mother of Zebedee's children with her sons, worshipping him, and desiring a certain thing of him. And he said unto her, What wilt thou? She saith unto him, Grant that these my two sons may sit, the one on thy right hand, and the other on the left, in thy kingdom.
>
> But Jesus answered and said, Ye know not what ye ask. Are ye able to drink of the cup that I shall drink of, and to be baptized with the baptism that I am baptized with? They say unto him, We are able. And he saith unto them, ye shall drink indeed of my cup, and be baptized with the baptism that I am baptized with; but to sit on my right hand, and on my left, is not mine to give, but it shall be given to them for whom it is prepared of my Father. And when the 10 heard it, they were moved with indignation against the two brethren. But Jesus called them unto him and said, Ye know that the princes of the Gentiles exercise dominion over them, and they that are great exercise authority upon them.
>
> But it shall not be so among you; but whosoever will be great among you, let him be your minister; and whosoever will be chief among you, let him be your servant; even as the Son of man came not to be ministered unto, but to minister, and to give his life a ransom for many.

Humility, Service Linked

Do you see how the Lord is striking at pride; how He wants us to have a humble spirit; how He will exalt us when we humble ourselves?

Did He not show us the greatest example in the world by being a servant himself, by serving other people, by touching them at the point of their need? By carrying their burdens, feeling their deepest needs, and going with them to the last mile of the way?

Jesus Christ wants a humble people. A serving people. A people who show, by their example, through humility, that their trust is in

God their source, who will supply their needs in due time.

Matthew 20:29-34

> And as they departed from Jericho, a great multitude followed him.
> And, behold, two blind men sitting by the way side, when they heard that Jesus passed by, cried out, saying, Have mercy on us, O Lord, thou son of David.
> And the multitude rebuked them, because they shall hold their peace: but they cried the more, saying, Have mercy on us, O Lord, thou son of David.
> And Jesus stood still, and called them, and said, What will ye that I shall do unto you?
> They say unto him, Lord, that our eyes may be opened.
> So Jesus had compassion on them, and touched their eyes; and immediately their eyes received sight, and they followed him.

When Jesus passed through Jericho, there was a tremendous multitude following him, hanging onto every word and watching every act. There were two blind men sitting by the wayside begging and they had heard that it was Jesus passing by.

They were galvanized into action, for they were two people who were looking for a miracle. Hearing about Jesus and putting everything together that they had heard, they decided that He was indeed the Son of David, the promised Messiah, that He was anointed to heal, and when He got near they yelled at the top of their voices, "Jesus, thou Son of David! Jesus, thou Son of David!"

They did not have any other way to get His attention. When they yelled, "Jesus, thou Son of David!" the Bible says that Jesus stood still.

Picture that scene. The whole crowd is engulfing Him with all kinds of noises and He hears these voices in unison: "Lord, thou Son of David!" That is what He had been listening for. He had been listening for faith and He said, "Bring those men to me." The crowd, of course, wanted them to shut up and not take their time. But they did not understand that a miracle was on the way.

Do you understand that a miracle is either coming toward you or going past you every day of your life? These men knew that because He was the Messiah, miracles were coming their way, and it was the miracle that would enable them to see again!

When they were brought to Him, He said, "Now, what is it you want Me to do for you?" Certainly He could see they were blind and He could see they wore beggar's robes which separated them from other people. He could see all that, but Jesus wants us to take action. To say something. To do something. Things have to be made to happen.

All these years I have dealt with all types of people, many of whom know that they must release their faith, they must learn how to do it, and they can do it. Others just lay back and say, "Well, if God wants to heal me He will." But that is not the spirit in which Jesus came.

He said, What is it that you want Me to do for you?

They said, "Lord, we want our eyes opened." Jesus had compassion and touched their eyes, and immediately they received their sight. In the other gospels we are also told that He said to them, "Thy faith hath saved thee." Do you realize that Jesus recognized the miracle-working power in their faith and that He recognizes the miracle-working power in the faith you have and the faith I have? If you have great faith, it is faith; if you have little faith, it is faith. If you will just release what faith you have — big faith, middle-sized faith, little faith — if you release that faith, it has miracle-working power in it. Their faith worked then just like it works today.

Matthew 21:1-11

> And when they drew nigh unto Jerusalem and were come to Bethphage unto the mount of Olives, then sent Jesus two disciples, saying unto them, Go into the village over against you, and straightway ye shall find an ass tied, and a colt with her: loose them, and bring them unto me. And if any man say ought unto you, ye shall say, The Lord hath need of them, and straightway he will send them.
>
> All this was done, that it might be fulfilled which was spoken by the prophet, saying, Tell ye the daughter of Sion, Behold, thy King cometh unto thee, meek, and sitting upon an ass, and a colt the foal of an ass. And the disciples went, and did as Jesus commanded them, and brought the ass and the colt and put on them their clothes, and they set him thereon. And a very great multitude spread their garments in the way; others cut down branches from the trees, and strawed them in the way. And the multitudes that went before, and that followed, cried, saying, Hosanna to the son of David! Blessed is he that cometh in the name of the Lord! Hosanna in the highest!
>
> And when he was come into Jerusalem, all the city was moved, saying, Who is this? And the multitude said, This is Jesus the prophet of Nazareth of Galilee.

A Glorious Entrance

This was just a few days before Jesus was crucified and He is now entering the city triumphantly. I will say more about this event later but I feel led to share this with you now. He knew that the great crowds would be expecting Him when He entered the capital city, so He asked His disciples to go find a colt for Him. They wondered where in the world they could do that and He said, "You go find a man who has a colt and you say to him, 'The Lord hath need of this colt,' and when you do, the man will let you have it." Jesus had revelational knowledge that this was going to happen. He could share it with His disciples in a believing way and they, too, would believe it and would go forth and find it so.

When they brought the colt we are told that they sat Him on it — a colt that had never been ridden. Jesus, the Master, mastered the colt. As He rode him down the hillside, it was reminiscent of scenes the people had seen when they had welcomed others who were kings as they had entered the city. This time, with an inner understanding that He was the Messiah, they began to shout at the top of their voices, "Hosanna to the Son of David!" And that phrase, of course, meant the Messiah, and "Blessed be He that cometh in the name of the Lord!"

The scene was so powerful that the city was deeply moved and agitated. It was disturbed about this person. In fact, the populace wanted to know who this person was that the crowd was magnifying, and they yelled, "This is Jesus, the prophet of Nazareth of Galilee!"

Matthew 21:12,13

> And Jesus went into the temple of God and cast out all them that sold and bought in the temple, and overthrew the tables of the moneychangers, and the seats of them that sold doves, and said unto them, It is written, My house shall be called the house of prayer; but ye have made it a den of thieves.

"It is written"

Jews from abroad were not allowed to use their own currency to pay the annual temple dues, and the moneychangers fixed a high rate of exchange. Poor people, who could only afford the cheapest sacrifice — two pigeons — were charged high prices. The priests turned a blind eye to all this.

Yet, when they criticized Jesus their indignation knew no bounds at what they called His "irreverence." He actually healed people in the temple courts — and they griped! With His eyes blazing, and remembering the Word of God, He said, "It is written."

You may recall that in the wilderness, with the three temptations Satan threw at Him, Jesus repulsed the devil all three times by saying, "It is written, it is written, it is written." Again He uses the Word of

God, "It is written that my house shall be called the house of prayer, but ye have made it a den of thieves."

Matthew 21:14-17

And the blind and the lame came to him in the temple; and he healed them. And when the chief priests and scribes saw the wonderful things that he did, and the children crying in the temple, and saying, Hosanna to the son of David; they were sore displeased, and said unto him, Hearest thou what these say? And Jesus saith unto them, Yea; have ye never read, Out of the mouth of babes and sucklings thou hast perfected praise? And he left them and went out of the city into Bethany; and he lodged there.

I want you to pay particular attention to the fact that when Jesus came into the temple, He was looking for prayer, for people who were seeking God. He also was looking for them to put "legs" on their prayers and have works with their faith. He demonstrated this by healing the blind and the lame as they came to Him in the temple. The healing power of Jesus Christ is especially to be manifested in the house of God. In every church service there is someone who needs healing. In every church service those in authority should be leading some phase of the healing ministry, showing people the mercy and compassion of Christ. In fact, all children of God should enter into the healing process with their prayers. The very atmosphere should be charged by faith to heal the people. Oh, there are those who will say that is not right for the house of God, just as the Pharisees and scribes were displeased when people were shouting with joy because Jesus was healing the afflicted in the temple, but it has always been like that. People of courage, of conviction, must take their stand and be like Jesus and heal the people as He did.

Matthew 21:18-22

Now in the morning as he returned into the city, he hungered. And when he saw a fig tree in the way, he came to it, and found nothing thereon, but leaves only, and said unto it, Let no fruit grow on thee henceforward for ever. And presently the fig tree withered away. And when the disciples saw it, they marvelled, saying, How soon is the fig tree withered away!

Jesus answered and said unto them, Verily I say unto you, If ye have faith, and doubt not, ye shall not only do this which is done to the fig tree, but also if ye shall say unto this mountain, Be thou removed, and be thou cast into the sea; it shall be done. And all things, whatsoever ye shall ask in prayer, believing, ye shall receive.

Here is Jesus, passing a fig tree, and everybody knew that when a fig tree put forth its leaves, the fruit came at the same time. Well, He saw nothing but leaves — leaves, but no fruit. That not only was against the way He had made nature, but it was also not the way that the kingdom of God operates. Therefore, He said to that fig tree, "You just wither away. You just go ahead and do what you are doing and get out of existence, because you are taking up space." What He meant was, You are all leaves and no fruit. You are all show but no go. You're all sowing but no reaping.

He is telling us that our Christian experience has got to be more than an experience inside our hearts, a private affair. It has to burst forth into real meaning, practical application for daily living and problems to be solved, and an action of it brought forth into the world by you, as your breath goes out of your mouth! In effect He is saying, "You breathe in, you breathe out. You put in, you take out. You sow, you reap. You receive, and from that receiving you give so that you may receive and give, receive and give."

Then He applied it to our prayer life. "If ye have faith and doubt not, ye shall not only do this which is done to the fig tree but also to this mountain." Now, Jesus is not speaking of some physical mountain, for there is no reference in the Bible that Jesus moved literal mountains. He is talking about a mountain of need and a mountain of problems. He says when you see this mountain, this need or problem, you shall speak to it and say, "You be removed," and it will be done. He is saying that our prayer is not just words.

Jesus was accustomed to hearing scribes and Pharisees and others pray their big, long, public prayers — a bunch of leaves but nothing else, no fruit, no results, no action! They were not really believing. They were saying but not believing. He is stating that when we truly believe, then we can say and whatever we say will happen. We can receive what we say, if it comes out of the believing of the inner being — believing of God that God is in the situation and our faith is rooted and grounded in Him, and that out of strength of that inner faith our words have real power against the things that are coming against us.

Matthew 21:23-32

And when he was come into the temple, the chief priests and the elders of the people came unto him as he was teaching, and said, By what authority doest thou these things? and who gave thee this authority?

And Jesus answered and said unto them, I also will ask you one thing, which if ye tell me, I in like wise will tell you by what authority I do these things. The baptism of John, whence was it? from heaven, or of men? And they reasoned with themselves, saying, If we shall say, From heaven; he will say unto us, Why did ye not then believe him? But if we shall say, of men; we fear the people; for all hold John as a prophet.

And they answered Jesus, and said, We cannot tell. And he said unto them, Neither tell I you by what authority I do these things.

But what think ye? A certain man had two sons; and he came to the first, and said, Son, go work to day in my vineyard. He answered and said, I will not; but afterward he repented, and went. And he came to the second and said likewise. And he answered and said, I go, sir; and went not.

Whether of them twain did the will of his father? They say unto him, The first. Jesus saith unto them, Verily I say unto you, That the publicans and the harlots go into the kingdom of God before you. For John came unto you in the way of righteousness, and ye believed him not; but the publicans and the harlots believed him; and ye when ye had seen it, repented not afterward, that ye might believe him.

Jesus Rejects Hypocrisy

Jesus is telling the so-called outwardly righteous who promise that they will do anything God tells them, but do not do it, That they will never enter the kingdom of God. But the sinners, who, when they finally hear God repent and obey, are the ones who will be going into the kingdom of God. I believe that Jesus is the most outraged at hypocrisy. His heart was open to people who had a need and recognized it. It was at the point of their need that they responded to God, just like it is today.

Matthew 21:33-46

Hear another parable: There was a certain householder, which planted a vineyard, and hedged it round about, and digged a winepress in it, and built a tower, and let it out to husbandmen, and went into a far country; and when the time of the fruit drew near, he sent his servants to the husbandmen, that they might receive the fruits of it. And the husbandmen took his servants, and beat one, and killed another, and stoned another. Again, he sent other servants more than the first; and they did unto them likewise. But last of all he sent unto them his son, saying, They will reverence my son. But when the husbandmen saw the son, they said among themselves, This is the heir; come, let us kill him, and let us seize on his inheritance. And they caught him, and cast him out of the vineyard, and slew him. When the lord therefore of the vineyard cometh, what will he do unto those husbandmen? They say unto him, He will miserably destroy those wicked men, and will let out his vineyard unto other husbandmen, which shall render him the fruits in their seasons. Jesus saith unto them, Did ye never read in the scriptures, The stone which the builders rejected, the same is become the head of the corner; this is the Lord's doing, and it is marvellous in our eyes? Therefore say I unto you, The kingdom of God shall be taken from you, and given to a nation bringing forth the fruits thereof. And whosoever shall fall on this stone shall be broken; but on whomsoever it shall fall, it will grind him to powder. And when the chief priests and Pharisees had heard his parables, they perceived that he spake of them. But when they sought to lay hands on him, they feared the multitude, because they took him for a prophet.

Many of the parables that Jesus gave were given in a way that was difficult for unbelieving people to understand. They had a spiritually hidden meaning which He later had to open up and explain. And He did this several times for His disciples. But here are some parables that had no hidden meaning. The chief priests and other leaders understood that He was speaking directly to them. The vineyard that He spoke of was Israel, the husbandmen were the spiritual leaders, the servants who came were the prophets sent down through the years (many of whom were killed), and finally, the son is sent by the Father and owner and the people kill him. By that time the chief priests and leaders of Israel were understanding very well because Jesus was reading the intent of their heart. They intended to kill Him. Two things stand out here. One is that the owner of the vineyard expected fruit and there was none. Jesus was saying that the Father in heaven truly expected Israel to be productive, to be carrying out the message of Abraham to be a light to the Gentiles, to the world, and to carry the chosen name of God to all people. But they had held it. They had polluted it and were even rejecting the Son of God himself. And the second thing is that Jesus told them of the scripture of how the builders had rejected the cornerstone, but the same had become the head of the corner and was the Lord's doing. And they knew that He was speaking directly to them about their treatment of Him — the Son of God. And then the Lord Jesus Christ spoke straight. He said because of your attitude, the kingdom of God will be taken from you and given to other nations who will bring forth fruit. And friend, that's what He is looking for. Not big words and pretenses in us, but our very hearts being in line with God's heart, thinking His thoughts, doing things the way He does them, and producing harvests from the seeds of faith that we plant.

Matthew 22:1-14

And Jesus answered and spake unto them again by parables, and said, The kingdom of heaven is like unto a certain king, which made a marriage for his son, and sent forth his servants to call them that were bidden to the wedding: and they would not come. Again, he sent forth other servants, saying, Tell them which are bidden, Behold, I have prepared my dinner: my oxen and my fatlings are killed, and all things are ready: come unto the marriage. But they made light of it, and went their ways, one to his farm, another to his merchandise; and the remnant took his servants, and entreated them spitefully, and slew them. But when the king heard thereof, he was wroth; and he sent forth his armies, and destroyed those murderers, and burned up their city. Then saith he to his servants, The wedding is ready, but they which were bidden were not worthy. Go ye therefore into the highways, and as many as ye shall find, bid to the marriage. So those servants went out into the highways, and gathered together all as many as they found, both bad and good: and the wedding was furnished with guests. And when the king came in to see the guests, he saw there a man which had not on a wedding garment: and he saith unto him, Friend, how camest thou in hither not having a wedding garment? And he was speechless. Then said the king to the servants, Bind him hand and foot and take him away, and cast him into outer darkness; there shall be weeping and gnashing of teeth. For many are called, but few are chosen.

The day will come when those who have been bidden and have refused will no longer be called. But newcomers will be listening to the voice of God. There will be those who, when they hear the gospel for the first time, will gladly receive it, while others who have repeatedly spurned the invitation of the Holy Spirit, will have hardened their hearts. Again, Jesus says, in Verse 14, "For many are called, but few are chosen." Let me emphasize that all are called but only a few choose their calling. It is not enough to feel God is calling you. There must be a leaping response in your heart so that you choose God's will for you. I think that more people struggle over this than anything else in the Bible or in their lives. If there ever was a time when we should be listening for God's call so that we can choose it, it is now.

Matthew 22:15-17

Then went the Pharisees, and took counsel how they might entangle him in his talk. And they sent out unto him their disciples with the Herodians, saying, Master, we know that thou art true, and teachest the way of God in truth, neither carest thou for any man; for thou regardest not the person of men. Tell us therefore, What thinkest thou? Is it lawful to give tribute unto Caesar, or not?

These Pharisees thought they were so smart that they could cross up Jesus, but we are told that Jesus perceived their wickedness. You know, we can never put anything over on God. And we need never try.

Matthew 22:18-34

But Jesus perceived their wickedness and said, Why tempt ye me, ye hypocrites? Shew me the tribute money. And they brought unto him a penny. And he saith unto them, whose is this image and superscription? They say unto him, Caesar's. Then saith he unto them, Render therefore unto Caesar the things which are Caesar's; and unto God the things that are God's. When they had heard these words, they marvelled and left him, and went their way. The same day came to him the Sadducees, which say that there is no resurrection, and asked him, saying, Master, Moses said, If a man die, having no children, his brother shall marry his wife, and raise up seed unto his brother. Now there were with us seven brethren; and the first, when he had married a wife, deceased, and, having no issue, left his wife unto his brother: likewise the second also, and the third, unto the seventh. And last of all the woman died also. Therefore in the resurrection whose wife shall she be of the seven? for they all had her. Jesus answered and said unto them, Ye do err, not knowing the scriptures, nor the power of God. For in the resurrection they neither marry, nor are given in marriage, but are as the angels of God in heaven. But as touching the resurrection of the dead, have ye not read that which was spoken unto you by God saying, I am the God of Abraham, and the God of Isaac, and the God of Jacob? God is not the God of the dead but of the living. And when the multitude heard this, they were astonished at his doctrine. But when the Pharisees had heard that he had put the Sadducees to silence, they were gathered together.

Remember, the Sadducees were the religious leaders who did not believe in the resurrection nor any of the miracles of God. They were simply trying to entangle Him in His words. But Jesus took that occasion to give us a great truth, by telling them that in the resurrection we do not marry, nor are we given in marriage, but we are like the angels of God in heaven. And then Jesus spoke of the continuity of God, proving the resurrection again. He said, I am the God of Abraham and the God of Isaac and the God of Jacob. And He could have said, I am the God of the children of Israel. I am the God of the disciples who first followed Christ. I am the God of you today, and tomorrow He will be saying, I am God. In eternity He will be saying, I am God. I am the God of the resurrection. No wonder the resurrection is the cornerstone of the Christian faith, because it means our God is from everlasting to everlasting.

Matthew 22:35-40

> Then one of them, which was a lawyer, asked him a question, tempting him, and saying, Master, which is the great commandment in the law? Jesus said unto him, Thou shalt love the Lord thy God with all thy heart and with all thy soul, and with all thy mind. This is the first and great commandment. And the second is like unto it, Thou shalt love thy neighbour as thyself. On these two commandments hang all the law and the prophets.

As you know, there were ten commandments, but Jesus reduced these down to two. First, thou shalt love the Lord thy God with all thy heart and soul and mind. And then secondly, you shall love your neighbor as you love yourself. And He said all the other things of the Bible hang on these two commandments. And notice that the very heart is love. Love God. And then love yourself. And after that, love your neighbor as you love yourself. Personally, I think there has been a lot of damage done by so-called overly religious people who say, God first, others second, and I am last. That simply is not scriptural. You cannot elevate someone by knocking yourself. You cannot love others by hating yourself. First, you love God with your total being. And after you love God with all your heart, then you love yourself. If you love God the most, you can never love yourself too much. That is, you cannot believe in yourself too much. But again, in order to harmonize your love for God and yourself, you love those whom God has created. You love your neighbor, the one who is in need, just like you love yourself.

Matthew 22:41-23:28

> While the Pharisees were gathered together, Jesus asked them, saying, What think ye of Christ? whose son is he? They say unto him, The son of David. He saith unto them, How then doth David in spirit call him Lord, saying, The Lord said unto my Lord, Sit thou on my right hand, till I make thine enemies thy footstool? If David then call him Lord, how is he his son? And no man was able to answer him a word, neither durst any man from that day forth ask him any more questions.

Then spake Jesus to the multitude, and to his disciples, saying, The scribes and the Pharisees sit in Moses' seat; all therefore whatsoever they bid you observe, that observe and do; but do not ye after their works; for they say, and do not. For they bind heavy burdens and grievous to be borne, and lay them on men's shoulders; but they themselves will not move them with one of their fingers. But all their works they do for to be seen of men; they make broad their phylacteries and enlarge the borders of their garments, and love the uppermost rooms at feasts, and the chief seats in the synagogues, and greetings in the markets, and to be called of men, Rabbi, Rabbi. But be not ye called Rabbi: for one is your Master, even Christ; and all ye are brethren. And call no man your father upon the earth: for one is your Father, which is in heaven. Neither be ye called masters: for one is your Master, even Christ. But he that is greatest among you shall be your servant. And whosoever shall exalt himself shall be abased; and he that shall humble himself shall be exalted. But woe unto you, scribes and Pharisees, hypocrites! for ye shut up the kingdom of heaven against men; for ye neither go in yourselves, neither suffer ye them that are entering to go in. Woe unto you, scribes and Pharisees, hypocrites! for ye devour widows' houses, and for a pretence make long prayer: therefore ye shall receive the greater damnation. Woe unto you, scribes and Pharisees, hypocrites! for ye compass sea and land to make one proselyte, and when he is made, ye make him twofold more the child of hell than yourselves. Woe unto you, ye blind guides, which say, Whosoever shall swear by the temple, it is nothing; but whosoever shall swear by the gold of the temple, he is a debtor! Ye fools and blind: for whether is greater, the gold, or the temple that sanctifieth the gold? And, whosoever shall swear by the altar, it is nothing, but Whosoever sweareth by the gift that is upon it, he is guilty. Ye fools and blind; for whether is greater, the gift, or the altar that sanctifieth the gift? Whoso therefore shall swear by the altar sweareth by it, and by all things thereon. And whoso shall swear by the temple sweareth by it, and by him that dwelleth therein. And he that shall swear by heaven, sweareth by the throne of God, and by him that sitteth thereon. Woe unto you, scribes and Pharisees, Hypocrites! for ye pay tithe of mint and anise and cummin, and have omitted the weightier matters of the law, judgment, mercy, and faith: these ought ye to have done and not to leave the other undone. Ye blind guides, which strain at a gnat, and swallow a camel. Woe unto you, scribes and Pharisees, hypocrites! for ye make clean the outside of the cup and of the platter, but within they are full of extortion and excess. Thou blind Pharisee, cleanse first that which is within the cup and platter, that the outside of them may be clean also. Woe unto you, scribes and Pharisees, hypocrites! for ye are like unto whited sepulchres, which indeed appear beautiful outward, but are within full of dead men's bones, and of all uncleanness. even so ye also outwardly appear righteous unto men, but within ye are full of hypocrisy and iniquity.

Therefore, why should I serve God? The hypocrites do even worse by becoming stumbling blocks to those hungry hearts out there in the world. Jesus seems to be cruel here, but I tell you He is kind. Because He is standing up for the purity of God's righteousness, and for the beauty of holiness in our lives. There is one thing I want to discuss with you and that is, in Verse 23, "woe unto you scribes and Pharisees, hypocrites! for ye pay tithe." And then He tells how that they pay tithes of even the smallest herbs in their gardens. He said, you pay tithe. These people had missed the very meaning of what God was saying in Malachi 3:10 and 11. God said, "Bring ye all the tithes and offerings into the storehouse and prove me now herewith, saith the Lord of hosts, if I will not open you the windows of heaven and pour you out a blessing, where there is not room enough to receive it. And I will rebuke the devourer for your sake . . . " Now, the principal of tithing was given before the law of Moses. It goes all the way back to Abraham, who gave tithes of all and God blessed him in all things. His son, Isaac, gave tithes of everything. And later his grandson, Jacob, gave tithes of all. And he taught it to his 12 sons who became the forefathers of the twelve tribes of Israel. So tithes go far beyond the law of Moses, though it was included in the law of Moses. But it was given as the first fruits. That was largely an agricultural land in those days. And God taught them that the tithe or the first tenth was holy, and it was the Lord's. Now, that made it different. God wanted the first fruits first, to teach them His ownership: second, for them to recognize his Lordship, and third, that there might be resources in His house which He could use for the kingdom of God upon the earth. He told them to give the first fruits, that is right off the top. He never told them to pay it. He told them to give it, to bring it in. And then He said it carried the greatest of rewards. He would actually open the windows of heaven. He is a God of abundant miracles. And then He added, "And I will rebuke the devourer for your sake." Now, when the people of Israel were at their height, they were all glad and happy tithers. They joyously gave to God. They would bring in their first fruits, waving them and saying, These are the Lord's. These are holy unto him. And now God is going to open the windows of heaven to us, and not only bless us in the natural, but supernaturally. And He is going to rebuke the devourer for our sake. It was a glorious thing, but later, the children of Israel drifted away from God, and the last bad thing they did was to stop giving Him their tithes and offerings. When they did, they cut themselves off. Heaven was closed, and God no longer rebuked the devourer for their sake. And it was not hard for Nebuchadnezzar to bring his mighty anti-God armies against Jerusalem and destroy it and lead them away captive into Babylon, where for 70 years they were captives. It was not hard for the oppressors and the devourer to come against them. And God ended the Old Testament, the book of Malachi, by urging them, Bring ye all the tithes and offerings into the storehouse and test Me. Test Me now, herewith. You do not have to wait till tomorrow or next year, but now.

Herewith, I will open the windows of heaven, and all the miracles of my kingdom I will pour upon you, and I will again rebuke the devourer for your sake. Four hundred years passed from Malachi's ending until we begin to read in Matthew of the birth of Jesus Christ. By that time, the Pharisees had risen up in their zeal to recapture the Glory of God, to restore the giving of tithes and offerings. But by now, they have gone away from God themselves. They have an outward pretense of religion. And now they are not giving tithes and offerings with a glad heart, and expecting miracles and trusting God to rebuke the devourer for their sake. They have descended to "paying" tithes. Now Jesus answered them and said, "You are not really giving out of joy. Your faith is not involved. Your giving of tithes is not an act of your joy and your faith, or of you acknowledging God as your King, as your Lord, as your Master. You are not treating the tithe as a holy thing. You are doing it that others may praise you. Therefore, you are not having miracles. I am not able to rebuke the devourer for your sake."

Friend, when Jesus gets after us, it is not just to make us feel bad. He is to remind us of the glory of God. The joy of salvation. The beauty of holiness, and the power of miracles. Truly, when you earn 10 dollars, the first dollar is God's. It is holy. And besides that, an offering of the nine dollars left is God's also. Therefore, when you bring your tithe and your offering right off the top and you give it to God, do it as an act of joy, and an act of your faith, and know that you know that you know from that moment God is going to open the windows of heaven to you, actually sending miracles upon you, and He will rebuke the devourer for your sake.

Matthew 23:29-39

Woe unto you, scribes and Pharisees, hypocrites! Because ye build the tombs of the prophets and garnish the sepulchres of the righteous, and say, If we had been in the days of our fathers, we would not have been partakers with them in the blood of the prophets. Wherefore ye be witnesses unto yourselves, that ye are the children of them which

> killed the prophets. Fill ye up then the measure of your fathers. Ye serpents, ye generation of vipers! how can ye escape the damnation of hell? Wherefore behold I send unto you prophets and wise men and scribes: and some of them ye shall kill and crucify; and some of them shall ye scourge in your synagogues and persecute them from city to city: that upon you may come all the righteous blood shed upon the earth, from the blood of righteous Abel unto the blood of Zacharias, son of Barachias, whom ye slew between the temple and the altar. Verily I say unto you, All these things shall come upon this generation. O Jerusalem, Jerusalem, thou that killest the prophets and stonest them which are sent unto thee, how often would I have gathered thy children together, even as a hen gathereth her chickens under her wings, and ye would not!
>
> Behold, your house is left unto you desolate. For I say unto you, Ye shall not see me henceforth till ye shall say, Blessed is he that cometh in the name of the Lord.

In Verse 37, we have our Lord with a broken heart. Although He apparently never stayed a single night in Jerusalem during His ministry, He was there quite often in the temple and in other places preaching, teaching, and healing. He was there as the Son of God and Son of Man, as the Messiah, as the Christ. He was offering them life. Life more abundantly. And they had totally rejected Him. And He cried, "Oh Jerusalem, Jerusalem, you have killed the prophets, you have stoned those that God sent to you. And now I have come and I have wanted to gather you to Me as a hen gathereth her chickens under her wings, but you would not listen. You wouldn't come. Therefore, I see your household will be left desolate. And you shall not see Me again until you say, Blessed is he that cometh in the name of the Lord." Time is winding down. Our Lord's earthly life is coming to an end and soon He will be hanging on the cross.

Matthew 24:1-14

> And Jesus went out and departed from the temple; and his disciples came to him for to shew him the buildings of the temple. And Jesus said unto them, See ye not all these things? verily I say unto you, There shall not be left here one stone upon another, that shall not be thrown down. And as he sat upon the mount of Olives, the disciples came unto him privately, saying, Tell us, when shall these things be? and what shall be the sign of thy coming, and of the end of the world? And Jesus answered and said unto them, Take heed that no man deceive you. For many shall come in my name, saying, I am Christ; and shall deceive many. And ye shall hear of wars and rumours of wars: see that ye be not troubled: for all these things must come to

> pass, but the end is not yet. For nation shall rise against nation, and kingdom against kingdom: and there shall be famines, and pestilences, and earthquakes in divers places. All these are the beginning of sorrows. Then shall they deliver you up to be afflicted, and shall kill you: and ye shall be hated of all nations for my name's sake. And then shall many be offended, and shall betray one another, and shall hate one another. And many false prophets shall rise, and shall deceive many. And because iniquity shall abound, the love of many shall wax cold. But he that shall endure unto the end, the same shall be saved. And this gospel of the kingdom shall be preached in all the world for a witness unto all nations; and then shall the end come.

You see, He speaks of wars, rumors of wars, earthquakes, famines, pestilences, and all kinds of things that have been going on in the world. We're not to be overly disturbed with these cataclysmic occasions.

We are to be concerned about something much more important: The preaching of the gospel of the kingdom of God. And the preaching and teaching of it for a witness unto all the nations. And then shall the end come. That is the key issue, friend. What we do in our preaching, teaching, and healing. Do we get the gospel out to the billions on this planet? Do the nations of the earth hear the Word of God? Do they have the opportunity to hear the people of God declare the wonderful works of the Lord and to give them the good news of the gospel? Now, when that is done, then shall the end come.

Matthew 24:15-22

> When ye therefore shall see the abomination of desolation, spoken of by Daniel the prophet, stand in the holy place, (whoso readeth, let him understand:) Then let them which be in Judaea flee into the mountains: let him which is on the housetop not come down to take any thing out of his house: neither let him which is in the field return back to take his clothes. And woe unto them that are with child, and to them that give suck in those days! but pray ye that your flight be not in the winter, neither on the sabbath day: for then shall be great tribulation, such as was not since the beginning of the world to this time, no, nor ever shall be. And except those days should be shortened, there should no flesh be saved: but for the elect's sake those days shall be shortened.

When Jesus mentioned the abomination of desolation here, His hearers understood well what He was saying because they knew that something like 200 years before, Antiochus Epiphanes had come into Jerusalem and destroyed hundreds of thousands of the chosen people and had taken a sow and sacrificed it on the altar in the temple of God itself. And that was an abomination of the temple and of God's great work. But Jesus is speaking of something far greater than that. He is saying that according to Daniel the prophet there is going to come somebody who will stand in the temple, in the holy place, and declare himself God. Now, He says when this happens it is going to be the beginning of the tribulation, the most dreaded time in history (in one place in the Bible called Jacob's trouble). And He says you better run for your lives, because unless those days are shortened, no one will be saved. He is referring to Antichrist's coming, the false prophets' arrival, Satan taking over the world — this unholy trinity mimicking the Father, the Son, and the Holy Ghost, and forming the government of the Antichrist, the last world dictatorship. And out of it this person will abominate the temple of God (which will be the abomination of desolation and will be the thing that sets off the wrath of God that will come in the battle of Armageddon).

Matthew 24:23-31

> Then if any man shall say unto you, Lo, here is Christ, or there; believe it not. For there shall arise false Christs, and false prophets, and shall shew great signs and wonders; insomuch that, if it were possible, they shall deceive the very elect. Behold, I have told you before. Wherefore if they shall say unto you, Behold, he is in the desert; go not forth: behold, he is in the secret chambers; believe it not. For as the lightning cometh out of the east, and shineth even unto the west; so shall also the coming of the Son of man be. For wheresoever the carcase is, there will the eagles be gathered together. Immediately after the tribulation of those days shall the sun be darkened, and the moon shall not give her light, and the stars shall fall from heaven and the powers of the heavens shall be shaken: and then shall appear the sign of the Son of man in heaven: and then shall all the tribes of the earth mourn, and they shall see the Son of man coming in the clouds of heaven with power and great glory. And he shall send his angels with a great sound of a trumpet, and they shall gather together his elect from the four winds, from one end of heaven to the other.

In the second coming of Jesus Christ, we believe the Bible teaches that He is first coming for His people and then afterward, He is coming back with those people. One is called the rapture, the other the revelation. When the Antichrist rises he will come in such a way that he will deceive the people and the nations. And later, he will change his nature and reveal himself as the true Antichrist. His wrath then will be turned against people. He will give them his number on their forehead or their right hand: the number 666. And those who take it will be damned. Those who do not take it will be destroyed by the devil. And so, the Lord is not going to let His people go through that tribulation period. When we come to I and II Thessalonians we will be talking about the rapture of the saints — the living and the raising of the dead in Christ — and then of the Lord coming back with His saints to this earth in the battle of Armageddon, revealing himself to all the world so that every eye shall see Him, every knee shall bow, and every tongue shall proclaim Him to be the Son of God. This is going to be an interesting study, my friend. The Bible holds the answer to everything in our future.

Matthew 24:32-35

> Now learn a parable of the fig tree; When his branch is yet tender, and putteth forth leaves, ye know that summer is nigh: so likewise ye, when ye shall see all these things, know that it is near, even at the doors. Verily I say unto you, This generation shall not pass, till all these things be fulfilled. Heaven and earth shall pass away, but my words shall not pass away.

Jesus said that this generation shall not pass until these things are fulfilled. He said that during His lifetime but He was speaking of the generation of man.

Matthew 24:36

> But of that day and hour knoweth no man, no, not the angels of heaven, but my Father only.

Christ's Return Unpredictable

This is a key statement of our Lord Jesus Christ. First, He says that no man knows the day and hour of His coming: second, the angels do not know: and third, only the Father knows and He has not said yet.

From time to time we notice people rising up and setting a date for our Lord's coming. Sometimes they will lead their followers out to a mountaintop or some other place, having sold all their property and goods to wait for the day that they have said He is coming.

Each time they have proved to be liars of the truth of God, because nobody knows, not even the angels, but our Father only. It is a matter of trust, of faith, of keeping our eyes on God and so living that we are ready for any hour or day when the Father decides to send His

Son back.

Matthew 24:37-39

> But as the days of Noah were, so shall also the coming of the Son of man be. For as in the days that were before the flood they were eating and drinking, marrying and giving in marriage, until the day that Noah entered into the ark, and knew not until the flood came, and took them all away; so shall also the coming of the Son of man be.

Live Prepared

Sin in Noah's day came to a climax before the flood. Before the second coming of Christ, sin must reach its final climax. Sin will be sin to its fullest, and man will have gone to his extremity away from God. There will be a great falling away, even among some of those of the elect; but the rest of the world will be carrying on business as usual. In other words, we are not to look for some extraordinary event, some world-shaking affair, so we can run around saying, "Look at that! That means the Lord is coming."

No, the coming of the Lord is going to catch unprepared people unaware. If we are looking for His coming, we will be so living that if He comes at any moment, day or night, we will be prepared. If we live like that, then we need not be disturbed by any world event.

Matthew 24:40-51

> Then shall two be in the field; the one shall be taken, and the other left. Two women shall be grinding at the mill: the one shall be taken, and the other left. Watch therefore; for ye know not what hour your Lord doth come.
>
> But know this, that if the goodman of the house had known in what watch the thief would come, he would have watched, and would not have suffered his house to be broken up. Therefore be ye also ready: for in such an hour as ye think not the Son of man cometh. Who then is a faithful and wise servant, whom his lord hath made ruler over his household, to give them meat in due season? Blessed is that servant, whom his lord when he cometh shall find so doing.
>
> Verily I say unto you, That he shall make him ruler over all his goods. But and if that evil servant shall say in his heart, My lord delayeth his coming; and shall begin to smite his fellowservants, and to eat and drink with the drunken; the lord of that servant shall come in a day when he looketh not for him, and in an hour that he is not aware of, and shall cut him asunder, and appoint him his portion with the hyprocrites: there shall be weeping and gnashing of teeth.

Expect His Coming

Jesus made it very clear that we can know the times and the seasons in which He will come, but not the hour or the day. There will be women who will be doing certain types of work together and men doing certain types of work together. And there will be men and women working together. One will be taken up in the rapture, the translation of the living saints of God. The other will be left to face the tribulation. One will be gone in a moment of time, and the other will stand there wondering where the other person went because the one left behind was not ready. Those who were ready were living as if He were coming the next moment, but working as if He would delay His coming a thousand years. He has called us to watchfulness, faithfulness, continuous serving of the Lord — day and night — expecting miracles, expecting His coming. But at the same time we are to be doing our work, living on this earth as human beings, as witnesses of Christ, carrying on the work of God, but being ready at any hour or moment for the coming of our Lord.

Matthew 25:1-13

> Then shall the kingdom of heaven be likened unto ten virgins, which took their lamps, and went forth to meet the bridegroom. And five of them were wise, and five were foolish. They that were foolish took their lamps, and took no oil with them; but the wise took oil in their vessels with their lamps.
>
> While the bridegroom tarried, they all slumbered and slept. And at midnight there was a cry made, Behold, the bridegroom cometh; go ye out to meet him. Then all those virgins arose and trimmed their lamps. And the foolish said unto the wise, give us of your oil; for our lamps are gone out. But the wise answered, saying, Not so; lest there be not enough for us and you; but go ye rather to them that sell, and buy for yourselves.
>
> And while they went to buy, the bridegroom came; and they that were ready went in with him to the marriage; and the door was shut. Afterward came also the other virgins, saying, Lord, Lord, open to us. But he answered and said, Verily I say unto you, I know you not. Watch therefore, for ye know neither the day nor the hour wherein the Son of man cometh.

Our Dual Citizenship

Jesus was making reference here to His coming to a wedding feast in Israel. The wedding feast took place before the wedding itself. It was a series of events, of parties and feasting; however, it could be interrupted at any time by the bridegroom, who would decide when the marriage would take place. For example, they may have had 10 days of partying without knowing when the bridegroom would come — early morning, noon, evening, midnight — no one knew when he would come. So he came at midnight, and five of the virgins had remained prepared along with the bride for such a moment. The other five were not ready for his arrival. They may have been carried away with the party. They went out to buy oil so they could follow the bride to the marriage, but it was too late. The bridegroom arrived while they were gone to buy oil.

Jesus is putting an urgency in the hearts of us who believe that not only are we to be children of God, but we are also to be alert, sensitive to the times around us, aware of what the Bible teaches, very conscious of the Holy Spirit's presence in our lives, ready at any moment should the Lord appear to catch us away for the wedding, that wedding of the bride of Christ to the Bridegroom himself.

He is telling us that the most important thing in our lives is to be ready. For example, if you and I knew that Jesus was coming in 10 days, but did not know the exact moment on that 10th day, we would be so spiritual, so involved in God's work, so careful in our prayer life and Bible study, looking unto Him, keeping our eyes on Him. He is saying we do not know exactly what that hour is, so we should be that way all the time.

Someone once said to me, "I could not even do my job or my work if I were to be working that way with my spirit in preparation of His coming." Oh, but Jesus says we can. We can live in this life and also be ready for the Lord's coming. We have our citizenship both here and in heaven. We sit together with Christ in heavenly places. We have the authority of a believer. What we must do is think these things over and then make the decision to put God first in our lives and follow Him, whatever we do, so that whatever we do and wherever we are in doing it, we look upon that as where God has placed us, and that is our witnessing field. It is like a flower that blooms where it is planted.

Matthew 25:14-30

> For the kingdom of heaven is as a man travelling into a far country, who called his own servants, and delivered unto them his goods. And unto one he gave five talents, to another two, and to another one; to every man according to his several ability; and straightway took his journey.
>
> Then he that had received the five talents went and traded with

the same, and made them other five talents. And likewise he that had received two, he also gained other two. But he that had received one went and digged in the earth, and hid his lord's money. After a long time the lord of those servants cometh, and reckoneth with them. And so he that had received five talents came and brought other five talents, saying, Lord, thou deliveredst unto me five talents: behold, I have gained beside them five talents more. His lord said unto him, Well done, thou good and faithful servant: thou hast been faithful over a few things, I will make thee ruler over many things: enter thou into the joy of thy lord.

He also that had received two talents came and said, Lord, thou deliveredst unto me two talents: behold, I have gained two other talents beside them. His lord said unto him, Well done, good and faithful servant; thou hast been faithful over a few things, I will make thee ruler over many things: enter thou into the joy of thy lord.

Then he which had received the one talent came and said, Lord, I knew thee that thou art an hard man, reaping where thou hast not sown, and gathering where thou hast not strawed: and I was afraid, and went and hid thy talent in the earth; lo, there thou hast that is thine. His lord answered and said unto him, Thou wicked and slothful servant, thou knewest that I reap where I sowed not, and gather where I have not strawed. Thou oughtest therefore to have put my money to the exchangers, and then at my coming I should have received mine own with usury. Take therefore the talent from him and give it unto him which hath ten talents. For unto every one that hath shall be given, and he shall have abundance: but from him that hath not shall be taken away even that which he hath. And cast ye the unprofitable servant into outer darkness: there shall be weeping and gnashing of teeth.

Jesus is still talking about His second coming. He illustrates it by saying there was a man who gave one of his servants five talents, another two, another one. The man with the five talents invested his and gained five more. The man with the two doubled his. But the man with the one talent would not risk. He hid his.

When the man returned he said, "Now look, I am not going to put up with this. I gave you these so you'd invest them and be rewarded. But you hid yours. You would not risk; you were not vulnerable; you just let it go by as though it were nothing."

As we consider these things in our time, we must remind ourselves that God does give people different numbers and types of talents. But that does not mean He loves one more than the other. That's according to His plan, that we can work together whether we have five talents, two talents, or one. The point is that we use what God has given us. He made a radical move. He took the one talent that was unused and gave it to the man with the five who had doubled his to 10, and this made 11 gifts or talents for him.

That is the way of God. All of life is like that. Use your arm, it becomes stronger. Use any muscle, it becomes greater. Do anything with yourself and you find yourself advancing. But just to lie down and quit means that God's law of multiplication and reward is not going to work in your life. So, in effect, Jesus is saying that there are rewards for God's people as we work our work, as we do our thing for God. God will bless us. This is the position we should be in at all times, because the Lord's coming will be at a time we do not know. So, we are busy laboring, working, investing, giving our best, and then expecting God's best.

Matthew 25:31-46

When the Son of man shall come in his glory, and all the holy angels with him, then shall he sit upon the throne of his glory. And before him shall be gathered all nations: and he shall separate them one from another, as a shepherd divideth his sheep from the goats. And he shall set the sheep on his right hand, but the goats on the left. Then shall the King say unto them on his right hand, Come, ye blessed of my Father, inherit the kingdom prepared for you from the foundation of the world; for I was an hungred, and ye gave me meat: I was thirsty, and ye gave me drink: I was a stranger, and ye took me in: naked, and ye clothed me: I was sick, and ye visited me: I was in prison, and ye came unto me.

Then shall the righteous answer him, saying, Lord, when saw we thee an hungred, and fed thee? or thirsty, and gave thee drink? When saw we thee a stranger, and took thee in? or naked, and clothed thee? Or when saw we thee sick, or in prison, and came unto thee?

And the king shall answer and say unto them, Verily I say unto you, Inasmuch as ye have done it unto one of the least of these my brethren, ye have done it unto me.

Then shall he say also unto them on the left hand, Depart from me, ye cursed, into everlasting fire, prepared for the devil and his angels: For I was an hungred, and ye gave me no meat: I was thirsty, and ye gave me no drink: I was a stranger, and ye took me not in: naked, and ye clothed me not; sick, and in prison, and ye visited me not.

Then shall they also answer him, saying, Lord, when saw we thee an hungred, or athirst, or a stranger, or naked, or sick, or in prison, and did not minister unto thee?

Then shall he answer them, saying, Verily I say unto you, Inasmuch as ye did it not to one of the least of these, ye did it not to me. And these shall go away into everlasting punishment: but the righteous into life eternal.

I want you to picture our Lord Jesus Christ coming in His glory. This is probably in reference to the battle of Armageddon when He is revealed to the whole world. At that time everyone shall look up and see Him coming. When He arrives it will be in Jerusalem. There in the city of God, the great King will gather before Him all the nations, and then He will separate them. Those who have followed God will be described as sheep and those who have not as goats. The sheep are set on the right hand and they are reminded of how they had works following their faith. Their hearts had the same compassion which Jesus had had for the needs and sufferings of people. He reminds them that they had cared for the unfortunate, the lost and the suffering. They had been so involved in obeying Jesus and carrying out His command through love and compassion, that they really were not aware of the greatness of their deeds or that Christ had even seen them. They wanted to know when they had done these things. He pointed them back to their lifetime of Christian service and told them now that they would be rewarded. Since they had done it unto the very least of human beings, they had done it unto Him, their Master. Then He told the goats that they were to be separated and would be put into hell prepared for the devil and his angels. Since they had insisted on living the life of the devil, they were to spend eternity with the devil and his demons. That is a great point. God never sends anybody to hell. Hell was not prepared for human beings, but for the devil and his angels. Therefore, anyone who goes to hell does so through his own deliberate choice. He deliberately, consciously, knowingly decides not to serve God, but to serve the devil, to follow the devil in his ways.

This is a passage in Matthew's gospel that we should study often, and put our lives up beside it, to examine our hearts, to see if we really care.

The end of Chapter 25 of Matthew's gospel is the end of Christ's public ministry and the beginning of the period of His sufferings.

Matthew 26:1-5

And it came to pass, when Jesus had finished all these sayings, he said unto his disciples, Ye know that after two days is the feast of the passover, and the Son of man is betrayed to be crucified.

Then assembled together the chief priests, and the scribes, and the elders of the people, unto the palace of the high priest, who was called Caiaphas, and consulted that they might take Jesus by subtilty and kill him. But they said, Not on the feast day, lest there be an uproar among the people.

God's Timetable

Jesus has now ended His public ministry and begins the period of His sufferings. He tells His disciples that it is only a couple of days until the Passover, and then the Son of Man will be betrayed and killed. Until the Romans became the overlords of Israel (which was about 100 years of intense rule over Palestine), the high priest was high priest for life. But when the Romans took charge, they upset that and decided a person could be high priest only as long as he did not agitate, but maintained peace so the Romans could rule in relative peace and quiet. Therefore, there were 28 high priests during this intense 100-year period of Roman rule. That turnover was evidence of their agitation against the Romans, revealing their desire to throw off the yoke. At this time they had a man named Caiaphas who really knew how to get along with the Romans. He advised those conspiring against Jesus not to kill Him during the Passover because that would create an uproar and he might lose his position as high priest.

However, Jesus knew He was to be killed during the Passover, and although Caiaphas and the chief priest had advised against it, they could not turn back the tide of prophecy. They were really trying to make God operate on man's timetable. But neither they nor anyone else has succeeded in doing that. Nor will they ever succeed. God's timetable is perfect.

Today many people try to operate on their own timetable by saying, "Well, when I decide, I will get around to serving God or to thinking about God." And they think that their timetable is the one that is accurate. But the scripture says you can only come to God when the Holy Spirit draws you. God has His own timetable for you and for me. There was a moment in my life at age 17. When that moment came, that was Oral Roberts' moment.

Someone says, "What if you had not obeyed God at that time?" I do not know what would have happened. I do not want to even think about it. The fact is that I did begin my obedience, and I obey Him now to the best of my knowledge.

The secret of deliverance with God is in instant obedience and continuous obedience.

Matthew 26:6-13

> Now when Jesus was in Bethany, in the house of Simon the leper, there came unto him a woman having an alabaster box of very precious ointment, and poured it on his head, as he sat at meat. But when his disciples saw it, they had indignation, saying, To what purpose is this waste? For this ointment might have been sold for much, and given

to the poor.

When Jesus understood it, he said unto them, Why trouble ye the woman? for she hath wrought a good work upon me. For ye have the poor always with you; but me ye have not always. For in that she hath poured this ointment on my body, she did it for my burial. Verily I say unto you, Wheresoever this gospel shall be preached in the whole world, there shall also this, that this woman hath done, be told for a memorial of her.

Give Best to God

We have an abrupt change. Whereas Caiaphas was trying to manipulate God's timetable, here was a woman who discerned in her spirit that God's time had come, that His Son was going to die. This woman came with very precious perfume and emptied it upon Jesus' head. Everybody smelled it and knew it was expensive. They said, "What a waste this is," and rebuked Jesus for it.

But Jesus said, "Don't you bother this woman, because she's wrought a great work upon Me. She has given the very best that she has, and it is a work of discernment. What she has done will be spoken of as a memorial of her throughout all generations." Here we are today fulfilling Jesus' word. We are speaking of this as a memorial to this woman. As we live close to God, and we put our highest value upon Him, some way, somehow, we are going to have a knowing about Him through which we will be led and prompted to do certain things for His glory. Never regret when you give your best to God.

Matthew 26:14-16

Then one of the twelve, called Judas Iscariot, went unto the chief priests and said unto them, What will ye give me, and I will deliver him unto you? And they covenanted with him for thirty pieces of silver. And from that time he sought opportunity to betray him.

"Son of Perdition"

It is very difficult to describe Judas Iscariot. We are told that he was the only one of the 12 apostles who did not come from Galilee. He was a man from the Judean area. He was a man outside the circle of the familiar Galilean group. This may explain why he was so aloof from them and somehow felt superior. Did Jesus know that Judas would ultimately betray him? In the later gospels we will understand that He did. Judas was the son of perdition. Yet we must remember he had the power of choice. Though there was to be a betrayer who would be called the son of perdition, it did not necessarily have to be this particular man. But, because of his choice, it turned out that Judas Iscariot became the betrayer.

As you may recall, Jesus had made him the treasurer of the group and he carried the money, and presumably paid the bills. But as we will learn in one of the other gospels, he was at heart a thief. Some think that Judas Iscariot carried the vision of the Herodians — that group of people who followed King Herod, who was looking for the restoration of the political kingdom of the people of Israel. Whatever it was, he was moved with a covetous heart, and he made a deal with the chief priests for 30 pieces of silver to deliver Jesus into their hands.

It is interesting that one of the 12 apostles turned against Jesus Christ and betrayed Him. It is true that at His crucifixion all the disciples deserted Him and fled, but they repented and came back. Judas Iscariot did not. Now, if you take this as one in 12 you might apply that to any group of 12 believers, where one will turn out wrong. In other words, there is always somebody going wrong, and it is virtually impossible to weed those people out until the time comes when they, by their own choice, enter into the betrayal that removes them.

Matthew 26:17-19

> Now the first day of the feast of unleavened bread the disciples came to Jesus, saying unto him, Where wilt thou that we prepare for thee to eat the passover? And he said, Go into the city to such a man and say unto him, The Master saith, My time is at hand; I will keep the passover at thy house with my disciples. And the disciples did as Jesus had appointed them; and they made ready the passover.

The Glory of Giving

There are always those remarkably humble, obedient people who, when Jesus calls upon them or impresses their heart to do something for Him, are always ready and obedient. We are not told who this man was who had the large house. But when Jesus sent His disciples to tell him of what Jesus had said, the man consented. Oh, the glory and the joy of being a giver, of sharing our best with the Lord Jesus Christ.

Matthew 26:20-30

> Now when the even was come, he sat down with the twelve. And as they did eat, he said, Verily I say unto you, that one of you shall

betray me. And they were exceeding sorrowful, and began every one of them to say unto him, Lord, is it I? And he answered and said, He that dippeth his hand with me in the dish, the same shall betray me.

The Son of man goeth as it is written of him: but woe unto that man by whom the Son of man is betrayed! it had been good for that man if he had not been born. Then Judas, which betrayed him, answered and said, Master, is it I? He said unto him, Thou hast said.

And as they were eating, Jesus took bread, and blessed it, and brake it, and gave it to the disciples, and said, Take, eat; this is my body. And he took the cup, and gave thanks, and gave it to them, saying, Drink ye all of it; for this is my blood of the new testament, which is shed for many for the remission of sins.

But I say unto you, I will not drink henceforth of this fruit of the vine, until that day when I drink it new with you in my Father's kingdom. And when they had sung an hymn, they went out into the mount of Olives.

Jesus in Control

No man except Jesus ever so completely controlled all situations. For example, the chief priests had determined that He would not be killed at Passover, but that He would be killed later. On the other side, Judas Iscariot had gone in with them and had made a covenant of blood with them, that for 30 pieces of silver he would betray Jesus Christ into the conspirators' hands. From that moment, he sought opportunity to betray Jesus. Jesus is eating His last meal right in the midst of the Passover. Here is Judas with a secret locked up inside of him. He was being Satan's catalyst. He really kept this secret away from Jesus and the disciples. At least, he thought he kept it away from Jesus. That night, when they were eating, Jesus said, "One of you shall betray me."

The moment He said that, all the 12 were deeply moved and wounded in their hearts and began to say, Is it I? When He got around to Judas, Judas asked, "Is it I?"

Jesus said, "You have said." In other words, he never fooled Jesus for one moment. Neither did the chief priests. Right in that situation, so utterly out of control from man's standpoint, Jesus was in perfect control. He then, right in the midst of the meal, took bread and wine and compared it with His body and His shed blood. In that most incredible situation at His last Passover, Jesus established the very beginning of the Holy Communion in the Christian faith. Jesus was absolutely in charge. He is in charge today. Do not ever doubt it. No matter what man is doing or what plans he is making or secrets he thinks he is keeping, Jesus is Lord. In I Corinthians 11, Paul spends quite some time explaining what Communion is to us today. I do my teaching there on the Communion, and it is "nowness" in our lives.

Matthew 26:31,32

> Then saith Jesus unto them, All ye shall be offended because of me this night: for it is written, I will smite the shepherd, and the sheep of the flock shall be scattered abroad. But after I am risen again, I will go before you into Galilee.

The Word and Faith

Especially where Jesus said, "It is written," I think we must remember that the two chief things Jesus used in His life were, first, the Word of God, and second, His faith in God — both of which are available to you and me today.

How can we say, "It is written," unless we know that it is written? Unless we study the Word of God? Unless we believe it and apply it to our lives! It was very strengthening to the humanity of our Lord Jesus Christ to know the scriptures.

Matthew 26:33-39

> Peter answered and said unto him, Though all men shall be offended because of thee, yet will I never be offended. Jesus said unto him, Verily I say unto thee, That this night, before the cock crow, thou shalt deny me thrice. Peter said unto him, Though I should die with thee, yet will I not deny thee. Likewise also said all the disciples.
>
> Then cometh Jesus with them unto a place called Gethsemane, and saith unto the disciples, Sit ye here, while I go and pray yonder. And he took with him Peter and the two sons of Zebedee, and began to be sorrowful and very heavy.
>
> Then saith he unto them, My soul is exceedingly sorrowful, even unto death: tarry ye here, and watch with me.
>
> And he went a little farther, and fell on his face, and prayed, saying, O my Father, if it be possible, let this cup pass from me: nevertheless not as I will, but as thou wilt.

Complete Control

Please notice that no man was ever in such complete control of a situation. As Jesus approached His death, the control He had during His ministry was climaxed. There was no scene that completely threw Him, not even when he was in Gethsemane, praying alone. Not even when He was on the cross did He lose control.

How wonderful it is to know that, as we know the Word of God, and release our faith to God, we are always in control of the situation. We need not fear being alone, because our faith in God will bring us through.

Matthew 26:40-42

> And he cometh unto the disciples, and findeth them asleep, and saith unto Peter, What, could ye not watch with me one hour? Watch and pray, that ye enter not into temptation: the spirit indeed is willing, but the flesh is weak. He went away again the second time, and prayed, saying, O my Father, if this cup may not pass away from me, except I drink it, thy will be done.

Obedience the Key

Obedience Is the main thing in the word of God. Obedience to God is what makes everything go right. It was disobedience that caused the fall of Lucifer, who became the devil. It was disobedience to God that caused Adam and Eve to fall and plunge the whole future human race into sin and despair, and in need of a Redeemer. But Jesus, as the second Adam, came with perfect obedience, determined to do the will of the heavenly Father, even to the giving of His life. Obedience, that is the key.

Matthew 26:43-56

> And he came and found them asleep again: for their eyes were heavy. And he left them, and went away again, and prayed the third time, saying the same words. Then cometh he to his disciples, and saith unto them, Sleep on now, and take your rest: behold, the hour is at hand, and the Son of man is betrayed into the hands of sinners. Rise, let us be going: behold, he is at hand that doth betray me.
>
> And while he yet spake, lo, Judas, one of the twelve, came, and with him a great multitude with swords and staves, from the chief priests and elders of the people.
>
> Now he that betrayed him gave them a sign, saying, Whomsoever I shall kiss, that same is he: hold him fast. And forthwith he came to Jesus, and said, Hail, master, and kissed him. And Jesus said unto him, Friend, wherefore art thou come? Then came they, and laid hands on Jesus, and took him.
>
> And behold, one of them which were with Jesus stretched out his hand, and drew his sword, and struck a servant of the high priest's,

and smote off his ear.
Then said Jesus unto him, Put up again thy sword into his place: for all they that take the sword shall perish with the sword. Thinkest thou that I cannot now pray to my Father, and he shall presently give me more than twelve legions of angels? But how then shall the scriptures be fulfilled, that thus it must be? In that same hour said Jesus to the multitudes, Are ye come out as against a thief with swords and staves for to take me? I sat daily with you teaching in the temple, and ye laid no hold on me. But all this was done, that the scriptures of the prophets might be fulfilled. Then all the disciples forsook him, and fled.

It is so striking to me that throughout Matthew's gospel, Jesus is revealed as the man of healing. He came to heal soul, mind, and body. He came to heal man's wrong situations. He came to heal man's Desperate ailments. He came to heal. My prayer is so often a prayer that we in the Church will come to know our Lord again, so that we can be moved with the compassion that He was moved with, and we will not act violently toward other people or be resentful of their behavior, but have a healing heart, and a healing hand.

Another important thing is Jesus' statement that He did not need anyone to defend Him with a sword or by violence. He could call thousands of angels down from heaven to defend Him, but He did not choose to do that because He had a purpose for His life. He came to give His life as a ransom for many, and for the forgiveness of our sins. Then it is added, all the disciples forsook Him and fled. I think there is no more desolate moment in the Lord's life than that His very own, who had been with Him day and night for those 3 years, and knew Him better than they knew anyone else, and loved Him so much, became afraid — afraid for themselves. They deserted Him, and ran away. We cannot deal too harshly with them, for have there not been times in our lives when we did not stand up? It need not be, because Jesus has given us power to stand against the enemy.

Matthew 26:57-75

And they that had laid hold on Jesus led him away to Caiaphas the high priest, where the scribes and the elders were assembled. But Peter followed him afar off unto the high priest's palace, and went in, and sat with the servants, to see the end. Now the chief priests, and elders, and all the council, sought false witness against Jesus, to put him to death; but found none: yea, though many false witnesses came, yet found they none. At the last came two false witnesses, and said, This fellow said, I am able to destroy the temple of God, and to build it in three days.

And the high priest arose, and said unto him, Answerest thou nothing? what is it which these witness against thee? But Jesus held his peace. And the high priest answered and said unto him, I adjure thee by the living God, that thou tell us whether thou be the Christ, the Son of God.

Jesus saith unto him, Thou hast said: nevertheless I say unto you, Hereafter shall ye see the Son of man sitting on the right hand of power, and coming in the clouds of heaven.

Then the high priest rent his clothes, saying, He hath spoken blasphemy; what further need have we of witnesses? behold, now ye have heard his blasphemy. What think ye? They answered and said, He is guilty of death. Then did they spit in his face, and buffeted him; and others smote him with the palms of their hands, saying, Prophesy unto us, thou Christ, Who is he that smote thee?

Now Peter sat without in the palace: and a damsel came unto him, saying, Thou also wast with Jesus of Galilee. But he denied before them all, saying, I know not what thou sayest. And when he was gone out into the porch, another maid saw him, and said unto them that were there, This fellow was also with Jesus of Nazareth. And again he denied with an oath, I do not know the man. And after a while came unto him they that stood by, and said to Peter, Surely thou also art one of them; for thy speech betrayeth thee.

Then began he to curse and to swear, saying, I know not the man. And immediately the cock crew. And Peter remembered the word of Jesus, which said unto him, Before the cock crow, thou shalt deny me thrice. And he went out, and wept bitterly.

Truth Will Prevail

The so-called "trial" of Jesus was a farce because they dealt with words, not with deeds, and they continually misquoted Him. No matter what He had said, when they alleged it, it was not what He had said. For example, in Verse 61 one witness claimed Jesus had said, "I am able to destroy the temple of God and to build it in 3 days." That was not what Jesus had said at all. He had said, "Destroy this temple (speaking of His body), and I will raise it again the third day." They spit on Him; they struck Him with the palms of their hands; they mocked Him; and they based their actions upon words, not upon the man's life or His actions.

Surely, that is a message of God to you and me today, not to judge people merely by words. Sometimes words can be so twisted, misinterpreted. They do not always mean what they sound like.

I think our Lord is trying to remind us to look into our own lives when we hear someone accused. Don't merely listen to the words, but look back of the words into the life, if possible. And in our own selves, be careful how we accuse others. When we are accused, be careful how we react, because God is the truth. It is truth that God is always going to use. In the end truth will prevail.

Matthew 27:1-5

> When the morning was come, all the chief priests and elders of the people took counsel against Jesus to put him to death:
>
> And when they had bound him, they led him away, and delivered him to Pontius Pilate the governor.
>
> Then Judas, which had betrayed him, when he saw that he was condemned, repented himself, and brought again the thirty pieces of silver to the chief priests and elders, saying, I have sinned in that I have betrayed the innocent blood. And they said, What is that to us? see thou to that. And he cast down the pieces of silver in the temple, and departed, and went and hanged himself.

Repent Before God

In light of the fact that the other apostles had denied Jesus Christ and fled but finally repented, receiving Him as Lord and Master, Judas Iscariot, when he turned against Christ by betraying Him, was condemned. And when he saw He was condemned he was sorry that he was caught and he even took back the money, which the chief priests would not receive. He repented all over the place. He repented to himself, he repented to the chief priests and elders, but he never went to God, which is the way true repentance works.

True repentance leads us to God with our wrong actions. We can have a "pity party" and go to different people, but that is not going to accomplish anything of value. Our repentance is to lead us to God. It is an about-face. We turn around from it, so we turn back to God, but Judas did not do that.

What if he had? I have often pictured it like this: When he threw the money down in the temple, he ran to the cross and threw his arms around Jesus' legs and looked up as the blood streamed down from Jesus' body and said, "Jesus, this terrible thing that I did, dear God, forgive me, give me another chance."

I have always believed, and I believe now, had Judas done that, we might have had the "gospel of the second chance" written by Judas Iscariot. But he did not do it. He went out and hung himself. The only thing I know to do with sin is to repent of it toward God, and I know that God will receive a sinner who repents. I feel strangely led to share this with you, that if you have sin in your life, let us pray. If you have something that has gone wrong in your life that needs to be righted. Let us take this moment to pray together. Will you pray with me now?

> *Father, I come to you in the name of Your Son, Jesus Christ of Nazareth. I come on behalf of this, my friend, who needs deliverance. I ask for the tendering of that heart, for the opening up of that spirit to God. I ask that the holy power of repentance will take charge of this one who will say, "Oh God, I am sorry, forgive me, heal me, deliver me." Father, I believe that you hear this prayer and we receive it through Jesus Christ our Lord. Amen and amen.*

Matthew 27:6-10

> And the chief priests took the silver pieces and said, It is not lawful for to put them into the treasury, because it is the price of blood. And they took counsel, and bought with them the potter's field, to bury strangers in. Wherefore that field was called, The field of blood, unto this day. Then was fulfilled that which was spoken by Jeremiah the prophet, saying, And they took the thirty pieces of silver, the price of him that was valued, whom they of the children of Israel did value; and gave them for the potter's field, as the Lord appointed me.

Prophecies Fulfilled

I think we should always bear in mind that Matthew is relating many prophecies that were fulfilled about the Messiah. Matthew's purpose was to reveal Him as the Messiah and to give the scriptures that pointed to His being the Messiah. Although we of the Gentile race can understand what he is saying, his words were addressed primarily to those of the covenant, to those who had once known the heavenly Father, but were unable to recognize their Messiah when He came. They could have recognized Him, had they merely listened, and had they observed, and above all, had they known the scripture.

Matthew 27:11-18

> And Jesus stood before the governor: and the governor asked him, saying, Art thou the King of the Jews? And Jesus said unto him, Thou sayest. And when he was accused of the chief priests and elders, he answered nothing. Then said Pilate unto him, Hearest thou not how many things they witness against thee? And he answered him to never

a word; insomuch that the governor marvelled greatly.

Now at that feast the governor was wont to release unto the people a prisoner, whom they would. And they had then a notable prisoner, called Barabbas.

Therefore when they were gathered together, Pilate said unto them, Whom will ye that I release unto you? Barabbas, or Jesus which is called Christ? For he knew that for envy they had delivered him.

Seeds of Destruction

Envy, jealousy, covetousness — these things really corrupt our lives, blind our vision, rob us of the ability to understand God, to carry out His purpose and to be like Him. And therefore, in the end, they destroyed us.

Matthew 27:19

When he was set down on the judgment seat, his wife sent unto him, saying, Have thou nothing to do with that just man: for I have suffered many things this day in a dream because of him.

Inspired Dreams

Pilate's wife was a woman whom God visited with dreams. She saw in the dream that Jesus was a just man. Now, she was a Roman lady. She knew nothing about the scriptures. She was not a child of the covenant, a descendant of Abraham. She really had not been with Jesus. But God in His infinite wisdom warned her with a dream. God still reveals himself in dreams and visions.

Matthew 27:20-25

But the chief priests and elders persuaded the multitude that they should ask Barabbas, and destroy Jesus. The governor answered and said unto them, Whether of the twain will ye that I release unto you? They said, Barabbas. Pilate saith unto them, What shall I do then with Jesus which is called Christ? They all say unto him, Let him be crucified. And the governor said, Why, what evil hath he done? But they cried out the more, saying, Let him be crucified.

When Pilate saw that he could prevail nothing, but that rather a tumult was made, he took water, and washed his hands before the multitude, saying, I am innocent of the blood of this just person: see ye to it. Then answered all the people, and said, His blood be on us, and on our children.

Portrait of Pilate

Let us take a look at this man Pilate. Pilate was not subject to the senate in Rome, but to the emperor himself. His headquarters was in Caesarea, but when he made his state visits, he went to Jerusalem. There he did everything to pacify the people. However, you can imagine how unhappy the Jews were under Roman rule, and they did everything they could to get out from under it.

They did have one power. If they felt that a Roman governor was really not fair, they could write Caesar himself and complain, which they did 2 or 3 years later after Jesus' death, and had the man removed. Pilate knew they had that authority. Yet, when he had to deal with Jesus, Pilate was moved by his wife's dream and he was also personally impressed with Jesus. He earnestly sought a way of escape for Jesus of Nazareth, and when all hell broke loose, the real nature of the man was revealed. Here he was trying to carry out Caesar's order and also attempting to pacify the Jews. Now this man is placed between Caesar and the Jews.

At this time every year the governor would release someone to the Jews to pacify them. So he gave them a clear choice: Barabbas (a murderer) or Jesus. They, of course, wanted Barabbas released rather than Jesus. Well, that left Pilate with Jesus on his hands, and he said, "Well, what in the world am I going to do with Jesus?" The man came right up to the moment of truth: Was he going to do what he believed to be right or was he going to let his fear of the Jews override the truth of Jesus that he felt he was experiencing?

Then he practiced a Jewish custom of washing his hands. This was not something the Romans did, but it dated 'way back in the history of the Jews. When they were not responsible for someone's murder, they would wash their hands. So, standing there in front of this enormous crowd, as they yelled and screamed for the blood of Jesus, Pilate called for a basin of water, dipped his hands in it, and publicly washed his hands and said, "I am innocent of the blood of this just person. You see to that."

Basically, Pilate gave in. Pilate knew that they had delivered Jesus up for the wrong reasons. He knew that He was an innocent man. He knew that He was a just man. He knew he had the power to overrule the Jews, but he made the choice against his own conscience. Now, we are faced with that all the time, and somewhere down the line you and I have to put our foot down against ourselves and say to ourselves, "Self, you're going to stand up for God and the truth, and let the chips fall where they will." God's Word backs up what I'm going to say to you now: You will triumph despite any temporary setbacks or loss or even martyrdom. You will win.

Matthew 27:26-53

Then released he Barabbas unto them: and when he had scourged Jesus, he delivered him to be crucified. Then the soldiers of the governor took Jesus into the common hall, and gathered unto him the whole band of soldiers. And they stripped him, and put on him a scarlet robe. And when they had platted a crown of thorns, they put it upon his head, and a reed in his right hand: and they bowed the knee before him, and mocked him, saying, Hail, King of the Jews!

And they spit upon him, and took the reed, and smote him on the head. And after that they had mocked him, they took the robe off from him, and put his own raiment on him, and led him away to crucify him. And as they came out, they found a man of Cyrene, Simon by name: him they compelled to bear his cross.

And when they were come unto a place called Golgotha, that is to say, a place of a skull, they gave him vinegar to drink mingled with gall: and when he had tasted thereof, he would not drink. And they crucified him, and parted his garments, casting lots: that it might be fulfilled which was spoken by the prophet, They parted my garments among them, and upon my vesture did they cast lots.

And sitting down they watched him there; and set up over his head his accusation written, THIS IS JESUS THE KING OF THE JEWS.

Then were there two thieves crucified with him, one on the right hand, and another on the left. And they that passed by reviled him, wagging their heads, and saying, Thou that destroyest the temple, and buildest it in three days, save thyself. If thou be the Son of God, come down from the cross.

Likewise also the chief priests mocking him, with the scribes and elders, said, He saved others; himself he cannot save. If he be the King of Israel, let him now come down from the cross, and we will believe him. He trusted in God; let him deliver him now, if he will have him: for he said, I am the Son of God. The thieves also, which were crucified with him, cast the same in his teeth.

Now from the sixth hour there was darkness over all the land unto the ninth hour. And about the ninth hour Jesus cried with a loud voice, saying, Eli, Eli, lama sabachthani? that is to say, My God, my God, why hast thou forsaken me?

Some of them that stood there, when they heard that, said, This man calleth for Elias. And straightway one of them ran, and took a sponge, and filled it with vinegar, and put it on a reed, and gave him to drink.

The rest said, Let be, let us see whether Elias will come to save him. Jesus, when he had cried again with a loud voice, yielded up the

> ghost.
>
> And, behold, the veil of the temple was rent in twain from the top to the bottom; and the earth did quake, and the rocks rent; and the graves were opened; and many bodies of the saints which slept arose, and came out of the graves after his resurrection, and went into the holy city, and appeared unto many.

After Jesus had made seven statements from the cross, as we see not only in Matthew but in the other gospels, He came to that greatest of moments and we are told in Verse 50, "When he had cried again with a loud voice, he yielded up the ghost." His cry was not addressed to anyone in particular. But it was the victory cry. It exclaimed the fact that what He had come to do was finished, and at that precise moment, as He expelled His life to God with a loud cry, God moved inside the temple and took hold of the veil, the veil that separated the holy from the most holy place into which only the high priest went once a year to confess the sins of the people. God took hold of that veil, a very thickly made veil, and He ripped it apart from top to bottom.

Someone said that Jesus, the true priest, had never been able to get inside that holy of holies, but now God went inside and worked His way outside. He burst forth by ripping the veil in twain and out came the power of God, not to dwell in one small place but in the unlimited life of Jesus Christ, His Son who has just shed His blood upon the cross.

Also at that moment, the earth shook, the rocks tore apart, and the graves of many of those who had died with faith opened. They rose up and many of them appeared in the city of Jerusalem.

It was a gigantic happening upon the face of this earth. We know that when he comes in the rapture to catch away His saints, He is coming in the very same way. We are told in I Thessalonians 4:16 that the Lord himself shall descend from heaven with a shout. That is right! With a shout! You talk about a voice that shall sound across the heavens and be heard in every nook and corner of this earth, it will almost burst the eardrums of the human race. That shout that shall be heard by those who have died in the faith and those who are alive up until His coming, that shout shall erupt into a rapture, a translation where the dead shall rise, brushing the dirt from their hair, rising to meet Christ in the clouds.

And we who might be alive at that time shall feel gravity lose its power upon our mortal flesh, and we shall defy it and jump on a passing cloud and meet the Lord in the air. Say "Hallelujah!" This is the victory cry of all time. Thank God we are on the winning side.

Matthew 27:54-66

Now when the centurion, and they that were with him, watching Jesus, saw the earthquake, and those things that were done, they feared greatly, saying, Truly this was the Son of God. And many women were there beholding afar off, which followed Jesus from Galilee, ministering unto him: among which was Mary Magdalene, and Mary the mother of James and Joses, and the mother of Zebedee's children.

When the even was come, there came a rich man of Arimathaea, named Joseph, who also himself was Jesus' disciple: he went to Pilate, and begged the body of Jesus. Then Pilate commanded the body to be delivered. And when Joseph had taken the body, he wrapped it in a clean linen cloth and laid it in his own new tomb, which he had hewn out in the rock: and he rolled a great stone to the door of the sepulchre, and departed. And there was Mary Magdalene, and the other Mary, sitting over against the sepulchre. Now the next day, that followed the day of the preparation, the chief priests and Pharisees came together unto Pilate, saying, Sir, we remember that that deceiver said, while he was yet alive, After three days I will rise again. Command therefore that the sepulchre be made sure until the third day, lest his disciples come by night, and steal him away, and say unto the people, He is risen from the dead: so the last error shall be worse than the first. Pilate said unto them, Ye have a watch: go your way, make it as sure as ye can. So they went, and made the sepulchre sure, sealing the stone, and setting a watch.

Securing the Grave

This was the sabbath day when the Jews and their leaders came to Pilate and said that "deceiver" said He was going to rise the third day. They asked Pilate to put a guard there so His own disciples could not steal Him away.

These were the same ones who accused Jesus of breaking the sabbath! Now they were doing the very same thing for which they condemned Him. When you tell one lie, it breeds another lie. I am told where there is one snake, there is always another. But Pilate saw through them. He said, "All right, you have a watch." That is, you have certain of my soldiers that you can use for this purpose. "You go out there and seal the stone and set the watch as you please." And they did.

Matthew 28:1,2

In the end of the sabbath, as it began to dawn toward the first day of the week, came Mary Magdalene and the other Mary to see the sepulchre.

And, behold, there was a great earthquake: for the angel of the Lord descended from heaven, and came and rolled back the stone from the door, and sat upon it.

Two Powers Combined

Here is a perfect picture of God acting through both His natural and supernatural powers. The earthquake was natural, but the supernatural consisted of the angel of the Lord coming down from heaven and then doing His mighty work — rolling the stone away and then sitting down upon it.

In this ministry of God's healing power that He committed to me to take to the people of my generation, I have from the beginning in 1947 understood that God heals through both His natural and supernatural powers. I have understood that this is the very nature of God, to use the things which He has created — both the natural and the supernatural. In the City of Faith Medical and Research Center we are combining prayer and medicine just like we breathe. It is no strange thing to us to use the chemicals of God's earth through the administration of skilled doctors, nurses, and other health professionals. At the same time, the patients, as praying people, believing people, are surrounded by trained prayer partners who come in to pray a prayer of faith with the doctors and nurses and others who are working with the sick.

I think it is time that believers begin to accept what they have said they have accepted all these years, and that is the incarnation.

The incarnation is the supernatural indwelling the natural. The human body of Jesus is as natural as your body or mine, but that indwelling Christ spirit is supernatural. Why should people who believe in medical help frown on prayer or even reject it? Why should people who believe that God heals through the agency or instrumentality of prayer reject medicine? Why should the supernatural reject the natural or the natural reject the supernatural? It is just as normal as breathing for them to work together.

Matthew 28:3-15

His countenance was like lightning, and his raiment white as snow: and for fear of him the keepers did shake, and became as dead men.

And the angel answered and said unto the women, Fear not ye: for I know that ye seek Jesus, which was crucified. He is not here: for he is risen, as he said. Come, see the place where the Lord lay. And go quickly and tell his disciples that he is risen from the dead; and, behold, he goeth before you into Galilee; there shall ye see him: lo, I have told you.

And they departed quickly from the sepulchre with fear and great joy; and did run to bring his disciples word.

And as they went to tell his disciples, behold, Jesus met them, saying, All hail. And they came and held him by the feet, and worshipped him.

Then said Jesus unto them, Be not afraid: go tell my brethren that they go into Galilee, and there shall they see me.

Now when they were going, behold, some of the watch came into the city, and shewed unto the chief priests all the things that were done. And when they were assembled with the elders, and had taken counsel, they gave large money unto the soldiers, saying, Say ye, His disciples came by night, and stole him away while we slept. And if this come to the governor's ears, we will persuade him, and secure you.

So they took the money, and did as they were taught: and this saying is commonly reported among the Jews until this day.

Matthew is the only one of the gospel writers who reported this scene. In effect, he was saying, "Now, when you hear this rumor that Jesus' disciples stole His body away at night, you remember how the rumor started and how money was paid to the soldiers to keep their mouths shut."

Thank God that it is recorded in the Bible, because many people still believe that rumor. But we know that they paid them money to compound their lie. We know that the angel rolled the stone away and Jesus is alive. We know because He is living inside us.

Matthew 28:16

Then the eleven disciples went away into Galilee, into a mountain where Jesus had appointed them. And when they saw him, they worshipped him: but some doubted.

And Jesus came and spake unto them, saying, All power is given unto me in heaven and in earth.

Go ye therefore, and teach all nations, baptizing them in the name of the Father, and of the Son, and of the Holy Ghost: teaching them to observe all things whatsoever I have commanded you: and, lo, I am with you alway, even unto the end of the world. Amen.

Here ends the reading of the gospel of Matthew. Matthew began his gospel with Abraham and David and throughout his writings, he gave confirmation of the covenant being fulfilled in Jesus Christ.

Now he comes to the end of the crucifixion and enters into the resurrection, where Jesus comes to His disciples in Galilee. There, as the Messiah rises from the dead, He declares that all power in heaven and in earth is given unto Him.

Then He does the most remarkable thing. You may recall in the book of Genesis that God called Abraham to be the father of all who have faith. It was with Abraham that He made the covenant. God told Abraham that He would make him a father of many nations, and that his seed would be like the stars of the sky and the sands of the sea. He was to take the light of God to all the nations.

This was something that had never been done by the Jewish race. They had lived in their land of Canaan, and somewhere back about 700 B.C., the 10 northern tribes had been taken into captivity by the Assyrians: about 586 B.C., the two southern tribes had been taken into captivity to Babylon. They had returned and had rebuilt the temple, Jesus had appeared, and they had not taken God's Word to the ends of the world. They had not taught the nations, and the light of God had not gone to all people.

Jesus says to His disciples, "Go ye, therefore, and teach all nations, baptizing them in the name of the Father, and of the Son, and of the Holy Ghost, teaching them to observe all things whatsoever I have commanded you, and lo, I am with you alway, even unto the end of the world."

What an ending, and what a beginning! The most Jewish of all the gospels closes with a word from the Messiah, Jesus, that throws the kingdom wide open to all people of all nations. Then He adds that His continued presence with believers will be there until He comes again.

I say that the closing of Matthew's gospel is the flinging wide of the doors to take the gospel to all men. No longer will it be confined to one little nation, but to all people, of all nations, of all generations. What a Savior! What a Lord! How honored I am to be a believer of our Lord Jesus Christ.

The Gospel according to Mark

The Gospel according to Mark

Mark was a young man who joined Paul on his missionary journey. Midway through the journey something happened to Mark's conscience or his determination, or his life-style, and he ran out on them. Later Mark regained control of himself, possibly through the strong faith that Barnabas had in him.

Later he met Peter and was with Peter, it is believed, in Rome. According to I Peter 5:13, that apostle defended Mark and said he was like a son to him. Mark was not one of the 12 apostles. But he had sat at Peter's feet. As we read the book of Mark, we can almost visualize Peter, since Peter was the source of most of the information about Jesus that Mark wrote. Peter's strong personality and vivid language are demonstrated in Mark's gospel. Mark presented Jesus differently than did Matthew. Matthew dealt mostly with the sayings of Jesus, tracing him back to Abraham. He wrote primarily to the Jewish people to convince them that Jesus was the Son of God. Mark dealt primarily with the Gentiles and especially the Romans who then ruled the world. The Romans loved power, especially military might. They had conquered the known world and were impressed only by power. Mark wrote to impress them with Jesus' action. While Matthew dealt more with what Jesus said, Mark was more concerned with what He did. Mark presented Jesus as the wonder-worker, the man of miracles, the man who could outdo any mortal power, including the entire Roman empire. Mark is a striking gospel! Some believe it was the first gospel written.

Mark 1:1

The beginning of the gospel of Jesus Christ, the Son of God

Peter's Influence Seen

Mark begins without apology or explanation by talking about the beginning and saying that Jesus Christ is the Son of God. Peter's influence upon young Mark is revealed again because this is the way Peter spoke of Jesus when he said, 'Thou art the Christ, the son of the living God.'

Mark 1:2,3

> As it is written in the prophets, Behold, I send my messenger before thy face, which shall prepare thy way before thee. The voice of one crying in the wilderness, Prepare ye the way of the Lord, make his paths straight.

Messiah Prophecy

This reference is to Isaiah 40 which prophesied that when the Messiah came, He would be preceded by a forerunner who would dash upon the scene with a message of preparation for people to get their lives in order, that they might be prepared to receive the Messiah.

Mark 1:4

> John did baptize in the wilderness, and preach the baptism of repentance for the remission of sins.

Repentance in the New Testament means to turn around, change your mind, and go in another direction.

Mark 1:5

> And there went out unto him all the land of Judaea, and they of Jerusalem, and were all baptized of him in the river of Jordan, confessing their sins.

Preaching Repentance

This kind of preaching strikes hard at the very root of sin. It has a shattering effect upon humanity and causes multitudes to repent of their sins and be baptized. Baptism is an outward symbol of the act of repentance itself, of the death and burial of their sins and resurrection into newness of life.

Mark 1:6,7

> And John was clothed with camel's hair, and with a girdle of a skin about his loins; and he did eat locusts and wild honey; and preached, saying, There cometh one mightier than I after me, the latchet of whose shoes I am not worthy to stoop down and unloose.

John the Baptist was referring to respect servants showed for their masters in the act of stooping down and unloosing the thongs of the leather shoes upon their feet.

Mark 1:8

> I indeed have baptized you with water but he shall baptize you with the Holy Ghost.

This is the first time that another baptism is mentioned, a baptism with the Holy Spirit through which the person of the Holy Spirit would be involved with the lives of the people of God on a grand scale. The Holy Spirit was present in the Old Testament, that is to say, the old covenant. Indeed, as Genesis tells us, it was the Spirit of God that brooded upon the face of the deep; Under the new covenant, however, the kingdom of God through Jesus Christ, the Holy Spirit would be at the very center of His activity.

Mark 1:9,10

> And it came to pass in those days, that Jesus came from Nazareth of Galilee, and was baptized of John in Jordan. And straightway coming up out of the water, he saw the heavens opened, and the Spirit like a dove descending upon him.

Jesus' Baptism

This word "straightway" is used in the New Testament 82 times. Mark alone uses it 41 times. Straightway means immediately, right now, or let's get it done. This trait reveals again the influence of Peter's personality on Mark, his protege.

Jesus went from Nazareth in Galilee to the River Jordan, probably near Jericho. There, he was baptized by John in the Jordan. As he "straightway" came up out of the water, as He came striding through the water, up toward the bank, He saw the heavens opened and the Holy Spirit like a dove descending upon Him.

Mark 1:11,12

> And there came a voice from heaven, saying, Thou art my beloved Son,

in whom I am well pleased. And immediately the spirit driveth him into the wilderness.

Jesus Spirit-filled!

The Spirit of God, the Holy Spirit, had everything to do with the life of our Lord. There was a divine impulse that Jesus felt by the indwelling Holy Spirit. Even Jesus, the divine Son of God, had to be filled with the Holy Spirit. How much more must those of us who are human beings be filled.

Mark 1:13-15

And he was there in the wilderness forty days, tempted of Satan; and was with the wild beasts; and the angels ministered unto him. Now after that John was put in prison, Jesus came into Galilee, preaching the gospel of the kingdom of God, And saying, The time is fulfilled, and the kingdom of God is at hand repent ye, and believe the gospel.

Old Law Repealed

Just as John the Baptist was telling people to repent, Jesus began to preach the same thing, and added, "Believe the gospel." It is noteworthy that the law of Moses had been in effect until John the Baptist came. The moment John the Baptist appeared and began to preach the coming of the kingdom of heaven, the old law of Moses was no longer in affect. It was replaced by the gospel of Jesus Christ.

Mark 1:16-18

Now as he walked by the sea of Galilee, he saw Simon and Andrew his brother casting a net into the sea for they were fishers. And Jesus said unto them, Come ye after me, and I will make you to become fishers of men. And straightway they forsook their nets and followed him.

Instant Decision

One of these fishermen was Simon Peter. Mark used the term "straightway" because Peter had emphasized to him how they had made an instant and firm decision to leave their fishing nets. Although their fishing business was quite large, they without hesitation chose to follow Jesus. So immense was the power of God, and so powerful was its effect upon these two brothers, that they saw something greater than their business. Instantly and "straightway," they just walked away and followed Jesus Christ.

The impact of Jesus Christ is the most powerful thing in the world. When He speaks to us today to follow Him as He does through the Holy Spirit, our action is to be the same. We are to get up and give it all we have.

Mark 1:19-21

And when he had gone a little farther thence, he saw James the son of Zebedee, and John his brother, who also were in the ship mending their nets. And straightway he called them and they left their father Zebedee in the ship with the hired servants, and went after him. And they went into Capernaum; and straightway on the sabbath day he entered into the synagogue, and taught.

Origin of Synagogues

The synagogues had been established during the Babylonian captivity of the children of Israel. At that time Nebuchadnezzar had destroyed their temple. Then in Babylon, in order to continue the work of God, the priests raised up synagogues in which to instruct the people in the law. They were also places of justice. It is said there were more than 400 synagogues in Jerusalem in Jesus' time. They were also all over the land of Israel, including Capernaum. In fact, wherever 10 Jews went, they were to build a synagogue and continue the work of the law of Moses.

Mark 1:22-28

And they were astonished at his doctrine for he taught them as one that had authority, and not as the scribes. And there was in their synagogue a man with an unclean spirit; and he cried out, Saying, let us alone; what have we to do with thee, thou Jesus of Nazareth? art thou come to destroy us? I know thee who thou art, the Holy One of God. And Jesus rebuked him, saying, Hold thy peace, and come out of him.

And when the unclean spirit had torn him, and cried with a loud voice, he came out of him. And they were all amazed, insomuch that they questioned among themselves, saying, What thing is this? what new doctrine is this? for with authority commandeth he even the unclean spirits, and they do obey him. And immediately his fame spread abroad throughout all the region round about Galilee.

Demons Exist

When Jesus spoke in the synagogue He spoke with authority, not like the scribes who were always quoting somebody else. In the midst of the service, a man with a demon cried out, and it was the demon speaking. Then the chief demon said, "I know who you are, the Holy One of God." Jesus rebuked him. He did not want the people to believe He was in league with demons. When that demon said, "I know who you are," the devil was trying to persuade people that Jesus was actually in league with the devil. Jesus did not want their satanic worship. He rebuked the demon and called him out. When the demon came out he tried to destroy the man's body.

The people were amazed, but they did not question the existence of demons. The people of Israel knew there were unclean spirits. I know today that there is a movement in the church of Jesus Christ to remove all teaching about demons, or to deny the existence of demons. How the devil must be laughing! Let me tell you; Wherever Jesus is, demon-possessed people are attracted today to His mighty presence. Demons who are in people always retain their spiritual power and their spiritual insights. They want to take over the spiritual kingdom of God. They want to stop the service of God. I say that we in the Church must return to our Lord Jesus Christ and do the mighty works that He did.

Mark 1:29-31

> And forthwith, when they were come out of the synagogue, they entered into the house of Simon and Andrew, with James and John. But Simon's wife's mother lay sick of a fever, and anon they tell him of her. And he came and took her by the hand, and lifted her up; and immediately the fever left her, and she ministered unto them.

Jesus at our Side

Let me say a special word about Jesus' healing Peter's mother-in-law of a fever. Notice that Mark introduces Jesus as the wonder-worker. In the opening scene of the introduction, John the Baptist has baptized Him in water, and as He comes up out of the water, the heavens are opened. The Spirit of God then drives Him into the wilderness to be tempted of the devil and then "straightway" He goes forward to cast out demons. He is in the role of the deliverer of humanity.

Then Mark inserts a very special scene in which Jesus deals with the individual and also with the needs of the family. When He arrived to eat dinner with Simon and his friends and family, He learned that

Peter's mother-in-law was very ill with a fever. Jesus went to her bedside, took her by the hand, and raised her up. Immediately the fever left her and she got out of bed and helped with the meal.

This reminds me so much of a man who said he had tried to love people but it was too hard. So he said he was going to "love the world." How different that is from Jesus who also loved the world, but the world to Jesus was made up of people, and people are individuals. Here is a mother, a mother-in-law, a woman who wants to be a vital part of life. She has many responsibilities. Jesus is at the home and she would like to have a part in ministering to Him. Jesus walks into her need and delivers her from the fever. One day, Evelyn, my darling wife, said to me that the fevers of life really try to demoralize us — the fevers of anxiety, fevers of bitterness, fevers of disappointment and frustration, fevers that rage inside us. Jesus cares about those fevers enough to cast them out so that we human beings will be free and normal again. Oh, I love this gospel because Mark brings Jesus right to our individual side.

Mark 1:32-34

> And at even, when the sun did set, they brought unto him all that were diseased, and them that were possessed with devils. And all the city was gathered together at the door. And he healed many that were sick of divers diseases, and cast out many devils; and suffered not the devils to speak, because they knew him.

The gospel of Jesus Christ, when it is preached in the fullness of its power, draws the sick and afflicted, the demon-possessed, the hurting people, often in large numbers. In contrast, some modern churches seem to be unable to minister to people's needs. Modern ministers attract no crowds of needy people. We must go back to Jesus, the founder of our faith, the Savior of our lives, the head of the Church, and be like Him.

I believe my ministry is a forerunner of the greatest healing revival this world has ever known. I believe what I have done has only scratched the surface of what is to come. I believe that as we read the New Testament and see Jesus, we are going to come alive in the Lord. And as we come alive in Christ, we will have compassion for the sick, the lost, and the suffering of our generation. We will invade the kingdom of darkness to cast out the devils, and to set the people free to follow and glorify Christ.

Mark 1:35

> And in the morning, rising up a great while before day, he went out, and departed into a solitary place, and there prayed. And Simon and

> they that were with him followed after him. And when they had found him, they said unto him, All men seek for thee. And he said unto them, Let us go into the next towns, that I may preach there also: for therefore came I forth.

After this tremendous healing scene in Capernaum, Jesus went out into a desert to be alone with God, and to pray. That really says something to you and me, doesn't it? The greater the anointing upon us, and the more results we have, the more we need to go off alone and pray. His disciples followed Him and told Him that all men sought for him. Of course they sought for Him! When people's hearts are touched by a manifestation of the power of God to set them free, they do seek those who have Jesus' power.

Mark 1:39-45

> And he preached in their synagogues throughout all Galilee, and cast out devils. And there came a leper to him, beseeching him, and kneeling down to him, and saying unto him, If thou wilt, thou canst make me clean. And Jesus, moved with compassion, put forth his hand, and touched him, and saith unto him, I will; be thou clean. And as soon as he had spoken, immediately the leprosy departed from him, and he was cleansed. And he straitly charged him, and forthwith sent him away; and saith unto him, See thou say nothing to any man but go thy way, shew thyself to the priest, and offer for thy cleansing those things which Moses commanded, for a testimony unto them. But he went out, and began to publish it much, and to blaze abroad the matter, insomuch that Jesus could no more openly enter into the city, but was without in desert places; and they came to him from every quarter.

Testimony

Notice that the gospels of Matthew and Mark are important to each other. While Matthew presented the sayings of Jesus, Mark is presenting him by telling about the things He did and the places He went. He was showing us that on the one hand there is the preaching and the teaching of the gospel, but on the other hand it must be confirmed by miracles, by healings, by exorcisms of demons, or casting out of unclean spirits. To have a balanced ministry of the Lord Jesus Christ, and to have a balanced Christ-like life as laymen and laywomen, we are to understand Jesus' full ministry of preaching.

Mark brought up an important issue through the lips of this leper who said to Christ, "If you will, you can heal me." Jesus told him that wasn't the question. He told him He would, and He healed him. Then

He told him to go and do the things that would prove that he was healed.

Any healing or miracle wrought by Jesus Christ will stand the test. It settles the issue. We urge people always to go back to their physicians, to be examined. If they are not healed, they need to know it. If they *are* healed, their testimony needs to be given to a world that is hurting to see and hear what God is doing. I cannot overemphasize the magnetic power of our Lord Jesus Christ upon people. That power is present today. It is available today. We must not settle for anything less. I believe it is time that we struck a blow for deliverance!

Mark 2:1-2

> And again he entered into Capernaum after some days; and it was noised that he was in the house. And straightway many were gathered together, insomuch that there was no room to receive them, no, not so much as about the door and he preached the word unto them. And they come unto him, bringing one sick of the palsy, which was borne of four. And when they could not come nigh unto him for the press, they uncovered the roof where he was and when they had broken it up, they let down the bed wherein the sick of the palsy lay.
>
> When Jesus saw their faith, he said unto the sick of the palsy, Son, thy sins be forgiven thee. But there were certain of the scribes sitting there, and reasoning in their hearts, Why doth this man thus speak blasphemies? who can forgive sins but God only? And immediately when Jesus perceived in his spirit that they so reasoned within themselves, he said unto them, Why reason ye these things in your hearts? Whether is it easier to say to the sick of the palsy, Thy sins be forgiven thee; or to say, Arise, and take up thy bed, and walk? But that ye may know that the Son of man hath power on earth to forgive sins, (he saith to the sick of the palsy,) I say unto thee, Arise, and take up thy bed, and go thy way into thine house. And immediately he arose, took up the bed, and went forth before them all; insomuch that they were all amazed, and glorified God, saying, We never saw it on this fashion.

The Healing Christ

Jesus always did the will of God. Whatever He did was in the will of God. He said He did the works of His Father. And if the healing of the sick is not the will of God, then Mark is presenting an impostor. If Jesus healing the sick is not of God, then He is working against the Father. You see how the devil wants to blind our eyes? When that paralyzed man was brought to Jesus, the crowd was so big inside the house that those carrying him went up on the roof and tore an entrance through the roof.

They raised the roof for victory, and the Bible says Jesus saw their faith! That was what He was looking for. Today, He is still looking for faith. When He saw their faith, He immediately dealt with the man with paralysis.

Jesus Christ used two things himself: faith and the Word of God. When He entered that house, He preached the word of God. He also had His faith. When He saw their faith, He said, "Son, thy sins be forgiven thee." Some of those present immediately criticized Him and called Him a blasphemer. He replied, "Which is easier, to forgive his sins or to heal him?"

Healing comes from the same Greek root word from which saving or salvation comes. "To save" and "to heal" come from the same Greek root word, and Jesus did not divide them. When He spoke the word of power it was to make a person whole — body, mind, and spirit.

This is what I see returning in the Church today. This is my mission on earth — to help prepare the way, to introduce this to the world. My mission is to be the John the Baptist of my time. In fact, that is what Christ told me in the early days of my ministry, that I was to be the John the Baptist of my time, to introduce the healing ministry, and to pave the way for people universally to see the healing Christ.

Mark 2:13-14

> And he went forth again by the sea side; and all the multitude resorted unto him, and he taught them. And as he passed by, he saw Levi the son of Alphaeus sitting at the receipt of custom, and said unto him, Follow me. And he arose and followed him.

Expect a Miracle!

Jesus said two short words, "Follow me," and the man got up and did it. Let us become aware of the power of the word of Jesus Christ, the power of His written word in the Bible, the power of the Word of God being spoken in faith by one of us with its power upon people. We should be expecting conversions, healings, and deliverances. As God said to me, "Expect a miracle. And tell the people to expect a miracle." I am telling you now, expect a miracle!

Mark 2:15-17

> And it came to pass, that, as Jesus sat at meat in his house, many publicans and sinners sat also together with Jesus and his disciples: for there were many, and they followed him. And when the scribes and Pharisees saw him eat with publicans and sinners, they said unto his disciples, How is it that he eateth and drinketh with publicans and

sinners? When Jesus heard it, he saith unto them, They that are whole have no need of the physician, but they that are sick: I came not to call the righteous, but sinners to repentance.

Christian Home Principles

It is said here that Jesus was in His own house, and that people came to His house. Primarily they were sinners, that is, people outside the kingdom of God. They were people whom the Jewish leaders called the scum of the earth, people who needed to be saved and to be healed. When the religious people, the Pharisees, saw it, they were deeply upset. They asked, Why is he eating and drinking with the scum of the earth? Jesus then spoke the principle of His kingdom: I came to call people who need salvation, not those who already have it.

Christians today have to redefine what it means to be people of God's kingdom. We must think of our homes as places in which to have prayer groups, or to have people come to receive our witness of the gospel. Being a Christian means that Jesus is the center of our lives and our activities.

Mark 2:18-22

And the disciples of John and of the Pharisees used to fast: and they come and say unto him, Why do the disciples of John and of the Pharisees fast, but thy disciples fast not? And Jesus said unto them, can the children of the bridechamber fast, while the bridegroom is with them? as long as they have the bridegroom with them, they cannot fast. But the days will come, when the bridegroom shall be taken away from them, and then shall they fast in those days.

No man also seweth a piece of new cloth on an old garment: else the new piece that filled it up taketh away from the old, and the rent is made worse. And no man putteth new wine into old bottles: else the new wine doth burst the bottles, and the wine is spilled, and the bottles will be marred: but new wine must be put into new bottles.

Reason for Fasting

It was well known that the disciples of John and the Pharisees fasted from the standpoint of doing without food only. Jesus talked about their fasting and compared it with sewing a piece of new cloth on an old garment, or to putting new wine in old bottles. He said, "It will not work. You Pharisees think you can merely do without food and that in itself will bring you closer to God. It will not. When you fast, you are not merely doing without food. Remember the true reason. You are seeking the presence of God, and His anointing upon your life."

Mark 2:23-28

> And it came to pass, that he went through the corn fields on the sabbath day; and his disciples began, as they went, to pluck the ears of corn. And the Pharisees said unto him, Behold, why do they on the sabbath day that which is not lawful? And he said unto them, Have ye never read what David did, when he had need, and was an hungred, he, and they that were with him? How he went into the house of God in the days of Abiathar the high priest, and did eat the shewbread, which is not lawful to eat but for the priests, and gave also to them which were with him?
>
> And he said unto them, The sabbath was made for man, and not man for the sabbath: therefore the Son of man is Lord also of the sabbath.

Honor Over Day

The chief characteristic of the old sabbath was to rest, so Jesus was saying, rest was made for man, not man for rest. There is much confusion about what day of the week one should keep the sabbath. The fact is that the sabbath is a part of the old covenant. In the new covenant it is not the day that counts; rather, it is the way we honor Christ. And we have, on the first day of the week, an established custom in the Christian faith, as we will see later in the New Testament, where the Christians meet together to celebrate Jesus' resurrection. It is not a sabbath in the same sense that the old Jewish sabbath was, for that was primarily a day of rest. The first day of the week among the Christians is primarily a day of worship. I, too, think that there should be a day of rest every week. Perhaps it is the sabbath day that one should rest, or maybe the second day, or the sixth day. But there should be a day when we take off and we rest from our labors, so that our strength is recuperated. The old sabbath was a day of rest and it was made for man. It was not a big religious issue. It was for the betterment of man. Jesus was saying, I am the Lord of the sabbath and I can arrange it the way I want.

Mark 3:1,2

> And he entered again into the synagogue; and there was a man there which had a withered hand. And they watched him, whether he would heal him on the sabbath day; that they might accuse him.

They were no longer concerned with whether or not Jesus would heal. They knew He would do that. Their concern was that He would not desecrate their so-called holy sabbath day by healing some suffering human being. That is a strange sort of religion, that one would put something like that above a human need! If there is anything religious people need to hear, it is that some of our traditions are not worth the paper they are printed on. Our concern should be with human beings and their needs of deliverance, and no matter what day it is, to do God's work.

Mark 3:3-5

> And he saith unto the man which had the withered hand, Stand forth. And he saith unto them, Is it lawful to do good on the sabbath days, or to do evil? to save life, or to kill? But they held their peace.
>
> And when he had looked round about on them with anger, being grieved for the hardness of their hearts, he saith unto the man, Stretch forth thine hand. And he stretched it out: and his hand was restored whole as the other.

Faith Must Act

There are two important things here. One is that Jesus looked round about them with "anger." Jesus did get angry. There is nothing wrong with getting angry as long as that anger is used in the right way.

The second thing is that He told that man to stretch forth his "withered" hand. In other words, Jesus was saying, whatever you can do with that withered hand, if you can move a finger or make some little slight movement, do it. Put your faith into action. And as the man began to try to move it, his hand was restored whole as the other.

Richard and I often pray for the sick and deal with people, especially those in wheelchairs, or those who have lost much feeling or activity in their bodies. We will say as we pray or speak the word of faith, "Move a finger if you can, or move a foot. Move your leg. Move some limb. Do something." No matter how sick one may be, when the time comes for healing, either by prayer or by medicine, one must do something; one must rise up in the inner man. The inner man has got to stand up inside the body. Even if it is not much physically at first, the inner man can do something, and it is amazing how the healing can come.

Mark 3:6-21

> And the Pharisees went forth, and straightway took counsel with the Herodians against him, how they might destroy him. But Jesus withdrew himself with his disciples to the sea: and a great multitude from Galilee followed him, and from Judaea, and from Jerusalem, and from Idumaea, and from beyond Jordan; and they about Tyre and Sidon, a great multi-

tude, when they had heard what great things he did, came unto him.
And he spake to his disciples, that a small ship should wait on him because of the multitude, lest they should throng him. For he had healed many; insomuch that they pressed upon him for to touch him, as many as had plagues.
And unclean spirits, when they saw him, fell down before him, and cried, saying, Thou art the Son of God. And he straitly charged them that they should not make him known. And he goeth up into a mountain, and calleth unto him whom he would: and they came unto Him.
And he ordained twelve, that they should be with him, and that he might send them forth to preach, and to have power to heal sicknesses, and to cast out devils: and Simon he surnamed Peter; and James the son of Zebedee, and John the brother of James; and he surnamed them Boanerges, which is, The sons of thunder; and Andrew, and Philip, and Bartholomew, and Matthew, and Thomas, and James the son of Alphaeus, and Thaddaeus, and Simon the Canaanite, and Judas Iscariot, which also betrayed him; and they went into an house.
And the multitude cometh together again, so that they could not so much as eat bread. And when his friends heard of it, they went out to lay hold on him; for they said, He is beside himself.

Even Friends Misunderstand

His friends thought that Jesus was a fanatic. Others thought He was out of his mind. Here He was, so involved with the gospel of the Good News, telling them the kingdom of heaven was at hand, to repent, and to receive the good things of God. Jesus thought that was the greatest thing in the world, but some of His friends had not caught the vision. They thought anyone who really gave himself in concern, compassion and faith toward lost and suffering people was out of his mind. Is it any different today?

Mark 3:22-35

And the scribes which came down from Jerusalem said, He hath Beelzebub, and by the prince of the devils casteth he out devils.
And he called them unto him, and said unto them in parables, How can Satan cast out Satan? And if a kingdom be divided against itself, that kingdom cannot stand. And if a house be divided against itself, that house cannot stand. And if Satan rise up against himself, and be divided, he cannot stand, but hath an end. No man can enter into a strong man's house, and spoil his goods, except he will first bind the strong man; and then he will spoil his house.
Verily I say unto you, All sins shall be forgiven unto the sons of men,

and blasphemies wherewith soever they shall blaspheme:

But he that shall blaspheme against the Holy Ghost hath never forgiveness, but is in danger of eternal damnation: because they said, He hath an unclean spirit. There came then his brethren and his mother, and, standing without, sent unto him, calling him. And the multitude sat about him, and they said unto him, Behold, thy mother and thy brethren without seek for thee. And he answered them, saying, Who is my mother, or my brethren?

And he looked round about on them which sat about him, and said, Behold my mother and my brethren! For whosoever shall do the will of God, the same is my brother, and my sister, and mother.

Holy Spirit Warning

Remember that the Scribes were the teachers of the law of Moses. They were the copiers, by hand, of the scriptures. They not only copied them, and studied them, but they interpreted them.

They had noticed different levels of demons as they were described in the Old Testament. There are different levels of authority within the devil's kingdom just as there are in God's kingdom of angels. The Scribes also noticed that when Jesus cast out devils, he would have cast out the biggest devil of all, the very prince of Satan's demons, Beelzebub. Jesus pointed out to them that if He indeed were casting out devils by the authority of the chief demon, Beelzebub, then the devil's kingdom was divided. He said any kingdom, or house, or family divided against itself cannot stand. Jesus explained, The thing that I do is to bind that chief demon, and then cast out any other demons." When He came to that point, He warned them against blaspheming against the Holy Spirit. He gave them so careful an explanation because they had said, "He hath an unclean spirit."

Jesus was warning them that while they might accuse him of casting out devils by the power of Beelzebub, they should never do it by accusing the Holy Spirit, because the Holy Spirit is the agent of salvation.

It is by the Spirit of God that a person's heart is touched, convicted of sin, and opened to God. It is by the Holy Spirit that the Messiah, the Savior, is revealed. It is by the Holy Spirit that a person is led to Christ and Christ enters into that person's life. Therefore, if the agent of that salvation is removed, there is no other way to be saved and there is no forgiveness in this life or the life to come.

Mark 4:1-34

And he began again to teach by the sea side: and there was gathered unto him a great multitude, so that he entered into a ship, and sat in the sea; and the whole multitude was by the sea on the land. And he taught them many things by parables, and said unto them in his doctrine,

Hearken; Behold, there went out a sower to sow. And it came to pass, as he sowed, some fell by the way side, and the fowls of the air came and devoured it up. And some fell on stony ground, where it had not much earth; and immediately it sprang up, because it had no depth of earth. But when the sun was up, it was scorched; and because it had no root, it withered away.

And some fell among thorns, and the thorns grew up, and choked it, and it yielded no fruit. And other fell on good ground, and did yield fruit that sprang up and increased; and brought forth, some thirty, and some sixty, and some an hundred.

And He said unto them, He that hath ears to hear, let him hear. And when he was alone, they that were about him with the twelve asked of him the parable. And he said unto them, Unto you it is given to know the mystery of the kingdom of God: but unto them that are without, all these things are done in parables: That seeing they may see, and not perceive; and hearing they may hear, and not understand; lest at any time they should be converted, and their sins should be forgiven them.

And He said unto them, Know ye not this parable? and how then will ye know all parables? The sower soweth the word. And these are they by the way side, where the word is sown; but when they have heard, Satan cometh immediately, and taketh away the word that was sown in their hearts.

And these are they likewise which are sown on stony ground; who, when they have heard the word, immediately receive it with gladness; and have no root in themselves, and so endure but for a time: afterward, when affliction or persecution ariseth for the word's sake, immediately they are offended.

And these are they which are sown among thorns; such as hear the word, and the cares of this world, and the deceitfulness of riches, and the lusts of other things entering in, choke the word, and it becometh unfruitful.

And these are they which are sown on good ground; such as hear the word, and receive it, and bring forth fruit, some thirtyfold, some sixty, and some an hundred.

And He said unto them, is a candle brought to be put under a bushel, or under a bed? and not to be set on a candlestick? For there is nothing hid, which shall not be manifested; neither was any thing kept secret, but that it should come abroad. If any man have ears to hear, let him hear.

And he said unto them, take heed what ye hear: with what measure ye mete, it shall be measured to you: and unto you that hear shall more be given. For he that hath, to him shall be given; and he that hath not, from him shall be taken even that which he hath.

And he said, So is the kingdom of God, as if a man should cast seed into the ground; and should sleep, and rise night and day, and the seed should spring and grow up, he knoweth not how. For the earth bringeth forth fruit of herself; first the blade, then the ear, after that the full corn in the ear. But when the fruit is brought forth, immediately he putteth in the sickle, because the harvest is come.

And he said, Whereunto shall we liken the kingdom of God? or with what comparison shall we compare it? It is like a grain of mustard seed, which, when it is sown in the earth, is less than all the seeds that be in the earth: but when it is sown, it groweth up, and becometh greater than all herbs, and shooteth out great branches; so that the fowls of the air may lodge under the shadow of it.

And with many such parables spake he the word unto them, as they were able to hear it. But without a parable spake he not unto them: and when they were alone, he expounded all things to his disciples.

Jesus as Communicator

A parable is a story Jesus used for illustration. God had told Him directly what He was to do when He came to this earth. He knew the eternal principles of the kingdom of God. He also knew how to explain them in the simplest terms. He realized it is difficult for people to understand complex issues. Therefore, He used stories to illustrate the deep truths of the eternal God. He knew that communication is in the hearer.

If we do not speak with the listener in mind, he will not understand. If we are only concerned about what we are saying, or what our witness is, without trying to understand the other person, and in what ways he can hear what we are saying, then we are virtually wasting our time. Communication is an art. Jesus was essentially a communicator who knew how to get through to a person's mind and spirit.

Mark 4:35-41

And the same day, when the even was come, he saith unto them, Let us pass over unto the other side. And when they had sent away the multitude, they took him even as he was in the ship. And there were also with him other little ships.

And there arose a great storm of wind, and the waves beat into the ship, so that it was now full. And he was in the hinder part of the ship, asleep on a pillow: and they awake him, and say unto him, Master,

> carest thou not that we perish? And he arose, and rebuked the wind, and said unto the sea, Peace, be still.
>
> And the wind ceased, and there was a great calm. And he said unto them, Why are ye so fearful? how is it that ye have no faith? And they feared exceedingly, and said one to another, What manner of man is this, that even the wind and the sea obey him?

Faith or Fear

When Jesus said, "Let us go over to the other side," that meant they couldn't go under for going over.

Jesus is the most positive of men. He knew that when He told a person to do something, that person could do it. He never sent His people off on blind errands or into situations they could not handle. He never permitted a temptation that was too much for a person. He said, "Let us go over to the other side," and when He said "Let us," that meant it was not just a one-sided affair. It meant that they would do it together. So He says to us today, "Let us walk together," and that means that we cannot be defeated. As long as we are doing what He says, we can't go under for going over.

Jesus believed His own word. Though He knew the storm would strike, He took a pillow, went down into the bottom of the ship, laid His head on the pillow, wrapped himself in the broad arms of faith and love, and went to sleep. The disciples, in the midst of the storm, seemed to forget that Jesus was on board. When trouble comes our way it has such a frightening voice and ferocious power that if we are not careful, it takes our full attention and we forget the Lord Jesus Christ is in us, that His Holy Spirit indwells us, and that our Father has promised never to leave us or forsake us. When water had filled the boat, and the ship was about to be blown away, the disciples remembered, and they said, "Jesus is on board." Someone said, "where?" Another one said, "He is down there asleep!"

He knew He couldn't go under for going over. Therefore, He could sleep well. They rushed down and cried, "Master, carest thou not that we perish?"

Notice that Jesus was not angered because they awakened Him or that they accused Him of not caring. That was a human reaction.

We should always feel free to say all that is on our heart, to unburden ourselves. Some people walk around as if they are walking on eggs, so far as God is concerned. They try to phrase every little statement in such a way that they will not offend God. The truth is that God wants to deal with you as you are. In this case, they cried out in fear as I have done many times, and wondered where God was. I have questioned whether God cared about Oral Roberts, or was interested in my ministry. I have said that to him. I have found that God appreciates honesty, and for us to be the way we are.

But then Jesus really did say something to them. When they had awakened Him, He said, "Why are ye so fearful?" In other words, fear is the reverse form of faith. Both faith and fear are forms of believing. Faith is when you believe in God and that God is going to honor your faith and take care of you.

Fear is faith reversed. Fear is when you do not believe God is going to take care of you. Fear is when you are unable to believe he will honor your faith. You do believe that you are going under, not over. That is one reason you and I become afraid, because of the absence of our faith at work.

He is saying to us that we should never doubt the power of our own faith in God, that when we release our faith it knocks fear out. The cure for fear is to be constantly releasing our faith in God.

The disciples were frightened after the storm, and said one to another, "What manner of man is this that even the wind and the sea obey him?" This statement, "what manner of man is this?" is very important to us today. He was man, when He was born of Mary in Bethlehem of Judaea. But He was God when at the age of 12 in the temple at Jerusalem He answered the questions of the doctors of the law and asked them questions they could not answer. He was man asleep on the pillow when the raging storm shook the boat that evening. But He was God when He stood at the bow of the ship, raised his hand. and said, "Peace, be still," and hushed the sea to sleep.

He was man when His friend Lazarus died and He shed bitter, salty tears. But He was God when He stood before the tomb and called His dead friend forth, saying, "Lazarus, come forth."

Jesus was man when He hung on the cross, crying, "My God, my God . . . Why hast thou forsaken me?" But He was God when He said, "It is finished," and, "Father, into thy hands I commend my spirit."

He was man when they took His lifeless body down from the cross and buried it in a newly made tomb. But on the third morning He was God, when He rose from the winding sheets of the dead, came forth from the tomb, looked over the silent cities of the dead and said, "Because I live, ye shall live also."

What manner of man is this that even the wind and the sea obey him? Oh, what a Savior! How we should throw our shoulders back, lift up our eyes, and rejoice that Jesus Christ is our personal Savior. We have someone who is in control. No one has ever been in such control as Jesus Christ.

Now I would like to pray for you as you face the storms of your life, and to remind you that Jesus really meant what He said: "Why are you so afraid? Don't you know that you have faith for this storm?" So as I pray for you today, I agree that you have faith, that you have faith to overcome the fear or the circumstance — the storm, this thing that is coming against you. Will you agree with me now in prayer as we pray together?

> *Father, through Jesus Christ who stilled the tempest, who rebuked the wind and said unto the sea, "Peace, be still" — In the name of Jesus of Nazareth, I lift up my voice and my heart and I pray, Storm, you cease. You lie down. You leave the life of my friend and partner. Go in the name of Jesus.*

And now, dear friend, I uphold you in the power of prayer. I reach out to you with all the faith of my heart, the full force of it, and I believe God with you. I expect miracles to happen to you. I expect miracles to begin very, very soon and to be completed until you too will say, What manner of Savior do I have — Jesus Christ — that He commands the storms of my life to obey Him, and they do obey Him? And I receive this answer, this victory with you today.

Mark 5:1-20

And they came over unto the other side of the sea, into the country of the Gadarenes. And when he was come out of the ship, immediately there met him out of the tombs a man with an unclean spirit, who had his dwelling among the tombs; and no man could bind him, no, not with chains: because that he had been often bound with fetters and chains, and the chains had been plucked asunder by him, and the fetters broken in pieces: neither could any man tame him.

And always, night and day, he was in the mountains, and in the tombs, crying, and cutting himself with stones. But when he saw Jesus afar off, he ran and worshipped him, and cried with a loud voice, and said, What have I to do with thee, Jesus, thou Son of the most high God? I adjure thee by God, that thou torment me not.

For He said unto him, Come out of the man, thou unclean spirit. And he asked him, What is thy name? And he answered, saying, My name is Legion; for we are many. And he besought him much that he would not send them away out of the country.

Now there was there nigh unto the mountains a great herd of swine feeding. And all the devils besought him, saying, Send us into the swine, that we may enter into them. And forthwith Jesus gave them leave. And the unclean spirits went out, and entered into the swine: and the herd ran violently down a steep place into the sea, (they were about two thousand;) and were choked in the sea.

And they that fed the swine fled, and told it in the city, and in the country. And they went out to see what it was that was done. And they come to Jesus, and see him that was possessed with the devil, and had the legion, sitting, and clothed, and in his right mind: and they were afraid.

And they that saw it told them how it befell to him that was possessed with the devil, and also concerning the swine. And they began to pray him to depart out of their coasts. And when he was come into the ship, he that had been possessed with the devil prayed him that he might be with him.

Howbeit Jesus suffered him not, but saith unto him, Go home to thy friends, and tell them how great things the Lord hath done for thee, and hath had compassion on thee. And he departed, and began to publish in Decapolis how great things Jesus had done for him: and all men did marvel.

Demon Possession is Real

In those days those people who were insane or those that were demon-possessed often lived in caves. In that particular mountainous and rocky area near the Sea of Galilee called the Gadarenes, nature had cut caves in the hillsides. The Gadarene demoniac lived among the caves, inhabited by an almost uncountable number of demons. Demons take up very little space, but they do seek human habitation. It is through man, by possessing him, that they can strike back at God. They are not against man so much as they are against God.

The battle over man is between God and the devil with his demons. The Gadarene known as Legion was possessed with so many demons that those in authority kept him in chains, except when he would break them. He lived out among the caves and graveyards. There he would take sharp stones and cut his own flesh and nobody could tame him.

The untameable people of this earth are usually possessed by demons — not new demons but the same old demons that have been in other people in the different generations of the past, the same demons that Jesus and His disciples dealt with 2,000 years ago. The important thing is that when the people of the area heard that Jesus had delivered Legion, they all came out to see. What did they see? They saw Legion sitting and clothed, and in his right mind. He had been naked. The first thing he did was to put on clothes. Afterward, He came and sat down in the presence of Jesus, perfectly whole.

The people were afraid. They had feared Legion, and barred him from their town. Then they became more afraid of the delivering power of Christ than they had been of the demon's power. What a strange world we live in. People are more frightened of the presence of Christ to convert and change a human being, to heal sickness, to cast out devils — they are more frightened of that than they are of an unconverted world. They fear the healing power of Jesus more than human beings who do terrible things to one another.

But Jesus said a very wonderful thing to this Gadarene. This person had wanted to go with Him, but the Lord said, No, you go home to your family and friends. You tell them what a great thing the Lord has done. He has had compassion on you, called the demons out, put you in your right mind, and you are a whole man again.

Mark 5:21-43

> And when Jesus was passed over again by ship unto the other side, much people gathered unto him: and he was nigh unto the sea. And behold, there cometh one of the rulers of the synagogue, Jairus by name; and when he saw him, he fell at his feet, and besought him greatly, saying, My little daughter lieth at the point of death: I pray thee, come and lay thy hands on her, that she may be healed; and she shall live. And Jesus went with him; and much people followed him, and thronged him.
>
> And a certain woman, which had an issue of blood twelve years, and had suffered many things of many physicians, and had spent all that she had, and was nothing bettered, but rather grew worse, when she had heard of Jesus, came in the press behind, and touched his garment. For she said, if I may touch but his clothes, I shall be whole. And straightway the fountain of her blood was dried up; and she felt in her body that she was healed of that plague.
>
> And Jesus, immediately knowing in himself that virtue had gone out of him, turned him about in the press, and said, Who touched my clothes?
>
> And his disciples said unto him, thou seest the multitude thronging thee, and sayest thou, Who touched me? And he looked round about to see her that had done this thing. But the woman fearing and trembling, knowing what was done in her, came and fell down before him, and told him all the truth.
>
> And He said unto her, Daughter, thy faith hath made thee whole; go in peace, and be whole of thy plague.
>
> While he yet spake, there came from the ruler of the synagogue's house certain which said, Thy daughter is dead: why troublest thou the Master any further? As soon as Jesus heard the word that was spoken, he saith unto the ruler of the synagogue, Be not afraid, only believe.
>
> And He suffered no man to follow him, save Peter, and James, and John the brother of James. And he cometh to the house of the ruler of the synagogue, and seeth the tumult, and them that wept and wailed greatly.
>
> And when he was come in, he saith unto them, Why make ye this

ado, and weep? The damsel is not dead, but sleepeth.

And they laughed him to scorn. But when he had put them all out, he taketh the father and the mother of the damsel, and them that were with him, and entereth in where the damsel was lying. And he took the damsel by the hand, and said unto her, Talitha cumi; which is, being interpreted, Damsel, I say unto thee, arise. And straightway the damsel arose, and walked; for she was of the age of twelve years. And they were astonished with a great astonishment. And he charged them straitly that no man should know it; and commanded that something should be given her to eat.

There are two marvelous healings, including the raising of the dead, and I want to comment upon them separately.

First, Jairus, the ruler of a synagogue, had a little girl who was very ill. Although it was unpopular for religious leaders to come into contact with Jesus, the illness of the man's daughter was so severe that he went to Jesus. There is something wonderful about Jesus concerning sickness or any other thing that hurts us. When we have a need, it is almost divinely built within us to think of God. That is one of the reasons why Jesus healed. People could relate to His healing power because everybody is sick in some way. The man told Him that his little daughter was near death and if He would come, his little daughter would live. He made his point of contact with Christ before the child died. He said, "If you will come and lay your hands on her, she will be healed, and live." Jesus said, "I will do it."

While they were on their way, someone came from the ruler's house and said, "Trouble Jesus no more; your little girl just died."

Oh, how cruel! And how badly they misunderstood Jesus. Instantly He said to the ruler, "Do not be afraid . . . only believe." The original meaning of "only believe" is, only believe and keep on believing. People say, "Oh, God is so great and so busy with the affairs of His universe, I do not want to bother Him. He cannot be bothered by me and the little concerns I have." Nobody is little in God's sight. Everybody is created in God's image. Everybody is a somebody.

Even as Jesus was going to heal the child, a woman who suffered from bloody hemorrhages made her way through the crowd. She could not be cured by the medicine of that day, but when she heard of Jesus, she believed on Him in her heart. But merely believing was not enough, as it is not enough today. If we believe with our heart and confess with our mouth, then God will do things in our lives. She did believe in her heart, but she also came saying, "If I can only touch his clothes, I shall be whole." Doubtless she was saying it over and over. Because of the hemorrhaging she was declared to be unclean. And therefore, people would not touch her, because if they touched a so-called "unclean" person, they had to go wash themselves and they could not touch anybody else for an entire day. So people in the great multitude were letting her through, and she finally came into the presence of Jesus. In her heart she is saying, "If I can touch Him, if I can touch Him, if I can touch Him." Her heart and her mouth were in agreement. Her spirit and her words were in faith. She reached out her trembling hand and touched the hem of Jesus' garment and immediately she felt in her body that the hemorrhages had stopped and that she was healed. She felt it.

Jesus felt something, too. He felt in His body that power had gone out of Him, and He asked, "Who touched me?" He knew the difference between people just brushing up against him and someone touching Him in faith. This is a different touch. It is the touch of faith in the living God. Someone says, "Oh, if I had lived back there, then." Yet, Jesus is alive today. He is closer to us than he was to that woman because He lives inside us. He lives in His people. We can touch Him.

It was not the touching of the clothes; that was merely a point of contact to help her release her faith. A point of contact is something you do physically. When you do it, you release your faith, just as you do when you flip on the light switch that is hooked up to the light company. When you flip that switch, it becomes the point of contact with electrical power and the light comes on. So when she touched His clothes with her hand, that was her point of contact to release her faith. For in touching His clothes, her faith was touching Him. And we can do it today. We are doing it today as we are releasing our faith. We are touching our Lord Jesus Christ and He is saying to us, "Your faith is making you whole."

Meanwhile, Jesus went on to Jairus' home and found that the little sick daughter had indeed died. When He went in with His disciples and with the parents, He saw a group of people who were professional mourners. They were hired people, professional mourners who could dry their tears in a moment and start laughing because they did not really care. They laughed Jesus to scorn. Often we read about religious people who do not have a caring heart. Jesus was never hard on sinners, only on religious pretenders, people who were religious outwardly, but really did not have inner salvation.

When they laughed Him to scorn, He put them all out. Jesus is strong and dynamic. He said, "Get out! Get out!" Then, surrounding himself with believers, He took the little girl by the hand and said in colloquial terms, "Little girl, it's time for you to get up." That is the real meaning of it. It's time for you to get up. Thank God that there is a time for each of us to be healed. When Jesus said, "Little girl, it is time for you to get up," she opened her eyes, got out of bed, and began walking around. Jesus said, "Give her something to eat." And the people were astonished.

Oh, let us recapture the astonishment of our heart about our Lord Jesus Christ. Let us again feel the thrill of the glory of our Lord. Let us never take a healing in a mundane way or think of it as something unimportant. Let us whet our appetite for the glory of the Lord to shine again upon our lives in our time. Let us believe as we never have before that our Christ is a healing Redeemer.

Mark 6:1-6

> And he went out from thence, and came into his own country; and his disciples follow him. And when the sabbath day was come, he began to teach in the synagogue: and many hearing him were astonished, saying, From whence hath this man these things? and what wisdom is this which is given unto him, that even such mighty works are wrought by his hands? Is not this the carpenter, the son of Mary, the brother of James, and Joses, and of Juda, and Simon? and are not his sisters here with us? And they were offended at him.
>
> But Jesus said unto them, a prophet is not without honour, but in his own country, and among his own kin, and in his own house.
>
> And he could there do no mighty work, save that he laid his hands upon a few sick folk, and healed them. And he marvelled because of their unbelief.

Seek God's Work

And he marvelled because of their unbelief. Jesus was always looking for faith. He was looking for people to believe. He marvelled because despite witnessing that each time people accepted His divine wisdom, he could do mighty works, they still did not believe for themselves. He marvelled. He was astonished. He was disappointed.

The message to you and to me is that we should always be sensitive. No matter who comes our way, if the power of God is working in their lives and God's wisdom is manifested in and through them, we should be open. Whether that person is a member of our own family or from our own town, or some other place, we should be trusting God, our source, and be always willing to receive the gospel.

Mark 6:6-13

> And he marvelled because of their unbelief. And he went round about the villages, teaching. And he called unto him the twelve, and began to send them forth by two and two; and gave them power over unclean spirits; and commanded them that they should take nothing for their

journey, save a staff only; no scrip, no bread, no money in their purse: But be shod with sandals; and not put on two coats. And he said unto them, In what place soever ye enter into an house, there abide till ye depart from that place. And whosoever shall not receive you, nor hear you, when ye depart thence, shake off the dust under your feet for a testimony against them. Verily I say unto you, It shall be more tolerable for Sodom and Gomorrah in the day of judgment, than for that city.

And they went out, and preached that men should repent. And they cast out many devils, and anointed with oil many that were sick, and healed them.

Repentance the Key

Their preaching began with repentance. Every one of us must repent, have a change of mind, a change of spirit, turn completely around. We must reverse directions and attitudes and believe on the Lord. When people repented, the way was provided for the disciples to begin casting out devils. They anointed with oil many who were sick and they were healed.

This is the first time the anointing oil is mentioned. Anointing oil is a form of the Holy Spirit. It means when we anoint with oil, which is simple olive oil, we are not depending on ourselves but upon the Holy Spirit through the name of Jesus, that the sick may be healed.

Mark 6:14-29

And king Herod heard of him; (for his name was spread abroad:), and he said, That John the Baptist was risen from the dead, and therefore mighty works do shew forth themselves in him.

Others said, That it is Elias. And others said, That it is a prophet, or as one of the prophets. But when Herod heard thereof, he said, It is John, whom I beheaded: he is risen from the dead.

For Herod himself had sent forth and laid hold upon John, and bound him in prison for Herodias' sake, his brother Philip's wife: for he had married her. For John had said unto Herod, It is not lawful for thee to have thy brother's wife. Therefore Herodias had a quarrel against him, and would have killed him; but she could not: for Herod feared John, knowing that he was a just man and an holy, and observed him; and when he heard him, he did many things, and heard him gladly.

And when a convenient day was come, that Herod on his birthday made a supper to his lords, high captains, and chief estates of Galilee; and when the daughter of the said Herodias came in, and danced, and pleased Herod and them that sat with him, the king said unto the damsel, Ask of me whatsoever thou wilt and I will give it thee. And he sware unto her, Whatsoever thou shalt ask of me, I will give it thee, unto the half of my kingdom. And she went forth, and said unto her mother, What shall I ask? And she said, The head of John the Baptist. And she came in straightway with haste unto the king, and asked, saying, I will that thou give me by and by in a charger the head of John the Baptist. And the king was exceeding sorry; yet for his oath's sake, and for their sakes which sat with him, he would not reject her.

And immediately the king sent an executioner, and commanded his head to be brought; and he went and beheaded him in the prison, and brought his head in a charger, and gave it to the damsel: and the damsel gave it to her mother. And when his disciples heard of it, they came and took up his corpse, and laid it in a tomb.

John a Martyr

Although I have commented upon this scene in Matthew's gospel, I would like to add these words. Herodias, who had been married to Philip, the brother of Herod, was now married to Herod. When her daughter danced before Herod, it was so sensually pleasing to the lusts of Herod that he gave in to those lusts and offered to give her up to half of his kingdom. Earlier, the mother had tried to kill John the Baptist because of his scriptural disapproval of the way she had lived. Also, the mother had previously told the daughter that this might happen and therefore, to ask the king for John's head. This was a grisly scene. They actually brought in his head, severed from his body. The king was very sorry. He had seen the works of God. John's preaching had touched his heart. But he had hardened himself. When individuals harden themselves against God, all restraints seem to be removed from them and they can do anything — kill people, mutilate people, ruin their reputations, say any evil thing they want to say, and act like the devil himself. This is an unforgettable scene. The forerunner of our Lord Jesus Christ, after having done his magnificent work, is put to death. I fear today that many Christians do not realize this depth of dedication to God. It may be that some of us, after we have completed our work, or in the midst of doing it, may be cut down. But the death of John the Baptist was not in vain. Nothing is in vain that is done for God.

Mark 6:30-32

And the apostles gathered themselves together unto Jesus, and told him all things, both what they had done, and what they had taught. And he said unto them, Come ye yourselves apart into a desert place, and rest a while: for there were many coming and going, and they had no leisure so much as to eat. And they departed into a desert place by ship privately.

Rest From Labors

After these disciples had gone out to preach, to cast out devils and bring healing to the sick, they returned to describe it all to Jesus. He said to them, You need to rest. Let us go apart in the desert and get away from the people so that we can be together privately. Many people have no understanding of what it means to preach the gospel, to cast out demons, to heal the sick, and the toll it takes upon one's life.

Remember that when the woman with the issue of blood came to Christ and touched the hem of His garment, He felt the power of God come out of Him. Every time Jesus gave of himself, something went out of Him. And for that reason, from time to time, He went to desert places and other places to rest.

Now, He recommends this to His disciples then and now. We need to take care of these precious bodies of ours which are indwelt by the Holy Spirit, and through which God works his mighty miracles among the people.

Mark 6:33-40

And the people saw them departing, and many knew him, and ran afoot thither out of all cities, and outwent them, and came together unto him. And Jesus, when he came out, saw much people, and was moved with compassion toward them, because they were as sheep not having a shepherd: and he began to teach them many things. And when the day was now far spent, his disciples came unto him, and said, This is a desert place, and now the time is far passed.

Send them away, that they may go into the country round about, and into the villages, and buy themselves bread: for they have nothing to eat. He answered and said unto them, Give ye them to eat. And they say unto him, Shall we go and buy two hundred pennyworth of bread, and give them to eat?

He saith unto them, How many loaves have ye? go and see.

And when they knew, they say, Five, and two fishes. And he commanded them to make all sit down by companies upon the green grass. And they sat down in ranks, by hundreds, and by fifties.

Order Needed

Do you see the organizational genius of our Lord Jesus Christ? He was in control of the situation. He knew exactly what to do. He organized the people. He placed them in ranks by hundreds and by fifties so they might be served more easily through the miracle He was going to do by multiplying the loaves and the fishes.

It is very important to you and me to know that we must have organization. So many times we criticize institutions, but we must have institutions, institutions of order and orderliness. However, when an institution gets out of touch with God, that is another thing. But we must always have order so people can be organized in a way that the work of God can go forth more perfectly.

Mark 6:41-49

> And when he had taken the five loaves and the two fishes, he looked up to heaven, and blessed, and brake the loaves and gave them to his disciples to set before them; and the two fishes divided he among them all.
>
> And they did all eat, and were filled. And they took up twelve baskets full of the fragments, and of the fishes. And they that did eat of the loaves were about five thousand men. And straightway he constrained his disciples to get into the ship, and to go to the other side before unto Bethsaida, while he sent away the people. And when he had sent them away, he departed into a mountain to pray.
>
> And when even was come, the ship was in the midst of the sea, and he alone on the land. And he saw them toiling in rowing; for the wind was contrary unto them: and about the fourth watch of the night he cometh unto them, walking upon the sea, and would have passed by them. But when they saw him walking upon the sea, they supposed it had been a spirit, and cried out.

You would have done the same thing if you had looked out from your boat upon the water and seen someone walking on top of it and walking faster than your boat was going!

Mark 6:50-52

> For they all saw him, and were troubled. And immediately he talked with them, and saith unto them, Be of good cheer: it is I; be not afraid.
>
> And he went up unto them into the ship; and the wind ceased: and they were sore amazed in themselves beyond measure, and wondered. For they considered not the miracle of the loaves: for their heart was hardened.

Master of All

In Matthew's gospel I commented at length upon this dramatic scene. I would like to add that the disciples were amazed beyond measure, for their heart hardened. They did not discern in their spirit what Christ was doing, that He was subduing the waves, revealing to them that Jesus Christ has all power in heaven and earth given unto Him and that He was their Master, and the Master of nature, that He was the Son of God in reality. Somehow they had not grasped the full meaning of His person.

Mark 6:53-56

> And when they had passed over, they came into the land of Gennesaret, and drew to the shore. And when they were come out of the ship, straightway they knew him, and ran through that whole region round about, and began to carry about in beds those that were sick, where they heard he was. And whithersoever he entered, into villages, or cities, or country, they laid the sick in the streets, and besought him that they might touch if it were but the border of his garment: and as many as touched him were made whole.

Touch Him with Faith

Jesus Christ had almost indescribable compassion. It was like a magnetic force pulling at people. Wherever they learned He was, they immediately began to gather up their sick and their deep needs and bring them to Jesus. Those people even desired to touch His clothes. While they touched His clothes with their finger tips, they touched Him with their faith. Now, that is very important to you and me today. We do not have His clothes to touch, but we do not need His clothes, because we can touch Him with our faith. It is our faith that does the job.

Mark 7:1-6

> Then came together unto him the Pharisees, and certain of the scribes, which came from Jerusalem. And when they saw some of his disciples eat bread with defiled, that is to say, with unwashen, hands, they found fault. For the Pharisees, and all the Jews, except they wash their hands oft, eat not, holding the tradition of the elders. And when they come from the market, except they wash, they eat not. And many other things there be, which they have received to hold, as the washing of cups, and pots, brasen vessels, and of tables.
>
> Then the Pharisees and scribes asked him, Why walk not thy disciples according to the tradition of the elders, but eat bread with unwashen hands?
>
> He answered and said unto them, Well hath Esaias prophesied of you

hypocrites, as it is written, This people honoureth me with their lips, but their heart is far from me.

Be "Little Christs"

Jesus is referring to Isaiah the 29th chapter, where the prophet foresaw the hypocrisy of the Jewish elders who would develop a doctrine that they would raise above the teaching of the Word of God. He saw that the people would respect and believe these traditions more than they would the word that God had written through His prophets of old. Now, it is amazing to me today how we are so divided in our denominations. One group will take a certain truth from the Bible and sometimes add to it, and if people refuse to go their way, they indicate or infer, at least, that these people will never make it. Now, all of this is just . . . human, with people Adding to what the Word of God teaches. Jesus condemns this. He wants us to take His pure word and to live by it through our spirit, not by Adding a variety of things that have been told through the generations until they become greater than the Word of God.

Let us leave this complexity of things and become simple . . . and see Jesus. That is what it is all about. If we are going to be Christians, we have to look to Christ. The word Christian itself means "little Christ" and we believers, as "little Christ," following in the footsteps of our Lord, can only do that when we see Jesus. Therefore, we who are in the ministry, who are preaching the gospel, must center everything we say and do on the Lord Jesus Christ, not on our denomination, though we appreciate and love our denomination. But we are to concentrate on Jesus Christ so that the people can be glad when they see Jesus in and through us.

Mark 7:7-13

Howbeit in vain do they worship me, teaching for doctrines the commandments of men. For laying aside the commandment of God, ye hold the tradition of men, as the washing of pots and cups: and many other such like things ye do.

And he said unto them, Full well ye reject the commandment of God, that ye may keep your own tradition. For Moses said, Honour thy father and thy mother; and, Whoso curseth father or mother, let him die the death. But ye say, If a man shall say to his father or mother, it is Corban, that is to say, a gift, by whatsoever thou mightest be profited by me; he shall be free. And ye suffer him no more to do ought for his father or his mother; making the word of God of none effect through your tradition, which ye have delivered: and many such like things do ye.

Word Over Tradition

Jesus was referring to those people who, when they got tired of supporting their parents, would make gifts, so-called gifts to God, and that supposedly released them from taking care of their parents even though it violated the commandment, "Honor thy father and thy mother." They did this because of tradition. How silly it is to believe every tradition that comes along in our churches, when we ought to be sticking close to the word of God.

Mark 7:14-30

And when he had called all the people unto him, he said unto them, hearken unto me every one of you, and understand:

There is nothing from without a man, that entering into him can defile him: but the things which come out of him, those are they that defile the man. If any man have ears to hear, let him hear.

And when he was entered into the house from the people, his disciples asked him concerning the parable. And he saith unto them, Are ye so without understanding also? Do ye not perceive, that whatsoever thing from without entereth into the man, it cannot defile him; because it entereth not into his heart, but into the belly, and goeth out into the draught, purging all meats?

And he said, That which cometh out of the man, That defileth the man. For from within, out of the heart of men, proceed evil thoughts, adulteries, fornications, murders, thefts, covetousness, wickedness, deceit, lasciviousness, an evil eye, blasphemy, pride, foolishness: All these evil things come from within, and defile the man.

And from thence he arose, and went into the borders of Tyre and Sidon, and entered into an house, and would have no man know it: but he could not be hid. For a certain woman, whose young daughter had an unclean spirit, heard of him, and came and fell at his feet: The woman was a Greek, a Syrophenician by nation; and she besought him that he would cast forth the devil out of her daughter.

But Jesus said unto her, Let the children first be filled: for it is not meet to take the children's bread, and to cast it unto the dogs. And she answered and said unto him, Yes, Lord yet the dogs under the table eat of the children's crumbs.

And he said unto her, For this saying go thy way; the devil is gone out of thy daughter.

And when she was come to her house, she found the devil gone out, and her daughter laid upon the bed.

Healing Requires Faith

The healing of the Syrophenician woman's child is of significance to you and me today for two reasons. First, faith is where you find it. Second, this woman, being a Gentile with such a desire to receive Jesus Christ and His healing power, was a preview of all those Gentiles who would be eagerly awaiting the opportunity to believe in Jesus when Peter and Paul and others were come after Jesus' ascension.

Jesus appeared to be unmoved when she came and asked Him to heal her little daughter. Jesus said something that seemed strange. He said, "Let the children first be filled, for it is not meet to take the children's bread and give it to dogs." He was referring to the Jewish people, that He had come to the lost sheep of the house of Israel. He also was referring to a custom of the Jews to call the Gentiles dogs. Dogs did not have the endearment to people then as they have in our time; then they were vicious, untamed, untrained, and unwanted. The only exception was a pet or a lap dog. This woman was so quick to notice that Jesus would not heal the child on the basis that she was not Jewish, and said, "It is not proper to take the children's bread and to give it to dogs."

Her faith refused to be denied. First, she understood that Jesus said healing belongs to the children of God. Second, when He said "dog," she immediately thought of a pet dog that would accept pieces of food cast under the table to it. She said, "Yea, Lord, even the dogs under the table eat of the children's bread, the crumbs." She was saying, "Lord, if the Jewish people would give the crumbs of the children's bread even to a pet dog, can't I qualify although I am a Gentile? Will you let me in? If I can't have a loaf, would you give me a crumb?" And He said unto her, "For this saying go thy way; the devil is gone out of thy daughter." And the little child was healed. What is the lesson? The lesson is what she believed in her heart. She accepted the fact that she had lived her life among Gentiles, but she also discerned the very nature of God. He would not even turn away a little hungry dog. Therefore, He would not turn her needy child away from deliverance. For that saying, Jesus delivered her daughter from demon possession.

When I began this ministry in 1947, many people did not believe that healing was for everybody. I was fought right and left when I said that God wants to heal everybody. People rose up and said, "Yes, in certain instances God will heal; with certain qualifications they can be healed. But outside of that, people are not generally accepted by the Lord to be healed." But I came against that with all the power of the Word of God. This is one of the scriptures I used, that healing is the children's bread. It belongs to those who will have faith.

Mark 7:31-37

And again, departing from the coasts of Tyre and Sidon, he came unto the Sea of Galilee, through the midst of the coasts of Decapolis. And they bring unto him one that was deaf, and had an impediment in his speech; and they beseech him to put his hand upon him. And he took him aside from the multitude, and put his fingers into his ears, and he spit, and touched his tongue; and looking up to heaven, he sighed, and saith unto him, Ephphatha, that is, Be opened.

And straightway his ears were opened, and the string of his tongue was loosed, and he spake plain. And he charged them that they should tell no man: but the more he charged them, so much the more a great deal they published it; and were beyond measure astonished, saying, He hath done all things well: he maketh both the deaf to hear, and the dumb to speak.

Point of Contact

When Jesus came to heal this man who was deaf and had an impediment in his speech, He did something beyond the ordinary. He put His fingers in His ears; then, He spit, and touched the man's tongue with it. I am referring to this because there are times in my own healing ministry that as I write to people who have written to me, I will ask them to do certain things as a point of contact to help them release their faith.

Point of contact is something that Jesus used and recommended to His followers, and it is something you do. When you do it, you release your faith; it sets the time. For example, if I said, "I will meet you" and you said, "Where?" and I said, "Oh, anywhere," we would never meet. If I said, "I will meet you" and you said, "where?" and I said, "At the post office downtown," and you said, "When?" and I said, "at 12 noon," then you would know to be at the post office downtown at 12 noon. That would be a point of contact to release you into action so you would do something to see to it that you would be there and be there on time.

A point of contact is something you do. And when you do it, it is the signal to cause you to release your faith to God. The laying on of hands is a point of contact that sets the time and the way for the releasing of our faith. The speaking of the word of faith to people to be healed is a point of contact, because, when the word is spoken, that sets the time and the way for us to release our faith. The writing of a letter, and saying, "Place this letter upon your body a moment and release your faith," that is a point of contact. To take a vial of olive oil and anoint your forehead, that is a point of contact to release your faith.

You might ask, "Oral Roberts, do these points of contact work?" They work when we work them, and since 1947, at the beginning of this ministry, I have been using points of contact for the healing of people and I can honestly tell you that tens of thousands of people have been able to release their faith through these various points of contact I have been led by the Lord to use. Yes, I use these points of contact gladly, and I hope you accept them in the spirit of the Lord.

Mark 8:1-9

In those days the multitude being very great, and having nothing to eat, Jesus called his disciples unto him, and saith unto them, I have compassion on the multitude, because they have now been with me three days, and have nothing to eat: And if I send them away fasting to their own houses, they will faint by the way: for divers of them came from far.

And his disciples answered him, From whence can a man satisfy these men with bread here in the wilderness? And he asked them, How many loaves have ye? And they said, Seven. And he commanded the people to sit down on the ground: and he took the seven loaves, and gave thanks, and brake, and gave to his disciples to set before them; and they did set them before the people.

And they had a few small fishes: and he blessed, and commanded to set them also before them. So they did eat, and were filled: and they took up of the broken meat that was left seven baskets. And they that had eaten were about four thousand: and he sent them away.

Jesus Cares

This is another time, a second time, that Jesus fed the multitude. He is so interested in our material needs. So many times it seems that we spiritualize everything in the gospel, but the gospel is for the whole person. Jesus is concerned about our souls, our minds, our bodies, our finances, our emotions, our food supply, our families, our eternal life — about us. Always have this picture of Christ in your mind — He cares about me, about everything concerning my life.

Mark 8:10-12

And straightway he entered into a ship with his disciples, and came into the parts of Dalmanutha. And the Pharisees came forth, and began to question with him, seeking of him a sign from heaven, tempting him. And he sighed deeply in his spirit, and saith, Why doth this generation seek after a sign? verily I say unto you, There shall no sign be given unto this generation.

It says Jesus sighed deeply in His spirit. He said, What is wrong with these people? These unbelievers who are not ever going to believe — I am not going to give such a people a sign. That is true today. If people continue in their unbelief, they simply will not be capable of seeing a sign, even if God reveals one to them.

Mark 8:13-21

> And he left them, and entering into the ship again departed to the other side. Now the disciples had forgotten to take bread, neither had they in the ship with them more than one loaf. And he charged them, saying, Take heed, beware of the leaven of the Pharisees, and of the leaven of Herod. And they reasoned among themselves, saying, It is because we have no bread.
>
> And when Jesus knew it, he saith unto them, Why reason ye, because ye have no bread? perceive ye not yet, neither understand? have ye your heart yet hardened? Having eyes, see ye not? and having ears, hear ye not? and do ye not remember? When I brake the five loaves among five thousand, how many baskets full of fragments took ye up? They say unto him, Twelve. And when the seven among four thousand, how many baskets full of fragments took ye up? And they said, Seven. And he said unto them, How is it that ye do not understand?

Discernment in our lives is very important. We have to be sensitive in our spirit as we deal with the things of the kingdom of God. If we live merely in our intellect, that is to say, in our mind, and use only our reasoning powers instead of feeling deep from within us, through the inner man, we are going to miss what Jesus Christ is really trying to tell us. How do we develop a discerning heart? We repent of our sins, believing on the Lord Jesus as our personal Savior, being filled with the Holy Spirit so that we can pray in the Spirit, sing in the spirit, think in the Spirit, and be sensitized by the Spirit. In that way, the Spirit of God deals with our spirit, and our spirit can understand what the Holy Spirit is doing. It will not be long until we are able to understand God's ways and choose them over the ways of men.

Mark 8:22-26

> And he cometh to Bethsaida; and they bring a blind man unto him, and besought him to touch him. And he took the blind man by the hand, and led him out of the town; and when he had spit on his eyes, and put his hands upon him, he asked him if he saw ought. And he looked up, and said, I see men as trees, walking. After that he put his hands again upon his eyes, and made him look up: and he was restored, and saw every man clearly. And he sent him away to his house, saying, Neither go into the town, nor tell it to any in the town.

Getting Enough of God

Notice that Jesus took the blind man by the hand and led him out of the town. Why did He lead him out of the town? Bethsaida had come to the point that despite all the miracles that Christ had done among the people there, the mass of the people had hardened their hearts. You must understand this. God works with believing believers and despite the fact that people can see the mighty works of God, some of them can still turn off those mighty works and keep their hearts filled with disbelief. You must understand that those of us who are in the healing ministry try to live by these rules of Jesus and attempt to do our work with believing believers. We simply have no power within ourselves to heal. We must do it in the name and the power of the Lord Jesus Christ. We must work according to the eternal principles of faith.

Jesus spit on the man's eyes and put His hands upon him and asked, "Now can you see?" The man looked up and said, "Why yes, I see men, but they are like trees and they are moving around but they look like trees." This is exactly what happens when people do not get enough of God. They do not really see people, they see them like trees. Today one of the major sins is that we can look at each other and not recognize each other's humanity. Even those of us who believe need another touch of God that we may see people as God sees them. Jesus then put His hands upon the man's eyes again. He said, Now sir, this time when you look up, look up expecting to see. In other words, this man had to do something. He did, and was restored and saw every man clearly. This man got a double healing. He got a healing of his physical eyesight and a healing of his spiritual eyesight.

We can get divided within ourselves and as a result divide people into sections. As a physician, a minister, as a believer in God, each of us should look upon one another as an entire person. Each of us is spirit, mind and body, with material needs, spiritual needs, and all the kinds of needs that we have as human beings on this earth.

Mark 8:27-30

> And Jesus went out, and his disciples, into the towns of Caesarea Philippi: and by the way he asked his disciples, saying unto them, Whom do men say that I am? And they answered, John the Baptist: but some say, Elias: and others, One of the prophets.
>
> And he saith unto them, But whom say ye that I am? And Peter answereth and saith unto him, Thou art the Christ. And he charged them that they should tell no man of him.

By this time the whole atmosphere was charged and people were sharply divided over Jesus Christ. Jesus knew that temporarily it would be better for His work to be done on a quieter basis. Then there would be time for the word to be spread later.

Mark 8:31-9:10

And he began to teach them, that the Son of man must suffer many things, and be rejected of the elders, and of the chief priests, and scribes, and be killed, and after three days rise again. And he spake that saying openly. And Peter took him, and began to rebuke him. But when he had turned about and looked on his disciples, he rebuked Peter, saying, Get thee behind me, Satan: for thou savourest not the things that be of God, but the things that be of men.

And when He had called the people unto him with his disciples also, he said unto them, Whosoever will come after me, let him deny himself, and take up his cross, and follow me. For whosoever will save his life shall lose it; but whosoever shall lose his life for my sake and the gospel's, the same shall save it.

For what shall it profit a man, if he shall gain the whole world, and lose his own soul? Or what shall a man give in exchange for his soul? Whosoever therefore shall be ashamed of me and of my words in this adulterous and sinful generation; of him also shall the Son of man be ashamed, when he cometh in the glory of his Father with the holy angels. And he said unto them, Verily I say unto you, That there be some of them that stand here, which shall not taste of death, till they have seen the kingdom of God come with power.

And after six days Jesus taketh with him Peter, and James, and John, and leadeth them up into an high mountain apart by themselves: and he was transfigured before them. And his raiment became shining, exceeding white as snow, so as no fuller on earth can white them.

And there appeared unto them Elias with Moses: and they were talking with Jesus. And Peter answered and said to Jesus, Master, it is good for us to be here: and let us make three tabernacles; one for thee, and one for Moses, and one for Elias. For he wist not what to say; for they were sore afraid.

And there was a cloud that overshadowed them: and a voice came out of the cloud, Saying, This is my beloved son: hear him. And suddenly, when they had looked round about, they saw no man any more, save Jesus only with themselves.

And as they came down from the mountain, he charged them that they should tell no man what things they had seen, till the Son of man were risen from the dead. And they kept that saying with themselves, questioning one with another what the rising from the dead should mean.

Focus on Resurrection

The Sadducees, that religious sect, did not believe in the resurrection. The Pharisees, did but the people of Israel were divided over the question of the resurrection. Although God had said, "I am the God of Abraham, and the God of Isaac, and the God of Jacob," meaning that He was the God of those who had gone on before, and that the resurrection was real, and that the continuity of life would never be broken in those who believed on Him, the people had departed from that teaching. Now, Jesus is reestablishing the belief in the resurrection and the disciples are beginning to question what it meant.

Mark 9:11-18

And they asked him, saying, Why say the scribes that Elias must first come? And he answered and told them, Elias verily cometh first, and restoreth all things; and how it is written of the Son of man, that he must suffer many things, and be set at nought. But I say unto you, That Elias is indeed come, and they have done unto him whatsoever they listed, as it is written of him. And when he came to his disciples, he saw a great multitude about them, and the scribes questioning with them. And straightway all the people, when they beheld him, were greatly amazed, and running to him saluted him. And he asked the scribes, What question ye with them? And one of the multitude answered and said, Master, I have brought unto thee my son, which hath a dumb spirit; and wheresoever he taketh him, he teareth him: and he foameth, and gnasheth with his teeth, and pineth away: And I spake to thy disciples that they should cast him out; and they could not.

Healing Commanded

And they could not. Just think of what is going on in the Christian Church today. What of the sick, the afflicted? When will preachers assume the mantle of the healing power of Jesus Christ for the suffering today? We men of God — pastors, evangelists, teachers, prophets, apostles — are under direct command of our Lord Jesus Christ to minister unto the sick. I believe the time is coming when there will be multiplied thousands upon thousands of preachers who will really start believing the Bible, following Jesus as He really is, letting the compassion roll up out of their heart and reach forth to minister God's healing power to the sick.

Mark 9:19-23

He answereth him, and saith, O faithless generation, how long shall I be with you? how long shall I suffer you? bring him unto me. And they brought him unto him: and when he saw him, straightway the spirit tare him; and he fell on the ground, and wallowed foaming. And he asked his father, How long is it ago since this came unto him? And he said, Of a child. And ofttimes it hath cast him into the fire, and into the waters, to destroy him: but if thou canst do any thing, have compassion on us, and help us. Jesus said unto him, If thou canst believe, all things are possible to him that believeth.

Willingness to Believe

The man said to Christ, "If thou canst." Jesus turned and said, "If thou canst." The implication is that there is a question about God's ability. The implication Christ gave is about man's willingness to believe. The man said, "Lord, if thou canst do anything." And Jesus said, "Sir, the question is not, can I do anything? The question is, can you believe? If you can, all things are possible to him that believeth."

Mark 9:24

And straightway the father of the child cried out, and said with tears, Lord, I believe; help thou mine unbelief.

Stimulate Faith

The man was so completely honest. He stood there hearing Christ say to him, "If you can believe, all things are possible, even the deliverance of your child." And the man, recognizing he was not really believing, began to cry, the tears rolling down his cheeks, and saying, "Lord, Lord."

So many times, people will come up to me and others in the healing ministry and say, "Can you help my child? Can you bring healing to my mother? Can you do this?" as if we have such great power in ourselves. We have to say to them, "no, we cannot." But there is a way: stimulating faith by preaching the Word of God. My faith does not work except on the Word of God and neither will yours. I know that there must be preaching, teaching, and healing in order for the people to be set free.

Mark 9:25-28

When Jesus saw that the people came running together, he rebuked the foul spirit, saying unto him, Thou dumb and deaf spirit, I charge thee, come out of him, and enter no more into him. And the spirit cried, and rent him sore, and came out of him: and he was as one dead: insomuch that many said, He is dead.

But Jesus took him by the hand, and lifted him up; and he arose. And when he was come into the house, his disciples asked him privately, Why could not we cast him out?

Seek Christ's Teaching

In this dramatic scene, the disciples were not able to cast out a demonic spirit. The point is that they were honest. They wanted to, but recognized they could not. They wanted to know why they had not been able to and how they could in the future.

Instead of being critical of all the healing power going on in the world today, we should all want to know more about how to do God's healing work. If we cannot do it, we should admit it. We should not stop with the admission of failure, but go to Christ and sincerely, faithfully ask Him to teach us. As we read and study the Word of God, we will learn.

Mark 9:29

And he said unto them, This kind can come forth by nothing, but by prayer and fasting.

Use Fasting Time

Jesus is not saying that prayer did the healing, or fasting did the healing, but He said, through prayer and fasting.

When we develop a prayerful spirit and fast from time to time, giving up a meal or two or three, we must use that time for prayer and meditation, for searching our hearts and for finding ways and means to release our faith. For then, we are prepared through the name of Jesus to accost the forces of Satan and to call them forth from the people.

Mark 9:30-32

And they departed thence, and passed through Galilee; and he would not that any man should know it. For he taught his disciples, and said unto them, The Son of man is delivered into the hands of men, and they shall kill him; and after that he is killed, he shall rise the third day. But they understood not that saying, and were afraid to ask him.

Don't Fear Resurrection

Many people today are afraid to talk about the resurrection. First, they do not want to think about death, which is an appointment. God said, "It is appointed unto man once to die and after this the judgment." We are going to put off this physical body and enter into a new life in the world to come. The second coming of Christ, is when He shall raise our bodies from the dead and we shall again become one — but we will be immortal and eternally whole. We should be very willing to talk about the resurrection, to ask questions, and to be certain in our own hearts of our own resurrection from the dead.

Mark 9:33-37

> And he came to Capernaum: and being in the house he asked them, What was it that ye disputed among yourselves by the way? But they held their peace: for by the way they had disputed among themselves, who should be the greatest.
>
> And he sat down, and called the twelve, and saith unto them, If any man desire to be first, the same shall be last of all, and servant of all. And he took a child, and set him in the midst of them: and when he had taken him in his arms, he said unto them, Whosoever shall receive one of such children in my name, receiveth me: and whosoever shall receive me, receiveth not me, but him that sent me.

"Number One"

This desire to be "number one" above all others is still among us humans today. Jesus said to be number one is to be humble like a servant and to meet the needs of people. That is what it means, to meet the needs of people. The better we serve, the more nearly God counts us as number one.

Mark 9:38-41

> And John answered him, saying, Master, we saw one casting out devils in thy name, and he followeth not us: and we forbad him, because he followeth not us. But Jesus said,
>
> Forbid him not for there is no man which shall do a miracle in my name, that can lightly speak evil of me. For he that is not against us is on our part. For whosoever shall give you a cup of water to drink in my name, because ye belong to Christ, verily I say unto you, he shall not lose his reward.

Eyes on the Harvest

Today when people are doing the work of God, many are tempted to say, "What church does he belong to? Does he belong to my denomination?" So many people, when they find you doing God's work and that you do not belong to their particular denomination, discount you and will have nothing to do with you. It is so unscriptural for people to think that their denomination is the only one. The Church is the Church militant. The Church is all the people who are born again, following Christ, and loving one another. God looks down and doesn't see all these denominational differences, He sees those of us who are truly loving Him.

On one of my trips to Europe, I was flying over Scotland and looked down and saw all the small farms that had rock fences around them. Each farm was separated from the other. On another trip I looked down and saw that the harvest time was on, and the crops had grown up and covered the rock walls. It looked like one vast productive farm. My heart leaped within me, and I thought, "That is the way it is. When we are not productive for Christ, there are walls among us, separating us. But when we are productive for the Lord, His work just spills over in our hearts and we have all the love we need for one another." All we have to do then is to reap the harvest, for people are ready to receive the gospel. When they see our love, then many are going to want our Lord Jesus Christ.

Mark 9:42-50

> And whosoever shall offend one of these little ones that believe in me, it is better for him that a millstone were hanged about his neck, and he were cast into the sea.
>
> And if thy hand offend thee, cut it off: it is better for thee to enter into life maimed, than having two hands to go into hell, into the fire that never shall be quenched; where their worm dieth not, and the fire is not quenched.
>
> And if thy foot offend thee, cut it off: it is better for thee to enter halt into life, than having two feet to be cast into hell, into the fire that never shall be quenched: where their worm dieth not, and the fire is not quenched.
>
> And if thine eye offend thee, pluck it out: it is better for thee to enter into the kingdom of God with one eye, than having two eyes to be cast into hell fire: where their worm dieth not, and the fire is not quenched.
>
> For every one shall be salted with fire, and every sacrifice shall be salted with salt. Salt is good: but if the salt have lost his saltness, wherewith will ye season it? Have salt in yourselves, and have peace one with another.

Hell is Real

Jesus Christ very definitely talks about hell and hell fire. He was saying that it is so much better not to go to hell that if any part of you offends you, remove it from your life. He was not speaking of physically mutilating your body. When He said, "Where their worm dieth not, and the fire is not quenched," He was referring to Gehenna, which is the Greek word used for hell. The Jews used the term to refer to a place just outside the walls of Jerusalem where they dumped their refuse. It was burned 24 hours a day and included the bodies of dead animals that were being eaten up with worms. Jesus used that well-known place as a reference or a descriptive phrase concerning hell fire.

When a person goes into hell, he goes against the wishes of God because hell was not made for man but for the devil and his angels. Any person going to hell goes there because he prefers the devil over God and the devil's life over the Christian life. Therefore, when he dies, he goes where the devil goes.

There are two distinguishing things about hell. One is that the inner spirit is not consumed. It is affected by the fires of hell but is never consumed. It is an everlasting experience. Another thing is that memory is never dimmed: rather, it takes one back to the life that might have been with "Why didn't I listen to God? Why didn't I respond to the movings of His Holy Spirit in my heart? Why didn't I read His Word and let it bring the faith up from my heart? Why didn't I release my faith to God? Why did I choose the devil's ways, to go my own way rather than God's way? Why did I reject the gospel?" That memory that never is dimmed is a part of hell. It is what makes hell, hell.

Jesus was giving warning. No matter who tells you there is no hell, do not believe them. Believe the Lord Jesus Christ because He knows. He says that when you leave this world you are going to heaven or you are going to hell. This is no laughing matter. Life is real, life is earnest, life is everlasting, either in hell or in heaven. If you do not know Jesus as your personal Savior, I hope you will open your heart right now and say, Jesus, come into my heart, I believe on you. Repenting of my sins I receive you as my personal Savior, to live for you forever and ever. Amen and amen.

Mark 10:1-16

And he arose from thence, and cometh into the coasts of Judaea by the farther side of Jordan: and the people resort unto him again; and, as he was wont, he taught them again.

And the Pharisees came to him, and asked him, Is it lawful for a man to put away his wife? tempting him.

And he answered and said unto them, What did Moses command you? And they said, Moses suffered to write a bill of divorcement, and to put her away. And Jesus answered and said unto them, For the hardness of your heart he wrote you this precept. But from the beginning of the creation God made them male and female. For this cause shall a man leave his father and mother, and cleave to his wife; and they twain shall be one flesh: so then they are no more twain, but one flesh. What therefore God hath joined together, let not man put asunder.

And in the house his disciples asked him again of the same matter. And he saith unto them, Whosoever shall put away his wife, and marry another, committeth adultery against her. And if a woman shall put away her husband, and be married to another, she committeth adultery.

And they brought young children to him, that he should touch them: and his disciples rebuked those that brought them. But when Jesus saw it, he was much displeased, and said unto them, Suffer the little children to come unto me, and forbid them not: for of such is the kingdom of God. Verily I say unto you, Whosoever shall not receive the kingdom of God as a little child, he shall not enter therein. And he took them up in his arms, put his hands upon them, and blessed them.

God Divided Marriage

Jesus is dealing with people under the law of Moses. At that time marriage had fallen to such a low estate that many of the Jewish girls did not even want to get married, for they feared what the hardhearted men among the Jews might do to them in marriage. The husband could simply declare that a marriage was dissolved, and it would be. Jesus was saying to them, That is not the way God created you. That is not the deal. That is not the goal that God set for the human race, and therefore you must take a new look by going all the way back to creation. In the beginning man and woman were of equal importance, and that is why the two of them became one, entering into a unity through which precious children were to be born and the family continued, providing the population of the human race to work out the plan of the almighty God.

The ordination of marriage is divine. On the one hand is God's ideal; on the other is the hardness of men's hearts that wants to separate, to divide, to cut asunder. Many marriages fall apart because of outside forces, fear relationships, other things coming in to take precedence and in effect to deny the original purpose of God, the divine ordination which is God's ideal.

Evelyn and I were joined together by God. We knew our marriage was of the Lord; therefore, we have had something to work for, to hold onto. But it was a joint effort. It wasn't merely Evelyn trying to hold the marriage together, nor was it Oral alone trying to hold the marriage together. It was Evelyn, Oral, and Jesus holding the marriage together.

The ideal of marriage is that God joins us together because from the very beginning He made us male and female. That rules out homosexuality of every type and brings together the male and the female in marriage.

The next thing that He deals with is an adulterous relationship where there is a third party. Satan comes in and the man, the woman, and Satan come together to join with some other person, a woman or a man, and adultery is committed.

Another thing He deals with is children. Now, children were not valued as highly then as they are now. These particular little children were not wanted. Jesus said, you are doing wrong by refusing little children the right to come to Me. Bring them to Me and do not forbid them, for of such is the kingdom of God. In effect, Jesus was saying, You people who are so mixed up in your marriages and so carried away with someone outside your marriage in an adulterous relationship, I tell you, start over and receive the kingdom of God as a little child. A little child is open to God, fresh out of heaven, and therefore is covered by the blood of Jesus.

He is telling such people they need a fresh start in the way they look at creation and the status of their marriage. Above all, they should realize that when they have an adulterous relationship, they are wrecking the marriage and their children's lives are in jeopardy. They either are not born or if they are born, they live in broken homes. Such parents have reduced themselves beyond the level of the innocence of a child and have in fact entered into a relationship with Satan, who rejects the kingdom of God. Jesus says little children receive the kingdom of God and they enter therein. When people are so adulterous — that is, breaking the union of one man and one woman who were united by God in marriage, going to some other woman or man for adultery — they threaten the very existence of the family that God has created. The family is God's plan. Whatever interrupts it or destroys it is not of God.

Mark 10:17

> And when he was gone forth into the way, there came one running, and kneeled to him and asked him, Good Master, what shall I do that I may inherit eternal life?

The number-one quest of man is the quest for eternal life. Instinctively we all know that this earthly life will end and there is a life beyond death. Whether we can take it in theologically or not, if we are true to our spirit, our spirit reflects our belief in a life beyond death.

Mark 10:18-22

And Jesus said unto him, Why callest thou me good? there is none good but one, that is, God. Thou knowest the commandments, Do not commit adultery, Do not kill, Do not steal, Do not bear false witness, Defraud not, Honour thy father and mother.

And he answered and said unto him, Master, all these have I observed from my youth. Then Jesus beholding him loved him, and said unto him, One thing thou lackest: go thy way, sell whatsoever thou hast, and give to the poor, and thou shalt have treasure in heaven: and come, take up the cross, and follow me.

And he was sad at that saying, and went away grieved: for he had great possessions.

Jesus Loves

One thing stands out here. When He dealt with this young ruler, and heard him out, the Bible says that Jesus loved him. Jesus loved him. That really breaks your heart and yet mends your heart at the same time. That we can come to Jesus and tell Him exactly how we feel and He still loves us.

The next thing is that He told this young man that he lacked something, but it was not something really great. It was only one thing to share what he had, to give.

Mark 10:23-25

And Jesus looked round about, and saith unto his disciples, How hardly shall they that have riches enter into the kingdom of God! And the disciples were astonished at his words. But Jesus answereth again, and saith unto them, Children, how hard is it for them that trust in riches to enter into the kingdom of God! It is easier for a camel to go through the eye of a needle, than for a rich man to enter into the kingdom of God.

"Trusting" Riches Sinful

Jesus seemed to be very hard on rich people here but He really was not. The reference to the eye of a needle is thought to refer to the holes in the side of the gates of Jerusalem, where when travelers came late in the day after the gates were closed, they could unload their camels, make them kneel, and then beat and push them through these holes called the "eye of a needle." The process sometimes took hours. It was virtually impossible, Jesus was saying. In the same way, it is nearly impossible for a rich man to enter God's kingdom, but, he can do it.

Then He added that line, "trusting" in riches. That is the key. If they trust in their riches, then that becomes their way of salvation and it leads them to destruction. But if they have riches without trusting in them, they can enter the kingdom of God. In fact, God needs people who are rich. How are the poor going to be helped? The poor cannot build factories. They cannot employ people. We need people with money who will provide employment and make things hum in this world.

Jesus certainly is not condemning riches because He had riches in heaven. He merely laid them aside temporarily to come to earth to be incarnated as man. But when He ascended back to His Father, it was to those riches. In Philippians 4:19 He said, "But my God shall supply all your need according to his riches in glory by Christ Jesus." Jesus is not striking at money. He is striking at a wrong spirit, a possessive spirit of the things of this world, rather than trusting to God and making God first in our lives so that whatever we possess becomes instrumental in our giving and receiving.

Mark 10:26-30

> And they were astonished out of measure, saying among themselves, Who then can be saved? And Jesus looking upon them saith, With men it is impossible, but not with God: for with God all things are possible.
>
> Then Peter began to say unto him, Lo, we have left all, and have followed thee.
>
> And Jesus answered and said, Verily I say unto you, There is no man that hath left house, or brethren, or sisters, or father, or mother, or wife, or children, or lands, for my sake, and the gospel's, but he shall receive an hundredfold now in this time, houses, and brethren, and sisters, and mothers, and children, and lands, with persecutions; and in the world to come eternal life.

Rewards for Today

It was easy for the disciples to become confused about what Jesus said concerning rich people and their difficulty in entering the kingdom of God. And Peter said, Lo, Lord, we have left everything and have followed thee. Then Jesus made the reference to the hundredfold return. If you have never understood before, understand this now because our Lord Jesus Christ wants to deal with you on the level where you are — whether you are rich, or not rich, or in-between. There is a tremendous message for you and me here. Jesus is saying that if you give up anything for the Lord — anything (and He specifies anything by naming houses, and lands, brothers, sisters, fathers, mothers) — and you do it for His sake and the gospel, you will receive a hundredfold now, in this time. But, if these loved ones and these things which are of enormous value come between us and the gospel, we must make a choice of whether we will continue that way or we will follow the Lord. If you make the gospel your highest priority, you are going to receive a hundredfold now, in this time.

This is something that people need to know and understand. For too long, they have heard a gospel of poverty, of giving up everything and having nothing until we die and go to heaven. Jesus is letting you and me know that when we get to heaven we will not need to receive anything, for heaven is heaven. It is everything that we are not and have not. It is the presence of God, and being in His presence is everlasting delight.

It is on this earth that we do not have everything we need. We live in this body 24 hours a day. Jesus says when we make a decision to give our best to God, then we should look to receive a hundredfold now in this life. He enumerates the things: houses, lands, loved ones, friends.

Then He adds, "with persecutions, and then, in the end, eternal life." Will you hear this? Jesus Christ is telling you that He is concerned about your life right now and for the rest of your mortal life on this earth. He is concerned about your having a hundredfold.

You are not going to be a victorious Christian if you are beaten down with the needs of this life, if you do not have enough to eat, if you cannot make your car payments or your house payments, if you are struggling through this world trying to be victorious and people all around you are looking at you as a witness of Christ, yet your faith is not working for your needs to be met.

Jesus is saying, expect to receive a hundredfold, and He even names houses and lands. If some of your loved ones have turned against you, there will be other loved ones who will take their place. If you have lost friends, there will be new friends take their place in a new relationship with you.

Then He cautions you by saying, you will have persecutions. People will not like it because you are a Christian and at the same time are receiving the hundredfold of this world. The devil claims this world. He is called the god of this world. But the Bible says that the earth is the Lord's and the fullness thereof. While the devil may claim this world civilization, he can lay no claim to God's earth nor to its fullness that includes space. In space we may have some of the greatest things we have ever known to meet our needs in the future. So Jesus is telling you and me that persecutions go hand in hand with our needs being met. When you turn that around, when our needs are met, then persecutions are going to strike us because the devil does not want us to have anything that he claims as his own. He claims every dollar, every piece of land, every house, every approval of your life by men in this world. Jesus says the devil does not have the power to stop His children who believe, who plant the seeds of faith and expect miracle harvests. The devil cannot stop that. God will break through, both naturally and supernaturally, with a hundredfold, now, in this time. God will supply our needs and with them we will have persecutions; I can testify to that. The more my needs are met, the more I am persecuted. But, when God meets my needs, I can stand the persecutions. Then, He adds, in the world to come — eternal life.

The question is, is it a "good deal" or a "bad deal" to serve the Lord? The devil says it is a bad deal. God says it is a good deal. He proves that with a hundredfold if we will receive it. Personally, I am expecting miracles. I am expecting God to meet my needs. I am expecting God to meet your needs.

Mark 10:31-45

> But many that are first shall be last; and the last first.
>
> And they were in the way going up to Jerusalem: and Jesus went before them: and they were amazed; and as they followed, they were afraid. And he took again the twelve, and began to tell them what things should happen unto him, saying, Behold, we go up to Jerusalem; and the Son of man shall be delivered unto the chief priests, and unto the scribes; and they shall condemn him to death, and shall deliver him to the Gentiles: And they shall mock him, and shall scourge him, and shall spit upon him, and shall kill him: and the third day he shall rise again.
>
> And James and John, the sons of Zebedee, come unto him, saying, Master, we would that thou shouldest do for us whatsoever we shall desire. And he said unto them, What would ye that I should do for you? They said unto him, Grant unto us that we may sit, one on thy right hand, and the other on thy left hand, in thy glory. But Jesus said unto them, Ye know not what ye ask: can ye drink of the cup that I drink of? and be baptized with the baptism that I am baptized with? And they said unto him, We can. And Jesus said unto them, Ye shall indeed drink of the cup that I drink of; and with the baptism that I am baptized withal shall ye be baptized: But to sit on my right hand and on my left hand is not mine to give: but it shall be given to them for whom it is prepared.
>
> And when the ten heard it, they began to be much displeased with James and John. But Jesus called them to him, and saith unto them, Ye

know that they which are accounted to rule over the Gentiles exercise lordship over them; and their great ones exercise authority upon them. But so shall it not be among you: but whosoever will be great among you, shall be your minister: and whosoever of you will be the chiefest, shall be servant of all. For even the Son of man came not to be ministered unto, but to minister, and to give his life a ransom for many.

Be a Blessing

The key to the 10th chapter of Mark's gospel is Verse 45: "For even the Son of man came not to be ministered unto, but to minister, and to give his life a ransom for many."

Jesus came to give, not to get. Jesus came to be a servant, not an overlord. Jesus came not to be overbearing but to be a humble, serving human being with God's nature resting in Him through the incarnation, and to be our example. When Jesus said, I have come to minister — to be a servant of all, to give My life a ransom for many, He was saying, If you want to be blessed, first be a blessing. I really believe that.

Mark 10:46-52

And they came to Jericho: and as he went out of Jericho with his disciples and a great number of people, blind Bartimaeus, the son of Timaeus, sat by the highway side begging. And when he heard that it was Jesus of Nazareth, he began to cry out, and say, Jesus, thou son of David, have mercy on me. And many charged him that he should hold his peace: but he cried the more a great deal, Thou son of David, have mercy on me.

And Jesus stood still, and commanded him to be called. And they call the blind man, saying unto him, Be of good comfort rise: he calleth thee.

And he, casting away his garment, rose, and came to Jesus. And Jesus answered and said unto him, What wilt thou that I should do unto thee? The blind man said unto him, Lord, that I might receive my sight. And Jesus said unto him, Go thy way; thy faith hath made thee whole.

And immediately he received his sight, and followed Jesus in the way.

Bartimaeus Featured

In Matthew, Chapter 20, you will remember there were two blind men in this scene, but there is only one mentioned here — Bartimaeus — because he is the more prominent of the two. Here the focus is upon Verse 50: "And he, casting away his garment, rose, and came to Jesus."

Cast Away Disbelief

He was beside the highway begging when Jesus noticed him. Of course, there is a highway side filled with millions of suffering people. But Bartimaeus was different in that he called out, recognizing that Jesus is the Lord, and he asked Him for help. When Jesus heard that cry, He told them to bring the blind man to Him. Jesus will hush every harp in heaven to hear somebody pray or to call His name.

When they told Bartimaeus that Jesus was calling for him, he did a significant thing that is applicable to you and to me in our need of healing: he cast away his beggar's robe.

There were no schools in those days for blind people, or government help for them. They were cast out along the highway sides of life to do the best they could. In order to be seen readily, they wore a special kind of garment that identified the blind. Bartimaeus had lived not only with physical blindness but had worn clothes that identified him as blind. Now, in the presence of Jesus, his faith in the Son of God has reached a point where he just took that old garment that identifies him as blind and tosses it aside, rises, and comes to Jesus. He has been preparing to get healed. He has burned every bridge behind him. He has struck a blow for deliverance. He has made up his mind that this is the Lord and that Jesus is a healer. Oh, I love that! I know some people do not like it. They do not like for us to have this audacity and boldness to come to God and in effect demand our healing, but it delights Jesus for us to do it.

When the Lord asked Bartimaeus what he wanted, he said he wanted to be healed and receive his sight. Jesus said to him, go your way, your faith has made you whole.

Jesus is telling us we have a great power within us. A faith-making power. It is our faith-making power and our faith that makes things happen. When we release that faith, we send it to God. We say to the faith in our heart, Come up, come up, go up to God, go up to God. It causes Christ's power to make us whole and to operate within us. I praise God that this scene is put in the Bible to encourage you and me in whatever form of need we have.

You may be physically blind or blind in some other way. There are many kinds of blindness: spiritual blindness, moral blindness, physical blindness, blindness to the fact that God can supply our needs, blindness to the fact that our faith can make us whole — all kinds of blindness. Jesus wants to make us whole. That includes healing whatever is wrong with us.

Finally, Bartimaeus followed Jesus in the way. You see, that is the key response. When we receive something from God, we are grateful. He is the source of our total supply. He becomes the center of our being and we follow Him.

I feel the spirit of prayer upon me because I see in this scripture the wondrous power of Jesus Christ and also the faith of this man who had been blind, who had heard Jesus say, "Thy faith hath made thee whole." Therefore I know you have faith. I have faith. I know that our faith has power with God. And let us agree together as we pray and let us pray that those things that seem to blind us, to baffle us and to hurt us, that God will just move them out of the way through the workings of our faith. Let us pray now.

Lord Jesus, I feel in my spirit that we can see You as You speak the word to this blind man and You tell him that his faith hath made him whole. I feel Your presence. And now I pray for this, my friend, my partner, my dear co-laborer in Christ. I pray that all the powers that can blind you, puzzle you, baffle you, get you down, will be cast out by our Lord Jesus, and that you are aware now that your faith is being released. Your faith is going up to God. In the name of Jesus. Amen and amen.

Mark 11:1-10

And when they came nigh to Jerusalem, unto Bethphage and Bethany, at the mount of Olives, he sendeth forth two of his disciples, and saith unto them, Go your way into the village over against you: and as soon as ye be entered into it, ye shall find a colt tied, whereon never man sat; loose him, and bring him. And if any man say unto you, Why do ye this? say ye that the Lord hath need of him; and straightway he will send him hither.

And they went their way, and found the colt tied by the door without in a place where two ways met; and they loose him. And certain of them that stood there said unto them, What do ye, loosing the colt? And they said unto them even as Jesus had commanded: and they let them go.

And they brought the colt to Jesus, and cast their garments on him; and he sat upon him. And many spread their garments in the way: and others cut down branches off the trees, and strawed them in the way.

And they that went before, and they that followed, cried, saying, Hosanna; Blessed is he that cometh in the name of the Lord. Blessed be the kingdom of our father David, that cometh in the name of the Lord: Hosanna in the highest.

Jesus Returns More

Jesus had a need, and there was someone who could supply that need. That someone in this instance was willing for Jesus to have his colt. That colt had never been ridden. I know, having grown up on a farm the first 14 years of my life, and dealing with livestock, that you do not ride an unbroken colt. First, you must break his spirit so the wildness is taken out of him, and then he can be a riding horse or a usable horse. Jesus was not only master of men and nature, He was master of His animals, and He was able to ride the unbroken colt.

This is very inspiring to me. He can change any of us. I remember at age 29, when God was dealing with me about this ministry. I felt so insignificant, obscure, and unworthy. I asked, Lord, why don't you get someone who is known, someone who has already made a reputation to take Your healing power to this generation? And in the depths of my heart He spoke, "I don't want somebody already made, I want somebody I can make, and I want to make you. I will make you like My Son Jesus, to heal the people as He did."

He could take my nature and change it. I discovered that Jesus could certainly tame my life, make me His ministering servant, mistakes and all. He could use me to reach millions of people as He is doing today.

When it was all over, Jesus sent the colt back. He sent the colt back. It was not the same. It had been mastered by Jesus. When we give something to Jesus, He does not keep it but gives it back, and it is always infinitely more. If we give Him money, the money He gives back is multiplied. If we give Him talent, that talent is made greater. If we give Him our time, our time becomes more unlimited. You cannot lose.

Mark 11:11-24

> And Jesus entered into Jerusalem, and into the temple: and when he had looked round about upon all things, and now the eventide was come, he went out unto Bethany with the twelve. And on the morrow, when they were come from Bethany, he was hungry. And seeing a fig tree afar off having leaves, he came, if happily he might find any thing thereon: and when he came to it, he found nothing but leaves; for the time of figs was not yet. And Jesus answered and said unto it, No man eat fruit of thee hereafter forever. And his disciples heard it. And they come to Jerusalem: and Jesus went into the temple, and began to cast out them that sold and bought in the temple, and overthrew the tables of the moneychangers, and the seats of them that sold doves; and would not suffer that any man should carry any vessel through the temple.
>
> And he taught, saying unto them, Is it not written, my house shall be called of all nations the house of prayer? but ye have made it a den of thieves.
>
> And the scribes and chief priests heard it, and sought how they might destroy him: for they feared him, because all the people was astonished at

his doctrine. And when even was come, he went out of the city. And in the morning, as they passed by, they saw the fig tree dried up from the roots. And Peter calling to remembrance saith unto him, Master, behold, the fig tree which thou cursedst is withered away. And Jesus answering saith unto them, Have faith in God. For verily I say unto you, that whosever shall say unto this mountain, Be thou removed, and be thou cast into the sea; and shall not doubt in his heart, but shall believe that those things which he saith shall come to pass; he shall have whatsoever he saith. Therefore I say unto you, what things soever ye desire, when ye pray, believe that ye receive them, and ye shall have them.

Faith Demands Action

When Jesus entered the outer court of the temple where the money exchangers were operating, He cleansed that area. He drove those people out and reminded them that the house of God was to be known among all nations as a house of prayer, but they had entered into thievery. They had mistreated the people, charged them too much, and so on. Oh, what power there is in a dedicated human being who comes with righteousness on his side, faith in his heart, motivated by love, and who is not afraid to face the things of the devil!

Jesus made an important point with the fig tree. Fig trees usually produce 10 months out of the year in the Holy Land. When Jesus and His disciples passed by a fig tree and wanted something to eat from it, it had only leaves. So He cursed it and said, You will never produce again. Later, when they returned, Peter noticed that the tree had dried up from its very roots.

Jesus used the incident to tell us how to use our faith, how to put our faith upon certain things in this world that we need, and how we can have them. He said have faith in God, literally, have the faith of God. God believes. The nature of God is not only love; His nature is to believe. Even when man rebelled and took all future humanity down with him into sin and death, God never ceased believing. He believes, and He believes whatever He says is going to happen. Therefore, since Jesus spoke to the fig tree and believed that what He said would happen, and it did happen, He told His disciples that when they spoke by faith against some mountain of need and had no doubt in their heart but believed that these things which they said would come to pass, they would have whatever they said. Therefore, whatever you desire when you pray, believe that you receive it and you shall have it.

Faith begins in the spirit, in the heart, where you begin to believe and not doubt. At that point, you reinforce what you believe in your heart by what you say. It is not enough to believe and hold it in your heart.

When you believe it, then you speak it and it will happen! It could happen without your being in a receptive mood to receive it, that is true. But it will happen, so you should be looking for it because you already have it in your heart. I had the healing ministry in my heart before I ever prayed for the first sick person. But in order for it to work I had to go out and speak the Word of faith from the Word of God and do something. Things have to be made to happen. Faith begins in the spirit, in the heart, where you begin to believe and
not doubt. At that point, you reinforce what you believe in your heart by what you say. It is not enough to believe and hold it in your heart. When you believe it, then you speak it and it will happen! It could happen without your being in a receptive mood to receive it, that is true. But it will happen, so you should be looking for it because you already have it in your heart. I had the healing ministry in my heart before I ever prayed for the first sick person. But in order for it to work I had to go out and speak the word of faith from the word of God and do something. Things have to be made to happen.

Mark 11:25-12:11

And when ye stand praying, forgive, if ye have ought against any: that your Father also which is in heaven may forgive you your trespasses. But if ye do not forgive, neither will your Father which is in heaven forgive your trespasses.

And they come again to Jerusalem: and as he was walking in the temple, there come to him the chief priests, and the scribes, and the elders, and say unto him, By what authority doest thou these things? and who gave thee this authority to do these things? And Jesus answered and said unto them, I will also ask of you one question, and answer me, and I will tell you by what authority I do these things.

The baptism of John, was it from heaven, or of men? answer me.

And they reasoned with themselves, saying, If we shall say, From heaven; he will say, Why then did ye not believe him? But if we shall say, Of men; they feared the people: for all men counted John, that he was a prophet indeed.

And they answered and said unto Jesus, We cannot tell. And Jesus answering saith unto them, Neither do I tell you by what authority I do these things. And he began to speak unto them by parables. A certain man planted a vineyard, and set an hedge about it, and digged a place for the wine vat, and built a tower, and let it out to husbandmen, and went into a far country. And at the season he sent to the husbandmen a servant, that he might receive from the husbandmen of the fruit of the vineyard. And they caught him, and beat him,
and sent him away empty. And again he sent unto them another servant; and at him they cast stones, and wounded him in the head, and sent

him away shamefully handled. And again he sent another; and him they killed, and many others; beating some, and killing some. Having yet therefore one son, his well-beloved, he sent him also last unto them, saying, They will reverence my son. But those husbandmen said among themselves, This is the heir; come, let us kill him, and the inheritance shall be ours. And they took him, and killed him, and cast him out of the vineyard.

What shall therefore the lord of the vineyard do? he will come and destroy the husbandmen, and will give the vineyard unto others. And have ye not read this scripture; The stone which the builders rejected is become the head of the corner: This was the Lord's doing, and it is marvellous in our eyes?

Christ the Cornerstone

Jesus is referring here to the 118th Psalm where David spoke of the stone which the builders rejected that is become the head of the corner. God is the divine and eternal architect. The builders were the children of Israel. God had set the cornerstone but they had rejected it. What was it all about? God had sent teachers, God had sent prophets, and finally He sent His only begotten Son. And each time they rejected them and finally they killed the Son. They rejected the cornerstone. Jesus was applying this to himself. And it is a great reminder to you and me that in spite of the rejection of Christ by this world, He is still the cornerstone.

Mark 12:12-27

And they sought to lay hold on him, but feared the people: for they knew that he had spoken the parable against them: and they left him, and went their way. And they send unto him certain of the Pharisees and of the Herodians, to catch him in his words. And when they were come, they say unto him, Master, we know that thou art true, and carest for no man: for thou regardest not the person of men, but teachest the way of God in truth: Is it lawful to give tribute to Caesar, or not? Shall we give, or shall we not give? But he, knowing their hypocrisy, said unto them, Why tempt ye me? bring me a penny, that I may see it.

And they brought it. And he saith unto them, Whose is this image and superscription? And they said unto him, Caesar's. And Jesus answering said unto them, Render to Caesar the things that are Caesar's, and to God the things that are God's. And they marvelled at him.

Then come unto him the Sadducees, which say there is no resurrection; and they asked him, saying, Master, Moses wrote unto us, If a man's brother die, and leave his wife behind him, and leave no children, that his brother should take his wife, and raise up seed unto his brother. Now there were seven brethren: and the first took a wife, and dying left no seed. And the second took her, and died, neither left he any seed: and the third likewise. And the seven had her, and left no seed: last of all the woman died also. In the resurrection therefore, when they shall rise, whose wife shall she be of them? for the seven had her to wife.

And Jesus answering said unto them, Do ye not therefore err, because ye know not the scriptures, neither the power of God? For when they shall rise from the dead, they neither marry, nor are given in marriage; but are as the angels which are in heaven. And as touching the dead, that they rise: have ye not read in the book of Moses, how in the bush God spake unto him, saying, I am the God of Abraham, and the God of Isaac, and the God of Jacob? He is not the God of the dead, but the God of the living; ye therefore do greatly err.

God not Mocked

The Sadducees did not believe in the resurrection, nor did they believe in angels or spirits. They believed in an historical Moses, but they did not believe all the teachings or the doctrine of Moses. The temptation that they took to Jesus with their questions concerning a woman who had been taken by seven brothers was not a sincere question. They were saying it in derision. And Jesus said, you simply do not know the Word of God. Neither do you know the power of God. Concerning the resurrection, He said, there is a continuity of life and it is shown when God spoke to Moses in the desert: "I am the God of Abraham, I am the God of Isaac, I am the God of Jacob. I am not the God of the dead." Life does not end when people die. God is a continuous God. Life is continuous, both in this world and in the world to come.

Mark 12:28-37

And one of the scribes came, and having heard them reasoning together, and perceiving that he had answered them well, asked him, Which is the first commandment of all?

And Jesus answered him, The first of all the commandments is, Hear, O Israel; the Lord our God is one Lord; and thou shalt love the Lord thy God with all thy heart, and with all thy soul, and with all thy mind, and with all thy strength: this is the first commandment. And the second is like, namely this, Thou shalt love thy neighbour as thyself. There is none other commandment greater than these. And the scribe said unto him, Well, Master, thou hast said the truth: for there is one God; and there is none other but he. And to love him with all the heart, and with all the understanding, and with all the soul, and with all the strength, and to love his neighbour as himself, is more than all whole burnt offerings and sacrifices.

And when Jesus saw that he answered discreetly, he said unto him, Thou art not far from the kingdom of God. And no man after that durst ask him any question.

And when Jesus answered and said, while he taught in the temple, How say the scribes that Christ is the son of David? For David himself said by the Holy Ghost, The Lord said to my Lord, Sit thou on my right hand, till I make thine enemies thy footstool.

David therefore himself calleth him Lord; and whence is he then his son?

This is a reference to II Samuel 23. Jesus reminded the people that David spoke by the Holy Spirit. The Holy Spirit was active in the Old Testament, but only with a certain group of people. He was not in all the people as He can be today, of every child of God. For when we believe on the Lord Jesus Christ, it is because the Holy Spirit brings Him to us and He enters us himself.

It is His spirit that bears witness with our spirit that we are the children of God. And now, starting with the last part of verse 37 . . .

Mark 12:37-44

And the common people heard him gladly. And he said unto them in his doctrine, Beware of the scribes, which love to go in long clothing, and love salutations in the marketplaces, and the chief seats in the synagogues, and the uppermost rooms at feasts: which devour widows' houses, and for a pretence make long prayers: these shall receive greater damnation. And Jesus sat over against the treasury, and beheld how the people cast money into the treasury: and many that were rich cast in much. And there came a certain poor widow, and she threw in two mites, which make a farthing.

And he called unto him his disciples, and saith unto them, verily I say unto you, that this poor widow hath cast more in, than all they which have cast into the treasury: for all they did cast in of their abundance; but she of her want did cast in all that she had, even all her living.

It is very important to understand that Jesus talked a lot about money in His ministry. Some have even said that He spent more time talking about money than He did about heaven. At any rate, we see Him now there in the temple area where the open treasury was located. He watched the people come to give of their money to the Lord. He saw that many rich people came. He did not condemn that, He just watched. Then a widow came, so poor that she had less than one penny. She walked up to the place and tossed the money in.

Here is one of the greatest teachings of the Bible and it really works in our Christian lives. You give to God out of your need, out of the deepest desires of your heart. This can turn your giving around. It can give you joy in your giving. It is not the amount that you give, for if it were the amount that is given, Jesus would have praised the rich people who gave out of their surplus. It is what comes out of your heart, out of sacrifice, out of need. You see, you get your money by work, by sweat, by toil. Money is not money in itself, money is you. When you give your money, you are giving of yourself.

When the rich men gave of their surplus, they were not giving of themselves, they were giving of something they did not need. But the woman giving of her need gave of herself. That is the way you plant your seed. That is the way you give your tithes and offerings unto the Lord. The tithes and offerings are the first fruits. The tithes and offerings are off the top. The tithes and offerings represent giving your best.

Growing up as a farm boy, my brother Vaden and I would often go out in the corn fields and gather in the corn, putting the ears of corn in the wagon and driving the wagon to the barn, shovelling the corn into the barn or into the corn bin. One day Papa said, "boys, you are doing that all wrong." We said, "what do you mean?" He said, "the best ears are our seed corn, and you never eat your seed corn. The seed is what we are going to use to plant next year's crop."

I never forgot that. I have learned not to eat my seed corn, not to keep the best for myself but to give it to God. If I give Him my best, He multiplies my best. If I give Him my worst, He multiplies my worst.

I also remember that after Papa became a preacher, people would give what they call poundings, or gifts of groceries. One day, two brothers came to our house and gave Papa a chicken, a frying chicken. We noticed it was a one-eyed chicken. Later that evening these two brothers returned and said, "Brother Roberts, did you notice that chicken had one eye?" Papa said, "yes." "Well," they said, "we've been convicted, and if you will give that one-eyed chicken back to us, we will give you another in its place that has two eyes, a healthier chicken." And Papa accepted it.

We do not give God our one-eyed chickens when we have two-eyed chickens we give God our best. If a one-eyed chicken is the best we have, we give that, but whatever we give is our best. We give it to God because it is what we give that God multiplies for us. Now, if we give Him nothing and God multiplies nothing, nothing is still nothing. The widow truly gave her best.

Mark 13:1-11

And as he went out of the temple, one of his disciples saith unto him, Master, see what manner of stones and what buildings are here!

And Jesus answering said unto him, Seest thou these great buildings? there shall not be left one stone upon another, that shall not be thrown down.

And as he sat upon the mount of Olives over against the temple, Peter and James and John and Andrew asked him privately, Tell us, when shall these things be? and what shall be the sign when all these things shall be fulfilled?

And Jesus answering them began to say, Take heed lest any man deceive you: For many shall come in my name, saying, I am Christ; and shall deceive many. And when ye shall hear of wars and rumours of wars, be ye not troubled: for such things must needs be: but the end shall not be yet. For nation shall rise against nation, and kingdom against kingdom: and there shall be earthquakes in divers places, and there shall be famines and troubles: these are the beginnings of sorrows.

But take heed to yourselves: for they shall deliver you up to councils; and in the synagogues ye shall be beaten: and ye shall be brought before rulers and kings for my sake, for a testimony against them. And the gospel must first be published among all nations.

But when they shall lead you, and deliver you up, take no thought beforehand what ye shall speak, neither do ye premeditate: but whatsoever shall be given you in that hour, that speak ye: for it is not ye that speak, but the Holy Ghost.

The Spirit Will Speak

Jesus says, "Do not try to figure out what to say, but depend upon the Holy Spirit within you." I would like to say that there is no human reasoning that the powers that be will receive. It is only what the Spirit gives us to say that will count in those times, and we can depend on the Holy Spirit.

Mark 13:12,13

Now the brother shall betray the brother to death, and the father the son; and children shall rise up against their parents, and shall cause them to be put to death. And ye shall be hated of all men for my name's sake; but he that shall endure unto the end, the same shall be saved.

The Tribulation Period

Jesus is speaking here of the great tribulation period, when people's homes will be divided and members of the family will kill one another. That is going to be a terrible time. But I do not intend to be here and neither should you, because I am looking for the catching away of the saints, the rapture of the children of God, before the tribulation.

Mark 13:14-20

> But when ye shall see the abomination of desolation, spoken of by Daniel the prophet, standing where it ought not, (let him that readeth understand,) Then let them that be in Judaea flee to the mountains. And let him that is on the housetop not go down into the house, neither enter therein, to take any thing out of his house: And let him that is in the field not turn back again for to take up his garment. But woe to them that are with child, and to them that give suck in those days! And pray ye that your flight be not in the winter. For in those days shall be affliction, such as was not from the beginning of the creation which God created until this time, neither shall be. And except that the Lord had shortened those days, no flesh should be saved: but for the elect's sake, whom he hath chosen, he hath shortened the days.

Beware the Antichrist

Jesus is speaking here — as I referred to it in Matthew's gospel — of the Antichrist's coming and how he will go into the rebuilt temple in Jerusalem and there stand, proclaim himself as God, and command the Jewish people to fall down and worship him. At that time the Jewish people will understand who is the Antichrist. They will know that their time of tribulation, called "Jacob's trouble," is now at hand. They will flee for their lives, and it will be terrible because there will not be any time to gather up goods or things of that nature. Jesus says unless God shortens those days, nobody will be spared. How important it is that you and I live ready for the coming of our Lord.

Mark 13:21-25

> And then if any man shall say to you, Lo, here is Christ; or, lo, he is there; believe him not. For false Christs and false prophets shall rise, and shall shew signs and wonders, to seduce, if it were possible, even the elect. But take ye heed: behold, I have foretold you all things. But in those days, after that tribulation, the sun shall be darkened, and the moon shall not give her light, and the stars of heaven shall fall, and the powers that are in heaven shall be shaken.

Spiritual Disturbance

Jesus is referring not only to physical things, but to those that are spiritual. Paul reminds us — as we will learn later in his teachings —

that the demons and the devil have their headquarters in the powers of the air. When Christ is ready to come back, even those powers, those principalities and kingdoms of the spirit world, will be shaken. They will be disturbed, for they will know that the end is nigh.

Mark 13:26-30

And then shall they see the Son of man coming in the clouds with great power and glory. And then shall he send his angels, and shall gather together his elect from the four winds, from the uttermost part of the earth to the uttermost part of heaven.

Now learn a parable of the fig tree; When her branch is yet tender, and putteth forth leaves, ye know that summer is near: So ye in like manner, when ye shall see these things come to pass, know that it is nigh, even at the doors. Verily I say unto you, that this generation shall not pass, till all these things be done.

He is speaking of the generation of man here.

Mark 13:32

Heaven and earth shall pass away: but my words shall not pass away: But of that day and that hour knoweth no man, no, not the angels which are in heaven, neither the Son, but the Father.

Jesus in His humanity was limited, just as we are limited in our humanity.

Mark 13:33-37

Take ye heed, watch and pray: for ye know not when the time is. For the Son of man is as a man taking a far journey, who left his house, and gave authority to his servants, and to every man his work, and commanded the porter to watch.

Watch ye therefore: for ye know not when the master of the house cometh, at even, or at midnight, or at the cockcrowing, or in the morning: lest coming suddenly he find you sleeping. And what I say unto you I say unto all, Watch.

This is as if Jesus is delaying His coming for a thousand years, but we should so live our lives for Christ, as if He is coming within the next split second.

Mark 14:1

After two days was the feast of the passover, and of unleavened bread: and the chief priests and the scribes sought how they might take him by craft, and put him to death.

A Snare is Set

This is the beginning of the end. Jesus has prepared His disciples for the end of time, for His second coming. He has told them to watch and pray. He has taught them to follow in the right path. Suddenly the scene shifts. Now it is only 2 days until the feast of the Passover and of unleavened bread. Jewish people from all over the world have congregated in Jerusalem for this commemoration of the deliverance of the children of Israel from Egyptian bondage. The chief priests, now knowing that things are coming to a climax through the influential power of Jesus Christ of Nazareth, lay a snare to take Jesus and put Him to death.

Mark 14:2

> But they said, Not on the feast day, lest there be an uproar of the people.

The people would be intent upon taking the Passover. They would be there for this holy season and they would not welcome an intrusion of death during this time; the chief priest would be most unpopular.

Mark 14:3-5

> And being in Bethany in the house of Simon the leper, as he sat at meat, there came a woman having an alabaster box of ointment of spikenard very precious; and she brake the box, and poured it on his head.
>
> And there were some that had indignation within themselves, and said, Why was this waste of the ointment made? For it might have been sold for more than three hundred pence, and have been given to the poor. And they murmured against her.

Healing and Murmuring

This scene took place in the home of a man named Simon, a leper who had been healed by Jesus Christ. First, it is one of the most remarkable indications that the healing power of Jesus Christ not only transforms a human being, but it lasts. It restores a person to full strength so that person can carry on his life. Second, when the woman anointed Jesus with the perfume, anointing Him because of discernment of His coming death, it was something the disciples themselves did not understand. They and other people there "murmured" against her. Murmuring against something holy, something of God, has always been condemned by the Lord. Murmuring has no place among God's people.

Mark 14:6

And Jesus said, Let her alone; why trouble ye her? she hath wrought a good work on me.

The Vision of Discernment

They had condemned the woman, not realizing her inner discernment. She knew that her Savior would soon be on the cross. They who had heard it from the very lips of Jesus and had never believed or understood it, now disapproved of someone who did. A little woman who was there because of an honest heart. Having discernment of coming events, she wanted to do this great work upon the person she believed to be the Son of God.

Mark 14:7-16

For ye have the poor with you always, and whensoever ye will ye may do them good: but me ye have not always. She hath done what she could: she is come aforehand to anoint my body to the burying. Verily I say unto you, Wheresoever this gospel shall be preached throughout the whole world, this also that she hath done shall be spoken of for a memorial of her.

And Judas Iscariot, one of the twelve, went unto the chief priests, to betray him unto them. And when they heard it, they were glad, and promised to give him money. And he sought how he might conveniently betray him.

And the first day of unleavened bread, when they killed the passover, his disciples said unto him, Where wilt thou that we go and prepare that thou mayest eat the passover?

And he sendeth forth two of his disciples, and saith unto them, Go ye into the city, and there shall meet you a man bearing a pitcher of water: follow him. And wheresoever he shall go in, say ye to the goodman of the house, The Master saith, Where is the guest-chamber, where I shall eat the passover with my disciples? And he will shew you a large upper room furnished and prepared: there make ready for us.

And his disciples went forth, and came into the city, and found as he had said unto them: and they made ready the passover.

The Ready Servant

There are two things going on here simultaneously. First, Judas Iscariot has now made up his mind that he is going to sell Jesus Christ by betraying Him into the hands of the chief priests. When they heard that, the chief priests were glad and promised to give him money, and Judas went about to find a convenient way to betray Him into their hands.

Second, Jesus was ready now to eat the last Passover. God always has somebody prepared who is willing and obedient to do the one special thing that must be done to advance the kingdom of God. A man who had a house with a large room was ready and eager to do what Jesus asked. Some believe this was the home of John Mark, the man who wrote this gospel, or the home of his mother, the same place where the Holy Spirit was poured out upon the day of Pentecost.

Mark 14:17-25

And in the evening he cometh with the twelve. And as they sat and did eat, Jesus said, Verily I say unto you, One of you which eateth with me shall betray me.

And they began to be sorrowful, and to say unto him one by one, Is it I? and another said, Is it I?

And He answered and said unto them, It is one of the twelve, that dippeth with me in the dish. The Son of man indeed goeth, as it is written of him: but woe to that man by whom the Son of man is betrayed! good were it for that man if he had never been born.

And as they did eat, Jesus took bread, and blessed, and brake it, and gave to them, and said, Take, eat: this is my body.

And he took the cup, and when he had given thanks, he gave it to them: and they all drank of it. And he said unto them, This is my blood of the new testament, which is shed for many. Verily I say unto you, I will drink no more of the fruit of the vine, until that day that I drink it new in the kingdom of God.

Communion Clarified

This is not transubstantiation or the doctrine that the wine and the bread in Communion are transformed into the actual body and blood of Jesus Christ. He had just said, "Me ye shall not always have with you." If the doctrine of transubstantiation is true, then we would still have the body, the physical body of Jesus, with us today. The Holy Communion is something taken by faith that brings forth the presence, the invisible, unlimited presence of our Lord Jesus Christ into our lives. I am a lover of the Holy Communion. I love to take it, and my life is always strengthened by it.

Mark 14:26,27

And when they had sung an hymn, they went out into the mount of

> Olives. And Jesus saith unto them, All ye shall be offended because of me this night: for it is written, I will smite the shepherd, and the sheep shall be scattered.

Learn What is "Written"

Jesus continues to say, "It is written." In the early part of St. Mark's gospel during the temptations, He repudiated the devil's attacks by saying, "It is written. It is written." Time after time He referred to the written Word of God from the book of Genesis through Malachi. At the very end of His life He still is saying, "It is written."

How in this world can you, a child of God, say, "It is written" unless you read and study the Bible? Take time to understand, to hear it preached, to meditate and pray about it, and to take it into your being so the Holy Spirit can manifest the Scriptures in you in times of stress and trial, as well as in times of glory and joy.

Mark 14:28-36

> But after that I am risen, I will go before you into Galilee. But Peter said unto him, Although all shall be offended, yet will not I. And Jesus saith unto him, Verily I say unto thee, That this day, even in this night, before the cock crow twice, thou shalt deny me thrice. But he spake the more vehemently, If I should die with thee, I will not deny thee in any wise. Likewise also said they all.

Jesus was still in command of the situation. Never lose sight that our Lord is in command. He was in command then, He is in command today, and He will be in command tomorrow and forever. He even knew that He would rise from the dead. He knew that Peter would deny Him. Before the rooster could crow twice that morning, Peter would have denied Him three times. We have to be careful about what we say because we can speak too quickly, too impulsively. We should measure our words and be careful that we lean upon the strength of God, for His strength is greater than ours.

Mark 14:32-36

> And they came to a place which was named Gethsemane: and he saith to his disciples, Sit ye here, while I shall pray. And he taketh with him Peter and James and John, and began to be sore amazed, and to be very heavy; and saith unto them, My soul is exceeding sorrowful unto death: tarry ye here, and watch.
>
> And he went forward a little, and fell on the ground, and prayed that, if it were possible, the hour might pass from him. And he said, Abba,

Father, all things are possible unto thee; take away this cup from me: nevertheless not what I will, but what thou wilt.

A Lesson in Humanity

Jesus was deeply distressed and troubled. Many people believe that his suffering at Gethsemane the night before the crucifixion was almost as much as it was on the cross. My own feeling is that the humanity of Jesus is shown here. I feel that for too long we Christians have not truly understood the incarnation. He was God, so He could do for us all that God himself could do, and that we could not do for ourselves. At the same time, He was fully man in order to enter into our humanity. To be bone of our bone and flesh of our flesh; to face the exact types of temptations, trials, and tribulations; to hurt, to be sorrowful, and to know precisely everything that you will know, or not know, in your humanity. He was sore amazed.

Some believe Jesus was concerned that the devil would try to talk Him out of going to the cross. But I believe Jesus knew what it meant to be separated from His Father. Having been with the Father from eternity past, He had come to earth as His beloved Son, and had never been separated from Him for one split second. When Jesus thought of being made sin for us, and bearing the sting of sin which He himself had never committed, and that He was doing it for us that we might be redeemed from it . . . as He thought of that separation and isolation from both God and man . . . it almost overwhelmed Him. So when He sweated, it was as if blood was coming from his body.

Oh, somehow, some way, the Spirit must let you and me understand what Gethsemane means, because we go through experiences like that, when we feel so isolated and separated. Aloneness, and loneliness strike us.

Jesus was going through all of this in Gethsemane the same as He would go through death on Calvary. Yet, He had control of His will.

You have got to understand the humanity of Jesus in order to understand His divinity. If you think solely of the Christ nature and not the human nature of Jesus, you are going to miss it. You must see the humanity of Jesus, that He was a person just as you and I are, who in trouble relied on the Word of God, and His faith in God. When you understand that, you become able to go through similar things. You too can know that you know, you can depend upon the Word of God and your faith to see you through in the same way Jesus did.

Mark 14:37, 38

And he cometh, and findeth them sleeping, and saith unto Peter, Simon, sleepest thou? couldest not thou watch one hour? Watch ye and pray, lest ye enter into temptation. The spirit truly is ready, but the flesh is weak.

Watch and Pray

Peter had said if everybody denies you, I will not. I will stand up for You. But he is the very one who went to sleep. The Lord awakened him, and said, "Simon, are you asleep? Remember what you said to me? Could you not even watch one hour. Simon, watch and pray lest ye enter into temptation. Your spirit is ready but the flesh is weak; therefore, watch and pray and that gives strength to your flesh." What a good word to you and me today.

Mark 14:39-41a

And again he went away, and prayed, and spake the same words. And when he returned, he found them asleep again (for their eyes were heavy,) neither wist they what to answer him. And he cometh the third time.

Don't Get Discouraged

Three different times the humanity of Jesus went out alone to wrestle with the challenge and the will of God. You do not always win the first time you pray or dedicate or commit yourself. It sometimes takes several times. It took three times for Jesus. Do not get discouraged if you do not quite get through the first or second or third time. Just hold on.

Mark 14:41-50

And he cometh the third time, and saith unto them, Sleep on now, and take your rest: it is enough, the hour is come; behold, the Son of man is betrayed into the hands of sinners. Rise up, let us go: lo, he that betrayeth me is at hand.

And immediately, while he yet spake, cometh Judas, one of the twelve, and with him a great multitude with swords and staves, from the chief priests and the scribes and the elders.

And he that betrayed him had given them a token, saying, Whomsoever I shall kiss, that same is he; take him, and lead him away safely. And as soon as he was come, he goeth straightway to him, and saith, Master, master; and kissed him.

And they laid their hands on him, and took him. And one of them that stood by drew a sword, and smote a servant of the high priest, and cut off his ear.

And Jesus answered and said unto them, Are ye come out, as against a thief, with swords and with staves to take me? I was daily with you in the temple teaching, and ye took me not: but the scriptures must be fulfilled.

And they all forsook him, and fled.

I do not think things are much different today. I think that when Christians have it too easy, they really cannot identify with Jesus. I do not think that the strength within you and me will ever be revealed until we come up against the hard things, when our lives are on the line.

Today the Church, the established organized Church, is starting to resemble a social club. It is so easy to join a church. It is so easy to go and sit, and it is almost like a one-way conversation where the minister does it all. It is just too easy today and I predict that this remnant, this charismatic outpouring of the Holy Spirit that is creating a dynamic Christian remnant of people, is going to be the leaven. This is going to be the pulling together of those children of God who really are determined to serve God through thick and thin, through life or death.

I say that because in my own experience of facing the devil's wrath against the healing ministry. When I face the unbelief of so many people, I can tell you, I have already tasted something of what Jesus tasted there in Gethsemane. I know Gethsemanes are coming in my life, and in your life as well as in the lives of all those people who have determined they are going to let Christ have His way and will in their lives. But, praise God, Gethsemane is followed by Calvary and Calvary is followed by the resurrection, and the resurrection is followed by the outpouring of the Holy Spirit and the outpouring of the Holy Spirit is followed by dynamic Christian witness. That Christian witness is followed by enduring to the end, and enduring to the end means we shall be saved eternally. It is worth it all.

Mark 14:51-59

And there followed him a certain young man, having a linen cloth cast about his naked body; and the young men laid hold on him: and he left the linen cloth, and fled from them naked.

And they led Jesus away to the high priest: and with him were assembled all the chief priests and the elders and the scribes. And Peter followed him afar off, even into the palace of the high priest: and he sat with the servants, and warmed himself at the fire. And the chief priests and all the council sought for witness against Jesus to put him to death; and found none. For many bare false witness against him, but their witness agreed not together.

And there arose certain, and bare false witness against him, saying, We heard him say, I will destroy this temple that is made with hands, and within three days I will build another made without hands. But neither so did their witness agree together.

The Christian faith has never been judged fairly. It never will be in this world. We Christians might as well accept that as a fact and get up and go on for God.

Mark 14:60,61a

And the high priest stood up in the midst, and asked Jesus, saying, Answerest thou nothing? what is it which these witness against thee? But he held his peace, and answered nothing.

Jesus Not Intimidated

Jesus, by knowing the Word of God and releasing His faith to the heavenly Father, was not intimidated by the so-called religious leader, even though he was the number-one man. Nor was Jesus intimidated by all the others surrounding Him. Nor was He intimidated by the fact they wanted to kill Him even with false witnesses.

He simply held His peace and did not answer. He just stood there.

Mark 14:61b,62

Again the high priest asked him, and said unto him, Art thou the Christ, the Son of the Blessed? And Jesus said, I am: and ye shall see the Son of man sitting on the right hand of power, and coming in the clouds of heaven.

He spoke to this high priest and said, "I am." The only unit of time He recognizes is the now. Whenever and wherever, it was always now. I am. Praise God.

Mark 14:63

Then the high priest rent his clothes, and saith, What need we any further witnesses? Ye have heard the blasphemy: what think ye? And they all condemned him to be guilty of death. And some began to spit on him, and to cover his face, and to buffet him, and to say unto him, Prophesy: and the servants did strike him with the palms of their hands.

Preach, Teach, Heal

Have you been through that? I do not think I have been through a whole lot. I have stood up for the glory of my Lord, trying to be like Him and to heal the people as He did. Despite my personal mistakes, I know that the chief opposition to this ministry is not because of my mistakes — because I am always going to make mistakes — but because of the reality of the risen Christ who shines forth in saving, healing, and delivering power as we stand up to preach, teach, and heal in His name.

Mark 14:66-15:1

> And as Peter was beneath in the palace, there cometh one of the maids of the high priest. And when she saw Peter warming himself, she looked upon him, and said, And thou also wast with Jesus of Nazareth. But he denied, saying, I know not, neither understand I what thou sayest. And he went out into the porch; and the cock crew.
>
> And a maid saw him again, and began to say to them that stood by, This is one of them. And he denied it again. And a little after, they that stood by said again to Peter, Surely thou art one of them: for thou art a Galilean, and thy speech agreeth thereto. But he began to curse and to swear, saying, I know not this man of whom ye speak.
>
> And the second time the cock crew. And Peter called to mind the word that Jesus said unto him, Before the cock crow twice, thou shalt deny me thrice. And when he thought thereon, he wept.
>
> And straightway in the morning the chief priests held a consultation with the elders and scribes and the whole council, and bound Jesus, and carried him away, and delivered him to Pilate.

Now they bring him before what we would call the supreme court. This is the court of final consultation and final authority. Then they took him from the council, the Sanhedrin, to Pilate, who was the Roman ruler, called procurator, whom Caesar had installed in the Holy Land at that time.

Mark 15:2,3

> And Pilate asked him, Art thou the king of the Jews? And he answering said unto him, Thou sayest it. And the chief priests accused him of many things: but he answered nothing.

Let God Defend You

One thing that Jesus taught and lived out in His own witness was not to strike back. Jesus said nothing when He could have said a lot. He could have defended himself. He could have taken all of that time to defend himself and thereby obscure the higher reason why He was there.

I have discovered that when you are doing God's work and your heart is clean and pure before Him, you can endure. Anything. Even when you are put in a bad light, if you hold your peace and do not hate, and do not strike back, God will fight your battles.

Mark 15:4-11

And Pilate asked him again, saying, answerest thou nothing? behold how many things they witness against thee. But Jesus yet answered nothing: so that Pilate marvelled.

Now at that feast he released unto them one prisoner, whomsoever they desired. And there was one named Barabbas, which lay bound with them that had made insurrection with him, who had committed murder in the insurrection. And the multitude crying aloud began to desire him to do as he had ever done unto them. But Pilate answered them, saying, Will ye that I release unto you the king of the Jews? For he knew that the chief priests had delivered him for envy. But the chief priests moved the people, that he should rather release Barabbas unto them.

"Religion" Without Christ

It was the chief religious leader who influenced the people and stirred them up that they should demand the release of Barabbas rather than Jesus Christ. It is true that religion without salvation, religion without inner conversion, religion without following Jesus Christ and putting Him first in your life can make you the cruelest person in the world.

Mark 15:12

And Pilate answered and said again unto them, What will ye then that I shall do unto him whom ye call the king of the Jews? And they cried out again, Crucify him. Then Pilate said unto them, Why, what evil hath he done? And they cried out the more exceedingly, Crucify him. And so Pilate, willing to content the people, released Barabbas unto them, and delivered Jesus, when he had scourged him, to be crucified.

This is the power structure. In every city there is a power structure. The temptation of those in the power structure is to be moved by what they feel is the majority opinion of the people. They do what will make them popular; therefore, they do not always stand up for what is right. It is not who is right, but it is what is right that really counts.

Mark 15:16-21

> And the soldiers led him away into the hall, called Praetorium; and they call together the whole band. And they clothed him with purple, and platted a crown of thorns, and put it about his head, and began to salute him, Hail, King of the Jews!
>
> And they smote him on the head with a reed, and did spit upon him, and bowing their knees worshipped him. And when they had mocked him, they took off the purple from him, and put his own clothes on him, and led him out to crucify him. And they compel one Simon a Cyrenian, who passed by, coming out of the country, the father of Alexander and Rufus, to bear his cross.

The Heavy Burden

As far as we know, Mark's gospel was the first of the four gospel's to be written. Scholars have tried to determine it was written 30 or 40 years after the death of Jesus. You may know that some of Paul's letters or books had already been written and at that time, Alexander and Rufus, who were sons of Simon of Cyrene, had become disciples and believers. This is a reference back to that time when they called this man to bear the cross of Jesus Christ. Simon may have been Jewish, but many believe he was black. I do not know. But if he were black, then all the black people can relate to him because they too have had heavy, grievous burdens laid upon them.

Mark 15:22-24

> And they bring him unto the place Golgotha, which is, being interpreted, The place of a skull. And they gave him to drink wine mingled with myrrh: but he received it not. And when they had crucified him, they parted his garments, casting lots upon them, what every man should take.

Gambling Crucifiers

The crucifiers were mostly paid by the clothes of the victim or whatever else he possessed on his person. Because the garment of Jesus was woven without seam from top to bottom, a very singular garment, they did not want to tear it into pieces. So they gambled for it. One of them won it.

Mark 15:25-30

> And it was the third hour, and they crucified him. And the superscription of his accusation was written over, THE KING OF THE JEWS. And with him they crucify two thieves; the one on his right hand, and the other on his left. And the scripture was fulfilled, which saith, and he was numbered with the transgressors. And they that passed by railed on him, wagging their heads, and saying, Ah, thou that destroyest the temple, and buildest it in three days, save thyself, and come down from the cross.

The spectators were referring to a statement Jesus had made about his own body. Destroy this body and I will raise it up the third day. They thought he was talking about the temple — destroy it, and in three days He would rebuild it. The carnal human mind cannot understand spiritually related things.

Mark 15:31,32

> Likewise also the chief priests mocking said among themselves with the scribes, He saved others; himself he cannot save. Let Christ the King of Israel descend now from the cross, that we may see and believe. And they that were crucified with him reviled him.

The key statement here is, Let Him come down from the cross and save himself that we may see and believe. When we reach the 11th chapter of St. John's gospel, we will see that Jesus turned that around, saying that when you believe, then you see. Some people say, show me and I will believe, and that is not true. One has to believe in order to see. They had it backwards.

Mark 15:33

> And when the sixth hour was come, there was darkness over the whole land until the ninth hour.

Noonday Darkness

The sixth hour was high noon and the ninth hour was three o'clock in the afternoon. For 3 hours a darkness came over everything. They could not even see their hand in front of their face. Out of that darkness something happened.

Mark 15:34-37

> And at the ninth hour Jesus cried with a loud voice, saying, Eloi, Eloi, lama sabachthani? which is, being interpreted, My God, my God, why

hast thou forsaken me? And some of them that stood by, when they heard it, said, Behold, he calleth Elias. And one ran and filled a sponge full of vinegar, and put it on a reed, and gave him to drink, saying, Let alone; let us see whether Elias will come to take him down. And Jesus cried with a loud voice, and gave up the ghost.

Jesus Absorbed All Sin

In the midst of the thick darkness when one could not see, the voice of Jesus rose, calling upon God — MY God — not just God — MY God, with that human question, Why hast thou forsaken me? God had to forsake Him because Jesus was there in the place of fallen man — including you and me. Had he not forsaken Him, there would have been no true redemption. Jesus cried out not only in His humanity, but He cried out by His spirit, for God had made His soul an offering for sin.

Nobody knows the sting of sin like Jesus does. It seems so easy for us to go out and commit some sin and think nothing of it. But God knows that sin destroys everything it touches and wipes out the instincts of man — the things that God has created in him — the highest aspirations, the everlasting soul, the immortal spirit, the human flesh, the hopes and goals of every human being of the whole human race, and of God's eternal purpose and plan. Jesus absorbed it, blow upon blow, sin upon sin, striking at Him until the whole of sin struck Him and He absorbed it all. Then He cried with a loud voice and gave up the ghost. But, He was in control. He never let things get out of control. It was He who gave up the ghost — they did not take it from Him. He gave it up.

Mark 15:38

And the veil of the temple was rent in twain from the top to the bottom.

The Blood Exchange

The veil, that large veil that separated the holy place from the other large parts of the temple, was torn in two from the top to the bottom. Invisible hands ripped it apart. And at that precise moment God fulfilled the old covenant and did away with the blood of bulls and goats and lambs, and took the shed blood of His only begotten Son, Jesus Christ, and redeemed us.

Mark 15:39-41

And when the centurion, which stood over against him, saw that he so cried out, and gave up the ghost, he said, Truly this man was the Son of God. There were also women looking on afar off: among whom was Mary Magdalene, and Mary the mother of James the less and of Joses, and Salome; (Who also, when he was in Galilee, followed him, and ministered unto him;) and many other women which came up with him unto Jerusalem.

The women were there. There is something about a woman's heart that is softer than that of most men. It seems that women are more spiritually inclined, more sensitive to the Holy Spirit. They had done so much for Him, even ministering to Him financially.

Mark 15:42,43

And now when the even was come, because it was the preparation, that is, the day before the sabbath, Joseph of Arimathaea, an honorable counsellor, which also waited for the kingdom of God, came, and went in boldly unto Pilate, and craved the body of Jesus.

Burial in God's Plan

This was a tremendously significant thing Joseph of Arimathea did. Joseph is thought to have been one of the members of the Jewish Sanhedrin, the highest "supreme court" of the land. He was a very highly thought of man, also rich. Recently he had hewn out a tomb for his own burial. But when he begged Pilate for the body, he saved Jesus from mass burial. Think a moment. If this had not happened, and Jesus' body had been taken down with the others who were crucified and buried in mass graves, what an implausible thing it would have been for people to believe He could have been raised from the dead. How would they have known which body had been raised? even in these infinitesimally small things, God was at work crossing the t's and dotting the i's, leaving nothing to chance. Never fret, Jesus is in control. There will always be somebody ready to be raised up or to come forward or to do a specific thing that must be done in harmony with the eternal plan of God.

Mark 15:44,45

And Pilate marvelled if he were already dead: and calling unto him the centurion, he asked him whether he had been any while dead. And when he knew it of the centurion, he gave the body to Joseph.

Pilate in Plan

Pilate did not even realize the significance of what he was doing. I am sure he did not know what motivated him, but God was using even the Roman ruler to fulfill prophecy.

Mark 15:46-16:3

> And he bought fine linen, and took him down, and wrapped him in the linen, and laid him in a sepulchre which was hewn out of a rock, and rolled a stone unto the door of the sepulchre. And Mary Magdalene and Mary the mother of Jesus beheld where he was laid.
>
> And when the sabbath was past, Mary Magdalene, and Mary the mother of James, and Salome, had bought sweet spices, that they might come and anoint him. And very early in the morning the first day of the week, they came unto the sepulchre at the rising of the sun. And they said among themselves, who shall roll us away the stone from the door of the sepulchre?

Tomb Officially Sealed

They did not know that the Jews had come to Pilate and prevailed upon him to put the government seal upon the tomb or upon the rock so that if anybody break the seal, it would mean that he would be put to death. The Jews were doing everything in their power so the Christians would not get away with saying that Jesus had risen from the dead.

Mark 16:4-7

> And when they looked, they saw that the stone was rolled away: for it was very great. And entering into the sepulchre, they saw a young man sitting on the right side, clothed in a long white garment; and they were affrighted.
>
> And he saith unto them, Be not affrighted: Ye seek Jesus of Nazareth, which was crucified: he is risen; he is not here: behold the place where they laid him. But go your way, tell his disciples and Peter that he goeth before you into Galilee: there shall ye see him, as he said unto you.

Our Mission His Concern

Jesus was concerned about Peter, as He is about any of us when we think we can do so much and yet in our weakness disappoint Christ. When we have so much promise, when we have the life that might have been, He is so concerned that we have the inner strength and the recognition of His love and mercy to be able to carry out our mission in life.

Mark 16:8

And they went out quickly, and fled from the sepulchre; for they trembled and were amazed: neither said they any thing to any man; for they were afraid.

Reality of Resurrection

First they were frightened, next they trembled, then they were amazed. Then they did not tell, anybody, and finally, they were terribly afraid. Why does God include such details in the account of the resurrection? He told it, as they say, "like it was." This was not fiction. This was reality and these women were reacting in a normal way.

Mark 16:9

Now when Jesus was risen early the first day of the week, he appeared first to Mary Magdalene, out of whom he had cast seven devils.

This woman who had been demon-possessed was delivered so completely and had served Him so devotedly that He now reveals himself to her.

Mark 16:10,11

And she went and told them that had been with him, as they mourned and wept. And they, when they had heard that he was alive, and had been seen of her, believed not.

Have you ever known something of God so deeply and so realistically that you just had to tell it, and yet you could not get anybody to believe you? That is what happened to Mary Magdalene. They did not believe her.

Mark 16:12-14

After that he appeared in another form unto two of them, as they walked, and went into the country. And they went and told it unto the residue: neither believed they them. Afterward he appeared unto the eleven as they sat at meat, and upbraided them with their unbelief and hardness of heart, because they believed not them which had seen him after he was risen.

Jesus Continued Caring

Jesus never accepts our unbelief or hardness of heart. He had told the angel to tell them to go into Galilee, and especially to tell Peter also that He would meet them there. He cared so much about them, but He cared so much that He told them the truth about their unbelief. He upbraided them for their hardness of heart. They not only had forsaken Him and fled from the cross, but now they did not believe what He had told them about his rising from the dead.

Mark 16:15,16

> And he said unto them, Go ye into all the world, and preach the gospel to every creature. He that believeth and is baptized shall be saved; but he that believeth not shall be damned.

"Go" with the Gospel!

Jesus shows us that this gospel has to be in movement, in motion, in activity. It is not to become sterile and stale and stagnant. He said go, and go ye, an imminently personal thing. Go ye. We should go to the house of God that we might be strengthened by the gospel of Jesus Christ and taught how to lift up the name of our Lord and reproduce His life in the world.

Then we are to go. Our main work is outside the church sanctuary. It is out there among the people. You either go or you send somebody, and you know that as you send them your heart goes with them. Also, when He said, "Go ye into all the world," He meant go into every man's world. That is to say, when we see the way men think and how they live, we enter into that situation with them to reproduce the life of Christ through our witness. He said, preach. Preach the gospel.

Mark 16:17,18

> And these signs shall follow them that believe; In my name shall they cast out devils; they shall speak with new tongues; they shall take up serpents; and if they drink any deadly thing, it shall not hurt them; they shall lay hands on the sick, and they shall recover.

Jesus' Directions Explained

When we cannot do certain things legally, we give that power to our attorneys so that when they speak, they are speaking for us, and we have put at their disposal all of our authority. Jesus is saying, when we believe, we will be saved, and when we believe, He gives us the power of His name and the power of attorney. In My name, Christ said, you shall cast out devils. You shall speak with new tongues. They shall take up serpents. This does not mean snake handling. If snake handling was going to bring deliverance, then we might as well get the snake handlers of Burma and India and other places. Their snake handling does not save souls, or heal the sick, or extend the gospel. This simply means as these people went forth into the world to preach the gospel to every creature, they might be bitten by a snake and they would be immune from that snake bite. It happened to Paul. Then, "If they drink any deadly thing, it shall not hurt them." The same would be true if enemies tried to poison them: they would be immune. Then, they that believe "shall lay hands on the sick, and they shall recover." That is not merely touching somebody with your hands. It is your heart and your faith working through your hands through the name of Christ. It causes the sick to recover.

Mark 16:19,20

> So then after the Lord had spoken unto them, he was received up into heaven, and sat on the right hand of God. And they went forth, and preached every where, the Lord working with them, and confirming the word with signs following. Amen.

This is the way Mark ended his gospel. He began it with action. He closed it with greater action. And what is the greater action? That these disciples went forth in the name of Christ to do His mighty deeds as if Jesus had never died. Through the one Jesus, there were thousands of "little Christs". The very things that Christ said would happen, did happen.

He worked with them and He confirmed and approved His word, with these signs following: devils were cast out; people spoke with new tongues, and nothing of serpents or poison destroyed them; they laid their hands on the sick and they recovered. That was the confirmation then and it is the confirmation today.

I praise God for the gospel of Mark. The man who showed us our Savior in action as no other did and who told us of the many places He went and the great things He did, ended his gospel by saying that we His followers can do the same thing. Amen and amen.

The Gospel According to Luke

The Gospel According to Luke

Luke, the writer of the gospel of Luke, also was the writer of the book of Acts. In effect Luke is a writer of two books in one, Luke and Acts. Luke was a medical doctor and probably a Greek. He joined Paul's evangelistic and missionary team as a full-time member and was very close to St. Paul. In Colossians 4:14, Paul calls him "the beloved physician," not the former beloved physician, not the nonpracticing beloved physician, but "the beloved physician." He was a man who continued the practice of medicine even as he became a full-time member of the evangelistic and missionary team of the apostle Paul.

We first hear of St. Luke In Acts 20:6, where in his most unassuming way Luke said,"we," and he used that little word, we, several times in that chapter. Luke had the inquiring mind of a doctor. He was profoundly interested in every facet of our Lord Jesus' life. By Luke's time the gospel had been established in the Holy Land by Peter, James, John, and others. Paul, upon his conversion, became a missionary, an evangelist to the world. On one of his journeys he met Dr. Luke and they hit it off immediately, becoming fast and intimate friends in the Lord.

Being a doctor, Luke believed in keeping records. He wanted to know the truth about the things which they most certainly believed. In writing both the gospel of Luke and the book of Acts, he addresses both works to a friend by the name of Theophilus. This man probably was a a nobleman in the Roman empire, a fellow believer who wanted his faith substantiated by the truth, by the facts.

Much of the information about Jesus Christ was communicated by word of mouth then and there were many distorted rumors. Luke, working while Paul was imprisoned in Caesarea, began a thorough investigation, back to Mary and including other personal eyewitnesses of the life of Jesus from the very beginning. It is noteworthy that only Matthew and Luke traced the genealogy of Jesus. Matthew went back to David and to Abraham, but Luke goes back to God. He was interested in Christ the Savior of the world. He uses the word "Savior" several times and he mentions Jesus as the Son of Man on countless occasions, more than any other writer. He was very interested in Jesus Christ, the Son of God, and in Jesus Christ, the Son of Man. When he refers to Son of Man, he is probably speaking primarily to the humanity of Jesus, who entered into your and my humanity, sitting where we sit, feeling what we feel, experiencing everything we go through, that He might be tested in every way that we are and be touched by the feelings of our infirmities. Through His humanity, depending on the Word of God, His faith in God, and the Holy Spirit, He would use only those things which are available to you and me as Christians today to overcome this world and the things in it and to be a triumphant child of God.

Luke is an accurate writer. He was careful to use the Septuagint, the Greek translation of the Hebrew Old Testament. He was trying to show the meaning of Hebrew names and Hebrew terms to the Gentile world.

Luke 1:1-17

Forasmuch as many have taken in hand to set forth in order a declaration of those things which are most surely believed among us, even as they delivered them unto us, which from the beginning were eyewitnesses, and ministers of the word; it seemed good to me also, having had perfect understanding of all things from the very first, to write unto thee in order, most excellent Theophilus, that thou mightest know the certainty of those things, wherein thou hast been instructed. There was in the days of Herod, the king of Judaea, a certain priest named Zacharias, of the course of Abiah, and his wife was of the daughters of Aaron, and her name was Elisabeth. And they were both righteous before God, walking in all the commandments and ordinances of the Lord blameless. And they had no child, because that Elisabeth was barren, and they both were now well stricken in years.

And it came to pass, that while he executed the priest's office before God in the order of his course, according to the custom of the priest's office, his lot was to burn incense when he went into the temple of the Lord. And the whole multitude of the people were praying without at the time of incense. And there appeared unto him an angel of the Lord, standing on the right side of the altar of incense. And when Zacharias saw him, he was troubled, and fear fell upon him. But the angel said unto him, Fear not, Zacharias: for thy prayer is heard; and

> thy wife Elisabeth shall bear thee a son, and thou shalt call his name John. And thou shalt have joy and gladness; and many shall rejoice at his birth. For he shall be great in the sight of the Lord, and shall drink neither wine nor strong drink; and he shall be filled with the Holy Ghost, even from his mother's womb. And many of the children of Israel shall he turn to the Lord their God. And he shall go before him in the spirit and power of Elias to turn the hearts of the fathers to the children, and the disobedient to the wisdom of the just; to make ready a people prepared for the Lord.

Prayer Can Surprise

In the days of King David, he instituted the custom of priests throughout the land going at least once a year to the great temple in Jerusalem to participate in its activities. There were 24 divisions of priests dating back to Aaron, the first of the high priests. It was Zacharias' time to go to Jerusalem and he was accompanied by his wife. There, in righteousness before God, walking in all the ways of the Lord, doing His will, Zacharias was working in the temple.

Zacharias and Elisabeth were like Abraham and Sarah, in that they were old but childless. There was a stigma attached to childlessness in those days, so God sent His angel to Zacharias and told him his prayer had been heard. When the angel told Zacharias that his prayer had been heard, Zacharias was frightened. When we pray and God begins to answer, we are often surprised. The angel told him God was going to visit them, and even though Elisabeth was barren and "well stricken in years," she would have a child and the child would be great. He would be the forerunner of Jesus Christ, John the Baptist, and would be like Samson of old, a Nazarite who would never drink strong drink, but be filled with the Spirit from his mother's womb.

The purpose of his coming was to turn the disobedient children of Israel back to the Lord. He would come in the power of the mightiest prophet that Israel had known, Elijah, who had been translated to heaven. Zacharias was afraid but he kept listening to the angel.

Luke 1:18-20

> And Zacharias said unto the angel, Whereby shall I know this? for I am an old man, and my wife well stricken in years. And the angel answering said unto him, I am Gabriel, that stand in the presence of God; and am sent to speak unto thee, and to shew thee these glad tidings. And, behold, thou shalt be dumb, and not able to speak, until the day that these things shall be performed, because thou believest

not my words, which shall be fulfilled in their season.

The penalty for unbelief in his case was that his speech was taken from him. The penalty for unbelief takes many forms but it is certain.

Luke 1:21

And the people waited for Zacharias, and marvelled that he tarried so long in the temple.

They were always frightened if a priest stayed too long because that might indicate he had done something wrong and the wrath of God had consumed him. They were anxious that Zacharias would come forth to them.

Luke 1:22-28

And when he came out, he could not speak unto them: and they perceived that he had seen a vision in the temple: for he beckoned unto them and remained speechless.

And it came to pass that, as soon as the days of his ministration were accomplished, he departed to his own house. And after those days his wife Elisabeth conceived, and hid herself five months, saying, Thus hath the Lord dealt with me in the days wherein he looked on me, to take away my reproach among men.

And in the sixth month the angel Gabriel was sent from God unto a city of Galilee, named Nazareth, to a virgin espoused to a man whose name was Joseph, of the house of David; and the virgin's name was Mary.

And the angel came in unto her, and said, Hail, thou that art highly favoured, the Lord is with thee: blessed art thou among women.

The Angel's Remark

The angel told Mary she was highly favored of God. He did not say, Hail Mary, full of grace. That statement is not in the Bible. He said, "Hail, thou that art highly favored. The Lord is with thee: blessed art thou among women."

Luke 1:29-33

And when she saw him, she was troubled at his saying, and cast in her mind what manner of salutation this should be. And the angel said unto her, Fear not, Mary: for thou hast found favour with God. And, behold, thou shalt conceive in thy womb, and bring forth a son, and shalt call his name JESUS.

> He shall be great, and shall be called the Son of the Highest: and the Lord God shall give unto him the throne of his father David.
> And he shall reign over the house of Jacob forever; and of his kingdom there shall be no end.

The Faithful Remnant

Mary, the young virgin, was a part of the remnant. Remember that Malachi, the last of the prophets of the Old Testament, ended his prophecy with a curse. There followed 400 so-called silent years in which there was no major prophet until the birth of Jesus Christ. While Malachi ended with the threat of a curse, the new testament begins with the promise of a Savior. While Israel was disobedient and backsliding there was always the faithful remnant — people who kept the law, the word, and the Spirit of God. Mary was one of them. We can be certain that however afar from God the world gets, if there is backsliding among the people of God or apostasy in the Church of Jesus Christ, there always will be a remnant, a remnant of holy and righteous people who are pleasing to God in every aspect of their life. God is going to work through them to do His mighty and everlasting works.

From the time David united the kingdom of Israel, until the exile of the people of Israel into Babylonian captivity, there had always been the promise of God that He would rule through the house of David, and of His kingdom there would be no end. Jesus Christ, the Son of David, took up this promise of God to fulfill it and God said of Him that there would be no end to His reign. Both Joseph and Mary descended from David. Joseph descended from Solomon and Mary from Nathan — both descendants of David through Bathsheba. It is very important that we know that.

Luke 1:34,35

> Then said Mary unto the angel, How shall this be, seeing I know not a man? And the angel answered and said unto her, The Holy Ghost shall come upon thee, and the power of the Highest shall overshadow thee: therefore also that holy thing which shall be born of thee shall be called the Son of God.

Reaching God Through Christ

Here we see the incarnation of God coming by His Spirit. First, God the Son, the everlasting God who created the world, then the

Holy Spirit who is everlasting God, who conceived the human body of the Son and who had coexisted with the Father from the beginning. We must understand that Mary bore His humanity but not the Christ part of Jesus. The Christ part was conceived by the Holy Spirit and coexisted with the Father from the beginning. In the mystery of the incarnation, God is becoming flesh and flesh is becoming God. God is so much man, it is as though He were not God, and man is so much God, it is as though He were not man. He is total God and total man — God, who is eternal, omniscient, omnipresent, omnipotent, and man that He might reflect what God is like.

Jesus was later to say in John 14 that "If you see me, you have seen the Father." Therefore, as we follow Jesus' life and study His ministry, understanding His preaching, teaching, healing, and doing good, we understand what God is like and we fall in love with God rather than having some fear of the mystery of Him, of His being so far removed from our sensibilities that we cannot grasp Him at all. It is through Jesus Christ that we really come into holy union, full union with the heavenly Father.

Luke 1:36-38

> And behold, thy cousin Elisabeth, she hath also conceived a son in her old age: and this is the sixth month with her, who was called barren. For with God nothing shall be impossible. And Mary said, Behold the handmaid of the Lord; be it unto me according to thy word. And the angel departed from her.

Obedience is Faith

Zacharias was full of doubt and unbelief about the angel's announcement of the birth of John the Baptist through him and his wife because they were both old and his wife was barren, but Mary was in a contrasting situation. She was sensitive to God. Willing and obedient. Although she did not understand, she said, "Here I am. Let the Lord do unto me as He wills. Behold, I am a servant girl of the Lord." Then the angel left because He knew he had found the obedient one. Obedience is the key to deliverance. It always has been the main thing with God and His people. When Israel disobeyed, they lost. When they obeyed, they gained everything. The key to your life and mine with God is obedience, simply to obey. Whether we understand or misunderstand, whether it is great or small, we simply must obey. That is faith.

Luke 1:39-41

> And Mary arose in those days and went into the hill country with

> haste, into a city of Juda; and entered into the house of Zacharias, and saluted Elisabeth. And it came to pass, that, when Elisabeth heard the salutation of Mary, the babe leaped in her womb; and Elisabeth was filled with the Holy Ghost.

Holy Ghost Experience

When we read the phrase "filled with the Holy Ghost," it is not the same as being baptized with the Holy Ghost. Later, John the Baptist was to say of Christ, "He shall baptize you with the Holy Ghost," and he said that after he had been filled with the Holy Ghost himself. In the first and second chapters of Luke's second book, Acts, we will learn that there is a baptism with the Holy Ghost.

Luke 1:42-44

> And she spake out with a loud voice, and said, Blessed art thou among women, and blessed is the fruit of thy womb. And whence is this to me, that the mother of my Lord should come to me? For, lo, as soon as the voice of thy salutation sounded in mine ears, the babe leaped in my womb for joy.

God is Joy

Joy is the surest sign of the presence of God. It is also the surest sign of the strength of God, for we are told by Nehemiah in the Old Testament that the joy of the Lord is thy strength. In some mysterious way, the babe, John the Baptist, leaped in Elisabeth's womb, and it was a leap of joy. The Christian faith was to be announced with joy and the keynote of it would be the joy of the Lord.

Luke 1:45

> And blessed is she that believed: for there shall be a performance of those things which were told her from the Lord.

Precious Prophetic Power

Blessed are those who believe, not those who spend their time in endless argumentation and asking millions of questions, but blessed are they who simply believe and obey. The one thing we can stake it all on is that God will be what He is and do what He said He would do. Elisabeth was speaking by the inspiration of the

Holy Spirit, or in a prophetic manner. There was no evidence that Mary was pregnant, because her body was not large then. Elisabeth had not been in communication with Mary. The Holy Spirit revealed to her the pregnancy of Mary, the great one who was in her, and that Mary was blessed of all women in her obedience to do what the Lord said, and the Lord would not let her down.

Oh, how precious is the prophetic power of the Holy Spirit! The dreams and visions of the Spirit are just as real today as they were then.

Luke 1:46,47

> And Mary said, My soul doth magnify the Lord, and my spirit hath rejoiced in God my Saviour.

Christ the Mediator

Mary says very clearly that God is her Savior. There is no such thing biblically as "immaculate conception," that is, that Mary was sinless herself. She was a normal follower of God, a daughter of Abraham, a descendant of David whose obedience was perfect as far as her ability was concerned, and who believed what God said. She was looking to Him as her Savior.

Mary was a marvelous, indescribable, incomparable woman, obedient, faithful, and willing, but that is all she was. In no way are we to pray to her or to think that she sits at God's side or that we have to go through her to get to her son. No! Jesus Christ is the mediator between God and man.

Luke 1:49-50

> For he hath regarded the low estate of his handmaiden: for, behold, from henceforth all generations shall call me blessed. For he that is mighty hath done to me great things; and holy is his name. And his mercy is on them that fear him from generation to generation.

Mercy Through Obedience

When she finishes glorifying God for doing great things in and through her, she then speaks of His same mercy being upon all who fear Him from generation to generation. She is saying that she is a person of low estate who, in her obedience to God, has been lifted up and therefore the same thing can happen to us. However lowly we may be, when we obey God, God shows His mercy to us and lifts us up in Him.

Luke 1:51-66

He hath shewed strength with his arm; he hath scattered the proud in the imagination of their hearts. He hath put down the mighty from their seats, and exalted them of low degree. He hath filled the hungry with good things; and the rich he hath sent empty away. He hath helped his servant Israel, in remembrance of his mercy; as he spake to our fathers, to Abraham, and to his seed for ever. And Mary abode with her about three months, and returned to her own house.

Now Elisabeth's full time came that she should be delivered; and she brought forth a son. And her neighbours and her cousins heard how the Lord had shewed great mercy upon her; and they rejoiced with her. And it came to pass, that on the eighth day they came to circumcise the child; and they called him Zacharias, after the name of his father. And his mother answered and said, Not so; but he shall be called John. And they said unto her, There is none of thy kindred that is called by this name. And they made signs to his father, how he would have him called. And he asked for a writing table, and wrote, saying, His name is John. And they marvelled all.

And his mouth was opened immediately, and his tongue loosed, and he spake, and praised God. And fear came on all that dwelt round about them: and all these sayings were noised abroad throughout all the hill country of Judaea. And all they that heard them laid them up in their hearts, saying, What manner of child shall this be! And the hand of the Lord was with him.

Prophecy Fulfillment Marvelous

When Zacharias had replied to the announcement of the angel, "How will I know this?" that was unbelief, and the angel had told him he would be mute. When the baby was born and they wanted to name him after Zacharias, his wife said "No." They turned to the father, Zacharias, who was still mute, and they knew this was a sign from the Lord. In order for this sign to be fulfilled and the muteness to be removed, Zacharias wrote the name John. Because of that, all the people were amazed and wondered at what manner of child he would be.

Luke 1:67-69

And his father Zacharias was filled with the Holy Ghost, and prophesied, saying, Blessed be the Lord God of Israel; for he hath visited and redeemed his people, and hath raised up an horn of salvation for us in the house of his servant David.

The term "horn of salvation " usually referred to the horns of oxen, which symbolized power. He was saying that God had raised up the power of salvation for those of the house of David.

Luke 1:70-75

As he spake by the mouth of his holy prophets, which have been since the world began: that we should be saved from our enemies, and from the hand of all that hate us; to perform the mercy promised to our fathers, and to remember his holy covenant; the oath which he sware to our father Abraham, that he would grant unto us, that we being delivered out of the hand of our enemies might serve him without fear, in holiness and righteousness before him all the days of our life.

Qualities of Faith

Zacharias, in his prophetic utterance under the inspiration of the Holy Spirit, is speaking of the mighty power of salvation that would come. And through our own faith we would be delivered from the hand of our enemies and serve God, first, without fear; second, in holiness; third, in righteousness; and fourth, we will be able to continue to endure all the days of our lives.

Luke 1:76-80

And thou, child, shalt be called the prophet of the Highest: for thou shalt go before the face of the Lord to prepare his ways; to give knowledge of salvation unto his people by the remission of their sins, through the tender mercy of our God; whereby the dayspring from on high hath visited us, to give light to them that sit in darkness and in the shadow of death, to guide our feet into the way of peace.

And the child grew, and waxed strong in spirit, and was in the deserts till the day of his shewing unto Israel.

We do know that later, when John the Baptist was grown, he was a man of the desert. Some have thought that his parents died. We do not know, but we do know that from an early age he went to the desert in his communion with God and in preparation to be the Elijah or the preparer of the way of the Messiah and to show the people there was great light in their darkness. Of course, in Israel, the deserts are never far away.

Luke 2:1-6

> And it came to pass in those days, that there went out a decree from Caesar Augustus, that all the world should be taxed. (And this taxing was first made when Cyrenius was governor of Syria.) And all went to be taxed, every one into his own city. And Joseph also went up from Galilee, out of the city of Nazareth, into Judaea, unto the city of David, which is called Bethlehem (because he was of the house and lineage of David): to be taxed with Mary his espoused wife, being great with child. And so it was, that, while they were there, the days were accomplished that she should be delivered.

God Used Caesar

Mary, the espoused wife of Joseph, was legally his wife although they had not come together as man and wife. Joseph has accompanied her to their own hometown, to be registered in the city of David, their father. It is important to understand that when Caesar decided to tax the world and take a census of the world, he thought it was his own idea, but God had to move in history and to rearrange things, people, and places in order for His Son to be born at the only moment in history that He could have been born.

There was no war in the world to take away from the event or to prohibit people from traveling. In addition, the Romans had built great, enduring roads, many parts of which remain today in the Mediterranean area. That meant people could travel and the news of the child's birth could spread by way of those hard-surfaced roads to the ends of the Roman Empire. It was a time of peace. It was a time of great roads, and it was a time when there was one universally understood language, meaning that the birth of Jesus could be told in one language and people could understand without distortion. These are just a few of the propitious things God brought together for the birth of His Son Jesus Christ.

Another outstanding thing is Jesus had to be born in Bethlehem to fulfill prophecy. The problem was how to get Joseph and Mary from Nazareth, in the north near Galilee, to Bethlehem, about a 3 day journey at that time. Old Augustus Caesar, sitting in Rome and making up his mind to tax the world and have a census, did not know God was going to use him to get Mary from Nazareth to Bethlehem, use his roads, use the language of commerce which he had chosen to use, and use the time of his forced peace. Oh, how mighty is God!

Luke 2:7-11

> And she brought forth her firstborn son, and wrapped him in swaddling

clothes, and laid him in a manger; because there was no room for them in the inn.

And there were in the same country shepherds abiding in the field, keeping watch over their flock by night. And, lo, the angel of the Lord came upon them, and the glory of the Lord shown round about them: and they were sore afraid. And the angel said unto them, Fear not: for, behold, I bring you good tidings of great joy, which shall be to all people. For unto you is born this day in the city of David a Saviour, which is Christ the Lord.

Gospel of Joy

When the angel came to any of those people, they were always afraid and immediately the angel said, "Fear not." There is a Satanic fear in the hearts of all of us, particularly when we come into contact with God, with things supernatural and eternal. I do not know what it is there unless it is the consequence of the fall of man in the garden of Eden, but God does not want us to live with fear. The angel told the shepherds, "I bring you good tidings of great joy which shall be to all people." The gloom that is over this world is of the devil, but I thank God that the gospel is a gospel of joy. Joy, joy, joy, to all people.

Luke 2:12

And this shall be a sign unto you; Ye shall find the babe wrapped in swaddling clothes, lying in a manger.

Finding Jesus

God has always used signs or particular manifestations by which people will know that it is God. Many of those signs were in the Old Testament. Here is another sign at the birth of Jesus and there will be many other signs and wonders. The angel also told those shepherds they would find the babe. Do not ever be concerned about finding the Lord. You can find Jesus. If you have any doubt in your heart, just stop it and understand, receive the truth, God will let you find His Son Jesus Christ.

Luke 2:13,14

And suddenly there was with the angel a multitude of the heavenly host praising God, and saying, Glory to God in the highest, and on earth peace, good will toward men.

Those shepherds heard the first song that was sung about our Savior, "Glory to God in the highest." In other words, "Hallelujah, praise God, glory to His name," because He has brought peace and goodwill toward men by the birth of His Son Jesus Christ.

Luke 2:15-18

And it came to pass, as the angels were gone away from them into heaven, the shepherds said one to another, Let us now go even unto Bethlehem, and see this thing which is come to pass, which the Lord hath made known unto us. And they came with haste, and found Mary, and Joseph, and the babe lying in a manger. And when they had seen it, they made known abroad the saying which was told them concerning this child. And all they that heard it wondered at those things which were told them by the shepherds.

The Overflowing Heart

Shepherds never leave their flocks by night. It would be too dangerous because the sheep might be destroyed. But these shepherds had heard a greater message: a greater one was awaiting them. They found the babe along with Mary and Joseph and there at the manger they looked, they listened, they heard the explanation, they believed it, and they went and told everybody concerning this child. There is not anybody who honestly meets Jesus Christ who can hold in the joy, or hold back the tide of telling the good news. The dawn breaks, the clouds lift, and the glory comes down! The joy wells up inside when you meet Jesus. When I met Him at 17, as I lay dying with tuberculosis, the joy filled my heart. His presence came up through my limbs, through my body, and I was praising God. My hands were up, I was glorifying the Lord. Your conversion may not be by the same methodology as mine, but it is going to be definite, I assure you of that, and you are going to have Him overflowing your heart.

Luke 2:19

But Mary kept all these things, and pondered them in her heart.

Mediating God's Ways

Mary did not know everything. Remember, it was not an immaculate conception. Mary was an obscure girl, a humble serving girl. She was a girl who loved the Lord and obeyed Him. She did not understand all. She simply said, "May this be unto me as the angel has said." She kept all those things in her heart and she meditated upon them and she set the stage for all of us to meditate upon the wondrous things of God, things that we do not understand about how God deals with us.

Luke 2:20-24

> And the shepherds returned, glorifying and praising God for all the things that they had heard and seen, as it was told unto them. And when eight days were accomplished for the circumcising of the child, his name was called JESUS, which was so named of the angel before he was conceived in the womb.
>
> And when the days of her purification according to the law of Moses were accomplished, they brought him to Jerusalem, to present him to the Lord. (As it is written in the law of the Lord, every male that openeth the womb shall be called holy to the Lord;) and to offer a sacrifice according to that which is said in the law of the Lord, A pair of turtledoves, or two young pigeons.

Intent Counts

This refers to people who were poor, who did not have a lot of money, but were never excluded from the Lord even though they would bring only a pair of turtledoves or young pigeons. It was the intent of the heart that counted then and now.

Luke 2:25,26

> And, behold, there was a man in Jerusalem, whose name was Simeon, and the same man was just and devout, waiting for the consolation of Israel: and the Holy Ghost was upon him. And it was revealed unto him by the Holy Ghost, that he should not see death, before he had seen the Lord's Christ.

Simeon had a secret. He knew something nobody else in the world knew. He was not frightened by death. The Holy Spirit had revealed to him that he could not die until his eyes had looked upon the babe, the Son of God. It is marvelous how the Holy Spirit can reveal things. When the Spirit reveals them to you, you need not worry about people disarranging them or causing them to stop, because the Holy Spirit is omnipotent, all-powerful, and He is going to bring to pass what He has said.

Luke 2:27-32

And he came by the Spirit into the temple: and when the parents brought in the child Jesus, to do for him after the custom of the law, then took he him up in his arms, and blessed God, and said, Lord, now lettest thou thy servant depart in peace, according to thy word: for mine eyes have seen thy salvation, which thou hast prepared before the face of all people; a light to lighten the Gentiles, and the glory of thy people Israel.

God's Covenant Intact

This reference goes all the way back to Isaiah's prophecy in Isaiah 42:6, but even beyond that to Abraham—Abraham who was told by God that he would be a light to the Gentiles, to the nations of the world. And here we see where the children of Israel were no longer that light nor a witness to the nations of the world. But God was not going to leave the nations and the people of the world without light or without a Redeemer. He was going to keep His covenant with Abraham and His love with all His race whom He created in His image. Simeon was so in touch with God that he knew this babe would be a light to light the way of all Gentiles and also be the glory of the people of Israel.

Luke 2:33-35

And Joseph and his mother marvelled at those things which were spoken of him. And Simeon blessed them, and said unto Mary his mother, Behold, this child is set for the fall and rising again of many in Israel; and for a sign which shall be spoken against (Yea, a sword shall pierce through thy own soul also); that the thoughts of many hearts may be revealed.

Mary's Soul Burden

Simeon's reference to a sword piercing the soul of Mary was a reference to the suffering she would have to endure. When the people called Jesus terrible names and finally killed Him, she had to stand by, to hear all that, to see all that, to feel all that to the very depths of her soul.

Luke 2:36-38

And there was one Anna, a prophetess, the daughter of Phanuel, of the tribe of Aser: she was of a great age, and had lived with an husband seven years from her virginity: and she was a widow of about fourscore and four years, which departed not from the temple, but served God with fastings and prayers night and day. And she coming in that instant gave thanks likewise unto the Lord, and spake of him to all them that looked for redemption in Jerusalem.

Anna's Destiny

Anna was not a woman who said, "Well, I will just retire and let the church take care of me." She entered into the service of God and therein the Lord provided for her, giving her proper revelations and at the right time bringing her forth. At the moment Simeon gave the last of his prophecy, she entered, reinforced it, and encouraged all those who looked for redemption.

Luke 2:39-50

And when they had performed all things according to the law of the Lord, they returned into Galilee, to their own city Nazareth. And the child grew, and waxed strong in spirit, filled with wisdom: and the grace of God was upon him. Now his parents went to Jerusalem every year at the feast of the passover. And when he was twelve years old, they went up to Jerusalem after the custom of the feast. And when they had fulfilled the days, as they returned, the child Jesus tarried behind in Jerusalem; and Joseph and his mother knew not of it. But they, supposing him to have been in the company, went a day's journey; and they sought him among their kinsfolk and acquaintance. And when they found him not, they turned back again to Jerusalem, seeking him.

And it came to pass, that after three days they found him in the temple, sitting in the midst of the doctors, both hearing them, and asking them questions. And all that heard him were astonished at his understanding and answers. And when they saw him, they were amazed: and his mother said unto him, Son, why hast thou thus dealt with us? behold, thy Father and I have sought thee sorrowing. And he said unto them, How is it that ye sought me? wist ye not that I must be about my Father's business? And they understood not the saying which he spake unto them.

Go Back for God

People seeking God today will turn to kinfolks and turn to friends and turn to this one and that one, but to find God you have to go back where you left Him. Where did you leave Him? You left Him, still being God, at that moment or time in your life when you really were sensitive toward God, when you were aware that God was real. He is still there. He is still real. They were gone a day, but took 3 days to find him because they had presumed something. With someone in your life as important as Jesus Christ, you must not presume, you must know! And you can know that you know that you know that Christ is with you! If He is not, you must not stop until you find Him.

It took them 3 days. It may take you even more, it may take you less. The important thing is to find Him. He was telling us there is a point in our lives when spiritual things take precedence over everything. The ethical, moral, spiritual laws of God are paramount. Even at the age of 12. A child at that age today can understand. They can understand a lot more than we think.

Luke 2:51

> And he went down with them, and came to Nazareth, and was subject unto them: but his mother kept all these sayings in her heart. And Jesus increased in wisdom and stature, and in favour with God and man.

Always Grow in Christ

The increase of Jesus' life is a remarkable demonstration for you and me to follow. Not only did He grow in His body but He grew in wisdom and He found favor with God and with people. He was busy. He obeyed His parents, He grew, He worked in the carpenter shop, He kept himself busy. As with every Jewish child, He learned a trade. He went to the synagogue schools. He went to the house of God on the sabbath days. He worshipped the Lord. He became a well-rounded human being. He grew as a whole man — in body, mind and spirit. As a follower of Christ, you should never stop growing. You should never stop learning. You should always be increasing yourself, growing in the Lord, growing in your mind, developing your health, and becoming more of a well-rounded human being every day of your life.

Luke 3:1-14

> Now in the fifteenth year of the reign of Tiberius Caesar, Pontius Pilate being governor of Judaea, and Herod being tetrarch of Galilee, and his brother Philip tetrarch of Ituraea and of the region of Trachonitis, and Lysanias the tetrarch of Abilene, Annas and Caiaphas

being the high priests, the word of God came unto John the son of Zacharias in the wilderness. And he came into all the country about Jordan, preaching the baptism of repentance for the remission of sins; as it is written in the book of the words of Esaias the prophet, saying, The voice of one crying in the wilderness, Prepare ye the way of the Lord, make his paths straight. Every valley shall be filled, and every mountain and hill shall be brought low; and the crooked shall be made straight, and the rough ways shall be made smooth; and all flesh shall see the salvation of God.

Then said he to the multitude that came forth to be baptized of him, O generation of vipers, who hath warned you to flee from the wrath to come? Bring forth therefore fruits worthy of repentance, and begin not to say within yourselves, We have Abraham to our father: for I say unto you, That God is able of these stones to raise up children unto Abraham. And now also the axe is laid unto the root of the trees: Every tree therefore which bringeth not forth good fruit is hewn down, and cast into the fire.

And the people asked him, saying, What shall we do then? He answereth and saith unto them, He that hath two coats, let him impart to him that hath none; and he that hath meat, let him do likewise.

Then came also publicans to be baptized, and said unto him, Master, what shall we do? And he said unto them, Exact no more than that which is appointed you. And the soldiers likewise demanded of him, saying, And what shall we do? And he said unto them, Do violence to no man, neither accuse any falsely; and be content with your wages.

God to the Point

Only in Luke are we told about the soldiers. They were Roman soldiers who brutalized the people of Israel, who were always accusing them falsely. John the Baptist challenged and instructed them how to behave, as he did with the publicans and the people of Israel. John pointed out to each of them specifically what they were to do. His teaching should remind us that God always comes to us at the point of our need, at the point where we should change. God deals with us in a specific way. He always individualizes His love for us, His concern and compassion, and His instructions for our lives.

Luke 3:15-22

And as the people were in expectation, and all men mused in their hearts of John, whether he were the Christ, or not; John answered, saying unto them all, I indeed baptize you with water; but one mightier than I cometh, the latchet of whose shoes I am not worthy to unloose; he shall baptize you with the Holy Ghost and with fire: whose fan is in his hand, and he will throughly purge his floor, and will gather the wheat into his garner; but the chaff he will burn with fire unquenchable. And many other things in his exhortation preached he unto the people.

But Herod the tetrarch, being reproved by him for Herodias his brother Philip's wife, and for all the evils which Herod had done, added yet this above all, that he shut up John in prison.

Now when all the people were baptized, it came to pass, that Jesus also being baptized, and praying, the heaven was opened, and the Holy Ghost descended in a bodily shape like a dove upon him, and a voice came from heaven, which said, Thou art my beloved son; in thee I am well pleased.

The Gap is Closed

John the Baptist was bringing the old covenant to an end, to its fulfillment, to that time when Jesus Christ, the Messiah, would arrive on the scene with His great power to baptize with the Holy Ghost and fire, to endue them with the Spirit of God so the Holy Spirit would cleanse and purify their lives and fill them with the very Spirit that created this universe — the Spirit of God, the Spirit that would give them life.

John the Baptist knew he was the forerunner of the Christ. His preaching rang through that countryside. He had preached repentance to tell the people to feel their sense of sin, their unworthiness and their deep need for the Messiah to come. He had told them it was a matter of life and death, that without Christ there would be no deliverance; therefore, they must repent and prepare for the coming of this wonderful Messiah who is Christ the Lord. John said, "When He comes He is going to do mightier things than I am doing." What was John the Baptist doing? He was preaching, teaching, and baptizing people in water, but he was not able to lead the people to the infilling of the Holy Spirit. As we study Luke and then John and Acts, we are going to see how the power of the Holy Spirit overshadows us and brings us into the new covenant, that covenant of grace, of light, of power, where we become new creatures in Jesus Christ. I thank God that John the Baptist was the one who closed the gap, who brought to an end or fulfillment the old and presented the new, and that Jesus arrived as the Son of the living God ready to fill the people with the Holy Spirit.

Luke 3:23-38

> And Jesus himself began to be about thirty years of age, being (as was supposed) the son of Joseph, who was the son of Heli, who was the son of Matthat, who was the son of Levi, who was the son of Melchi, who was the son of Janna, who was the son of Joseph, who was the son of Mattathias, who was the son of Amos, who was the son of Naum, who was the son of Esli, who was the son of Nagge, who was the son of Maath, who was the son of Mattathias, who was the son of Semei, who was the son of Joseph, who was the son of Juda, who was the son of Joanna, who was the son of Rhesa, who was the son of Zorobabel, who was the son of Salathiel, who was the son of Neri, who was the son of Melchi, who was the son of Addi, who was the son of Cosam, who was the son of Elmodam, who was the son of Er, who was the son of Jose, who was the son of Eliezer, who was the son of Jorim, who was the son of Matthat, who was the son of Levi, who was the son of Simeon, who was the son of Juda, who was the son of Joseph, who was the son of Jonan, who was the son of Eliakim, who was the son of Melea, who was the son of Menan, who was the son of Mattatha, who was the son of Nathan, who was the son of David, who was the son of Jesse, who was the son of Obed, who was the son of Booz, who was the son of Salmon, who was the son of Naasson, who was the son of Aminadab, who was the son of Aram, who was the son of Esrom, who was the son of Phares, who was the son of Juda, who was the son of Jacob, who was the son of Isaac, who was the son of Abraham, who was the son of Thara, who was the son of Nachor, who was the son of Saruch, who was the son of Ragau, who was the son of Phalec, who was the son of Heber, who was the son of Sala, who was the son of Cainan, who was the son of Arphaxad, who was the son of Sem, who was the son of Noe, who was the son of Lamech, who was the son of Mathusala, who was the son of Enoch, who was the son of Jared, who was the son of Maleleel, who was the son of Cainan, who was the son of Enos, who was the son of Seth, who was the son of Adam, who was the son of God.

The lineage is traced to Adam. In Verse 31 of Luke 3, we are told that Jesus is traced to the son of Nathan who was the son of David. That is Mary's genealogy. Joseph descended from Solomon, David's son by Bathsheba, and Mary by Nathan, David's son by Bathsheba.

Luke 4:1

> And Jesus being full of the Holy Ghost returned from the Jordan, and was led by the Spirit into the wilderness . . .

It is Luke who reminds us repeatedly that it was the Holy Spirit who anointed Jesus. He went in the power of the Holy Spirit and it was the witness of the Spirit to Jesus' spirit that gave Him power as the Son of Man to be the full Son of God in order to deliver the people. People who are operating under the charismatic power of the Holy Spirit today are reaching into the depths of more people, touching them at the deepest levels of their being. They are the ones whom God is using more than any others to bring healing to the sick, to cast out devils, to bring a new inspiration and anointing of the Holy Spirit. Let me start with Verse 1 again . . .

Luke 4:1-13

And Jesus being full of the Holy Ghost returned from the Jordan, and was led by the Spirit into the wilderness, being forty days tempted of the devil. And in those days he did eat nothing: and when they were ended, he afterward hungered. And the devil said unto him, If thou be the Son of God, command this stone that it be made bread.

And Jesus answered him, saying, It is written, That man shall not live by bread alone, but by every word of God.

And the devil, taking him up into an high mountain, shewed unto him all the kingdoms of the world in a moment of time. And the devil said unto him, All this power will I give thee, and the glory of them: for that is delivered unto me; and to whomsoever I will I give it. If thou therefore wilt worship me, all shall be thine.

And Jesus answered and said unto him, Get thee behind me, Satan: for it is written, Thou shalt worship the Lord thy God, and him only shalt thou serve. And he brought him to Jerusalem, and set him on a pinnacle of the temple, and said unto him, If thou be the Son of God, cast thyself down from hence: for it is written, He shall give his angels charge over thee, to keep thee: and in their hands they shall bear thee up, lest at any time thou dash thy foot against a stone.

And Jesus answering said unto him, It is said, Thou shalt not tempt the Lord thy God.

And when the devil had ended all the temptation, he departed from him for a season.

Defeating the Devil

The devil is a personality, just as Jesus is a personality, except he is a fallen archangel while Jesus is the Son of God. Do not forget that the devil talks and people hear him. They either hear his voice or they feel his impressions or they are persuaded by him, but Jesus talked back. Jesus kept saying, "It is written." The only thing Jesus replied to the devil was that which God had said. We must not argue with the devil; we must use the Word of God and stand on it. In Verse 13, when it said the temptation had ended, it did not mean the devil would not tempt the Lord Jesus again. He simply left him "for a season."

When we triumph over the devil by the Word of God and our faith in the Lord Jesus, then the devil may leave us for a particular period of time, but he will return because his battle is a battle with God and we are the ones who are the prize. The devil simply withdraws until he has another opportunity and then he returns to tempt us. Meanwhile, we are studying and knowing the Word of God, immersing ourselves in His teaching, building up our faith in the Lord and preparing ourselves so we can withstand the devil on every and any issue at any time, any place.

Luke 4:14,15

> And Jesus returned in the power of the Spirit into Galilee; and there went out a fame of him through all the region round about. And he taught in their synagogues, being glorified of all.

Synagogue's Origin

When the temple was destroyed during the Babylonian captivity, when Israel was held in Babylon, the Hebrew people established the synagogue, a type of building in which they instructed their children as well as the adults. The synagogue institution was returned with them to the Holy Land and the temple was rebuilt. Synagogues were scattered throughout Jerusalem and the towns and villages of the land.

Luke 4:16,17

> And he came to Nazareth, where he had been brought up: and, as his custom was, he went into the synagogue on the sabbath day, and stood up for to read. And there was delivered unto him the book of the prophet Esaias. And when he had opened the book, he found the place where it was written...

The "book" handed to Jesus was actually a scroll that unwound from both top and bottom as it was read. It was very rare and terribly expensive because every word was copied by hand and there was usually only one scroll of any book of the Bible in a synagogue at one time.

Luke 4:18,19

> The Spirit of the Lord is upon me, because he hath anointed me to preach the gospel to the poor; he hath sent me to heal the brokenhearted, to preach deliverance to the captives, and recovering of sight to the blind, to set at liberty them that are bruised, to preach the acceptable year of the Lord.

Deliverance Through Jesus

Jesus said, "The Spirit of the Lord is upon me." Not even the incarnate Son of God attempted to do God's work without the Holy Spirit being upon Him. It is sad today that many in the Christian Church do not even know who the Holy Spirit is. We must come back to the fountain of knowledge, the Word of God, and see again that our Lord Jesus Christ came in the "power of the Spirit" and said that the Holy Spirit was intimately and powerfully upon Him! Then He adds, "because he has anointed me." "He has anointed me." I have often said the anointing is that power of God that comes upon you and then separates you from yourself and fills you with the glory, so that when you speak, it is like God speaking: when you act, it is like God acting. The anointing is so precious to me that when I began this ministry in 1947, I made a vow to God that I would never enter the pulpit to preach without first having experienced the anointing of the Holy Spirit going through me, that is to say, the Holy Spirit's power would come upon me and separate Oral Roberts from himself, and so fill him with the glory of God that when he spoke it would be like God speaking, and when he acted it would be like God acting. That vow has been very precious to me. The Word of God is already anointed, but I must be anointed myself, and so must everybody else who deals with the Word of God. Jesus said that He was sent to preach the gospel to the poor, to the deprived, to the disenfranchised.

Luke had an eye for the social outcast, for the sick and afflicted, for those who did not have anything. Doctors have such a keen eye for suffering people — people who have lost their health, lost their money — and Jesus came to preach to these poor people. What did He preach? The power of the gospel. The good news that Jesus can deliver even from poverty.

So many times in the Christian church today we hold up poverty as a virtue. Poverty exists to be wiped out. Jesus said He was sent to preach deliverance to people who were captive — those in bondage in the yoke of sin, in the thrall of disease, of fear and torment. The anointing breaks the yoke. It breaks the yoke of sin.

It breaks the yoke of disease. It breaks the yoke of demon possession. It breaks the yoke of fear and torment. It releases us.

Jesus said He was sent to recover sight to the blind, and that refers not only to physical blindness, but also to that terrible blindness of spirit and soul. He said He was sent to set at liberty those who are bruised, those who are beaten and bruised, and knocked about in the battle of life. Look at them all around you. Look at yourself at times when you feel beaten up — whether by someone's fist or just by the circumstances of life. You are bruised. Jesus came to set you free. To heal those bruises.

Finally Jesus said He came to preach the acceptable year of the Lord. That was the message of mercy. He did not add, the vengeance of the Lord. At that time He was coming in mercy to deliver the people.

Luke 4:20,21

> And he closed the book, and he gave it again to the minister, and sat down. And the eyes of all them that were in the synagogue were fastened on him. And he began to say unto them, This day is this scripture fulfilled in your ears.

In other words, He was saying, In the now, right now, this moment, this split second, all I have read is right here, resident in Me, and I am present to deliver you.

Luke 4:22-30

> And all bare him witness, and wondered at the gracious words which proceeded out of his mouth. And they said, Is not this Joseph's son? And he said unto them, Ye will surely say unto me this proverb, Physician, heal thyself; whatsoever we have heard done in Capernaum, do also here in thy country.
>
> And he said, Verily I say unto you, No prophet is accepted in his own country. But I tell you of a truth, many widows were in Israel in the days of Elias, when the heaven was shut up three years and six months, when great famine was throughout all the land; but unto none of them was Elias sent, save unto Sarepta, a city of Sidon, unto a woman that was a widow.
>
> And many lepers were in Israel in the time of Eliseus the prophet; and none of them was cleansed, saving Naaman the Syrian.
>
> And all they in the synagogue, when they heard these things, were filled with wrath, and rose up, and thrust him out of the city, and led him unto the brow of the hill whereon their city was built, that they might cast him down headlong. But he passing through the midst of them went his way.

Jesus is speaking of Elijah and Elisha, the two prophets whom the Israelites thought were their greatest. Jesus compared himself to Elijah when Elijah helped the widow of Zarephath by asking her to give him something, first as a man of God, and then promising her that the rest would be multiplied and would take care of her through the famine. Then He compared himself with Elisha, the prophet who brought healing to Naaman, the general of Syria who was a Gentile. When they understood what Jesus was saying, they were offended because of who they thought He was. To them, He was Joseph's boy. They had seen Him grow up in their town. Now here He was speaking such impressive words, and speaking them so graciously, that they were offended. Their hostility overcame them and they rose up against Him, and seized Him and led Him to the brow of the hill upon which the city was built and tried to cast him headlong to His death, but Jesus performed a mighty miracle. He did not fight them; He just walked through them and went on about His work.

Jesus was pointing up religious bias and was telling them that the gospel was for the whole world, for the Gentile world as well as the Hebrews. Remember that Abraham, the father of all who had faith, was called of God to take the light of God to all the nations and the peoples of the world. If you have faith you're a true son or daughter of Abraham and you should be willing to share your faith with whosoever will, so that all of us will get the good news of our God to this lost, suffering, and benighted world.

Luke 4:31,32

> And came down to Capernaum, a city of Galilee, and taught them on the sabbath days. And they were astonished at his doctrine; for his word was with power.

Power Plus Anointment

His Word was with power. No excuses. No quoting different people. His Word was simply coming from the Word of God, backed by the anointing of the Holy Spirit. His word was with power. Oh, give us ministers who speak with the power of God! Give us lay people who witness and testify with the power of God! Give us people who are anointed by the Holy Spirit and I will tell you, we will turn this world upside down again.

Luke 4:33-36

> And in the synagogue there was a man, which had a spirit of an unclean devil, and cried out with a loud voice, saying, Let us alone;

> what have we to do with thee, thou Jesus of Nazareth? art thou come to destroy us? I know thee who thou art; the Holy One of God. And Jesus rebuked him, saying, Hold thy peace, and come out of him. And when the devil had thrown him in the midst, he came out of him, and hurt him not.
>
> And they were all amazed, and spake among themselves, saying, What a word is this! for with authority and power he commandeth the unclean spirits, and they come out.

Importance of "Rebuke"

Pay particular attention to the word "rebuke." In Malachi 3:10,11, it says that when we bring our tithes and offerings unto God, He will open the windows of heaven and give us access to more miracles than we can receive. He will rebuke the devourer, another name for the devil, who is called a devourer, a deceiver, an adversary. Jesus rebuked the devourer, that is, He was rebuking that unclean spirit. He did not want that spirit of a fallen angel calling His name.

Luke 4:37-39a

> And the fame of him went out into every place of the country round about. And he arose out of the synagogue, and entered into Simon's house. And Simon's wife's mother was taken with a great fever; and they besought him for her. And he stood over her, and rebuked the fever . . .

Note the word "rebuke" again. He "rebuked" the fever.

Luke 4:39b-41a

> And it left her; and immediately she arose and ministered unto them.
>
> Now when the sun was setting, all they that had any sick with divers diseases brought them unto him; and he laid his hands on every one of them and healed them. And devils also came out of many, crying out, and saying, Thou art Christ the Son of God. And he rebuking them . . .

Note the word "rebuke" again. He "rebuked" the fever.

Remember "Rebuke"

The word "rebuke" is used again. Always keep the word "rebuke" in your mind, because when you give your tithes and offerings to God, He will rebuke the devourer for your sake.

Luke 4:41b-44

And he rebuking them suffered them not to speak: for they knew that he was Christ.

And when it was day, he departed and went into a desert place: and the people sought him, and came unto him, and stayed him, that he should not depart from them. And he said unto them, I must preach the kingdom of God to other cities also: for therefore am I sent. And he preached in the synagogues of Galilee.

In Luke 5, we are going to read about the net-breaking, boat-sinking load of fish that Jesus helped Peter and the disciples catch. I want to point out that Dr. Luke is the only one of the gospel writers who records this great event.

Luke 5:1-11

And it came to pass, that, as the people pressed upon him to hear the word of God, he stood by the lake of Gennesaret, and saw two ships standing by the lake: but the fishermen were gone out of them and were washing their nets. And he entered into one of the ships, which was Simon's, and prayed him that he would thrust out a little from the land. And he sat down, and taught the people out of the ship.

Now when he had left speaking, he said unto Simon, Launch out into the deep, and let down your nets for a draught. And Simon answering said unto him, Master, we have toiled all the night, and have taken nothing: nevertheless at thy word I will let down the net. And when they had this done, they inclosed a great multitude of fishes: and their net brake. And they beckoned unto their partners, which were in the other ship, that they should come and help them. And they came, and filled both the ships, so that they began to sink.

When Simon Peter saw it, he fell down at Jesus' knees, saying, Depart from me; for I am a sinful man, O Lord. For he was astonished, and all that were with him, at the draught of the fishes which they had taken.

And so was also James, and John, the sons of Zebedee, who were partners with Simon. And Jesus said unto Simon, Fear not; from henceforth thou shalt catch men. And when they had brought their ships to land, they forsook all, and followed him.

This Is Seed-Faith

Notice the interplay between Jesus and this man. The first thing Jesus did was ask Him to do something, to let Him have something of his, that is, to plant a seed. The next thing was that when the seed got into Jesus' hands, He multiplied it. He not only used it for a higher purpose, but He gave back to those same disciples who had given of their very living to Him. When they launched out and threw the net over, it was the same body of water, the same place they had thrown the nets over the night before, the place of failure. But everything was changed because they now had gotten into harmony with Jesus. They had become seed-faithers, givers, sharers with God of what they had. Then God began to open the windows of heaven. He began to rebuke the devourer, to rebuke the failure of the fish, to strike the net. And they came at it from every side and filled it so full that when Peter and the others began to haul it into the boat, it began to break up. When they got the fish into the boat, there were so many the boat began to shake and seemed as though it would sink. It was a net-breaking, boat-sinking load. It was a miracle of deliverance because they had planted a seed of faith; they had sown it, Christ had grown it, and now they were going to reap it.

And then Peter and the others fell down at Christ's feet once they got on the shore and said, We are sinful people, Lord. We don't feel comfortable in your presence. Leave us.

They were absolutely stunned by the catch of fish. I have never seen this fail. When a miracle of God happens, it most often settles the issue. It gets the job done. It brings people to a point of decision. That is what happened here. When they saw that God multiplied their giving, and as they depended upon His Word, he rebuked the failure and brought them more success than they were accustomed to. Yet they were intimidated. But the Lord said, You just follow Me. Follow Me and I will make you fishers of men.

Notice the word "make." Jesus was "making power." The making power of God is as real now in your life as it was when He said to Peter, I will make you. This story is exactly what it says. It says God will honor our giving and our depending on His Word by giving us a net-breaking, boat-sinking load of his miraculous power of deliverance and supply, and He will also make us throughout our lives, make our character, make our influence, make our witness, that we may become fishers of men, winners of souls, causing people to come to Christ.

Luke 5:12-14

> And it came to pass, when he was in a certain city, behold a man full of leprosy: who seeing Jesus fell on his face, and besought him, saying, Lord, if thou wilt, thou canst make me clean.
>
> And He put forth his hand and touched him, saying, I will: be thou clean. And immediately the leprosy departed from him. And he

charged him to tell no man: but go, and shew thyself to the priest, and offer for thy cleansing, according as Moses commanded, for a testimony unto them.

The Healing Christ

The concern of this man with leprosy was Jesus' willingness. He knew He could heal him, but would He? Was it His will? Was that within the purpose of his coming to the earth, to heal sick people? Many people have never settled that issue, even today, but Jesus settled it then once and for all. He said, "I will. Be thou clean." And he was healed. This is never to be doubted again because it is what Christ came to do. The healing of sick people by prayer, or by medicine, or by climate, or by nutrition, or by love, or by any good thing in this earth has been established by our Lord. We are never to doubt His will. He can and He will heal us.

All He wanted the leper to do after his healing was go to the priest and get what amounted to a health certificate. Lepers were not allowed to mingle with people in the towns, but were forced to live alone. Jesus wanted the man restored in himself and among the people, but only the priests could give that health certificate so the person could be restored to human society.

This is the Savior I know. I know the healing Christ. I know the Christ who heals us supernaturally and naturally. I know He is the one who combines medicine and prayer. I know it is His will to heal. This is why we go to doctors. This is why we use the chemicals of God's earth in the form of medicines. This is why we listen to our physicians. This is why we pray the prayer of faith — because God wants us well.

Some people believe that God heals only through prayer. Others believe that cures come only through medicine. They are both wrong, because God is the source of all healing. Whether it comes supernaturally alone, or naturally alone, or whether we are supernaturally natural or naturally supernatural, it is all God.

Luke 5:15,16

But so much the more went there a fame abroad of him: and great multitudes came together to hear, and to be healed by him of their infirmities. And he withdrew himself into the wilderness, and prayed.

Jesus' Prayer Life

Dr. Luke pays more attention to Jesus' prayer life than the

other gospel writers. Time after time Luke shows us that right in the midst of a great success or a terrible thing that Jesus had to pass through, He went apart to pray. He was a man of prayer.

Luke 5:17

> And it came to pass on a certain day, as he was teaching, that there were Pharisees and doctors of the law sitting by, which were come out of every town of Galilee, and Judaea, and Jerusalem: and the power of the Lord was present to heal them.

That crowd included Pharisees who hated Jesus. It included the doctors of the law of Moses, theologians who misinterpreted nearly everything Jesus said and did, and yet when they arrived, the power of the Lord was present to heal them. They needed it. The people today who oppose the power of God need to be healed. Wherever the opposition is to the Lord, there is also the power of the Lord present to heal. I praise God because He is omnipresent. He is everywhere at the same time and He is the same yesterday, today, and forever.

Luke 5:18-26

> And, behold, men brought in a bed a man which was taken with a palsy: and they sought means to bring him in, and to lay him before him. And when they could not find by what way they might bring him in because of the multitude, they went upon the housetop, and let him down through the tiling with his couch into the midst before Jesus.
>
> And when he saw their faith, he said unto him, Man, thy sins are forgiven thee.
>
> And the scribes and the Pharisees began to reason, saying, Who is this which speaketh blasphemies? Who can forgive sins, but God alone? But when Jesus perceived their thoughts, he answering said unto them, What reason ye in your hearts? Whether is easier, to say, Thy sins be forgiven thee; or to say, Rise up and walk? But that ye may know that the Son of man hath power upon earth to forgive sins, (he said unto the sick of the palsy,) I say unto thee, Arise, and take up thy couch, and go into thine house.
>
> And immediately he rose up before them, and took up that whereon he lay, and departed to his own house, glorifying God. And they were all amazed, and they glorified God, and were filled with fear, saying, We have seen strange things today.

Sharing Healing Faith

There are two powerful things present here. Number one, the

power of the Lord was present to heal the people, and number two, there were people who were taking advantage of that power, coming themselves, and bringing people who were close to them who were very ill. In this instance, Jesus was surrounded by critics and yet the power of God was present to heal. He was full of the healing power of God and nothing these critics could do or say could change that. In the midst of His discussion with those critics, men arrived who tore the roof off to let down, into the midst of the people, a man who was taken with palsy. Doubtless they were close to this man and they had taken his illness into their hearts and believed by their faith that Jesus Christ could change his situation.

How well I remember when I was diagnosed as having tuberculosis and was at that fateful time in my life when I could not help myself. The E.M. Roberts family, my family, came to my aid. My brother Vaden fell across my bed and my body and said, "Lord, put this TB on me, for I have always been stronger than Oral. I can bear it and he cannot." My sister, Jewel, said, "Oral, God is going to heal you." My brother Elmer, the oldest one in the family, borrowed a car and took me to be prayed for by an evangelist in a nearby city who was there praying for the healing of the sick. My parents held me up so that I would not fall as this evangelist laid his hands on me and prayed in the name of Christ that I would be healed. I can witness personally, that the men who brought their sick friend to be healed by Jesus are men to be looked at and considered in the light of our needs today.

In my crusades, most of the people who are really ill are brought by someone else. Some are sent by groups of people who collect money to send them by bus or by plane so that the person will have a chance to come into our healing line. They are people like this whose hearts are stirred and touched by the illnesses of others. They are also moved by a greater power — the power of faith, believing that if they could only get the ill person there, something good would happen. And something good did happen, all because these men got the sick brother on their hearts, went out of their way, planted their seeds of faith, and gave of their love, their faith, and their expectations of miracles, and that is also for you and me today. If you really believe in Jesus' healing power and you know where prayer is being offered, you can be a part of a healing. The four men are mentioned by Dr. Luke as a notable part of a miracle of the restoration of a fellow human being. You can imagine they never forgot it as long as they lived. Neither will you forget the part you play in helping someone be healed by the Lord Jesus Christ.

Luke 5:27-32

And after these things he went forth, and saw a publican, named Levi, sitting at the receipt of custom: and he said unto him, Follow me. And he left all, rose up, and followed him. And Levi made him a great feast in his own house: and there was a great company of publicans and of others that sat down with them. But their scribes and Pharisees murmured against his disciples, saying, Why do ye eat and drink with publicans and sinners? And Jesus answering said unto them, They that are whole need not a physician: but they that are sick. I came not to call the righteous, but sinners to repentance.

God to the Point

When this tax gatherer, Levi, who is really Matthew, accepted Christ, he immediately opened his great house to Him and all of his friends and many others, and they came and met Jesus. The scribes and Pharisees also were there and when they saw Jesus eating with people they despised, sinners and others, they asked why. Jesus told them flatly, "They that are sick need a physician."

I wish and pray that we will all hear that. We need physicians. We need men and women who care, who train themselves and who have a listening ear, and an open heart to suffering people in the world today. We must remove this supposed divider between the natural and supernatural. We must understand that both heaven and earth are God's, and that God is concerned about us at the point of our need. He sends people with the gospel whom we call preachers, evangelists, apostles, prophets, and others.

He also sends physicians and others who come to the point at people's needs because they have need. I thank God for a balanced Christian life. I thank God above all that He cares for us, for each of us, coming to us always at the point of our need.

Luke 5:33-39

And they said unto him, Why do the disciples of John fast often, and make prayers, and likewise the disciples of the Pharisees; but thine eat and drink?

And he said unto them, Can ye make the children of the bridechamber fast, while the bridegroom is with them? But the days will come, when the bridegroom shall be taken away from them, and then shall they fast in those days.

And he spake also a parable unto them; No man putteth a piece of new garment upon an old; if otherwise, then both the new maketh a rent, and the piece that was taken out of the new agreeth not with

> the old. And no man putteth new wine into old bottles; else, the new wine will burst the bottles, and be spilled, and the bottles shall perish. But new wine must be put into new bottles; and both are preserved. No man also having drunk old wine straightway desireth new, for he saith, The old is better.

Bigger Than the Book

Jesus is appealing both to men and women. He knows women understand that in sewing a garment, they do not put a piece of a new garment upon an old because it will be torn from its place. He knows men understand that they are to put new wine into new skins because the fermentation process expands and contracts the skins (or bottles) and new ones will hold and preserve their form instead of bursting and the wine will not be spilled. He is really saying more than that. He is saying something new has arrived. "It is new to you people because you have been looking for it so long. You have been living by the law of Moses. The law of Moses principally has been given you to teach you a sense of your sinfulness, that you cannot save yourself and you must have a Redeemer. All the old types of animal sacrifices have played their part and you cannot institute them into the new. You must go from the old animal sacrifices to Me, the Redeemer, the divine sacrifice who takes away your sins forever and makes you a new creature." In other words, He is saying, "We have to be open to the new things of the Holy Spirit."

So many people today hold onto a tradition they learned long ago. For example, here is the Bible, we have it in writing and there is no more revelation of God. Yet, we are told again and again that God will pour out His spirit. "Your young men shall see visions and your old men shall dream dreams and your young women shall prophesy." Theirs is revelational knowledge. They have and are the gifts of the Spirit. There is more knowledge being poured out day by day by the Lord Jesus Christ in His resurrected form through the Holy Spirit than any of us realize. Therefore, be open. Let God continue to reveal himself to you because God is bigger than the book. God is God and He is a continuing God.

Luke 6:1-11

> And it came to pass on the second sabbath after the first, that he went through the corn fields; and his disciples plucked the ears of corn, and did eat, rubbing them in their hands. And certain of the Pharisees said unto them, Why do ye that which is not lawful to do on the sabbath days?

And Jesus answering them said, Have ye not read so much as this, what David did, when himself was an hungred, and they which were with him; how he went into the house of God, and did take and eat the shewbread, and gave also to them that were with him; which is not lawful to eat but for the priests alone?

And he said unto them, That the son of man is Lord also of the Sabbath.

And it came to pass also on another sabbath, that he entered into the synagogue and taught: and there was a man whose right hand was withered. And the scribes and Pharisees watched him, whether he would heal on the sabbath day; that they might find an accusation against him.

But he knew their thoughts, and said to the man which had the withered hand, Rise up, and stand forth in the midst. And he arose and stood forth. Then said Jesus unto them, I will ask you one thing; Is it lawful on the sabbath days to do good, or to do evil? to save life, or to destroy it?

And looking round about upon them all, he said unto the man, Stretch forth thy hand. And he did so: and his hand was restored whole as the other.

And they were filled with madness; and communed one with another what they might do to Jesus.

Righteousness Has a Price

In Deuteronomy there was the law that you could pluck corn if you were hungry, but not on the sabbath. Christ's critics said, "It is not lawful for you to do this," and they began a campaign they carried on until the day He was nailed to the cross.

Jesus replied, in effect, that His Father had instituted that law and the law of the sabbath, but He had never put the sabbath above man. He reminded them of David. "Do you not remember the man who was king, whom you have revered above all the people of the Old Testament, who went into the tabernacle where the twelve loaves of the shewbread were offered every morning to God and because of his hunger ate of the shewbread? Well, you have said nothing about that. Don't you understand that our heavenly Father puts our needs above such things? That human need comes first? That is why I have come into the world, because of human need. Don't you understand that man is number one with God?"

Then a sabbath or two later, Jesus was accosted by them again as they accused Him of healing on the sabbath. And He said, "Don't you understand that the sabbath is given to do good? To save life?"

And looking round about them He said to the man who was paralyzed in his arm, "Stretch forth your hand." And he did, and Jesus healed that hand and arm.

The Bible says in Verse 11 that they were filled with madness and communed what they might do to Jesus. That was the continuing argument, that He violated the sabbath. You and I can get carried away with some rule of our denomination and put it above a miracle of deliverance, put it above the salvation of a soul, put it above an act of love and mercy, and still think we are doing the will of God. We have got to work from the inside out, not the outside in. Our hearts have got to be the ruling power — our hearts, touched by the Spirit of God, our hearts moved in the spirit of Jesus so that we are like Jesus, and we who do these things in alleged violation of the rules of men and are persecuted for it should remember that Jesus did it. We ought to be willing to be persecuted when we know we are loving, showing mercy, and bringing deliverance to lost and suffering humanity.

Luke 6:12

> And it came to pass in those days, that he went out into a mountain to pray, and continued all night in prayer to God.

Luke is the only one who mentions that Jesus spent that entire night in prayer. Even Jesus felt the need at times to spend such a period in prayer before God.

Luke 6:13-19

> And when it was day, he called unto him his disciples: and of them he chose twelve, whom also he named apostles; Simon, (whom he also named Peter,) and Andrew his brother, James and John, Philip and Bartholomew, Matthew and Thomas, James the son of Alphaeus, and Simon called Zelotes, and Judas the brother of James, and Judas Iscariot, which also was the traitor.
>
> And he came down with them, and stood in the plain, and the company of his disciples, and a great multitude of people out of all Judaea and Jerusalem, and from the sea coast of Tyre and Sidon, which came to hear him, and to be healed of their diseases; and they that were vexed with unclean spirits: and they were healed. And the whole multitude sought to touch him: for there went virtue out of him, and healed them all.

Power, Faith Unchanged

That same power is in Christ today and the faith with which we touch Him works in our lives the same as it did in theirs. Jesus is the same. Faith is the same. Touching Him with our faith is the same. Releasing our faith to God, saying,"Faith, go up to God, faith, go up to God," is the same and it produces the same results.

Luke 6:20-37

> And he lifted up his eyes on his disciples, and said, Blessed be ye poor: for yours is the kingdom of God. Blessed are ye that hunger now: for ye shall be filled. Blessed are ye that weep now: for ye shall laugh. Blessed are ye, when men shall hate you, and when they shall separate you from their company, and shall reproach you, and cast out your name as evil, for the Son of man's sake. Rejoice ye in that day, and leap for joy: for, behold, your reward is great in heaven: for in the like manner did their fathers unto the prophets.
>
> But woe unto you that are rich! for ye have received your consolation. Woe unto you that are full! for ye shall hunger. Woe unto you that laugh now! for ye shall mourn and weep. Woe unto you, when all men shall speak well of you! for so did their fathers to the false prophets.
>
> But I say unto you which hear, Love your enemies, do good to them which hate you, bless them that curse you, and pray for them which despitefully use you. And unto him that smiteth thee on the one cheek offer also the other; and him that taketh away thy cloak forbid not to take thy coat also. Give to every man that asketh of thee; and of him that taketh away thy goods ask them not again.
>
> And as ye would that men should do to you, do ye also to them likewise. For if ye love them which love you, what thank have ye? for sinners also love those that love them. And if ye do good to them which do good to you, what thank have ye? for sinners also do even the same. And if ye lend to them of whom ye hope to receive, what thank have ye? for sinners also lend to sinners, to receive as much again.
>
> But love ye your enemies, and do good, and lend, hoping for nothing again; and your reward shall be great, and ye shall be the children of the Highest: for he is kind unto the unthankful and to the evil. Be ye therefore merciful, as your Father also is merciful.
>
> Judge not, and ye shall not be judged: condemn not, and ye shall not be condemned: forgive, and ye shall be forgiven . . .

Jesus' Revolutionary Doctrine

In Luke's account of the Beatitudes that are so beautifully recorded in Matthew's gospel and on which I have commented in detail, Jesus was not on a mountain or mountainside, but was in the plain. This suggests to us that Jesus did not simply give a sermon on the mount one time. It meant that He preached these things wherever He went, time and time and time again. Now, we have been taught from childhood to recite these things. We have heard them read, but we really do not understand today how truly revolutionary they were. For example, in Verse 35, He says, "Love your enemies, do good and lend, hoping for nothing again, and your reward shall be great." Then He says, "You are blessed when people hate you and separate you from their company and reproach you and cast out your name as evil for the sake of the Son of Man." That is revolutionary. It is revolutionary today when we actually do it. Jesus is striking at the root level of the way we conduct our lives. He is saying there is a different way to relate to our enemies. We do not go talk about them the way they talk about us. We do not strike them back when they strike us. We do good to them.

I remember very well when we were building the City of Faith Health Care Center and all kinds of things were brought against us. The Lord gave me one thing right out of the Sermon on the Mount: The people who were opposing us did not understand. The newspapers and the media repeated again and again that Oral Roberts says, "They do not understand." Sometimes they would put it like this: "Oral Roberts will only say, They do not understand."

What could I gain by striking back at people who did not understand God's call upon my life to combine the healing streams of prayer and medicine? Why should I consume my time striking at them? They were not against me. They simply did not understand. If they did understand and were still against me, so what? That should not change what I was doing in obedience to my heavenly Father.

And I can say, in retrospect, in looking back upon every incident in my life, when I put Christ first, doing the opposite thing of what typical people do, that I would go back and do it over if I had the opportunity. It worked. It did good.

Luke 6:38

> Give, and it shall be given unto you; good measure, pressed down, and shaken together, and running over, shall men give into your bosom. For with the same measure that ye mete withal it shall be measured to you again.

The Lesson of Giving

Jesus says, "Give." The old popular feeling of the past is, we are to receive first and then if we have anything left over, and we have a right feeling about it, we give some of it to God. Christ reverses the order, and it is very important that you understand the ways of the Lord. If you find out the way God does things and you do them the way He does, then they are going to work. God's ways comprise an irresistible force for accomplishment, the success that God has ordained for each of us as His children.

Give and it shall be given unto you. What God gives back is so much more than what we give. His description of what is given back is in good measure, pressed down, shaken together, and running over.

It also is in the form of what men do, that is, given through men. So often we say, "When we give, then God is going to give." God always gives, of course, but He uses different instrumentalities through which He gives. Jesus said, ". . . shall men give unto your bosom." Does that mean when we give to people we ought to expect those same people to give back to us? No, because they're not your source. If they are, they are a mighty poor source because sometimes they feel like helping you and sometimes they don't. God is your source. He is the source of your total supply.

You do not give to people in order for them to give back to you. You give to God as your source, remembering that God will move upon somebody you know or do not know, somebody you have helped or not helped. And those people will give to you.

Be expectant because you know not just which one God is going to speak to, to give to you. Just know that with what measure of generosity and faith you give, that is the same measure God will use to give back to you. Get into the joy of giving and giving first. Get into the cheerfulness of giving God your best and then expecting God to give you His best.

Luke 6:39-46

> And he spake a parable unto them, Can the blind lead the blind? shall they not both fall into the ditch? The disciple is not above his master: but every one that is perfect shall be as his master.
>
> And why beholdest thou the mote that is in thy brother's eye, but perceivest not the beam that is in thine own eye? Either how canst thou say to thy brother, Brother, let me pull out the mote that is in thine eye, when thou thyself beholdest not the beam that is in thine own eye? Thou hypocrite, cast out first the beam out of thine own eye, and then shalt thou see clearly to pull out the mote that is in thy brother's eye.
>
> For a good tree bringeth not forth corrupt fruit; neither doth a corrupt tree bring forth good fruit. For every tree is known by his own fruit. For of thorns men do not gather figs, nor of a bramble bush

gather they grapes.

A good man out of the good treasure of his heart bringeth forth that which is good; and an evil man out of the evil treasure of his heart bringeth forth that which is evil: for of the abundance of the heart his mouth speaketh.

And why call ye me, Lord, Lord, and do not the things which I say?

The main point Jesus is making here is in Verses 45 and 46 where He says, "Out of the abundance of the heart the mouth speaketh. And why call me Lord and do not the things which I say?"

He is saying that your heart and your mouth have to be in unity. What you say with your mouth must correspond with what your heart believes because if you really believe it, you are going to do it. Jesus was striking at the hypocrisy of pointing out other people's mistakes and blowing them all out of proportion while you can do anything you want to and expect to get by with it.

I remember hearing an outstanding preacher tell the story of how he became overly critical during one stage of his life. He went to a preachers' conference and the speaker that day did not look very good to him. His tie was not tied properly and his clothes were not well tailored. He was sitting there saying, "Now, isn't that a sight, that man up there trying to preach the gospel looking like that?" Suddenly, he felt something touch the back of his neck. The person sitting behind him had reached out and pulled down the preacher's collar. He said to himself, "Oh, thank you, God, for showing me my critical spirit. Here I had forgotten to turn the collar of my coat down. And I'm criticizing the preacher in the pulpit."

That made a tremendous impression upon me. I believe Jesus is telling us to get rid of a critical spirit and also to do what we say. We want other people to do certain things — let us do them. We want them to be the best — let us be the best. We want them to serve God — let us serve God.

Luke 6:47-49

Whosoever cometh to me, and heareth my sayings, and doeth them, I will shew you to whom he is like: he is like a man which built an house, and digged deep, and laid the foundation on a rock: and when the flood arose, the stream beat vehemently upon that house, and could not shake it: for it was founded upon a rock. But he that heareth, and doeth not, is like a man that without a foundation built an house upon the earth; against which the stream did beat vehemently, and immediately it fell; and the ruin of that house was great.

Count God In

In Jesus' time, as it is today in the Holy Land, the desert areas are crisscrossed with very shallow river beds. When flash floods come, they just sweep everything away. Jesus said, in effect, "Look at that. You would not be foolish enough to go out there and take the easy way and build your house on that sand. No, you would build your house on a rock. You would drive the pilings down to the solid rock and when the flash floods and the big winds and storms struck, the house would stand like the Rock of Gibraltar." He is saying, "If you would do that naturally, then do not take the easy way out in anything."

Count God in. God is the eternal one. God is the one who endures. God is the one who will be standing when man's greatest efforts are swept aside by the flash floods of this world. Build your life pattern upon God. Never take the easy way out. Do not do something today that will hurt you 10 days from now or 6 months from now. If you want a "high," do not get on drugs for a temporary benefit. Get on a high with God, who will take care of you today, 6 months from now, 6 years from now, 60 years from now, a lifetime or eternity.

Do not cheat today, thinking, "Well, if I do not cheat today I will never get hold of this money or this piece of merchandise." Think of the time ahead. Build your life pattern upon the things that endure, not something that tickles your fancy today or sounds right or appears to be easy and does not require any major effort. Do it the tough way and you will stand all the way.

Luke 7:1-10

> Now when he had ended all his sayings in the audience of the people, he entered into Capernaum. And a certain centurion's servant, who was dear unto him, was sick, and ready to die. And when he heard of Jesus, he sent unto him the elders of the Jews, beseeching him that he would come and heal his servant. And when they came to Jesus, they besought him instantly, saying, That he was worthy for whom he should do this: for he loveth our nation, and he hath built us a synagogue.
>
> Then Jesus went with them. And when he was now not far from the house, the centurion sent friends to him, saying unto him, Lord, trouble not thyself: for I am not worthy that thou shouldest enter under my roof: wherefore neither thought I myself worthy to come unto thee: but say in a word, and my servant shall be healed. For I also am a man set under authority, having under me soldiers, and I say unto one, Go, and he goeth; and to another, Come, and he cometh; and to my servant, Do this, and he doeth it.

When Jesus heard these things, he marvelled at him, and turned him about, and said unto the people that followed him, I say unto you, I have not found so great faith, no, not in Israel.

And they that were sent, returning to the house, found the servant whole that had been sick.

Jesus found a man who had the faith to believe that He had authority above all authority; therefore, distance and space were no hindrances. He could speak the word where He was and the word of faith would affect the sick person at a distance, which it did.

Luke, a doctor, was not accustomed to medical practice having such power. He was astounded by it and so should we be. On the other hand, we should not be surprised because there is no distance in prayer.

Luke 7:11-18

And it came to pass the day after, that he went into a city called Nain; and many of his disciples went with him, and much people. Now when he came nigh to the gate of the city, behold, there was a dead man carried out, the only son of his mother, and she was a widow: and much people of the city was with her.

And when the Lord saw her, he had compassion on her, and said unto her, Weep not.

And he came and touched the bier: and they that bare him stood still. And he said, Young man, I say unto thee, Arise.

And he that was dead sat up, and began to speak. And he delivered him to his mother. And there came a fear on all: and they glorified God, saying, That a great prophet is risen up among us; and, that God hath visited his people. And this rumour of him went forth throughout all Judaea, and throughout all the region round about. And the disciples of John shewed him of all these things.

The Physician's Example

This is the first time in all of Luke's writing that he has called Jesus "Lord," and Luke also is the only one who described the scene of the raising of the widow's son at Nain. Luke, the physician, wrote the gospel of Luke and as he tells the story of the raising of the dead son of the widow of Nain, he emphasizes what doctors do, and he means do. They do not just talk or look or consider, they do something about it. They become involved with the sicknesses and the health of people.

Luke showed Jesus as the Great Physician, as the one who is

touched in the deepest way. He represented to those people that this was not just another funeral to be weeping over, though weeping certainly was in order. He is saying, "I am moved. I am touched." He touched the bier and said, "Young man, I say unto thee, arise." Jesus showed the continuity of life, that life could be called back because life is not extinguished at death. And the dead man sat up and spoke and Jesus delivered the young man back to his mother. The people glorified God, saying that God had visited His people.

God has indeed visited His people. He is visiting His people today through every prayer, every song of the gospel, every word of God, every touch of the hand, through faith, through every look of compassion, through the eyes of one human being toward another. Yes, Jesus is involved. He is where the need is and that is where we look for Him, where the need is.

As you read the Bible with me and you share with me in the teaching of it, remember that as Jesus moves in your life, you are moved, you are touched by other people's sufferings. You get involved. You become part of the answer rather than remaining a mere part of the problem.

Luke 7:19-23

> And John calling unto him two of his disciples sent them to Jesus, saying, Art thou he that should come? or look we for another? When the men were come unto him, they said, John Baptist hath sent us unto thee, saying, Art thou he that should come? or look we for another? And in that same hour he cured many of their infirmities and plagues, and of evil spirits; and unto many that were blind he gave sight.
>
> Then Jesus, answering, said unto them, Go your way, and tell John what things ye have seen and heard; how that the blind see, the lame walk, the lepers are cleansed, the deaf hear, the dead are raised, to the poor the gospel is preached. And blessed is he, whosoever shall not be offended in me.

The Blessed Faithful

There is something about John the Baptist we should remember today. He grew up in the desert, in the wide open spaces. When he presented Jesus Christ as the Messiah, it was with the great sky over him and the broad expanse of the land going, going in every direction. You can imagine seeing him throw up his hands and saying, "Behold the Lamb of God that taketh away the sins of the world." There were the tremendous crowds, the ovation, and the Holy Spirit descending on Jesus' head in the bodily form of a dove. John was used to action, to seeing results.

Suddenly the end comes. He is thrown into a dungeon. There is no light, no expanse, no sky, no sun rising in the morning or moon shining at night, no great crowds, no freedom to preach, no further opportunity to witness the mighty miracle-working power of the one of whom he was the forerunner, and darkness closed in on him and honest doubts assailed. He was no different from you or me when trouble struck. It is so hard to remember the good times. When the darkness of sickness, bereavement, personal loss and tragedy, financial harm and hurt all come at us and our world shrinks to that one little point in time where we feel like a cipher, when nobody cares and there is no way out, we wonder, "Where is God? Is He real?" John, in effect, was saying, "Is He real? Is this a mirage? Is this just something I am dreaming about?" It is hard to understand how John could have had the tremendous experiences in presenting Christ, and then in this loneliest of moments have honest doubts.

John was a flesh and blood man. He knew that the Christ would be the real Christ if He were doing all that the prophets had said He would do, including what he himself had said that Christ would do. So he sent messengers to ask Jesus. Jesus very kindly said, "You tell John what things you have seen and heard — the blind see, the lame walk, the lepers are cleansed, the deaf hear, the dead are raised, the poor are having the gospel preached to them. Blessed is he who doesn't lose faith in me." Then no more do we hear of John's doubts.

I like it because Jesus is honest and deals honestly with honest questions. You can be assured that if the night is dark, dark, dark and the way is lonely and you feel all alone, that you can really say whatever you want to say and Jesus will understand. But, when you say it, do something about it. Turn yourself to the Lord or to some of His servants. Ask the right questions and you are going to get the right answers. God's Book says you will. I say you will, I know you will.

Luke 7:24-28

> And when the messengers of John were departed, he began to speak unto the people concerning John, What went ye out into the wilderness for to see? A reed shaken with the wind? But what went ye out for to see? A man clothed in soft raiment? Behold, they which are gorgeously apparelled, and live delicately, are in kings' courts. But what went ye out for to see? A prophet? Yea, I say unto you, and much more than a prophet.
>
> This is he, of whom it is written, Behold, I send my messenger before thy face, which shall prepare thy way before thee. For I say unto you, among those that are born of women there is not a greater

> prophet than John the Baptist: but he that is least in the kingdom of God is greater than he.

Now, John the Baptist was not the greatest prophet of the New Testament or of the old covenant. He was great, that is, none greater, because of his special calling to come as the forerunner and the preparer of the way. Yet, he had not tasted of Calvary, of the resurrection, of the outpouring of the Holy Spirit on the day of Pentecost, of the new covenant. He was the bridge between the old and the new, signifying one was ending and the other beginning, but he had not tasted of the gospel of Jesus Christ in the way that the least of us do who are Christians today.

I thank God that Jesus showed the difference — that greater is the new covenant than the old, for it fulfilled the old and it brought the revelation of God through His Son Jesus Christ and brought God with every one of us so that whosoever of us calls upon Jesus, can be saved. How wonderful it is to be a Christian!

Luke 7:29-32

> And all the people that heard him, and the publicans, justified God, being baptized with the baptism of John. But the Pharisees and lawyers rejected the counsel of God against themselves, being not baptized of him. And the Lord said, Whereunto then shall I liken the men of this generation? and to what are they like? They are like unto children sitting in the marketplace, and calling one to another, and saying, We have piped unto you, and ye have not danced; we have mourned to you, and ye have not wept.

Opposition Can Unite

Children such as Jesus mentioned would have a play funeral and would mourn, but the other children would not mourn. Then they would have a play wedding and tell everybody to rejoice, and nobody would. In other words, nothing could please them. Jesus is saying to the people of any generation who reject God, "No matter what I do, you are not going to be pleased."

So many times in my ministry when I was opposed so savagely, I would change some methodology, hopeful that the people would see that I was sincere and that I was not bound to some particular method. I was trying to follow God's principles. No matter, when I changed that method to another, they were against me even more. It didn't make any difference. They did not like me because I was preaching the gospel of deliverance. I was lifting up Jesus as the

healer and deliverer, as the source of all healing and supply. All it did was bring out more opposition. But it did something else. It brought together those of us who really believe.

Luke 7:33-50

For John the Baptist came neither eating bread nor drinking wine; and ye say, He hath a devil. The Son of man is come eating and drinking; and ye say, Behold a gluttonous man, and a winebibber, a friend of publicans and sinners! But wisdom is justified of all her children. And one of the Pharisees desired him that he would eat with him. And he went into the Pharisee's house, and sat down to meat. And, behold, a woman in the city, which was a sinner, when she knew that Jesus sat at meat in the Pharisee's house, brought an alabaster box of ointment, and stood at his feet behind him weeping, and began to wash his feet with tears, and did wipe them with the hairs of her head, and kissed his feet, and anointed them with the ointment.

Now when the Pharisee which had bidden him saw it, he spake within himself, saying, This man, if he were a prophet, would have known who and what manner of woman this is that toucheth him: for she is a sinner.

And Jesus answering said unto him, Simon, I have somewhat to say unto thee. And he saith, Master, say on.

There was a certain creditor which had two debtors: the one owed five hundred pence, and the other fifty. And when they had nothing to pay, he frankly forgave them both. Tell me therefore, which of them will love him most?

Simon answered and said, I suppose that he, to whom he forgave most. And he said unto him, Thou hast rightly judged.

And he turned to the woman, and said unto Simon, Seest thou this woman? I entered into thine house, thou gavest me no water for my feet: But she hath washed my feet with tears, and wiped them with the hairs of her head. Thou gavest me no kiss: but this woman since the time I came in hath not ceased to kiss my feet. My head with oil thou didst not anoint: But this woman hath anointed my feet with ointment. Wherefore I say unto thee, Her sins, which are many, are forgiven; for she loved much: but to whom little is forgiven, the same loveth little.

And he said unto her, Thy sins are forgiven. And they that sat at meat with him began to say within themselves, Who is this that forgiveth sins also?

And he said to the woman, Thy faith hath saved thee; go in peace.

The Heart Counts

The woman, recognizing her sins, her need of forgiveness and cleansing, received a deep forgiveness and cleansing, but the one who needed it even more, that Christ-rejecting, God-defying Pharisee, did not receive any. That is what Jesus is trying to teach us today. It is not our outward pretentions, but the inner feelings of our heart that counts with Him.

Luke 8:1-3

> And it came to pass afterward, that he went throughout every city and village, preaching and shewing the glad tidings of the kingdom of God: and the twelve were with him, and certain women, which had been healed of evil spirits and infirmities, Mary called Magdalene, out of whom went seven devils, and Joanna the wife of Chuza Herod's steward, and Susanna, and many others, which ministered unto him of their substance.

Christ's Giving Followers

Those women are called by name. Jesus honored women. Women took on a new stature when Jesus came to this earth. It is not of Jesus' doing that women are not treated as highly as they ought to be. Jesus was born of a woman. He was her firstborn son. He allowed women to minister financially to Him. He trusted women. They were close to Him in their devotion and faith. He had important things for them to do and it is the same today.

I praise God for the ministry of men. I equally praise God for the ministry of women. We need each other. We should never be separate or apart.

We should remember that Jesus had financial needs, not only for himself, as the Son of God, but as the man, the human being who was engaged in doing God's work, the most important work in the world. It took money, the same as it does today. I praise God for people who give, and I am one of those givers who provide finance for the kingdom of God and who count it an honor. If it were not an honor, Jesus would have refused it, but He was an imminently practical, pragmatic man who knew it takes money to live on this earth.

Let us as Christians not hang our heads about finances. Let us receive the finances because the giver is going to be blessed time and time again, some thirtyfold, some sixtyfold, some a hundredfold, and God will always give us back more than we give.

Luke 8:4-18

And when much people were gathered together, and were come to him out of every city, he spake by a parable:

A sower went out to sow his seed: and as he sowed, some fell by the way side; and it was trodden down, and the fowls of the air devoured it. And some fell upon a rock; and as soon as it was sprung up, it withered away, because it lacked moisture. And some fell among thorns; and the thorns sprang up with it, and choked it. And other fell on good ground, and sprang up, and bare fruit an hundredfold.

And when he had said these things, he cried, He that hath ears to hear, let him hear.

And his disciples asked him, saying, What might this parable be?

And he said, Unto you it is given to know the mysteries of the kingdom of God: but to others in parables; that seeing they might not see, and hearing they might not understand.

Now the parable is this: The seed is the word of God.

Those by the way side are they that hear; then cometh the devil, and taketh away the word out of their hearts, lest they should believe and be saved. They on the rock are they, which, when they hear, receive the word with joy; and these have no root, which for a while believe, and in time of temptation fall away. And that which fell among thorns are they, which, when they have heard, go forth, and are choked with cares and riches and pleasures of this life, and bring no fruit to perfection.

But that on the good ground are they, which in an honest and good heart, having heard the word, keep it, and bring forth fruit with patience.

No man, when he hath lighted a candle, covereth it with a vessel, or putteth it under a bed; but setteth it on a candlestick, that they which enter in may see the light.

For nothing is secret, that shall not be made manifest; neither any thing hid, that shall not be known and come abroad.

Take heed therefore how ye hear: for whosoever hath, to him shall be given; and whosoever hath not, from him shall be taken even that which he seemeth to have.

Rooted in the Word

Jesus told the parable of the sower and the seed and the disciples wanted to know what He meant. In our manner of speaking He was saying that some of us are living our lives on the surface; we don't have any depth to us. We are so carried away with the things of this world that His Word has no opportunity to grow in us because there is not enough depth or care. When something comes along to get our attention, we are not rooted in the Word of God, which tells of eternal values rather than temporary and temporal ones, and we yield to temptation and go on into sin. We respond too quickly to the bright lights, to the easy buck, to doing it the easy way, to finding a way that suits us better than the Word of God teaches.

Jesus says, in effect, "How foolish can you be? You would not go out into a field and plant seed like that because if you plant in improper soil, the seed won't grow. The seed I am talking about is the Word of God."

The Bible, God's Word, must have foremost place in your life. In order to think God's thoughts and to do things the way God does them, we have to know the Word of God. The Word of God is the seed we plant to form our character, our relationship to the world, our ability to withstand in times of temptation and trial. It is the force that makes us immovable when the storms are striking. The Word of God gives us understanding and light so we can unravel something that is mysterious. Through the Word of God, we can get to the key issue of a matter in order to know how to act, how to be. Jesus emphasizes the Word of God.

When you go to church do not say, "Well, the preacher or the pastor is reading the Bible. Why should I read the Bible at home? Why should I learn it? Why shouldn't I allow him to teach me everything in the Bible?" For one thing, he can't teach you everything in the Bible. He does not have time to teach you everything in the Bible. He can only read a few verses and comment on them in any service. The Bible is yours. The Word of God is for you to study as well as to hear the minister preach. I thank God that I had parents who taught me upon my conversion to start reading the Bible. I did not know I was going to be a preacher, an evangelist, and be known worldwide. I did not know those things then. I only knew that Christ had come into my heart and I did not know how to deal with life. But my parents very wisely told me to study the Bible, to read it, to hear it preached, to hear it taught, and to think God's thoughts, and to do things the way Jesus did them, applying His way to my own personal life. This parable of sowing is about sowing the Word of God in our lives so that we have good harvests.

Luke 8:19-24a

> Then came to him his mother and his brethren, and could not come at him for the press. And it was told him by certain which said, Thy mother and thy brethren stand without, desiring to see thee.
>
> And he answered and said unto them, My mother and my brethren are these which hear the word of God, and do it.

> Now it came to pass on a certain day, that he went into a ship with his disciples: and he said unto them, Let us go over unto the other side of the lake. And they launched forth. But as they sailed he fell asleep: and there came down a storm of wind on the lake; and they were filled with water, and were in jeopardy. And they came to him, and awoke him, saying, Master, Master, we perish. Then he arose, and rebuked the wind.

Rebuking the Rebuker

Jesus uses the word "rebuked" frequently. God rebukes the rebuker. The devil is a rebuker, a deceiver, a devourer, a killer, a destroyer, an enemy, a liar. Jesus rebuked the wind just like He rebukes other things of the devil that come against us. When we give God our best, then we can fully believe that He will rebuke the devourer for our sake that we might have His best. Bear this in mind. Meditate on it. Read Verse 24 again;

Luke 8:24,25

> And they came to him, and awoke him, saying, Master, Master, we perish. Then he arose, and rebuked the wind and the raging of the water: and they ceased, and there was a calm.
>
> And he said unto them, Where is your faith? And they being afraid wondered, saying one to another, What manner of man is this! for he commandeth even the winds and water, and they obey him.

When the storm struck, the disciples had the good sense to go to Jesus. I cannot say anything better than when the storm strikes us, we go to Christ. Our nature is to go to everybody else or just to try to obscure it as if the storm is not happening. Sometimes we go off in hiding or we live inside ourselves. Sometimes we think it is beyond all solving. Sometimes we act as if there is no God.

Do you realize that they took that trip because Jesus told them to do it? He said, "Let us go over unto the other side of the lake." They did not go until He told them to go. When they went to Him it was not like going to just anybody. They went to the one who had the power to command the winds and the water and to compel them to obey Him. When it was over He said something that is so meaningful to us today. In effect, He said, "Where is your faith? You had faith for this. You really could have manifested your faith and loosed it. You could have said, 'Faith, go up to God. Faith, go up to God.' You could have handled this because of your faith." The wonderful thing is that back of our faith is He who commands even the winds and the waters, and they obey Him. Our faith is based upon Jesus Christ. We do have faith. In my experience in dealing with thousands upon thousands of people, most of the time they do not think they have any faith. Jesus did not accuse them of not having any. He just wanted to know where it was. He does not accuse you of not having any faith. He just wants to know, what are you doing with it? Are you loosing it? Are you sending it to God? Are you saying, "Faith, go up to God"? Or are you going to pieces?

I have had experience along these lines. I have gone to pieces at times. I have forgotten I even had faith. One thing about a storm: If you are not careful, it will blot out the presence of God. It will make you think you do not have any faith. It will bring you to a point where you believe you are not going to make it, but Jesus is saying you have the faith to make it. And I can testify to that, too. So many times I have remembered that I have faith. I have released it — and I have stood amazed at the miracles, at how God brought me through, or brought somebody through as I prayed for them. He says, "You have faith, use it. You have got what it takes."

Luke 8:26-35

> And they arrived at the country of the Gadarenes, which is over against Galilee. And when he went forth to land, there met him out of the city a certain man, which had devils long time, and ware no clothes, neither abode in any house, but in the tombs. When he saw Jesus, he cried out, and fell down before him, and with a loud voice said, What have I to do with thee, Jesus, thou Son of God most high? I beseech thee, torment me not. (For he had commanded the unclean spirit to come out of the man. For oftentimes it had caught him: and he was kept bound with chains and in fetters; and he brake the bands, and was driven of the devil into the wilderness.)
>
> And Jesus asked him, saying, What is thy name? And he said, Legion: because many devils were entered into him.
>
> And they besought him that he would not command them to go out into the deep. And there was there an herd of many swine feeding on the mountain: and they besought him that he would suffer them to enter into them. And he suffered them. Then went the devils out of the man, and entered into the swine: and the herd ran violently down a steep place into the lake, and were choked.
>
> When they that fed them saw what was done, they fled, and went and told it in the city and in the country.
>
> Then they went out to see what was done; and came to Jesus, and found the man, out of whom the devils were departed, sitting at the feet of Jesus, clothed, and in his right mind: and they were afraid.

People of this world have always been frightened of people in their right mind, people who have the mind of Christ.

Luke 8:36-40

They also which saw it told them by what means he that was possessed of the devils was healed. Then the whole multitude of the country of the Gadarenes round about besought him to depart from them; for they were taken with great fear: and he went up into the ship, and returned back again. Now the man out of whom the devils were departed besought him that he might be with him: but Jesus sent him away, saying,

Return to thine own house, and shew how great things God hath done unto thee. And he went his way and published throughout the whole city how great things Jesus had done unto him. And it came to pass, that, when Jesus was returned, the people gladly received him: for they were all waiting for him.

People Welcome Witnessing

Here is the power of a single witness. When you are really saved from something, you know it. By that I mean that you know that you know you are saved from sin, or you are healed from a disease, or God has met some significant need in your life so that Jesus is alive in you. It is not hard to be a witness. People want to experience a person who has met Christ and in so many, many instances they will welcome the Lord into their own lives.

Luke 8:41-53

And, behold, there came a man named Jairus, and he was a ruler of the synagogue: and he fell down at Jesus' feet, and besought him that he would come into his house: for he had one only daughter, about twelve years of age, and she lay a dying. But as he went the people thronged him.

And a woman having an issue of blood twelve years, which had spent all her living upon physicians, neither could be healed of any, came behind him, and touched the border of his garment: and immediately her issue of blood stanched.

And Jesus said, Who touched me? When all denied, Peter and they that were with him said, Master, the multitude throng thee and press thee, and sayest thou, Who touched me?

And Jesus said, Somebody hath touched me: for I perceive that virtue is gone out of me.

And when the woman saw that she was not hid, she came trembling, and falling down before him, she declared unto him before all the people for what cause she had touched him, and how she was healed immediately.

And he said unto her, Daughter, be of good comfort: thy faith hath made thee whole; go in peace.

While he yet spake, there cometh one from the ruler of the synagogue's house, saying to him, Thy daughter is dead; trouble not the Master. But when Jesus heard it, he answered him, saying, Fear not: believe only, and she shall be made whole.

And when he came into the house, he suffered no man to go in, save Peter, and James, and John, and the father and the mother of the maiden.

And all wept, and bewailed her: but he said, Weep not; she is not dead, but sleepeth.

And they laughed him to scorn, knowing that she was dead.

When Jesus said, "She sleepeth," He meant that she would wake again. Jesus was saying that life is not over. They were saying that at death, life ends. And they scorned Him.

Luke 8:54

And he put them all out, and took her by the hand, and called, saying, Maid, arise.

Faith People

In those days, at a funeral, they often hired professional mourners. It was customary to have people come in and weep as loudly as they could. Not that they cared; they were weeping for pay. He just told them, "Get out!" And they did. That is what it takes today. We in the gospel have to take authority over the scorners, putting them out so the place will be filled with faith people like Peter, James, and John. Faith people produce faith.

Luke 8:55

And her spirit came again, and she arose straightway: and he commanded to give her meat.

Jesus is the most practical of men. He knows that we have to have the necessary things of life.

Luke 8:56

And her parents were astonished: but he charged them that they should tell no man what was done.

These people were tempted to tell others that Jesus was so great,they presumed every deed He did was leading toward restoration of the political kingdom of Israel, and Jesus did not want to be identified with the revolutionary elements that were active at that time. Jesus wanted them to understand that He had not come for some political reason, but for the complete restoration of His people and the opening up of the kingdom of God to all humanity.

Luke 9:1,2

> Then he called his twelve disciples together, and gave them power and authority over all devils, and to cure diseases. And he sent them to preach the kingdom of God, and to heal the sick.

Extensions of Jesus

They were to be an extension of Jesus himself. In order to be His followers, they were to follow Him as a person and also exemplify His deeds. We, too, are an extension of our Lord. Also, work of preaching, teaching, and healing is an extension of Jesus Christ. People with needs who are suffering with torments, pursued by the devil, oppressed by him, and often possessed, are looking for Jesus.

Luke 9:3

> And he said unto them, Take nothing for your journey, neither staves, nor scrip, neither bread, neither money; neither have two coats apiece.

Don't Underestimate Faith

He was telling them essentially to go by faith alone. Somehow the whole Christian life is based upon faith. Paul is to say later, "The just shall live by their faith." In my own life, I have discovered that God has never given us a surplus. I had to start with nothing, the same ingredient He used when He made the world. I had to do it by faith and to share with my partners the idea that they too had to help by faith. Let us not underestimate the power of faith.

Luke 9:4,5

> And whatsoever house ye enter into, there abide, and thence depart. And whosoever will not receive you, when ye go out of that city, shake off the very dust from your feet for a testimony against them.

God Will Meet You

Deliver your soul. Give God your best, then expect God to give you His best. And do not look back upon where you had an apparent failure. Walk away with your whole faith, your entire life not being discouraged or feeling defeated. Go on to the next place and God will meet you there.

Luke 9:6

And they departed, and went through the towns, preaching the gospel, and healing every where.

Christ's Pattern

Here is the pattern that Jesus set for himself and then for all of His followers. There is no substitute for preaching the gospel, but the gospel is to be confirmed with the signs of healing the people.

Luke 9:7-9

Now Herod the tetrarch heard of all that was done by him: and he was perplexed, because that it was said of some, that John was risen from the dead; and of some, that Elias had appeared; and of others, that one of the old prophets was risen again. And Herod said, John have I beheaded: but who is this, of whom I hear such things? And he desired to see him.

Holy Spirit At Work

There is inherent in every human being a desire to see the Lord. There is a God-consciousness in everyone. Herod, even though he had committed murder, adultery, and other sins, still desired to see Jesus.

When we are ministering the gospel, we have the advantage that the Holy Spirit has already gone before us and has stirred up the hearts of the people, giving them an inner desire. If we only remember that, we're going to have a new enthusiasm as we approach people to bring deliverance to them.

Luke 9:10,11

And the apostles, when they were returned, told him all that they had done. And he took them, and went aside privately into a desert place belonging to the city called Bethsaida. And the people, when they knew it, followed him: and he received them, and spake unto them of the kingdom of God, and healed them that had need of healing.

Recognizing Needs

That particular group of people had a need not only for healing, they knew they had the need. Everybody in some way has a need for healing, but not everybody recognizes this need. People must be taught to recognize their need for healing, and at that point of need is where we believers have our best opportunity to be an extension of Jesus Christ in the now of our lives.

Luke 9:12-26

And when the day began to wear away, then came the twelve, and said unto him, Send the multitude away, that they may go into the towns and country round about, and lodge, and get victuals: for we are here in a desert place. But he said unto them, Give ye them to eat. And they said, We have no more but five loaves and two fishes; except we should go and buy meat for all this people.

For they were about five thousand men. And he said to his disciples, Make them sit down by fifties in a company.

And they did so, and made them all sit down. Then he took the five loaves and the two fishes, and looking up to heaven, he blessed them, and brake, and gave to the disciples to set before the multitude. And they did eat, and were all filled: and there was taken up of fragments that remained to them twelve baskets.

And it came to pass, as he was alone praying, his disciples were with him: and he asked them, saying, Whom say the people that I am? They answering said, John the Baptist; but some say, Elias; and others say, that one of the old prophets is risen again.

He said unto them, But whom say ye that I am? Peter answering said, The Christ of God.

And he straitly charged them, and commanded them to tell no man that thing; saying, The Son of man must suffer many things, and be rejected of the elders and chief priests and scribes, and be slain, and be raised the third day. And he said to them all, If any man will come after me, let him deny himself, and take up his cross daily, and follow me. For whosoever will save his life shall lose it: but whosoever will lose his life for my sake, the same shall save it. For what is a man advantaged, if he gain the whole world, and lose himself, or be cast away? For whosoever shall be ashamed of me and of my words, of him shall the Son of man be ashamed, when he shall come in his own glory, and in his Father's, and of the holy angels.

Christianity Is Reality

It is St. Luke who specifically writes, "If any man will come after me, let him deny himself and take up his cross daily, and follow me."

As an illustration, how would you like to be a person who knew the end from the beginning? At this period of Jesus' life He knew what awaited him: rejection, false accusation, suffering, the cross. He knew that the resurrection would follow. He is telling us that we are going to lose our lives, the lives that seem commonplace in this world. We are to attach ourselves to Jesus so closely that we spiritually follow Him and in a sense literally follow Him, knowing in advance that we are going to be hit, struck, misrepresented, knocked down, misunderstood, falsely accused — all the things that a cross can bring.

How many of us take up our cross daily, 7 days a week, to follow the steps of the Master? That is what God is looking for, our willingness to lose our ordinary daily lives in order to one day take up that great resurrected life.

Jesus asked, "What are you advantaged if you should gain the whole world and lose your own soul?" For one thing you can only eat one meal at a time. If you eat more, you will become ill. You can only wear one set of clothes or you will be overdressed. You can only drive one car at a time. If you owned all the money in the world you could only spend a little of it.

Christianity is a joyous experience but it is total reality.

Luke 9:27-31

> But I tell you of a truth, there be some standing here, who shall not taste of death, till they see the kingdom of God.
>
> And it came to pass about an eight days after these sayings, he took Peter and John and James, and went up into a mountain to pray. And as he prayed, the fashion of his countenance was altered, and his raiment was white and glistening. And, behold, there talked with him two men, which were Moses and Elias, who appeared in glory and spake of his decease which he should accomplish at Jerusalem.

Jesus Prepared

Moses exemplified the law and Elijah, the prophets. Moses was buried by the Lord and nobody knew the location. Elijah was translated, and both of them appeared there and talked to Jesus about His decease or His death. An even better word is His exodus, His exit from this world. The cross was of supreme importance to the heavenly councils. Even then God was making every preparation, preparing Jesus himself, even to the extent of sending these two men to talk to Him about His approaching death.

Luke 9:32-34

> But Peter and they that were with him were heavy with sleep, and when they were awake, they saw his glory, and the two men that stood with him. And it came to pass, as they departed from him, Peter said unto Jesus, Master, it is good for us to be here: and let us make three tabernacles; one for thee, and one for Moses, and one for Elias: not knowing what he said. While he thus spake, there came a cloud, and overshadowed them: and they feared as they entered into the cloud.

Cloud of Glory

The cloud that overshadowed them is much like the shekinah glory of God that came in the tabernacle and later in the temple and particularly that filled the temple when Solomon was at prayer before God.

Luke 9:35-45

> And there came a voice out of the cloud, saying, This is my beloved son: hear him. And when the voice was past, Jesus was found alone. And they kept it close, and told no man in those days any of those things which they had seen.
>
> And it came to pass, that on the next day, when they were come down from the hill, much people met him. And, behold, a man of the company cried out, saying, Master, I beseech thee, look upon my son: for he is mine only child. And, lo, a spirit taketh him, and he suddenly crieth out; and it teareth him that he foameth again, and bruising him hardly departeth from him. And I besought thy disciples to cast him out; and they could not.
>
> And Jesus answering said, O faithless and perverse generation, how long shall I be with you, and suffer you? Bring thy son hither.
>
> And as he was yet a coming the devil threw him down, and tare him. And Jesus rebuked the unclean spirit, and healed the child, and delivered him again to his father.
>
> And they were all amazed at the mighty power of God. But while they wondered everyone at all things which Jesus did, he said unto his disciples, Let these sayings sink down into your ears: for the Son of man shall be delivered into the hands of men.
>
> But they understood not this saying, and it was hid from them, that

> they perceived it not: and they feared to ask him of that saying.

In Chapter 8 we talked about Jesus having the power over the winds and the waters, the natural winds and waters, subduing them and bringing peace to the people. In Chapter 9 the storm is on the inside of the people, not on the outside. Here is a father with a demon-possessed child whose little spirit is troubled. The storm is raging and nothing has been able to set him free. And thank God, Jesus rebuked the unclean spirit. I repeat, He rebuked the unclean spirit, healed the child, and handed him back to his father. The people were just as amazed at that as the disciples had been after Jesus had stilled the tempest, the great storm there on the Sea of Galilee.

Jesus rebuked the unclean spirit. Time after time in this teaching I will be referring to Malachi 3:10,11. As we bring our tithes and offerings to Him, He says, "I will open the windows of heaven and pour you out a blessing where there is not room enough to receive it, and I will rebuke the devourer for your sake." Time and time again, Jesus is in the posture of rebuking the storms, the enemies, the devourer that comes against our lives. And I think that you hold in mind at all times that Jesus rebukes the forces that come to destroy you. Jesus said, "Let these words sink down into your ears, into your heart." That is good advice for us today, for His words to sink into our thoughts, our way of thinking, our way of doing. The Word of God is our strength.

Luke 9:46-51

> Then there arose a reasoning among them, which of them should be greatest. And Jesus, perceiving the thought of their heart, took a child, and set him by him, and said unto them, Whosoever shall receive this child in my name receiveth me: and whosoever shall receive me receiveth him that sent me: for he that is least among you all, the same shall be great.
>
> And John answered and said, Master, we saw one casting out devils in thy name; and we forbad him, because he followeth not with us.
>
> And Jesus said unto him, Forbid him not: for he that is not against us is for us. And it came to pass, when the time was come that he should be received up, he stedfastly set his face to go to Jerusalem . . .

The Turning Point

Here is probably the exact turning point in the ministry of our Lord Jesus. He set his face toward Jerusalem and everything that was going to meet Him there. There is a point in the life of every believer who carries his cross daily for Christ, when he or she, too, shall know that the turning point of his life has begun.

Luke 9:52-56

> And sent messengers before his face: and they went, and entered into a village of the Samaritans, to make ready for him. And they did not receive him, because his face was as though he would go to Jerusalem. And when his disciples James and John saw this, they said, Lord, wilt thou that we command fire to come down from heaven, and consume them, even as Elias did?
>
> But he turned, and rebuked them, and said, Ye know not what manner of spirit ye are of. For the Son of man is not come to destroy men's lives, but to save them. And they went to another village.

Saving and Healing

Again we read the word "rebuke." I am going to remind you of this word rebuke again and again.

Jesus is moving in the spirit of the power of rebuking the forces that are against God and against people.

He rebukes the spirit of destruction. The anxiety and the murderous intent of James and John were not of God. And Jesus rebuked them.

They were apostles, believers, bearing their cross daily, but in a moment of forgetfulness and anger, they wanted these people to be destroyed. So Jesus rebuked them. Then He said, "For the Son of man (speaking of himself) is not come to destroy men's lives, but to save them." The Greek root word for "save" is also "heal" and it would read, "for the Son of man is not come to destroy men's lives, but to save or heal them." Remember, Jesus came to preach, to teach, and to heal, to save the soul, to heal the mind and body, that is, whole-person healing.

Luke 9:57,58

> And it came to pass, that, as they went in the way, a certain man said unto him, Lord, I will follow thee whithersoever thou goest. And Jesus said unto him, Foxes have holes, and birds of the air have nests; but the Son of man hath not where to lay his head.

Worldly "Home" Rejected

This is not to be taken quite so literally because Jesus did have a place to stay. One of his favorite places was at the home of Mary and Martha. He had a home in Capernaum. He was not speaking here of living a poverty-stricken life, of having no bed to sleep on, or roof over His head, of being a penniless man. But He was speaking primarily socially and politically. The people of the power structure had no place for this man. And we who really take up our cross daily and follow Christ have no place to lay our heads.

What do we mean by that? There is no place for us in the world's power structure, in the supreme councils of human authority and power. God has promised to supply all our needs according to His riches by Christ Jesus in glory. But He has not promised that we will take over the power structure before His second coming. Generally speaking, we are the same as our Lord. We are to look to Him as our source and not to the world's power structure.

Luke 9:59,60

> And he said unto another, Follow me. But he said, Lord, suffer me first to go and bury my father. Jesus said unto him, Let the dead bury their dead: but go thou and preach the kingdom of God.

Priorities Established

This seems very unsympathetic of Jesus, but remember what He was really saying. Jesus said that while the burial of the loved one is very important, the preaching of the kingdom of God is of absolute importance.

Luke 9:61,62

> And another also said, Lord, I will follow thee; but let me first go bid them farewell, which are at home at my house. And Jesus said unto him, No man, having put his hand to the plough, and looking back, is fit for the kingdom of God.

Path to Glory

Jesus is saying, in effect, It is a straight line to glory, and to follow God we have to walk with our eyes forward, our minds looking into the future with our Lord, and not looking backward to the past.

Luke 10:1,2

> After these things the Lord appointed other seventy also, and sent them two and two before his face into every city and place, whither

> he himself would come. Therefore said he unto them, The harvest truly is great, but the labourers are few: pray ye therefore the Lord of the harvest, that he would send forth labourers into his harvest.

Faith Leaps to Harvest

The urgency is so great and the time is so short. At the same time, the harvest is so ripe, pray that God will thrust people forth, that He will stir them up until they understand it is the most important thing in the world to go out to win men and women to Christ.

There is another thought here that has to do with seed-faith. Many people who love the Lord have planted seeds of faith time and time again, but without a harvest. The harvest truly is ripe, and those of us who believe in seed-faith, who give our tithes and offerings as seed-faith to God, are told to pray that God will thrust us into reaping, into the harvest that is ripe.

Luke 10:3

> Go your ways: Behold, I send you forth as lambs among wolves.

Avoid Corruption

We are to go with a pure heart, with an innocence about us that is like our Lord's. We are to understand we are in a world of wolves. The Lord tells us that we are lambs, we are babes in Christ, we don't know our way; therefore, we must keep our eyes on Him. We're innocent; therefore, we should never be corrupted by the wolflike characteristics of this world.

Luke 10:4-7a

> Carry neither purse, nor scrip, nor shoes: and salute no man by the way. And into whatsoever house ye enter, first say, Peace be to this house. And if the son of peace be there, your peace shall rest upon it: if not, it shall turn to you again. And in the same house remain, eating and drinking such things as they give: for the labourer is worthy of his hire.

God's Workers Worthy

It seems that in the gospel work, those who do God's work are expected to live on starvation wages. But God says that the laborer is worthy of his hire. If the laborer does not eat more, sleep better, be better cared for, then he will not be able to labor as well. Really, he must be treated in the most extraordinary way as we would any other worker. God's true people are never going to abuse that which is given to them. They are going to use it right — not only me, but every child of God who is laboring in the service of our Lord is worthy. If anybody has a right to prosper for the glory and honor of God, it is one who serves the God who owns this earth and the fullness thereof. Laborers must be taken care of and God wants it done, and He will bless those who make it possible.

Luke 10:7b-9

> Go not from house to house. And into whatsoever city ye enter, and they receive you, eat such things as are set before you: and heal the sick that are therein, and say unto them, The kingdom of God is come nigh unto you.

Whole-Person Healing

Tell them that the healing of the sick means that the kingdom of God has come in the now, that God is near, God is working, God is meeting people at the point of their need. Always keep healing foremost, especially in its broadest sense. Whole-person healing — soul, mind, body, and circumstances.

Luke 10:10-22

> But into whatsoever city ye enter, and they receive you not, go your ways out into the streets of the same, and say, even the very dust of your city, which cleaveth on us, we do wipe off against you: notwithstanding be ye sure of this, that the kingdom of God is come nigh unto you. But I say unto you, that it shall be more tolerable in that day for Sodom, than for that city.
>
> Woe unto thee, Chorazin! woe unto thee, Bethsaida! for if the mighty works had been done in Tyre and Sidon, which have been done in you, they had a great while ago repented, sitting in sackcloth and ashes. But it shall be more tolerable for Tyre and Sidon at the judgment, than for you. And thou, Capernaum, which art exalted to heaven, shalt be thrust down to hell. He that heareth you heareth me; and he that despiseth you despiseth me; and he that despiseth me despiseth him that sent me.
>
> And the seventy returned again with joy, saying, Lord, even the devils are subject unto us through thy name.

> And he said unto them, I beheld Satan as lightning fall from heaven. Behold, I give unto you power to tread on serpents and scorpions, and over all the power of the enemy: and nothing shall by any means hurt you. Notwithstanding in this rejoice not, that the spirits are subject unto you; but rather rejoice, because your names are written in heaven.
>
> In that hour Jesus rejoiced in spirit, and said, I thank thee, O Father, Lord of heaven and earth, that thou hast hid these things from the wise and prudent, and hast revealed them unto babes: even so, Father; for so it seemed good in thy sight.
>
> All things are delivered to me of my Father: and no man knoweth who the Son is, but the Father; and who the Father is, but the Son, and he to whom the son will reveal him.

Jesus Laughed!

They returned with joy. Now when they returned with joy, telling the Lord that even the devils were subject to them, He made two statements.

First, He said He had seen the devil as lightning fall from heaven. He remembered the time in the infinite past when Lucifer had rebelled against the Father in heaven. God had seen sin in his heart and said, "You shall be cast down to the earth." And like a stroke of lightning, this mighty fallen archangel streaked his way to the earth. Jesus said, "I was there and I saw it." The second thing He said to them was, "I want you to know that I give you power like this, power to tread on snakes and scorpions (meaning enemies). I give unto you power to overcome your enemies, over all the power of the enemy. Do not worry about being hurt. There will be nothing fashioned in this world that will be able ultimately to hurt you. But do not just rejoice in this; rejoice because your names are written in heaven."

Here Jesus points out for the first time that there is a writer in heaven who inscribes the names of believers in the city of God. When He finished talking, in that very hour, He had joy. He began to rejoice in spirit.

Luke 10:21

> In that hour Jesus rejoiced in spirit . . .

He is ecstatic as He thanks God and rejoices in spirit, His face flooded with the sunshine of heaven, a laugh crinkling the corners of His mouth, a joy bounding up from within the inner man. Certainly

Jesus laughed. He held little children, patted them, laughed with them. He laughed with His disciples. He was a man of joy. What about being a man of sorrows? Those were our sorrows, not His. Jesus did not come into the world with personal sorrows; those were our sorrows that He bore. He was a man of joy and when His disciples had joy, He had joy, and He thanked God.

Luke 10:23-37

> And he turned him unto his disciples, and said privately, Blessed are the eyes which see the things that ye see. For I tell you, that many prophets and kings have desired to see those things which ye see, and have not seen them; and to hear those things which ye hear, and have not heard them.
>
> And, behold, a certain lawyer stood up, and tempted him, saying, Master, what shall I do to inherit eternal life? He said unto him, What is written in the law? How readest thou? And he answering said, Thou shalt love the Lord thy God with all thy heart, and with all thy soul, and with all thy strength, and with all thy mind; and thy neighbor as thyself. And he said unto him, Thou hast answered right: this do, and thou shalt live.
>
> But he, willing to justify himself, said unto Jesus, And who is my neighbour?
>
> And Jesus answering said, A certain man went down from Jerusalem to Jericho, and fell among thieves, which stripped him of his raiment, and wounded him, and departed, leaving him half dead. And by chance there came down a certain priest that way: and when he saw him, he passed by on the other side. And likewise a Levite, when he was at the place, came and looked on him, and passed by on the other side.
>
> But a certain Samaritan, as he journeyed, came where he was: and when he saw him, he had compassion on him, and went to him, and bound up his wounds, pouring in oil and wine, and set him on his own beast, and brought him to an inn, and took care of him. And on the morrow when he departed, he took out two pence, and gave them to the host, and said unto him, Take care of him; and whatsoever thou spendest more, when I come again, I will repay thee.
>
> Which now of these three, thinkest thou, was neighbour unto him that fell among the thieves?
>
> And he said, He that shewed mercy on him. Then said Jesus unto him, Go, and do thou likewise.

Jericho, at that time, had about 10,000 priests living there. It was a sunny area, a beautiful place to live, only 17 or 18 miles from Jerusalem. Many of the priests had to go to and from, and they knew the dangers of the Jericho road. It was infested with thieves and robbers.

Jesus related the story of a man who went from Jerusalem to Jericho and was robbed, stripped, and wounded and left for dead. By chance, one of the priests came by, looked at him, and passsed on. Then a Levite came, looked at him, and passed on. They would not touch him because they would soil their hands ceremonially, that is, they were not allowed to touch a dead person although they did not know for certain he was dead.

But a Samaritan, Jesus said, who was not liked, and was not one of them, came by and was moved with compassion. He took care of the victim. He paid 2 days' wages and promised more if it were needed.

Jesus asked the doctor of law, "Which one of the three people is the neighbor?" He replied, "The one who helped the man." Jesus said, "You have been asking the question. You go and do likewise."

Jesus knew the lawyer was trying to trap him. He knew he was not a good neighbor. He knew he was not keeping the law. He knew he did not have mercy and compassion. And he tells every one of us that when it comes to helping people, we are not to stand back because of the particular ceremonies of our religion. We are to strip ourselves of the outward veneer, get down to our hearts, and there prove ourselves. If we are taking up our cross daily and following Jesus, we are not going to stand on ceremony. We are going to touch people at the point of their need and it does not matter who they are.

Luke 10:38-42

> Now it came to pass, as they went, that he entered into a certain village: and a certain woman named Martha received him into her house. And she had a sister called Mary, which also sat at Jesus' feet, and heard his word. But Martha was cumbered about much serving, and came to him, and said, Lord, dost thou not care that my sister hath left me to serve alone? bid her therefore that she help me.
>
> And Jesus answered and said unto her, Martha, Martha, thou art careful and troubled about many things: but one thing is needful: and Mary hath chosen that good part, which shall not be taken away from her.

I do not think Jesus was speaking of Martha's service, but of the "overcare" she was exhibiting. She was more anxious than necessary that everything went right. He was not condemning her for serving them, but in the manner that she did.

Luke 11:1-4

> And it came to pass, that, as he was praying in a certain place, when

> he ceased, one of his disciples said unto him, Lord, teach us to pray, as John also taught his disciples.
>
> And he said unto them, When ye pray, say, Our Father which art in heaven, Hallowed be thy name. Thy kingdom come. Thy will be done, as in heaven, so in earth. Give us day by day our daily bread. And forgive us our sins; for we also forgive every one that is indebted to us. And lead us not into temptation; but deliver us from evil.

The disciples had seen Jesus praying. They listened to His prayers. They were impressed that He prayed so often, that He depended upon prayer, that He prayed as a link between Him and His Father. They hung on every word, on everything that He did, and they knew that Jesus knew how to pray.

Jesus tells us that when we pray, we are to be reverential toward our Father. To know that God is our Father, that His name is hallowed. And we are to pray for the kingdom of God to come to this earth so that God's will, which is always done in heaven, will also be done here on earth. You may call Jesus an idealist, but He wanted the best. He loved people.

Then He told us to pray for God to give us day by day our daily bread. Some people do not think God is concerned when they have need of groceries, but Jesus tells us God is so concerned that we are to incorporate it into our prayers. To ask God to give us day by day our daily bread, which also includes the Word of God.

Then He told us to pray for God to forgive our sins in the same way that we pray for the forgiveness of those who wrong us. Right here He gives a penetrating thought, that the basis upon which we ask God for forgiveness of our wrongs is dependent upon the way we are so willing to forgive other people.

Then He says, "Pray that there will be no temptation too great for you to bear." We are not exempt from temptation, but our Lord is teaching us to think in terms that God will not allow any temptation which is bigger than we are to touch us. Then He says that we pray to be delivered from evil. Evil is not for God's people. We are not to be part of evil in this world.

Luke 11:5-13

> And he said unto them, Which of you shall have a friend, and shall go unto him at midnight, and say unto him, Friend, lend me three loaves; for a friend of mine in his journey is come to me, and I have nothing to set before him?
>
> And he from within shall answer and say, Trouble me not: the door is now shut, and my children are with me in bed; I cannot rise and give thee.

I say unto you, Though he will not rise and give him, because he is his friend, yet because of his importunity he will rise and give him as many as he needeth. And I say unto you, Ask, and it shall be given you; seek, and ye shall find; knock, and it shall be opened unto you. For everyone that asketh receiveth; and he that seeketh findeth; and to him that knocketh it shall be opened.

If a son shall ask bread of any of you that is a father, will he give him a stone? or if he ask a fish, will he for a fish give him a serpent? Or if he shall ask an egg, will he offer him a scorpion? If ye then, being evil, know how to give good gifts unto your children: how much more shall your heavenly Father give the Holy Spirit to them that ask him?

Luke is the only one who refers to this statement by our Lord Jesus Christ. It is of supreme importance to us particularly when we are asking for the Holy Spirit. If you ask your own father or mother for something, they are not going to give you the opposite. If they are that good, how much more is God good? How much more is He inclined to give us the Holy Spirit?

You Must Ask

If anybody has a right to ask God anything, it is His own children. If anybody has a right to ask for help to spread the gospel, it is God's people. There is one thing certain: If you do not ask, you will not receive. If you do not seek, you will not find. If you do not knock, the door will not open to you. And you will never know the goodness of God. Jesus says, How much more shall your heavenly Father do for you than your human Father? Always remember God is a good God and God is always a good God.

Luke 11:14-26

And he was casting out a devil, and it was dumb. And it came to pass, when the devil was gone out, the dumb spake; and the people wondered. But some of them said, He casteth out devils through Beelzebub the chief of the devils. And others, tempting him, sought of him a sign from heaven.

But he, knowing their thoughts, said unto them, every kingdom divided against itself is brought to desolation; and a house divided against a house falleth. If Satan also be divided against himself, how shall his kingdom stand? because ye say that I cast out devils through Beelzebub. And if I by Beelzebub cast out devils, by whom do your sons cast them out? therefore shall they be your judges. But if I with the finger of God cast out devils, no doubt the kingdom of God is

> come upon you.
>
> When a strong man armed keepeth his palace, his goods are in peace: but when a stronger than he shall come upon him, and overcome him, he taketh from him all his armour wherein he trusted, and divideth his spoils. He that is not with me is against me: and he that gathereth not with me scattereth. When the unclean spirit is gone out of a man, he walketh through dry places, seeking rest; and finding none, he saith, I will return unto my house whence I came out. And when he cometh, he findeth it swept and garnished. Then goeth he, and taketh to him seven other spirits more wicked than himself; and they enter in, and dwell there: and the last state of that man is worse than the first.

Jesus' Multiple Messages

When the scribes and Pharisees became very upset about Jesus casting out devils, He reminded them that there were people among them who were casting out devils, and they were not saying a word about it.

It may be that He referred to Solomon. Solomon was the wisest man who ever lived and had the great wisdom of God. We are told by the rabbis that Solomon, in his great wisdom, knew how to use herbs in a medical way and to combine them with prayer and cast out demons so they would never return. This same practice from Solomon was being carried on up until the time Jesus appeared on the scene. Jesus knew that. He realized that they had accepted it, were practicing it, and now, because He cast out devils, they were criticizing Him. He said the only way a strong man's house can be pillaged or plundered by someone else would be for the one coming to be stronger than the man who owned the house. In effect, He is saying, "I am that stronger one. I am doing far more than Solomon did, far more than your sons are doing. I am casting out devils by the very finger of God."

The bottom line Jesus was addressing was that these people did not really understand the power of God and therefore were making wild accusations. That is certainly true today. There are people in the Church who do not understand the charismatic power of God, the gifts of the spirit, or even the prayer language of the spirit, of speaking in tongues and interpreting. There are people who, because they do not understand it, say that it is of the devil and therefore it is of no value. Jesus is telling us that just because we do not understand something doesn't mean it is not true. Who understands the atom? Yet, scientists are discovering it, harnessing it, and using it. Who understands light or darkness? I do not even know how a television set works, but I certainly turn one on. One of the main things we can do as Christians and believers is to keep an open mind. The next thing Jesus talked about was the unclean spirit. When such a spirit is cast out of a man, he walks through dry places seeking satisfaction, seeking rest, and finds none, so he decides he will attempt to enter that same person. But being unable to do so alone, he finds seven other demons to join with him to overpower resistance. He discovers that once he is out of that person, the soul is clean. It is empty, but it is clean. However, with seven other demons more powerful than himself, he is able to enter that clean but empty soul. Jesus is telling us that it is not enough to have our souls empty of the devil, or clean of this world, but that we are to be constantly filled with the Spirit of God so God's Spirit fills us up.

Remember Paul saying in Ephesians 5:18 for us not to be drunk on wine wherein is excess, but to be filled with the Holy Spirit. I remember Jesus talking about seed-faith. If you have a clean field and you do not plant, then weeds grow back and take the field over. If you have your soul cleaned by God and you do not go on with God, studying His Word, doing His will, and constantly being filled with the Spirit again and again, then the devil's power returns and the devil always brings reinforcements in order to overcome that empty soul. So our souls must not be clean but empty; we must be filled with God.

Luke 11:27-36

> And it came to pass, as he spake these things, a certain woman of the company lifted up her voice, and said unto him, Blessed is the womb that bare thee, and the paps which thou hast sucked. But he said, Yea rather, blessed are they that hear the word of God, and keep it.
>
> And when the people were gathered thick together, he began to say, This is an evil generation: they seek a sign; and there shall no sign be given it, but the sign of Jonas the prophet. For as Jonas was a sign unto the Ninevites, so shall also the Son of man be to this generation.
>
> The queen of the south shall rise up in the judgment with the men of this generation. And condemn them: for she came from the utmost parts of the earth to hear the wisdom of Solomon; and, behold, a greater than Solomon is here.
>
> The men of Nineveh shall rise up in the judgment with this generation, and shall condemn it: for they repented at the preaching of Jonas; and, behold, a greater than Jonas is here.
>
> No man, when he hath lighted a candle, putteth it in a secret place, neither under a bushel, but on a candlestick, that they which come

> in may see the light.
>
> The light of the body is the eye: therefore when thine eye is single, thy whole body also is full of light; but when thine eye is evil, thy body also is full of darkness.
>
> Take heed therefore that the light which is in thee be not darkness. If thy whole body therefore be full of light, having no part dark, the whole shall be full of light, as when the bright shining of a candle doth give thee light.

"Signs" Within Us

Now this woman was carried away with the emotion and passion of the moment when she saw the outstanding way that Jesus answered the opposers, and she cried out, "Blessed is the womb that bear thee and the paps which thou hast sucked." But Jesus was not necessarily with the emotion of her heart; He simply replied to her to obey God. It is better to obey God than to be carried away with some emotion about how we feel about God.

Then Jesus, being surrounded by this tremendous multitude, told them they were always seeking a sign, and there would be no sign given other than the sign of Jonah the prophet. When the people of Nineveh saw and heard Jonah, they accepted him and his message as a sign of God that they should repent, and they did. When the Queen of Sheba visited Solomon, she accepted the event as a sign from God that she should accept Solomon's God. And she did.

Jesus says that when the people of Nineveh and the Queen of Sheba come to the judgment, they are going to reprove this world and judge this world because God's greatest sign of himself was to send Jesus Christ, His only begotten Son ,and the existence of Christ upon the earth, showing us what the Father is like, going to the cross, being raised from the dead, sending the Holy Spirit to indwell us — that is the sign by which we will be judged when we go to the judgment seat of Christ.

He referred to the eye. When the eye is "single," when it is seeing straight, then it brings light to the inner man. But when it does not it fills the life with darkness. Here He is speaking of the heart of man. When the heart is right with God, filled with the Spirit of God constantly, then we have all the signs of God we will ever need because we are indwelt by the Lord Jesus Christ himself.

Let us pray that we will not miss Jesus by looking for some celestial sign rather than the reality of our Lord in the Word of God.

Father, we thank you today and we stand in agreement with

You that You have given the sign of yourself in the Lord Jesus Christ and we receive that sign of your presence in the world, of your reality to mankind, and your own personal relationship with us.

We receive You into our lives and we respond with our whole heart to follow the Word of God, to know You and your personal presence, and the infilling of the Spirit of our hearts, and to walk daily with You in the Spirit. And, dear friend and partner, I pray for you to be so filled with the Spirit of God that never again will the thought occur to you of some sign at all because God has already given His greatest sign, the Lord Jesus Christ, to live in your heart and work through your being forever and ever. Amen and amen.

Luke 11:37-54

And as he spake, a certain Pharisee besought him to dine with him: and he went in, and sat down to meat. And when the Pharisee saw it, he marvelled that he had not first washed before dinner.

And the Lord said unto him, Now do ye Pharisees make clean the outside of the cup and the platter; but your inward part is full of ravening and wickedness. Ye fools, did not he that made that which is without make that which is within also? But rather give alms of such things as ye have; and, behold, all things are clean unto you.

But woe unto you, Pharisees! for ye tithe mint and rue and all manner of herbs, and pass over judgment and the love of God: these ought ye to have done, and not to leave the other undone. Woe unto you, Pharisees! for ye love the uppermost seats in the synagogues, and greetings in the markets. Woe unto you, scribes and Pharisees, hypocrites! for ye are as graves which appear not, and the men that walk over them are not aware of them.

Then answered one of the lawyers, and said unto him, Master, thus saying thou reproachest us also.

And he said, Woe unto you also, ye lawyers! for ye lade men with burdens grievous to be borne, and ye yourselves touch not the burdens with one of your fingers. Woe unto you! for ye build the sepulchres of the prophets, and your fathers killed them. Truly ye bear witness that ye allow the deeds of your fathers: for they indeed killed them, and ye build their sepulchres.

Therefore also said the wisdom of God, I will send them prophets and apostles, and some of them they shall slay and persecute: that the blood of all the prophets, which was shed from the foundation of the world, may be required of this generation; from the blood of Abel unto the blood of Zacharias, which perished between the altar and the temple: verily I say unto you, It shall be required of this generation.

Woe unto you, lawyers! for ye have taken away the key of knowledge: ye entered not in yourselves, and them that were entering in ye hindered.

And as he said these things unto them, the scribes and the Pharisees began to urge him vehemently, and to provoke him to speak of many things: laying wait for him, and seeking to catch something out of his mouth, that they might accuse him.

Respect Today's Godly

Jesus was talking to religious leaders who had drifted so far away from God in their hearts that they had nothing much left but an outward observance of the things of God.

That incident reminds me so much of the now that we live in. I have been so shocked at times by high religious people who, when I have a vision or a dream of God, will criticize me or criticize somebody else who has had them. They praise God for Martin Luther, for John Wesley, or other great men and women of God in the past. Yet when they come into confrontation with anointed men and women today, it really seems that in their heart, they would like to do away with us. This is why they do not have the power of God in their life. They do not really believe. They do not care. They do not believe the Bible. They say they do, but if Paul rose from the dead and came back to preach in our cities, it wouldn't take long until they would throw him in jail again.

While we revere the people of the Bible and great godly leaders in the past, we must not let that blind our judgment to true leaders of the gospel today. For God's leaders today are just as important as those of other generations.

As we obey God, The devil is going to stir up people against us. Be careful when you criticize someone who is serving God with his whole heart, because you do not understand everything he says or does. Wait. Wait on God. Look for the fruit to be produced in his life.

Luke 12:1-10

In the mean time, when there were gathered together an innumerable multitude of people, insomuch that they trode one upon another, he began to say unto his disciples first of all, Beware ye of the leaven of the Pharisees, which is hypocrisy.

For there is nothing covered, that shall not be revealed; neither hid, that shall not be known. Therefore whatsoever ye have spoken in darkness shall be heard in the light; and that which ye have spoken in the ear in closets shall be proclaimed upon the housetops.

And I say unto you my friends, Be not afraid of them that kill the body, and after that have no more that they can do. But I will forewarn you whom ye shall fear: Fear him, which after he hath killed hath power to cast into hell; yea, I say unto you, Fear him.

Are not five sparrows sold for two farthings, and not one of them is forgotten before God? But even the very hairs of your head are all numbered. Fear not therefore: ye are of more value than many sparrows.

Also I say unto you, Whosoever shall confess me before men, him shall the Son of man also confess before the angels of God: but he that denieth me before men shall be denied before the angels of God.

And whosoever shall speak a word against the Son of man, it shall be forgiven him: but unto him that blasphemeth against the Holy Ghost it shall not be forgiven.

When Jesus referred to blaspheming against the Holy Ghost, He was talking about people — men and women. Do you realize that only man blasphemes? No other creature does. No other creature blasphemes the Maker. Only man. Jesus continues to talk about the opposition of the scribes and Pharisees and other enemies that He faced who were declaring that all His good works were done by the spirit of the devil rather than by the Spirit of God.

He counts each of these arguments by pointing out to them the things they know very well. He tells them of the goodness of God, God's act of knowing them so well, so intimately, that He has numbered the hairs on their heads. It has been estimated that a typical head of hair has at least 100,000 separate hairs. Jesus urges the people to turn away from the hypocrisy of the scribes and Pharisees and to accept Him, to confess Him before men because, He says, "If you confess me before men, I shall confess you before the angels of God. But if you deny me before men I shall deny you before the angels of God."

There is something very powerful here and it is in reference to activating the angels on our behalf. For when we confess Christ before men, it immediately causes the Son of Man to call the angels together and to proclaim before them that Oral Roberts, or you, or someone else has confessed Him as the Savior. On the other hand, if we come to the point where we finally deny him before men, He again calls the angels and declares to them that this individual has denied Him. So what we do activates the angels.

He says you can speak anything you want to against the Son of Man and it can be forgiven, but if you blaspheme against the Holy Spirit, there shall never be any forgiveness. Why? Because the Holy Spirit is the spirit by which Christ came into the world, even born of the Virgin Mary. The Holy Spirit came upon Him as a dove when He was baptized by John the Baptist in the River Jordan. The Holy Spirit filled Him, led Him, directed Him. Through the Spirit He was able to cast out demons and do all of His mighty works. If people blaspheme the Spirit by which God does His work, then there is no other way for them to be saved. They can never come to God. There will never be any forgiveness. Therefore, He warns us against finally blaspheming the Holy Spirit to the point we will have nothing to do with the Spirit of God.

Luke 12:11-21

> And when they bring you unto the synagogues, and unto magistrates, and powers, take ye no thought how or what thing ye shall answer, or what ye shall say: for the Holy Ghost shall teach you in the same hour what ye ought to say.
>
> And one of the company said unto him, Master, speak to my brother, that he divide the inheritance with me.
>
> And he said unto him, Man, who made me a judge or a divider over you?
>
> And he said unto them, Take heed, and beware of covetousness: for a man's life consisteth not in the abundance of the things which he possesseth.
>
> And he spake a parable unto them, saying, The ground of a certain rich man brought forth plentifully: And he thought within himself, saying, What shall I do, because I have no room where to bestow my fruits? And he said, This will I do: I will pull down my barns, and build greater; and there will I bestow all my fruits and my goods. And I will say to my soul, Soul, thou hast much goods laid up for many years; take thine ease, eat, drink, and be merry.
>
> But God said unto him, Thou fool, this night thy soul shall be required of thee: then whose shall those things be, which thou hast provided?
>
> So is he that layeth up treasure for himself, and is not rich toward God.

Beware Covetousness

What is He saying? Well, first, He is talking about seed-faith. He is talking about how we plant our seed, reap our harvest, and give of what we have, how we share it with other people, how we are stewards of what we possess. That man said, "These are all mine. What am I going to do with mine? I will tear down my barn. I will build bigger barns for myself." Jesus teaches us to sow seeds of faith and love, to give of our best. But that man sowed bad seeds. He sowed seeds of covetousness. Some people just never get enough.

A deeper truth is the unplanted seed. That man quit planting seeds. He took the increase and stored it up and quit planting. A seed not planted is a seed that cannot be harvested. If you sow nothing, you will reap nothing. Seed-faith is infinitely precious because it causes you to sow your best to God. Then as God grows your best and multiplies it, you can reap God's best.

Luke 12:22-32

> And he said unto his disciples, Therefore I say unto you, Take no thought for your life, what ye shall eat; neither for the body, what ye shall put on. The life is more than meat, and the body is more than raiment.
>
> Consider the ravens: for they neither sow nor reap; which neither have storehouse nor barn; and God feedeth them: how much more are ye better than the fowls? And which of you with taking thought can add to his stature one cubit? If ye then be not able to do that thing which is least, why take ye thought for the rest?
>
> Consider the lilies how they grow: they toil not, they spin not; and yet I say unto you, that Solomon in all his glory was not arrayed like one of these. If then God so clothe the grass, which is today in the field, and tomorrow is cast into the oven; how much more will he clothe you, O ye of little faith?
>
> And seek not ye what ye shall eat, or what ye shall drink, neither be ye of doubtful mind. For all these things do the nations of the world seek after: and your Father knoweth that ye have need of these things.
>
> But rather seek ye the kingdom of God; and all these things shall be added unto you. Fear not, little flock; for it is your Father's good pleasure to give you the kingdom.

Needs in Perspective

Jesus is not disparaging your need of food or clothes or shelter or money or things that are material. He is simply telling you that this is all the world thinks about, and the worldly are going straight to hell. The worldly are not thinking about God or their proper relationship with God and their fellow man. They are thinking about material things. Jesus is saying God considered them in their proper order.

God set before us His heavenly kingdom, the greatest kingdom of all. He says to get straight with that and then God will add the things to you that you need. He is not going to subtract. He is going to add. God knows the vital importance of things in our lives. We live on a material earth. Our bodies are made of matter. We have to travel, to eat, to sleep, to work, to play; all these require material things. It is uppermost in God's mind that we have the things that are necessary for us to live as His people on His earth before we get to His heaven. In heaven we will need none of these things.

Our number-one search is to be for God and His kingdom, putting our affection upon things above and wearing the things of this earth as a loose garment so at any moment we can cast it off and be lifted up to be with God.

Remember that both sections of Luke 12:31 are actives. One, you are active in seeking the kingdom of God. Two, you are active in working for the things that God will add to you. You need God to add them to you because you cannot do them by yourself. But neither will God do them by himself. Without God, you cannot. Without you, He will not. Understand that without God, you cannot. But without you, God will not.

Things have to be made to happen. You have to work. Using talents, and enthusiasm, and not only enthusiasm in what you are doing, but in doing it thoroughly and adding to that the faith for the things God has promised to us. So it's a divine human reciprocity. It's God and you working together, not only for His kingdom, but for the things that you need and that His work needs on this earth. If anybody has a right to the things of God's earth, it is God's people.

Luke 12:33,34

> Sell that ye have, and give alms; provide yourselves bags which wax not old, a treasure in the heavens that faileth not, where no thief approacheth, neither moth corrupteth. For where your treasure is, there will your heart be also.

The Men's Desire

What He is saying here is being stated to a group of people who have an outward pretense of inner spirituality but are fully carried away with a material kind of life. It is only to that type of person that this scripture can apply. He is making a contrast of where your heart is. If your treasure is serving God, knowing God is going to add to you all the things that you need, that is where your heart will be. If your treasure is with this materialistic world, this world system, without God having first place in your life, that is where your heart will be.

Luke 12:35-40

Let your loins be girded about, and your lights burning; and ye yourselves like unto men that wait for their Lord, when he will return from the wedding; that when he cometh and knocketh, they may open unto him immediately.

Blessed are those servants, whom the lord when he cometh shall find watching: verily I say unto you, that he shall gird himself, and make them to sit down to meat, and will come forth and serve them. And if he shall come in the second watch, or come in the third watch, and find them so, blessed are those servants.

And this know, that if the goodman of the house had known what hour the thief would come, he would have watched, and not have suffered his house to be broken through. Be ye therefore ready also: for the Son of man cometh at an hour when ye think not.

Be Prepared, Active

The Lord is speaking to us of being watchful, diligent, occupied until He comes, and being very active in His divine service, rather than being carried away with the things of this world which blind our inner sight from watchfulness, of being prepared for whatever He wants us to do on this earth and also for His return.

Luke 12:41-53

Then Peter said unto him, Lord, speakest thou this parable unto us, or even to all?

And the Lord said, who then is that faithful and wise steward, whom his lord shall make ruler over his household, to give them their portion of meat in due season? Blessed is that servant, whom his lord when he cometh shall find so doing. Of a truth I say unto you, that he will make him ruler over all that he hath. But and if that servant say in his heart, My lord delayeth his coming; and shall begin to beat the menservants and maidens, and to eat and drink, and to be drunken; the lord of that servant will come in a day when he looketh not for him, and at an hour when he is not aware, and will cut him in sunder, and will appoint him his portion with the unbelievers. And that servant, which knew his lord's will, and prepared not himself, neither did according to his will, shall be beaten with many stripes. But he that knew not, and did commit things worthy of stripes, shall be beaten with few stripes. For unto whomsoever much is given, of him shall be much required: and to whom men have committed much, of him they will ask the more.

I am come to send fire on the earth; and what will I, if it be already

> kindled? But I have a baptism to be baptized with: and how am I straitened till it be accomplished! Suppose ye that I am come to give peace on earth? I tell you, Nay; but rather division: for from henceforth there shall be five in one house divided, three against two, and two against three. The father shall be divided against the son, and the son against the father; the mother against the daughter, and the daughter against the mother; the mother-in-law against her daughter-in-law, and the daughter-in-law against her mother-in-law.

I think that Jesus is trying to show us that it is our responsibility to put first things first, to seek His kingdom first, and to live our lives in the spirit of what He came to do on this earth. However, Jesus says that when you give yourselves to the Lord with your whole heart, it will bring people to a confrontation with the issues of life, and they will have to make a decision whether they serve the Lord or they do not. In one's own house, there will be some who will choose the Lord and some who will not. The choice will be so strongly made that there will be a division. It happens all the time. We should not be surprised by it. We simply should remember that our choice of the Lord is right.

Luke 12:54-57

> And he said also to the people, When ye see a cloud rise out of the west, straightway ye say, There cometh a shower; and so it is. And when ye see the south wind blow, ye say, There will be heat; and it cometh to pass.
>
> Ye hypocrites, ye can discern the face of the sky and of the earth; but how is it that ye do not discern this time? Yea, and why even of yourselves judge ye not what is right?

Spiritual Smartness

Palestine was east of the Mediterranean Sea. If the people looked out there and saw a cloud, they knew it was going to rain. South of Jerusalem was desert and when the wind began to blow from the south, they knew that it was going to get hot. Jesus said, "If you are so smart in things of this earth, why is it that you do not grasp through your inner man the things of God? Why is it that you cannot be as smart spiritually as you are with your physical senses?"

Luke 12:58-13:5

> When thou goest with thine adversary to the magistrate, as thou art in the way, give diligence that thou mayest be delivered from him;

lest he hale thee to the judge, and the judge deliver thee to the officer, and the officer cast thee into prison. I tell thee, thou shalt not depart thence, till thou hast paid the very last mite. There were present at that season some that told him of the Galilaeans, whose blood Pilate had mingled with their sacrifices.

And Jesus answering said unto them, Suppose ye that these Galilaeans were sinners above all the Galilaeans, because they suffered such things? I tell you, Nay; but, except ye repent, ye shall all likewise perish.

Or those eighteen, upon whom the tower in Siloam fell, and slew them, think ye that they were sinners above all men that dwelt in Jerusalem? I tell you, Nay: but, except ye repent, ye shall all likewise perish.

A New Path

Jesus is saying that repentance is the way into the kingdom of God. Whether we are called great sinners or ones not so deeply bound by sin, repentance is still the way to God. Repentance means that you really change your mind, you change your attitude, you turn around, away from a life of sin, and direct yourself to God, asking Him to give you a new birth, a new heart, to regenerate you and put you on a new path.

Luke 13:6-9

He spake also this parable; A certain man had a fig tree planted in his vineyard; and he came and sought fruit thereon, and found none. Then said he unto the dresser of his vineyard, Behold, these three years I come seeking fruit on this fig tree, and find none: cut it down; why cumbereth it the ground? And he answering said unto him, Lord, let it alone this year also, till I shall dig about it, and dung it: and if it bear fruit, well: and if not, then after that thou shalt cut it down.

Gospel of Second Chance

Jesus is pointing out to us that we are a very favored people. We are planted. When we do not reproduce after our kind, after our own faith, we are takers and not givers. Therefore we are not multiplied in any way. In the fig tree parable, Jesus declares the gospel of a second chance, giving us every opportunity we need in order to look into our hearts, decide for Christ, and make our lives as a seed we plant. When we do that we begin to bear fruit. Our seed-faith really turns into reproduction and multiplication and our lives are changed.

But what if everything we have is taken from us? When we study Romans we will see where Paul said in Romans 1:14, "I am debtor. I am debtor both to the wise and unwise, the Greeks, the barbarians. I am debtor to everyone I come in contact with because I have really received Christ, His salvation into my life." Jesus is telling us that we are debtors. We are to share, we are to plant our seeds of faith. We are to be givers because it is in our giving that we have our receiving.

Luke 13:10-17

> And he was teaching in one of the synagogues on the sabbath. And, behold, there was a woman which had a spirit of infirmity eighteen years, and was bowed together, and could in no wise lift up herself.
>
> And when Jesus saw her, he called her to him, and said unto her, Woman, thou art loosed from thine infirmity.
>
> And he laid his hands on her: and immediately she was made straight, and glorified God.
>
> And the ruler of the synagogue answered with indignation, because that Jesus had healed on the sabbath day, and said unto the people, There are six days in which men ought to work: in them therefore come and be healed, and not on the sabbath day.
>
> The Lord then answered him, and said, Thou hypocrite, doth not each one of you on the sabbath loose his ox or his ass from the stall, and lead him away to watering? And ought not this woman, being a daughter of Abraham, whom Satan hath bound, lo, these eighteen years, be loosed from this bond on the sabbath day?
>
> And when he had said these things, all his adversaries were ashamed: and all the people rejoiced for all the glorious things that were done by him.

Succeeding for God

You see, the ruler of the synagogue looked for a minute detail. His mind was on rule-making more than it was upon people — healing, or people-deliverance. Jesus could not stand for the people called by His name to put things, even the tiniest things, above the deliverance of an immortal soul, a human body and mind bound by Satan himself.

The Word says that while Christ was teaching, He saw that woman. He never fails to do that. That is why you and I often feel such an urgency toward sick people, or suffering people. That is the Christ in us, wanting us to see and to pay attention to people like them.

I believe it is right here that we in the kingdom of God are going to succeed for God or we are going to fail. If we are concerned that God will be God, and that means He is a God of deliverance, we are going to preach and teach the God of deliverance. We are going to bring healing through His name as He did. We are going to see people and meet them at the point of their need, people who are ill in any way — spiritually, physically, emotionally, financially, in their families — you name it.

Somehow, we will be drawn to them because the love of God draws us to sinners, to sick people, to demon-possessed individuals, to those who have great need. This is our Savior at work and this is what will turn the Church around. This is what will fill any building that we have with earnest-hearted, God-seeking, needy people. It is going to put a new resiliency in us to endure, a holy enthusiasm to magnify God. It is going to help us rise above the little idiosyncrasies, the religious pretentions that we face in whatever denomination we belong to.

Luke 13:18-22

> Then said he, Unto what is the kingdom of God like? and whereunto shall I resemble it? It is like a grain of mustard seed, which a man took, and cast into his garden; and it grew, and waxed a great tree; and the fowls of the air lodged in the branches of it. And again he said, Whereunto shall I liken the kingdom of God? It is like leaven, which a woman took and hid in three measures of meal, till the whole was leavened. And he went through the cities and villages, teaching, and journeying toward Jerusalem.

Jesus' Last Journey

This is Jesus' last journey. It would not be long until He was in Jerusalem for His arrest and trial and crucifixion. This is Jesus' last journey on His way to the cross, but He is continuing to talk with people as He walks along the way. He tells them about the mustard seed again because that is one of the most commonly planted seeds in the land of Israel and it grows into a tremendous bush, 10 or 12 feet high. He refers them to that and then to the woman who is always making her meals and getting the bread ready to bake.

In effect, He is saying that our seed-faith is more than just some single act of giving; it is the constant flow of what we have from God inside which we are planting into His kingdom. We are giving our prayers, our compassion, our time, our love and faith. We are going out of the way to help someone. We are in the house of God not only to receive the Word and fellowship from others, but to give fellowship and to be a part of the service — not just sit there on the church pew like a knot on a log.

We are to be part of what is going on in the house of God. We are to be part of what is going on in the kingdom of God in the everydayness of our lives. Even the smallest things have a major part in the way God looks upon us and receives us as His children.

Luke 13:23-30

> Then said one unto him, Lord, are there few that be saved? And he said unto them, Strive to enter in at the strait gate; for many, I say unto you, will seek to enter in, and shall not be able. When once the master of the house is risen up, and hath shut to the door, and ye begin to stand without and to knock at the door, saying, Lord, Lord, open unto us; and he shall answer and say unto you, I know you not whence ye are: then shall ye begin to say, We have eaten and drunk in thy presence, and thou hast taught in our streets. But he shall say, I tell you, I know you not whence ye are; depart from me, all ye workers of iniquity.
>
> There shall be weeping and gnashing of teeth, when ye shall see Abraham, and Isaac, and Jacob, and all the prophets, in the kingdom of God, and you yourselves thrust out. And they shall come from the east, and from the west, and from the north, and from the south, and shall sit down in the kingdom of God.
>
> And, behold, there are last which shall be first, and there are first which shall be last.

Jesus on Judgment

Things are serious. He does not have time left to tell them anything. He tells them candidly that there is a responsibility and that everybody is going to meet an end, that they are going to face what they have lived through and what they have done with their lives.

This statement, "weeping and gnashing of teeth," has been written by Luke seven times. Throughout the Bible it is mentioned 118 times and not once is it used in a figurative sense. It is referring to hell, the judgment. And at that time, there will be people who will be coming from the north, south, east, and west, and from all generations, and those present will be surprised at some who make it and surprised at others who do not make it. He is trying to say, "Get to the key issue. Serve God with your whole heart."

Luke 13:31-33

> The same day there came certain of the Pharisees, saying unto him, Get thee out, and depart hence: for Herod will kill thee. And he said unto them, Go ye, and tell that fox, Behold, I cast out devils, and I do cures today and tomorrow, and the third day I shall be perfected. Nevertheless I must walk today, and tomorrow, and the day following: for it cannot be that a prophet perish out of Jerusalem.

He has about 3 days left. The Pharisees are aware that Herod is on His trail. This is one of the few times Jesus speaks rather harshly, calling Herod a name — a fox with cunning ways. And He says, "You go tell him that today I am casting out devils. Today and tomorrow I am healing the sick. The third day I am going to come to the perfection of myself as a man on this earth. However, there is no way that a prophet is going to perish outside of Jerusalem. I will not be in his jurisdiction." You may remember that Pontius Pilate had been appointed by Rome to be governor over Jerusalem and that area.

Luke 13:34,35

> O Jerusalem, Jerusalem, which killest the prophets, and stonest them that are sent unto thee; how often would I have gathered thy children together, as a hen doth gather her brood under her wings, and ye would not!
>
> Behold, your house is left unto you desolate: and verily I say unto you, Ye shall not see me, until the time come when ye shall say, Blessed is he that cometh in the name of the Lord.

Jesus Offers Protection

Jesus knew that there was great calamity coming to Jerusalem. In A.D. 70, the Roman general Titus would burn and sack the city, kill at least a million Jews, and disperse most of the survivors. Jesus told them that a day of desolation was coming, that He had tried so hard to love them, to gather them all as a hen calls her little chickens and puts them under her wings of protection.

There is something about the heart that, if it does not repent and let God in, it simply cannot see the future. Are you sensitive to the Holy Spirit and to the signs of the times? Jesus is saying to you, "Oh, I want to gather you in My arms and protect you because there are times coming which no person can stand."

Luke 14:1-6

And it came to pass, as he went into the house of one of the chief Pharisees to eat bread on the sabbath day, that they watched him. And, behold, there was a certain man before him which had the dropsy.

And Jesus answering spake unto the lawyers and Pharisees, saying, Is it lawful to heal on the sabbath day?

And they held their peace. And he took him, and healed him, and let him go; and answered them, saying, Which of you shall have an ass or an ox fallen into a pit, and will not straightway pull him out on the sabbath day?

And they could not answer him again to these things.

Healing Ministry Emphasized

As Jesus' life draws to a close, He seems to be taking special pains to point out to us the absolute value of the saving and healing ministry of the kingdom of God. Nothing can take that place.

Luke 14:7-14

And he put forth a parable to those which were bidden, when he marked how they chose out the chief rooms; saying unto them, When thou art bidden of any man to a wedding, sit not down in the highest room; lest a more honourable man than thou be bidden of him; and he that bade thee and him come and say to thee, Give this man place; and thou begin with shame to take the lowest room.

But when thou art bidden, go and sit down in the lowest room; that when he that bade thee cometh, he may say unto thee, Friend, go up higher: then shalt thou have worship in the presence of them that sit at meat with thee.

For whosoever exalteth himself shall be abased; and he that humbleth himself shall be exalted.

Then said he also to him that bade him, When thou makest a dinner or a supper, call not thy friends, nor thy brethren, neither thy kinsmen, nor thy rich neighbours; lest they also bid thee again, and a recompence be made thee. But when thou makest a feast, call the poor, the maimed, the lame, the blind: and thou shalt be blessed; for they cannot recompense thee: for thou shalt be recompensed at the resurrection of the just.

See God's Viewpoint

Jesus tells us to look at people from heaven's viewpoint, that God looks at people at the point of their need, not at the strata of society that man has established. God is looking to deliver people. What we are interested in is the continuity of our lives, here and in eternity, standing in the presence of God at all times. Seeing from His viewpoint.

Luke 14:15-24

And when one of them that sat at meat with him heard these things, he said unto him, Blessed is he that shall eat bread in the kingdom of God.

Then said he unto him, A certain man made a great supper, and bade many. And sent his servant at supper time to say to them that were bidden, Come; for all things are now ready.

And they all with one consent began to make excuse. The first said unto him, I have bought a piece of ground, and I must needs go and see it: I pray thee have me excused. And another said, I have bought five yoke of oxen, and I go to prove them: I pray thee have me excused.

And another said, I have married a wife, and therefore I cannot come.

So that servant came, and shewed his lord these things. Then the master of the house being angry said to his servant, Go out quickly into the streets and lanes of the city, and bring in hither the poor, and the maimed, and the halt, and the blind.

The servant said, Lord, it is done as thou hast commanded, and yet there is room. And the lord said unto the servant, Go out into the highways and hedges, and compel them to come in, that my house may be filled. For I say unto you, That none of those men which were bidden shall taste of my supper.

Jesus Extends Invitation

Now, the Pharisees in the room knew Jesus was talking about them. He was also opening up the kingdom to the Gentiles. Always, as Jesus dealt with this small nation of Israel, He was trying to pry open their minds and open them up to the whole world. Certainly, God is concerned about His kingdom being filled because His greatest concern is for humanity, for people; whether they are Jews or Gentiles, they are just human beings.

Luke 14:25-35

And there went great multitudes with him: and he turned, and said unto them, If any man come to me, and hate not his father, and mother, and wife, and children, and brethren, and sisters, yea, and his own life also, he cannot be my disciple.

And whosoever doth not bear his cross, and come after me, cannot be my disciple.

For which of you, intending to build a tower, sitteth not down first, and counteth the cost, whether he have sufficient to finish it? Lest haply, after he hath laid the foundation, and is not able to finish it, all that behold it begin to mock him, saying, This man began to build, and was not able to finish.

Or what king, going to make war against another king, sitteth not down first, and consulteth whether he be able with ten thousand to meet him that cometh against him with twenty thousand? Or else, while the other is yet a great way off, he sendeth an ambassage, and desireth conditions of peace.

So likewise, whosoever he be of you that forsaketh not all that he hath, he cannot be my disciple.

Salt is good: but if the salt have lost his savour, wherewith shall it be seasoned? It is neither fit for the land, nor yet for the dunghill, but men cast it out. He that hath ears to hear, let him hear.

Here are great multitudes following Jesus, hanging onto every word, trying to see every little thing that happens, but they are not getting the key issue, the number-one thing. They are not understanding that He is calling upon them to give God their best. They are just traveling along, listening and looking and talking with one another, but not absorbed in the main thrust of what Christ is trying to do in their lives. It is pretty easy to do that today, to be carried away with the different details of life without truly keeping our heart sensitive to what the Spirit of God is saying to us.

Luke 15:1-10

Then drew near unto him all the publicans and sinners for to hear him. And the Pharisees and scribes murmured, saying, This man receiveth sinners, and eateth with them.

And he spake this parable unto them, saying, What man of you, having an hundred sheep, if he lose one of them, doth not leave the ninety and nine in the wilderness, and go after that which is lost, until he find it? And when he hath found it, he layeth it on his shoulders, rejoicing. And when he cometh home, he calleth together his friends and neighbours, saying unto them, Rejoice with me; for I have found my sheep which was lost.

I say unto you, that likewise joy shall be in heaven over one sinner that repenteth, more than over ninety and nine just persons, which need no repentance.

Either what woman having ten pieces of silver, if she lose one piece, doth not light a candle, and sweep the house, and seek diligently till she find it? And when she hath found it, she calleth her friends and her neighbours together, saying, Rejoice with me; for I have found the piece which I had lost. Likewise, I say unto you, there is joy in the presence of the angels of God over one sinner that repenteth.

Joy in Salvation

There is that word "joy" again. There is joy in the presence of the angels of God. Our salvation is one of joy! It is not a long-faced religion, as if we had been eating sauerkraut or crab apples,or like a disaster going off to happen. It is a joyous salvation that puts a shine on our face, a sparkle in our eye, a lift to our shoulder, a spring in our feet, and joy in our heart. There is joy! Do not settle for less than joy in your salvation.

Luke 15:11-32

And he said, A certain man had two sons: and the younger of them said to his father, Father, give me the portion of goods that falleth to me. And he divided unto them his living. And not many days after the younger son gathered all together, and took his journey into a far country, and there wasted his substance with riotous living. And when he had spent all, there arose a mighty famine in that land; and he began to be in want.

And he went and joined himself to a citizen of that country; and he sent him into his fields to feed swine. And he would fain have filled his belly with the husks that the swine did eat: and no man gave unto him. And when he came to himself, he said, How many hired servants of my father's have bread enough and to spare, and I perish with hunger! I will arise and go to my father, and will say unto him, Father, I have sinned against heaven, and before thee, and am no more worthy to be called thy son: make me as one of thy hired servants.

And he arose, and came to his father. But when he was yet a great way off, his father saw him, and had compassion, and ran, and fell on his neck, and kissed him. And the son said unto him, Father, I have sinned against heaven, and in thy sight, and am no more worthy to be called thy son.

But the father said to his servants, Bring forth the best robe, and put it on him; and put a ring on his hand, and shoes on his feet: and bring hither the fatted calf, and kill it; and let us eat, and be merry:

For this my son was dead, and is alive again; he was lost, and is found. And they began to be merry.

Now his elder son was in the field: and as he came and drew nigh to the house, he heard music and dancing. And he called one of the servants, and asked what these things meant. And he said unto him, Thy brother is come; and thy father hath killed the fatted calf, because he hath received him safe and sound.

And he was angry, and would not go in: therefore came his father out, and intreated him.

And he answering said to his father, Lo, these many years do I serve thee, neither transgressed I at any time thy commandment: and yet thou never gavest me a kid, that I might make merry with my friends: but as soon as this thy son was come, which hath devoured thy living with harlots, thou hast killed for him the fatted calf.

And he said unto him, Son, thou art ever with me, and all that I have is thine. It was meet that we should make merry, and be glad: for this thy brother was dead, and is alive again; and was lost, and is found.

We Can Change

The story of the prodigal son, his father, and his elder brother is probably the best known story that Jesus ever told. The younger son represents the way we are created by God to use our will in the freest way, because that is the way God designed us. God had such love that He made man His masterpiece, made him different from all other creatures, and gave him the power of choice. Although the father knew the younger son was wrong, he let him do it.

People ask, "Why are all the wars in the world? Why does God permit all this? Why doesn't He just come down and stop it all?" What they are saying unknowingly is, "Why doesn't God take away man's freedom of choice?" Should that happen, we would cease to be human beings.

God risked His all. He put His faith on the line, that before it was over enough people would come to their senses and use their choice in the right way, and His kingdom would triumph.

Now, the elder brother was terribly upset, and he said to his father, I have always done what you told me to do and you have never done anything for me. His father said, "Son, all that I have is yours."

God has put everything in this world to our use and at our disposal.

Then he said to the elder son, "Your younger brother did all that you said, but he has repented. He has changed his attitude and returned home. Son, this is what life is all about."

When we make a mistake, correct it. When we fall, get up. When we do wrong, repent. Get in line with the kingdom of God. The father in Jesus' story represents your heavenly Father who, by this demonstration of love and mercy, is showing us,through His Son

Jesus Christ, that we can change. We can turn to Him no matter if we are like the younger brother or like the older brother. We can come to Him and all that He has is ours.

Luke 16:1-8

> And he said also unto his disciples, There was a certain rich man, which had a steward; and the same was accused unto him that he had wasted his goods. And he called him, and said unto him, How is it that I hear this of thee? give an account of thy stewardship; for thou mayest be no longer steward.
>
> Then the steward said within himself, What shall I do? for my lord taketh away from me the stewardship: I cannot dig; to beg I am ashamed. I am resolved what to do, that, when I am put out of the stewardship, they may receive me into their houses.
>
> So he called every one of his lord's debtors unto him, and said unto the first, How much owest thou unto my lord? And he said, An hundred measures of oil. And he said unto him, Take thy bill, and sit down quickly, and write fifty.
>
> Then said he to another, And how much owest thou? And he said, An hundred measures of wheat. And he said unto him, Take thy bill, and write fourscore.
>
> And the lord commended the unjust steward, because he had done wisely: for the children of this world are in their generation wiser than the children of light.

Get Smart For God

The Lord is not commending this man for the deed. He is simply commending him for the wisdom that he used in disposing of this difficult situation. Then He adds that the people of the world are smarter than we who are in the kingdom of God. In other words, they use their minds better. We have fallen into the old syndrome that the soul is everything; if our souls are saved and right with God, then what use is there to develop our minds or to develop our bodies or to be a whole person? But the children of this world are thinking all the time, trying to get the best out of the situation. Frankly, the Lord is trying to tell us to "smarten up."

Luke 16:9-15

> And I say unto you, Make to yourselves friends of the mammon of unrighteousness; that, when ye fail, they may receive you into everlasting habitations.
>
> He that is faithful in that which is least is faithful also in much: and

> he that is unjust in the least is unjust also in much. If therefore ye have not been faithful in the unrighteous mammon, who will commit to your trust the true riches? And if ye have not been faithful in that which is another man's, who shall give you that which is your own?
>
> No servant can serve two masters: for either he will hate the one, and love the other; or else he will hold to the one, and despise the other. Ye cannot serve God and mammon. And the Pharisees also, who were covetous, heard all these things: and they derided him. And he said unto them, Ye are they which justify yourselves before men; but God knoweth your hearts: for that which is highly esteemed among men is abomination in the sight of God.

Jesus is saying that we must get our priorities straight because we cannot serve two masters at the same time. We have got to know the difference between the material riches of this world and the spiritual riches of the eternal world. Mammon is the riches of this world in contrast with the true riches of God. The Lord is saying, If we are not faithful in handling money or dealing with the riches of the earth and of mankind, how in the world can we be faithful in dealing with the things of God? There is a difference between a possession and a treasure. When you possess something, you possess it for a particular length of time and when you die you leave it behind. A treasure is something of God. It is something that no possession can buy. A treasure comes out of your heart by your faith, your love, your hope. A treasure reflects the things of the Lord, even the miraculous, including your salvation, and these can never be taken from you.

Luke 16:16

> The law and the prophets were until John: since that time the kingdom of God is preached, and every man presseth into it.

Great Principles Continue

The coming of John the Baptist as the forerunner of Jesus Christ was the signal that the law and the prophets were fulfilled. John the Baptist was now introducing the Messiah, who would open up a new kingdom. Other people thought that when the Messiah came, He would restore the political kingdom of Israel. John the Baptist knew better. When Jesus came, He made it clear that His kingdom was not of this world.

Also, there is to be a pressing forward, a deep effort made. We're to do something about it. We are to make things happen through the kingdom of God.

Another thing that Jesus referred to is when John the Baptist came (which signaled the fulfilling of the law of Moses), it did not mean that the great eternal laws and principles of God ceased. But it did refer to the cessation of those little regulations that put a crimp in your spiritual style, that cause a person to get his eyes upon the outward rather than the inward. He is saying that the great eternal principles of God continue. The principle of love, the principle of faith, the principle of hope, the principle of loving others as you love yourself, of loving your neighbor as you love yourself, the principle of putting God first in your life. You are not doing away with any of these great eternal principles. He is saying, in effect, that people were not able to grasp them because they got carried away with the nonessential things.

Luke 16:17-31

> And it is easier for heaven and earth to pass, than one tittle of the law to fail.
>
> Whosoever putteth away his wife, and marrieth another, committeth adultery: and whosoever marrieth her that is put away from her husband, committeth adultery.
>
> There was a certain rich man, which was clothed in purple and fine linen, and fared sumptuously every day: and there was a certain beggar named Lazarus, which was laid at his gate, full of sores, and desiring to be fed with the crumbs which fell from the rich man's table: moreover the dogs came and licked his sores. And it came to pass, that the beggar died, and was carried by the angels into Abraham's bosom: the rich man also died, and was buried; and in hell he lift up his eyes, being in torments, and seeth Abraham afar off, and Lazarus in his bosom.
>
> And he cried and said, Father Abraham, have mercy on me, and send Lazarus, that he may dip the tip of his finger in water, and cool my tongue; for I am tormented in this flame. But Abraham said, Son, remember that thou in they lifetime receivedst thy good things, and likewise Lazarus evil things: but now he is comforted, and thou art tormented.
>
> And beside all this, between us and you there is a great gulf fixed: so that they which would pass from hence to you cannot; neither can they pass to us, that would come from thence.
>
> Then he said, I pray thee therefore, father, that thou wouldest send him to my father's house: for I have five brethren; that he may testify unto them, lest they also come into this place of torment.
>
> Abraham saith unto him, They have Moses and the prophets; let them hear them.
>
> And he said, Nay, father Abraham: but if one went unto them from

the dead, they will repent.

And he said unto him, If they hear not Moses and the prophets, neither will they be persuaded, though one rose from the dead.

Resurrection Changed Everything

Somewhere in the bowels of the earth there was a place which in Hebrew was called "sheol," in Greek "hades," in English "hell." It was a place of departed souls.

Now, it was in two compartments. One compartment was for the souls of the unrighteous, the other for the righteous. Those in the upper part, called paradise, could not go from paradise down to the lower part called hell. They that were in hell could not pass from there to paradise, the upper part. They were forever separated but they could see each other.

Jesus went to that place, and both Paul and Peter specifically tell us that Christ preached to the spirits in prison, to Abraham, Isaac, Jacob, Moses, Isaiah — to all who died in the faith. He proclaimed His death on the cross and the promise of His resurrection.

While His body was in the grave in Jerusalem, He was down there, proclaiming his victory and saying that He was going to deliver them into the immediate presence of God. On the third morning when the angel rolled the stone away from the tomb and Christ arose, somewhere in that mighty incomparable resurrection scene Jesus led captivity captive. That is, He gathered up the souls of the righteous dead and when He ascended to His Father, He took those souls with Him, straight to glory, and laid them at the feet of the Father. Since that time, when we who believe on Christ die, at that moment our soul leaves our body and is placed in the hands of the angels and they take us, not down to paradise somewhere in the bowels of the earth, but directly into the presence of the heavenly Father — absent from the body but present with the Lord.

Hell remains. It is in the same place it was and will be there until the final judgment when God will lift those who are there out and they will go into the lake of fire, which is the second death. Be assured, if you have believed on the Lord and are carrying His cross daily, you are a saved person, you are delivered from hell. Sin does not have dominion over you any longer. You are a child of God. If you should die any moment, they may bury your body or do with it whatsoever they will, but it is God who will deal with your soul. He will send His angels to lift your soul out of your body and wing it to glory in a moment of time. You see, they are pointing out here that the soul is conscious, not only while it is in the body, but after it leaves the body. "Divies" is the traditional name of this man who went to hell. Divies did not go to hell because he was rich. And Lazarus did not go to heaven because he was poor. It was the attitude of the two men toward God that made the difference.

Faith is faith. You either decide by choice to manifest faith in God or you decide by choice not to.

Luke 17:1-10

Then said he unto the disciples, It is impossible but that offences will come: but woe unto him, through whom they come! It were better for him that a millstone were hanged about his neck, and he cast into the sea, than that he should offend one of these little ones.

Take heed to yourselves: If thy brother trespass against thee, rebuke him; and if he repent, forgive him. And if he trespass against thee seven times in a day, and seven times in a day turn again to thee, saying, I repent: thou shalt forgive him.

And the apostles said unto the Lord, Increase our faith.

And the Lord said, If ye had faith as a grain of mustard seed, ye might say unto this sycamine tree, Be thou plucked up by the root, and be thou planted in the sea; and it should obey you.

But which of you, having a servant plowing or feeding cattle, will say unto him by and by, when he is come from the field, Go and sit down to meat? And will not rather say unto him, Make ready wherewith I may sup, and gird thyself, and serve me, till I have eaten and drunken; and afterward thou shalt eat and drink?

Doth he thank that servant because he did the things that were commanded him? I trow not. So likewise ye, when ye shall have done all those things which are commanded you, say, We are unprofitable servants: we have done that which was our duty to do.

Doing Our Duty

The first thing that Jesus is saying to us here is that we should always have a forgiving spirit. It is better to be wronged than to wrong someone else.

The next thing He addresses is the faith of the disciples. He is saying, "Use it, release your faith," and your faith grows by releasing it. The more your faith goes up to God, the stronger your faith gets, the larger it becomes.

Then He tells us that when we have used our faith and by our faith have done the greatest things possible, we are not to rest on our laurels and say, "Look what I have done," but to say, "We are unprofitable servants because we have done only what we are supposed to do." The praise should be to God, for without God, we are nothing.

Luke 17:11-19

And it came to pass, as he went to Jerusalem, that he passed through the midst of Samaria and Galilee. And as he entered into a certain village, there met him ten men that were lepers, which stood afar off: and they lifted up their voices, and said, Jesus, Master, have mercy on us.

And when he saw them, he said unto them, Go shew yourselves unto the priests. And it came to pass, that, as they went, they were cleansed.

And one of them, when he saw that he was healed, turned back, and with a loud voice glorified God, and fell down on his face at his feet, giving him thanks: and he was a Samaritan.

And Jesus answering said, Were there not ten cleansed? But where are the nine? There are not found that returned to give glory to God, save this stranger. And he said unto him, Arise, go thy way: thy faith hath made thee whole.

Location of Faith

Jesus was looking for faith. He was not looking for certain types of folks, their color, their culture, and so on. He was looking for faith, and when He found the faith it was not always where people expected it to be. So many times in my crusades, in praying for thousands and thousands of sick people, I was amazed that some people I thought would be healed did not get healed, and some I thought would not, were healed. It is always this element of faith that counts, not how sick you are, not how poor you are, not how rich you are, not how smart you are, but where the faith is found. Jesus was looking for faith because faith makes one whole. Faith not only heals the body, it heals the whole person.

Luke 17:20-32

And when he was demanded of the Pharisees, when the kingdom of God should come, he answered them and said, The kingdom of God cometh not with observation. Neither shall they say, Lo here! or,lo there! for, behold, the kingdom of God is within you.

And he said unto the disciples, The days will come, when ye shall desire to see one of the days of the Son of man, and ye shall not see it. And they shall say to you, See here; or, see there: go not after them, nor follow them. For as the lightning, that lighteneth out of the one part under heaven, shineth unto the other part under heaven; so shall also the Son of man be in his day.

But first must he suffer many things, and be rejected of this generation.

And as it was in the days of Noah, so shall it be also in the days of the Son of man. They did eat, they drank, they married wives, they were given in marriage, until the day that Noah entered into the ark, and the flood came, and destroyed them all. Likewise also as it was in the days of Lot; they did eat, they drank, they bought, they sold, they planted, they builded; but the same day that Lot went out of Sodom it rained fire and brimstone from heaven, and destroyed them all.

Even thus shall it be in the day when the Son of man is revealed. In that day, he which shall be upon the housetop, and his stuff in the house, let him not come down to take it away: and he that is in the field, let him likewise not return back. Remember Lot's wife.

Don't Expect Notice

Christ is saying here when that day comes, it will not be so extraordinary as people think, for as in the days of Noah, people were conducting their lives in the usual way, eating, and drinking, and marrying, and getting married, and going through the motions of life. Nothing was drastic or unusual. They did this until the very day the flood came. The same with Lot, Abraham's nephew, who lived in Sodom. In that wicked place, people were carrying on their lives the same as usual until the very day God rained fire and brimstone down and destroyed them all.

He is saying not to look for cataclysmic events to signal the coming of the Lord. It will just be ordinary affairs, and for that reason you must be ready. There will be no forewarning. Two will go to bed, one will be prepared in the Lord to be caught up, the other will not. He is telling us that we should be ready at all times.

And then He added, "Remember Lot's wife," who looked back at the fire and brimstone destroying the cities out of which she was delivered along with her husband, Lot, and she was turned into a pillar of salt. We cannot look back to the beggarly elements of this world from which we have been saved by the grace of God. We must keep our eyes on the Lord. Put first things first and be ready, for it will be in the twinkling of an eye when the Lord catches up His people.

Luke 17:33-37

Whosoever shall seek to save his life shall lose it; and whosoever shall lose his life shall preserve it. I tell you, in that night there shall be two men in one bed; the one shall be taken, and the other shall be left. Two women shall be grinding together; the one shall be taken, and the other left. Two men shall be in the field; the one shall be taken, and the other left.

And they answered and said unto him, Where, Lord? And he said unto them, Wheresoever the body is, thither will the eagles be gathered together.

Share Christian Experience

Jesus is continuing to speak of the second coming of Christ and He is telling us that if we hold onto this world in order to save our lives in it by making the world the fulfillment of everything we desire, we are really going to lose out. We are not going to save our lives because we will miss the second coming of Christ if we do that. But if we submit our lives to Christ, and in the light of men actually lose it, we are actually holding onto it because we shall be ready when the Lord Jesus Christ comes.

He says we should not look upon mere human intimacy or friendship as a preparation for our souls and lives to be ready for Christ's second coming. There will be two people working; one will be snatched up into heaven and the other will not. His statement, "Wheresoever the body is, there will the eagles be gathered together," means that a thing will come to pass when all the conditions are fulfilled. God will act when that time comes. You must submit your life to him at all times so that when all conditions are fulfilled, you will be ready and will be in connection with the Lord to be caught up to meet Him face to face.

How can we apply that to our lives today? Often we work side by side with a friend or a loved one and somehow the devil wants to make us reluctant to share our witness or to talk about the Lord. When you love someone you talk about them. There are times when you can say certain things that you feel deep within yourself which will prompt a question or reply from that person. Then you can say what you really feel in your heart. We simply cannot live together in close friendship without ever sharing our Christian experience and faith.

Luke 18:1

And he spake a parable unto them to this end, that men ought always to pray, and not to faint . . .

Avoid Easy Way

It is so easy to lose heart in this world of sin where we are opposed by the devil and where every step we take must be taken by faith. But Jesus says we are not to take the easy way, which is to lose heart and give way, but we ought to pray, because prayer changes things.

Luke 18:2-8

Saying, There was in a city a judge, which feared not God, neither regarded man: and there was a widow in that city; and she came unto him, saying, Avenge me of mine adversary. And he would not for a while: but afterward he said within himself, Though I fear not God, nor regard man; yet because this widow troubleth me, I will avenge her, lest by her continual coming she weary me.

And the Lord said, Hear what the unjust judge saith. And shall not God avenge his own elect, who cry day and night unto him, though he bear long with them? I tell you that he will avenge them speedily. Nevertheless when the Son of man cometh, shall he find faith on the earth?

Persistent Prayer Succeeds

The persistent kind of prayer always gets through. In its persistence, it overcomes all opposition and because the opposition is overcome, a straight and clear road is opened up for the Lord to give victory.

Luke 18:9-14

And he spake this parable unto certain which trusted in themselves that they were righteous, and despised others: Two men went up into the temple to pray; the one a Pharisee, and the other a publican. The Pharisee stood and prayed thus with himself, God, I thank thee, that I am not as other men are, extortioners, unjust, adulterers, or even as this publican. I fast twice in the week, I give tithes of all that I possess.

And the publican, standing afar off, would not lift up so much as his eyes unto heaven, but smote upon his breast, saying, God be merciful to me a sinner.

I tell you, this man went down to his house justified rather than the other: for every one that exalteth himself shall be abased; and he that humbleth himself shall be exalted.

Seek God's Mercy

Jesus was looking for the inner heart of all people to be open to Him, to recognize in themselves a tendency to sin and to be reminded of their sins and their need of a Messiah, a Christ, a Redeemer. This publican who was a sinner did that. He did not try to justify himself but smote his breast, saying, "Lord, be merciful to me a sinner."

I have used that prayer with hundreds of thousands of unsaved people throughout America and 46 nations. I think God will hush every heart in heaven to hear a sinner pray, "Lord, be merciful to me a sinner." There's no prayer quite so precious as this prayer, "Lord, be merciful to me a sinner." Have you prayed that prayer? Isn't it time you did? I assure you, if you will pray it with all the sincerity and believing of your heart, God will hear your prayer and save you.

Now this other man was bragging, and God hates bragging. He says, "He that humbleth himself shall be exalted." Jesus wants to lift you up. He does not want you down, beaten by your adversaries, eaten up by the devourers of your life. He wants you to humble yourself so that you give yourself away to God, that God may give himself away to you. In your receiving God and His fullness, you are lifted to God's kind of exaltation, the kind that brings the miracles of God into our life, His peace to fill your heart, and the true ability to witness in His name.

The Pharisee was not really praying. He was giving a testimonial to himself. The publican, the tax collector, was not doing that at all. In fact, the scripture says here, "God be merciful to me a sinner," but the original says, "God be merciful to the sinner." Paul said, I am the sinner of sinners. Jesus is telling us when we pray to feel our absolute need of God, our own deepest unworthiness. Let us pray right now.

Heavenly Father, deliver us from ever praying for ourselves, as a testimonial to how good we think we are. Allow us to recognize the mistakes and failures we make and the shortcomings we have. And God, be merciful to us, to me, to this reader, my friend and partner. Be merciful to us because we come to You in agreement that we need You. We rely upon You. You are the source of our total supply. You are the God of our life, the Savior of our souls, minds, and bodies, now and forever. Be merciful to us. Father, we receive Your mercy through Jesus Christ right now. Amen and amen.

Luke 18:15

And they brought unto him also infants, that he would touch them:

but when his disciples saw it, they rebuked them.

Well, these unspiritual disciples of His turned their rebuking power around. I pray that this word "rebuke" will be driven into your spirit so that you'll understand that it is to be used only in God rebuking the devourer of our lives. We're not to use it, we're not to be part of a rebuking spirit; it's God alone who knows how to rebuke.

Luke 18:16,17

But Jesus called them unto him, and said, Suffer little children to come unto me, and forbid them not: for of such is the kingdom of God.

Verily I say unto you, Whosoever shall not receive the kingdom of God as a little child shall in no wise enter therein.

Throw Off Unbelief

Little children are so fresh from God that they have not lost their faith. He is telling us to be like a little child, to throw off the unbelieving spirit of the people of this world, humble ourselves so childlike faith can reenter our heart. Then, believing in God will not be a chore. It will be a joy.

Luke 18:18-30

And a certain ruler asked him, saying, Good Master, what shall I do to inherit eternal life?

And Jesus said unto him, Why callest thou me good? none is good, save one, that is, God. Thou knowest the commandments, Do not commit adultery, Do not kill, Do not steal, Do not bear false witness, Honour thy father and thy mother.

And he said, All these have I kept from my youth up. Now when Jesus heard these things, he said unto him, Yet lackest thou one thing: sell all that thou hast, and distribute unto the poor, and thou shalt have treasure in heaven: and come, follow me.

And when he heard this, he was very sorrowful: for he was very rich.

And when Jesus saw that he was very sorrowful, he said, How hardly shall they that have riches enter into the kingdom of God! For it is easier for a camel to go through a needle's eye, than for a rich man to enter into the kingdom of God.

And they that heard it said, Who then can be saved? And he said, The things which are impossible with men are possible with God.

Then Peter said, Lo, we have left all, and followed thee, and he said unto them, Verily I say unto you, There is no man that hath left house,

> or parents, or brethren, or wife, or children, for the kingdom of God's sake, who shall not receive manifold more in this present time, and in the world to come life everlasting.

"Riches" Not Christ's Point

This certain ruler came to Christ by saying "good Master." Among the Jews they did not use that term concerning a rabbi, and Jesus was a rabbi. That was a sort of flattery, and Jesus realized he was trying to flatter Him. And then Jesus drove him right back to God and to His Word. In effect He is saying, "Look, the Jewish people are taught not to call men good but to call God good. You know the commandments. These are things that you should have your mind on: God and His commandments." Jesus knew this man was full of flattery, that he never gave anything away, and his real God was comfort and selfishness and worshipping his own possessions. And when He called upon him to start giving so that God should fill up the empty soul that he had, he said, "You will have treasures in heaven as you follow Me." And the man went away very sorrowful because he was rich.

Rich, in this instance, means a lot of material possessions which he had his heart set on. We can be rich whether we have money or not and have a bad spirit about it. We can be selfish, we can depend upon ourselves, we can really worship ourselves. This man went away sorrowful because all he had was possessions and no treasures in heaven. When Jesus saw him going away, He said, "It is easier for a camel to go through a needle's eye than for a rich man to enter into the kingdom of God."

I heard one reference to this that He was referring to the ropes of a ship, that it is easier to take one of those big ropes and thread a needle with it than it is for a person who has the spirit of the riches of this world in his heart — rather than the treasures of God's salvation and the treasure of following Christ everyday — to enter God's kingdom.

When the disciples turned to Jesus and said, "Who then can be saved?" they really meant, "Who then can win his way with God?" Jesus says, "You cannot. There is no way you can win your way with God by the amount of things that you possess in this world, because it is impossible. But it is possible with God for you to come to Him."

Some people take this to mean that Jesus is condemning riches. He is not. He is condemning having a wrong spirit, a possessiveness toward riches, substituting them in the place of having a personal relationship with Jesus Christ and having Him first in your life. Then

He is saying, "I want you to know that I am concerned about you in this life — spiritually, physically, financially — and about your loved ones, your circumstances, and I am going to see to it that you will receive and you will receive much more than you ever gave up and you will receive it in this present time. Then when you come down to leave this world, you will come into life everlasting which began when you received Me into your heart." I tell you, serving Christ is the best deal in the world.

Luke 18:31-34

> Then he took unto him the twelve, and said unto them, Behold, we go up to Jerusalem, and all things that are written by the prophets concerning the Son of man shall be accomplished. For he shall be delivered unto the Gentiles, and shall be mocked, and spitefully entreated, and spitted on: and they shall scourge him, and put him to death: and the third day he shall rise again.
>
> And they understood none of these things: and this saying was hid from them, neither knew they the things which were spoken.

Exalt Our Death Day

You know, there are so many Christians who seemingly have a dread of their own death, of their own homegoing to God. But we should be in command of ourselves because of our relationship with Christ. We are pilgrims and strangers on this earth. Our citizenship is in heaven, our names are written there. The Lord has gone and prepared a place for us. We should exalt in our life, despite the agonizing of death itself at being the last enemy. We should exalt in the passing of our soul from our bodies to God because that last enemy is destroyed.

Better than our birthday is our death day because it is a passage. It is entrance into the everlasting kingdom of God. He has promised every believer his or her resurrection. No longer will the devil have any power over our bodies. It is a precious thing because it is the final defeat of the devil over our personal lives. Praise God that someday we will go to be with Him.

Luke 18:35-41a

> And it came to pass, that as he was come nigh unto Jericho, a certain blind man sat by the way side begging: and hearing the multitude pass by, he asked what it meant. And they told him, that Jesus of Nazareth passeth by. And he cried, saying, Jesus, thou Son of David, have mercy on me.

And they which went before rebuked him, that he should hold his peace: but he cried so much the more, Thou Son of David, have mercy on me.

And Jesus stood, and commanded him to be brought unto him: and when he was come near, he asked him, saying, What wilt thou that I shall do unto thee?

Business With God

The sweetest sound to His ears is our cry of need and faith. There He was striding through that crowd, and here came this voice out of it pleading, "Son of David, have mercy on me." Jesus hears it, and while His disciples are trying to get him to shut up, Jesus stops the whole procession! He stops everything when one of us calls out to Him from our need and in our faith. Jesus knew what the man wanted. He could see he was blind because all blind people in those days dressed in a way so people would know they were blind. But He wanted this man to be specific, and prayer is specific. Our needs are specific. God wants us to transact business with Him in a way that is serious and complete in itself.

Luke 18:41b-43

And he said Lord, that I may receive my sight. And Jesus said unto him, Receive thy sight: thy faith hath saved thee. And immediately he received his sight, and followed him, glorifying God: and all the people, when they saw it, gave praise unto God.

Keep "Receiver" Busy

Jesus said, "Receive your sight." Our receiver has to go into action. Our believing is an act, the act of releasing our faith to God. Our receiving is a similar act. It is the action of receiving what God is sending us. Therefore, we must keep our receiver busy all the time, receiving from God.

Luke 19:1-6

And Jesus entered and passed through Jericho. And, behold, there was a man named Zacchaeus, which was the chief among the publicans, and he was rich. And he sought to see Jesus who he was, and could not for the press, because he was little of stature. And he ran before, and climbed up into a sycamore tree to see him: for he was to pass that way.

And when Jesus came to the place, he looked up, and saw him, and said unto him, Zacchaeus, make haste, and come down; for today I must abide at thy house.

And he made haste, and came down, and received him joyfully.

Christ Gives Joy

There again is that word "received."

And there again is that word "joy." Look at this part of the gospel, which is the very heart of it: receiving because of our believing brings us into a state of joy. That is what our hearts are hurting for — joy, victory, the spirit of light in our hearts. This is the true Spirit of God when joy comes. There is no truer sign of God's presence than the joy of Christ in our hearts.

Luke 19:7,8

And when they saw it, they all murmured, saying, That he was gone to be guest with a man that is a sinner. And Zacchaeus stood, and said unto the Lord; Behold, Lord, the half of my goods I give to the poor; and if I have taken any thing from any man by false accusation, I restore him fourfold.

Jesus' Power Reveals Sins

Zacchaeus was the head tax man for the Romans. He was a Jew who hired himself out to the occupying Roman forces to collect their taxes, and the only money he made was over and above the amount of taxes he was able to collect for the Romans. He added his income onto what the Romans had assessed. Therefore he said, "The half of my goods I give to the poor" because he knew that half he had gotten wrongly. And he said, "If I have done this to any man I will restore him fourfold," and it was apparent that he had taken four times as much as he should. Therefore, when Jesus' convicting power came upon him, it revealed his sins. They came before him like a moving picture — and he saw them.

Luke 19:9,10

And Jesus said unto him, This day is salvation come to this house, forsomuch as he also is a son of Abraham. For the Son of man is come to seek and to save that which was lost.

God Our Supply

Jesus was so overjoyed with the repentance of Zacchaeus and his faithful pledge to make restitution, He said, "Today salvation is come to him and to his house." He was saying, "This is the spirit of Abraham." In Genesis 14 you will see that Abraham said, "I will not take even a shoe latchet from anybody."

Once we are saved, God is our supply. We no longer misrepresent, or vilify, or rebuke people, or take things from them that are theirs. We trust God just as this man was doing.

Luke 19:11-27

And as they heard these things, he added and spake a parable, because he was nigh to Jerusalem, and because they thought that the kingdom of God should immediately appear.

He said therefore, A certain nobleman went into a far country to receive for himself a kingdom, and to return. And he called his ten servants, and delivered them ten pounds, and said unto them, Occupy till I come.

But his citizens hated him, and sent a message after him, saying, We will not have this man to reign over us. And it came to pass, that when he was returned, having received the kingdom, then he commanded these servants to be called unto him, to whom he had given the money, that he might know how much every man had gained by trading.

Then came the first, saying, Lord, thy pound hath gained ten pounds. And he said unto him, Well, thou good servant: because thou hast been faithful in a very little, have thou authority over ten cities.

And the second came, saying, Lord, thy pound hath gained five pounds. And he said likewise to him, Be thou also over five cities.

And another came, saying, Lord, behold, here is thy pound, which I have kept laid up in a napkin: for I feared thee, because thou art an austere man: thou takest up that thou layedst not down, and reapest that thou didst not sow.

And he saith unto him, Out of thine own mouth will I judge thee, thou wicked servant. Thou knewest that I was an austere man, taking up that I laid not down, and reaping that I did not sow: wherefore then gavest not thou my money into the bank, that at my coming I might have required mine own with usury? And he said unto them that stood by, Take from him the pound, and give it to him that hath ten pounds. (And they said unto him, Lord, he hath ten pounds.)

For I say unto you, That unto every one which hath shall be given; and from him that hath not, even that he hath shall be taken away from him.

But those mine enemies, which would not that I should reign over them, bring hither, and slay them before me.

Work, Sow to Reap

There are two things to observe here. One is Christ's statement, "Occupy till I come." This is His direct statement that we are to be busy in His work. Since we do not know the hour of His coming, whether today or tomorrow or next year or even beyond our lifetime, we are to occupy, we are to be doing His work.

Second, Jesus' parable about giving to these people is a direct statement about seed-faith. Fear is the thing that keeps us from sowing our seeds of faith. We are afraid we will not receive anything back. Instead, we will have less. I know when God began to reveal seed-faith to me, I caught a vision of how what I gave, God would multiply back, but if I gave nothing and God multiplied nothing, it would still be nothing.

This is what is happening to so many people, even Christians; they are not getting their needs met because they are not giving to God, or when they give they do not expect to receive.

God sends it, it passes them by, and they wonder, "Why does God forget me?" God has not forgotten them. They are to receive from what they plant.

Don't you see how God loves you? How He has a plan for meeting your needs? Get into the rhythm of sowing and reaping.

Luke 19:28-40

And when he had thus spoken he went before, ascending up to Jerusalem. And it came to pass, when he was come nigh to Bethphage and Bethany, at the mount called the mount of Olives, he sent two of his disciples, saying, Go ye into the village over against you; in the which at your entering ye shall find a colt tied, whereon yet never man sat: loose him, and bring him hither. And if any man ask you, Why do you loose him? thus shall ye say unto him, Because the Lord hath need of him.

And they that were sent went their way, and found even as he had said unto them. And as they were loosing the colt, the owners thereof said unto them, Why loose ye the colt? And they said, The Lord hath need of him.

And they brought him to Jesus: and they cast their garments upon the colt, and they set Jesus thereon. And as he went, they spread their clothes in the way. And when he was come nigh, even now at the descent of the mount of Olives, the whole multitude of the disciples began to rejoice and praise God with a loud voice for all the mighty works that they had seen; saying, Blessed be the King that cometh in the name of the Lord: peace in heaven, and glory in the highest.

And some of the Pharisees from among the multitude said unto him, Master, rebuke thy disciples.

And he answered and said unto them, I tell you that, if these should hold their peace, the stones would immediately cry out.

Prince of Peace

In those days, when a king went forth to fight a battle, he rode a great horse. When he won the war and came back with his trophies, he rode a donkey. Riding the horse was an emblem of going forth to war. Riding the donkey was an emblem of peace. Jesus was saying, as He rode the donkey, "I am not the military warrior you seek, but I am the Prince of peace bringing you glad tidings of the kingdom of God." The people understood what He was saying and a great cry of praise went up as they gave glory to God for the mighty works they had seen. They said, "Blessed be the King that cometh in the name of the Lord. Peace in heaven and glory in the highest." Well, the Pharisees, of course, did not like it and they said, "Master, rebuke thy disciples." He said, "If they hold their peace, the stones on these hillsides will cry out to the glory of God." Understand this: Jesus Christ is coming back. When we read in I Thessalonians we will study the two stages of His second coming. The first stage will be the rapture or the catching away of His bride, those who have died in the faith and those who are alive up to the very moment he appears in the heavens and catches us away. The second stage will be His second coming down to this earth, fighting in the battle of Armageddon. In Revelation 19 we will enjoy how He describes riding a great horse, a white charger, and how upon His thigh is written, "King of kings and Lord of lords."

Luke 19:41-44

And when he was come near, he beheld the city, and wept over it, saying, If thou hadst known, even thou, at least in this thy day, the things which belong unto thy peace! but now they are hid from thine eyes. For the days shall come upon thee, that thine enemies shall cast a trench about thee, and compass thee round, and keep thee in on every side, and shall lay thee even with the ground, and thy children within thee; and they shall not leave in thee one stone upon another; because thou knewest not the time of thy visitation.

Prophecy of Doom

Jesus knew that in A.D. 70, the Roman general Titus would destroy the city of Jerusalem. He was predicting their doom. And He wept. He wept because they did not receive the King of Glory and avert the coming disaster.

Luke 19:45-48

> And he went into the temple, and began to cast out them that sold therein, and them that bought; saying unto them, It is written, My house is the house of prayer: but ye have made it a den of thieves.
>
> And he taught daily in the temple. But the chief priests and the scribes and the chief of the people sought to destroy him. And could not find what they might do: for all the people were very attentive to hear him.

God's House Is Spiritual

Time and time again, Jesus met the problems of life by saying, "It is written." But how could Jesus have said it is written, had He not studied the Word of God? How could His faith have come forth? How can our faith come forth unless we study and know the Word of God?

This is the third cleansing of the temple by the Lord Jesus Christ. By this time He was fed up with these people who were making the house of God into a den where thieves were actually stealing from the people by improper exchanges of money. We do not have the same type of house of God today as was the temple of Jerusalem. We have a place to go have fellowship one with another, to hear the Word preached and to learn how better to serve the Lord. We do not have sacrifices to make such as these people did. We do not have to exchange our money for temple money, so He is not talking to us in that precise term. He is saying to us that when we enter into any place of worship, it should be with a prayerful spirit and a trust in God.

Luke 20:1-8

> And it came to pass, that on one of those days, as he taught the people in the temple, and preached the gospel, the chief priests and the scribes came upon him with the elders, and spake unto him, saying, Tell us, by what authority doest thou these things? or who is he that gave thee this authority?
>
> And he answered and said unto them, I will also ask you one thing;

and answer me: the baptism of John, was it from heaven, or of men?

And they reasoned with themselves, saying, If we shall say, From heaven; he will say, Why then believed ye him not? But and if we say, Of men; all the people will stone us: for they be persuaded that John was a prophet.

And they answered, that they could not tell whence it was.

And Jesus said unto them, Neither tell I you by what authority I do these things.

The Wisest Question

The 20th chapter of Luke is often called "the day of questions." The chief priests cornered Jesus and came at Him with every conceivable type of question, trying to trap Him. The chief priests usually consisted of the ex-high priest, the scribes, and elders, who made up the membership of the Jewish council, their supreme court called the Sanhedrin. They claimed to have authority to govern Israel and to answer all questions. When one of them answered a question, he would cite the authority of some great rabbi or other leader who was alive or who had lived, but Jesus came with a single authority. He did not give any authority other than God, and that He had come as the Son of God.

Jesus asked them a question which, if they answered it, would answer their own question to Him. He asked, "Who gave John the Baptist his authority?" That was the wisest question he could ask. John the Baptist had proclaimed the coming of the Messiah and that he was the forerunner of Him, and when Jesus arrived he said, "Behold the lamb of God that taketh away the sin of the world." And he proclaimed Him to be the Messiah. Jesus asked, "Who gave him his authority to say that?" If they accepted the fact that God gave John the Baptist the authority to recognize Jesus as the Messiah, they would have to accept John's authority that Jesus is the Son of God. They said, "we do not know." Therefore, Jesus did not have to answer the question. They answered it themselves by not replying to His question.

We do not always have to answer every question we are asked. Jesus answered them by asking one.

Luke 20:9-20

Then began he to speak to the people this parable;

A certain man planted a vineyard, and let it forth to husbandmen, and went into a far country for a long time. And at the season he sent a servant to the husbandmen, that they should give him of the fruit of the vineyard: but the husbandmen beat him, and sent him away empty. And again he sent another servant: and they beat him also, and entreated him shamefully, and sent him away empty. And again he sent a third: and they wounded him also, and cast him out.

Then said the lord of the vineyard, What shall I do? I will send my beloved son: it may be they will reverence him when they see him. But when the husbandmen saw him, they reasoned among themselves, saying, This is the heir: come, let us kill him, that the inheritance may be ours. So they cast him out of the vineyard, and killed him. What therefore shall the lord of the vineyard do unto them? He shall come and destroy these husbandmen, and shall give the vineyard to others. And when they heard it, they said, God forbid.

And he beheld them, and said, What is this then that is written, The stone which the builders rejected, the same is become the head of the corner? Whosoever shall fall upon that stone shall be broken; but on whomsoever it shall fall, it will grind him to powder.

And the chief priests and the scribes the same hour sought to lay hands on him; and they feared the people: for they perceived that he had spoken this parable against them.

And they watched him, and sent forth spies, which should feign themselves just men, that they might take hold of his words, that so they might deliver him unto the power and authority of the governor.

Warning to Israel

Jesus had come in triumph through the city of Jerusalem where the people were magnifying Him and giving praise to God. He had cleansed the temple, He had submitted himself to the question of the chief priest concerning John the Baptist and answered it, and now, He turns to the crowd and says, "I want to tell you a story. There was a man who had a vineyard and he went away. While he was away he put it in the hands of the husbandmen and after a while, he sent one of his servants to collect what was due him from the crops. They decided to beat him. So he sent a second servant. They beat him. He sent a third and they beat him up. Finally he said, 'I will send my own. They certainly will respect him.' But when the son came they put him to death."

The chief priests present as He told this story knew the story was against them. The scribes said, "God forbid." Jesus said, "That is right. Here is what you should do. You must understand that the nation of Israel is this vineyard. The leaders, the rulers of the Jews, are the ones who are attending God's vineyard. But when He sent His prophets to you, you have persecuted and killed them. Now He has sent His only begotten Son and you are going to kill Him. I tell you, particularly those of you who have rejected the Son, unless you break your will, give up your own will and accept the Son of God as the stone that is the cornerstone, then you are going to fall into judgment with God and be ground into destruction." When the chief priests heard that, they wanted to lay hands on Him and kill Him right there, but they feared the people. Then they watched Him and sent spies to catch Him in His word, but they were unable to do it until God's own time came for the cross.

Luke 20:21-26

And they asked him, saying, Master, we know that thou sayest and teachest rightly, neither acceptest thou the person of any, but teachest the way of God truly. Is it lawful for us to give tribute unto Caesar, or no? But he perceived their craftiness, and said unto them, Why tempt ye me?

Shew me a penny. Whose image and superscription hath it? They answered and said, Caesar's.

And he said unto them, Render therefore unto Caesar the things which be Caesar's, and unto God the things which be God's.

And they could not take hold of his words before the people: and they marvelled at his answer, and held their peace.

Jesus Not Entrapped

When they tried to take hold of His words, they could not do it because He only spoke as the Holy Spirit directed Him. Therefore, they sought other ways that He might be condemned. Since they could not trap Him in any way, there was nothing left for them except to find Judas, one of the 12 who coveted money, and to make a deal with him.

Luke 20:27-47

Then came to him certain of the Sadducees, which deny that there is any resurrection; and they asked him, saying, Master, Moses wrote unto us, If any man's brother die, having a wife, and he die without children, that his brother should take his wife, and raise up seed unto his brother. There were therefore seven brethren; and the first took a wife, and died without children. And the second took her to wife, and he died childless. And the third took her; and in like manner the seven also: and they left no children, and died. Last of all the woman died also.

Therefore in the resurrection whose wife of them is she? for seven had her to wife.

And Jesus answering said unto them, The children of this world marry, and are given in marriage: but they which shall be accounted worthy to obtain that world, and the resurrection from the dead, neither marry, nor are given in marriage: neither can they die any more: for they are equal unto the angels; and are the children of God, being the children of the resurrection.

Now that the dead are raised, even Moses shewed at the bush, when he calleth the Lord the God of Abraham, and the God of Isaac, and the God of Jacob. For he is not a God of the dead, but of the living: for all live unto him.

Then certain of the scribes answering said, Master, thou hast well said. And after that they durst not ask him any question at all.

And he said unto them, How say they that Christ is David's son? And David himself saith in the book of Psalms, The Lord said unto my Lord, Sit thou on my right hand, till I make thine enemies thy footstool. David therefore calleth him Lord, how is he then his son?

Then in the audience of all the people he said unto his disciples, Beware of the scribes, which desire to walk in long robes, and love greetings in the markets, and the highest seats in the synagogues, and the chief rooms at feasts; which devour widows' houses, and for a shew make long prayers: the same shall receive greater damnation.

Resurrection Involves All

As the chief priests continued asking Jesus questions, they finally got down to the key issue — the resurrection. They told about a woman whose husband having died, was married to his different brothers. They wanted to know, at the resurrection, which of the men would be her husband. He replied, "You have missed the whole issue because they neither marry nor are given in marriage then. The resurrection is about the continuity of God, for God is the God of Abraham, the God of Isaac, and the God of Jacob. He is not a God of the dead but of the living, for all live unto him." Then they stopped questioning him.

Then He said, "This ties in with David, in the Psalms, who had a vision of the Messiah in which he saw God saying to him, 'Sit thou on my right hand,' and David called him Lord." Yet, Jesus says, "You know that the Messiah is going to come through the house of David and will be called the Son of David."

What they had missed is that Jesus is Lord. David had recognized that Jesus is Lord and before they could accept Him as the Son of David, they had to accept Him as Lord, or His coming as the Son of

David would come to naught. In other words, God is alive. He is alive from everlasting to everlasting.

It involves your personal relationship with Him. Is Christ your personal Savior? Is He whom God sat on His right hand, your Lord? Or are you thinking of Jesus as a mere historical figure, set in a group of parables in the Bible and without real personal meaning to your life? Jesus is saying that you can know Him as your own personal Lord.

Luke 21:1-4

> And he looked up, and saw the rich men casting their gifts into the treasury. And he saw also a certain poor widow casting in thither two mites. And he said, Of a truth I say unto you, that this poor widow hath cast in more than they all: for all these have of their abundance cast in unto the offerings of God: but she of her penury hath cast in all the living that she had.

Giving From Spirit

Turn back to the 12th chapter of St. Mark's gospel and read again my explanation of what Jesus meant about this precious widow. She was in the courtyard where there were 13 offering boxes shaped like trumpets, and each one provided a place where one could make a special offering for the sacrifices or for the wood of the sacrifices or to polish the gold vessels and similar things. People were coming and giving. Some were giving for show, making a great pretense of giving a lot of money. Then here came this little woman without any pretense at all and she reached down in the deepest part of her need and gave all she had, which was less than a penny. Maybe the thought had come to the woman that she could not give anything because she did not have much in comparison with those who had a lot. But when she reached down deep inside and gave of her spirit in the form of that little coin, that was all the Lord wanted to know. She is on His side. She believed that when she gave, God would give to her . . . and He will.

Luke 21:5-9

> And as some spake of the temple, how it was adorned with goodly stones and gifts, he said, As for these things which ye behold, the days will come, in the which there shall not be left one stone upon another, that shall not be thrown down.
>
> And they asked him, saying, Master, but when shall these things be? and what sign will there be when these things shall come to pass?

And he said, Take heed that ye be not deceived: for many shall come in my name, saying, I am Christ; and the time draweth near: go ye not therefore after them. But when ye shall hear of wars and commotions, be not terrified: for these things must first come to pass; but the end is not by and by.

Service Is Readiness

The Lord said, You will hear of wars and commotions, but do not be terrified, for these things must first come. They must come and run their course. There is going to be an entirely different happening in the world when the Lord comes, for we have already read where He said, "as it was in the days of Noah." They were acting normally every day as they were accustomed to, eating and drinking and giving in marriage. There was nothing cataclysmic going on. That is why He said, "Therefore, watch, for in such an hour as you think not, the Son of man cometh." People will not even be thinking about it. That is also why He said, "Occupy till I come."

Be busy serving the Lord. Keep your mind on the Lord. That will take care of the coming of the Lord. It will take care of your readiness and of my readiness. Therefore, we will not be upset by every war or every commotion that is in the world.

Luke 21:10-19

Then said he unto them, Nation shall rise against nation, and kingdom against kingdom: and great earthquakes shall be in divers places, and famines, and pestilences; and fearful sights and great signs shall there be from heaven.

But before all these, they shall lay their hands on you, and persecute you, delivering you up to the synagogues, and into prisons, being brought before kings and rulers for my name's sake.

And it shall turn to you for a testimony. Settle it therefore in your hearts, not to meditate before what ye shall answer: for I will give you a mouth and wisdom, which all your adversaries shall not be able to gainsay nor resist.

And ye shall be betrayed both by parents, and brethren, and kinsfolks, and friends; and some of you shall they cause to be put to death. And ye shall be hated of all men for my name's sake.

But there shall not an hair of your head perish. In your patience possess ye your souls.

We Perish Not

As He describes the fearful things that will happen to various people of God because of the devil's wrath, He tells us that even if some of us are killed, not a hair of our head will perish. He is going to be in charge of our death. Jesus is really saying there is a big difference between dying and perishing. We are going to die, whether we die for the glory of God or not, for it is appointed unto man once to die and after that face judgment. But here He speaks of perishing. There shall not a hair of your head perish. You will not lose your soul. It is in your faith, your perseverance, your holding onto God. Though your body may die, you yourself will never perish. In fact, your body will be raised from the dead and you will live with Christ forever.

Luke 21:20-24

> And when ye shall see Jerusalem compassed with armies, then know that the desolation thereof is nigh. Then let them which are in Judaea flee to the mountains; and let them which are in the midst of it depart out and let not them that are in the countries enter thereinto. For these be the days of vengeance that all things which are written may be fulfilled.
>
> But woe unto them that are with child, and to them that give suck, in those days! for there shall be great distress in the land, and wrath upon this people. And they shall fall by the edge of the sword, and shall be led away captive into all nations: and Jerusalem shall be trodden down of the Gentiles, until the times of the Gentiles be fulfilled.

A Major Prophecy

Jesus is speaking of two different events. First, He talks about Jerusalem being compassed about with armies, and that the desolation thereof being nigh. He warns them to flee Jerusalem lest they be killed. He is talking about A.D. 70, a future time then, when the Roman general Titus would burn and sack the city of Jerusalem and destroy hundreds of thousands of Jews. From that moment they would be scattered throughout the nations of the world, and Jerusalem would be trodden down by the Gentiles. We know now that that happened.

Then He adds in Verse 24, "until the times of the Gentiles be fulfilled." He is saying that the condition of Jerusalem, which would be emptied of the Jewish people and fall under the control of Gentiles, also would change.

We believe that when Israel became a nation, something highly significant began. In 1948, a part of Jerusalem was taken by the Jews. In the "Six-Day War" in 1967, the rest of Jerusalem was put under control of the Jews, that is, the nation of Israel. Now the nation of Israel is trying to stabilize itself, including what the media calls the West Bank.

We who believe the Bible know that Israel is going to take all the land promised it. How soon we cannot say. However, this statement of Jesus refers not only to A.D. 70, the scattering of the Jews to the nations and then the eventual return of a remnant of the Jewish people to retake Jerusalem and the land of promise. He is also talking about the end of time, the coming of Antichrist, that moment Daniel speaks of and that Christ speaks of in Matthew 24, the abomination of desolation. Then the Antichrist, that world personality, will take over this present world system politically and religiously as well as economically, and during his reign the Jews who have returned to Jerusalem will make a covenant with him. But in the midst of Antichrist's reign there will be a terrible abomination of desolation, the very term that Daniel used and that Christ used in Matthew 24, when the Antichrist will enter the rebuilt temple. They will rebuild their temple on the very site that it once occupied, on Moriah, and the Antichrist will go into that temple, including his image, and that image will be given the power to speak. Then the Jews will realize that it is the abomination of desolation, and that the prophecy of Daniel has come to pass and that this is a false God. When they have been compelled to bow down to Antichrist they will refuse, and then, of course, there will begin another reign of terror against them such as the world has never known. In fact, if those days are not shortened, they will not be able to bear it.

Then while they are being scattered, the times of the Gentiles will be rapidly coming to a close. When we get to Romans I will be sharing with you how that up to that time of Christ's coming the Hebrew nation was a more select nation. They were a people whose commission of God was to take God's light to the Gentiles and to all nations, but that commission had degenerated until Christ came. And even after He had been resurrected, His first disciples had had great difficulty believing that the Gentiles could be brought into the kingdom. In the 10th chapter of Acts we will read how Peter goes into the house of Cornelius, a Gentile, and there opens the kingdom to the Gentiles. But it was Paul who took the gospel to the Gentile world and the times of the Gentiles then became very important for, in effect, they were grafted into the original olive plant which was symbolic of Israel. The Gentiles of the world began to open up to the gospel at the same time the Jews rejected Christ. A great blindness came over their eyes and that blindness is there until this day. In the reign of the Antichrist, when he brings the abomination of desolation into the temple in Jerusalem, they will have their eyes opened, and as they flee they will begin to realize that Jesus is the Christ.

In the second coming, the part which is the revelation when Christ is revealed in the heavens and every eye shall see Him, they will look up and see Him. And as one of the old prophets said, they will say, "Where did you get those marks in your hands?" And He will say, "In the house of my friends," and the nation will be born in a day. All Israel will be saved, Paul said. There will be a switching back at that time from the Gentiles to the original olive tree, the Jewish people, and during that time the Gentiles, in effect, will close their minds to the gospel of Jesus Christ. Because of that, Antichrist will be able to bring his armies against the coming of Jesus Christ, because the devil will know about the second coming. They will gather their armies at Armageddon, and when Christ is revealed in His glory with a sword of fire issuing forth from His nostrils, riding the great white charger (which we will discover in the book of Revelation), that will be the battle of Armageddon when Christ will wipe out the armies of Antichrist.

He will also land on the Mount of Olives with His own feet touching the soil of Israel. A great valley shall be created, as told to us by the prophet Zechariah, down through which Christ, followed by His raptured saints, shall enter the city of Jerusalem. There, the people who have come with Him and those who have hidden out because of their faith in Christ will gather to crown him King of kings and Lord of lords and He will begin His millenial and everlasting reign.

Luke 21:25-28

> And there shall be signs in the sun, and in the moon, and in the stars; and upon the earth distress of nations, with perplexity; the sea and the waves roaring; men's hearts failing them for fear, and for looking after those things which are coming on the earth: for the powers of heaven shall be shaken.
>
> And then shall they see the Son of man coming in a cloud with power and great glory. And when these things begin to come to pass, then look up, and lift up your heads; for your redemption draweth nigh.

Jews' Salvation Planned

Our Lord now skips to that period of time when Israel is fully reestablished, and the Antichrist has risen and taken over world powers and has entered into an alliance with Israel for a brief period of time, probably for economic reasons, possibly political ones. But there will be terrible things going on, from God's point of view, in the sun, in the moon, in the stars, in the waters of the oceans. Men will not understand what is going on. Great fear will grip them and the heavens themselves will be shaken because Jesus said that at that time they would see the Son of Man coming. He is really speaking of Armageddon, when Antichrist breaks his covenant with Israel, goes into the temple (which has been rebuilt and reestablished), and proclaims himself as God. That is the signal to the Jews that they have made the worst mistake of their existence, for they will not bow down to any God. They never have and they never will. Then terrible things will happen to them, for the wrath of the Antichrist will be turned against them and many will be killed; others will flee and will be hiding out somewhere in the earth. Things come to a climax rather quickly, for the power of the Antichrist is such that he would try to supplant forever even the authority of God in the earth. So Christ will reveal himself. That is, He will show himself in the heavens. In some gigantic way He will appear so that every eye shall see Him, and He shall fight that battle of Armageddon. It will be His power coming forth. He is coming to bring redemption to the earth and many of us believe that is the time the Jews will look up and see Him. The prophet of old tells how they will see the scars and the stripes and they will say, "Where did you get these scars?" He will reply, "In the house of my friends," and a nation will be born in a day.

We believe that is when the Jewish people will be saved, reestablished, so that when Christ comes down to the earth, He lands on the Mount of Olives and according to Zechariah's prophecy, it splits and He proceeds down through the valley, into the city of Jerusalem, up to His kingdom to be the King over all the earth forever.

Luke 21:29-33

> And he spake to them a parable; Behold the fig tree, and all the trees; when they now shoot forth, ye see and know of your own selves that summer is now nigh at hand. So likewise ye, when ye see these things come to pass, know ye that the kingdom of God is nigh at hand. Verily I say unto you, This generation shall not pass away, till all be fulfilled. Heaven and earth shall pass away: but my words shall not pass away.

Imperishable Word

The Word of God is the one imperishable in the world. So line yourself up with the Word of God.

Luke 21:34-36

And take heed to yourselves, lest at any time your hearts be overcharged with surfeiting, and drunkenness, and cares of this life, and so that day come upon you unawares.

For as a snare shall it come on all them that dwell on the face of the whole earth.

Watch ye therefore, and pray always, that ye may be accounted worthy to escape all these things that shall come to pass, and to stand before the Son of man.

A Clear Statement

Verse 36 may be the first time that Jesus directly refers to the rapture of the saints who are not to go through the tribulation period. A terrible holocaust will ensue. Some believe that the Christians who are alive at that time will go through it. I do not. I believe that Luke 21:36 is a very clear statement: "Watch ye therefore and pray always, that ye may be accounted worthy to escape all these things that shall come to pass and to stand before the Son of man."

Luke 21:37-22:3

And in the day time he was teaching in the temple; and at night he went out, and abode in the mount that is called the mount of Olives. And all the people came early in the morning to him in the temple, for to hear him.

Now the feast of unleavened bread drew nigh, which is called the Passover. And the chief priests and scribes sought how they might kill him; for they feared the people. Then entered Satan into Judas surnamed Iscariot, being of the number of the twelve.

The Way to Hell

Judas had been flirting with the devil. He had been on the edge for a long time. He had been doing one thing that led to another that led to another until they became big enough for the devil to take over his life and they became one. That is what happens. That is why we have to stop the little things before they become big things. And we are not to flirt with the devil and his crowd. We are to cut it off and separate ourselves from anything that would cause us not to have a close walk with our Lord. I have noticed that sin becomes a pattern in a person's life. Sometimes I tell people in my preaching that there is a difference between a sinner and a sin-ner. The thing about sin is that people can go along in sin, sort of carried away with it, and come under conviction by the Holy Spirit and then repent and come to the Lord. On the other hand, there are those people who set themselves against God and His Holy Word and they develop a pattern and this pattern becomes stronger every day till they become sin-ners.

You can know whether you are going to hell or not, because hell enters into people before they enter into hell. You can know if you are going to heaven because heaven enters into you before you enter into it. Heaven is righteousness and peace and joy in the Holy Spirit and you can have that right here. It is a terrible thing to develop sin in your life as a pattern until you become a sinner. It is very hard to reach a sinner, very hard for the Holy Spirit and His convicting power to be felt by such a person. Even when felt, it is very hard for that person to choose the Lord. It is not impossible, for nothing is impossible with God. I warn people all the time, do not develop a pattern of sin. I warn myself, I warn you against sin. Come to God and let God break that pattern of sin.

Luke 22:4-12

> And he went his way, and communed with the chief priests and captains, how he might betray him unto them. And they were glad, and covenanted to give him money. And he promised, and sought opportunity to betray him unto them in the absence of the multitude.
>
> Then came the day of unleavened bread, when the passover must be killed. And he sent Peter and John, saying, Go and prepare us the passover, that we may eat. And they said unto him, Where wilt thou that we prepare? And he said unto them, Behold, when ye are entered into the city, there shall a man meet you, bearing a pitcher of water; follow him into the house where he entereth in. And ye shall say unto the goodman of the house, The Master saith unto thee, Where is the guestchamber, where I shall eat the passover with my disciples? And he shall shew you a large upper room furnished: there make ready.

Spirit of Discernment

Do you see the discerning of the Lord and the word of knowledge? He knew in advance where He was going, the man who had the pitcher of water, and everything connected with it. Do not think for one moment that the spirit of discerning has been removed or that we no longer have the gift of the word of knowledge. Through the

Holy Spirit these things still are happening today.

Luke 22:13-20

> And they went, and found as he had said unto them: and they made ready the passover.
>
> And when the hour was come, he sat down, and the twelve apostles with him.
>
> And he said unto them, With desire I have desired to eat this Passover with you before I suffer: for I say unto you, I will not any more eat thereof, until it be fulfilled in the kingdom of God. And he took the cup, and gave thanks, and said, Take this, and divide it among yourselves: for I say unto you, I will not drink of the fruit of the vine, until the kingdom of God shall come.
>
> And he took bread, and gave thanks, and brake it, and gave unto them, saying, This is my body which is given for you: this do in remembrance of me. Likewise also the cup after supper, saying, This cup is the new testament in my blood, which is shed for you.

Meaning of Communion

I am going to comment upon this in detail when I come to John's gospel concerning the things St. Luke records about this final supper that Jesus eats with His disciples. It commemorates the passage of Israel from Egyptian bondage. As they ate the Passover that last night, the devouring angel passed over them because the blood was on the doorpost, and these people were eating the Passover lamb.

Jesus had taken that to represent the giving of His own life. As they eat it, He stops and takes bread, gives thanks, breaks it, and gives to them to eat and says, "This is My body which is given for you. You eat it and when you eat it remember Me."

Everybody wants to be remembered. Nobody wants to be forgotten. Each of us has so much in our life with such deep feelings that we want a remembrance of our existence, a notice that we are human beings. Jesus wanted that, too, but not because He was only passing through the world; He was giving His life on the cross that we might live. Therefore, He gives them some symbols — the bread and the cup — to eat and to drink to help them remember. To remember Jesus is the number-one thing in life. The Communion takes on a much greater meaning when we come to eat the bread and drink of the cup. We are not dealing with bread and the cup; we are dealing with the living Lord, our Lord and our Savior. If we miss that, we have only a form in our communion. But if we remember Him, He comes alive in us.

Luke 22:21-24

But, behold, the hand of him that betrayeth me is with me on the table.

And truly the Son of man goeth, as it was determined: but woe unto that man by whom he is betrayed!

And they began to inquire among themselves, which of them it was that should do this thing.

And there was also a strife among them, which of them should be accounted the greatest.

Strife Is Satanic

Strife. There was strife among the men closest to Christ. There was strife among them while they were in His presence, while they were in the presence of one another. This is so Satanic. So unlike God, so unwanted in God's kingdom. Certainly there is strife today. There is strife in nearly every church, strife in nearly every gathering. It is Satan's business to tempt God's people to get into strife. But we do not have to do it. We can resist the devil and he will flee from us.

Luke 22:25-32

And he said unto them, The kings of the Gentiles exercise lordship over them; and they that exercise authority upon them are called benefactors.

But ye shall not be so: but he that is greatest among you, let him be as the younger; and he that is chief, as he that doth serve.

For whether is greater, he that sitteth at meat, or he that serveth? is not he that sitteth at meat? but I am among you as he that serveth.

Ye are they which have continued with me in my temptations.

And I appoint unto you a kingdom, as my Father hath appointed unto me;

that ye may eat and drink at my table in my kingdom, and sit on thrones judging the twelve tribes of Israel.

And the Lord said, Simon, Simon, behold, Satan hath desired to have you, that he may sift you as wheat:

But I have prayed for thee, that thy faith fail not: and when thou art converted, strengthen thy brethren.

Jesus' Intimate Care

The devil is described in the Bible as the tempter and the accuser of the brethren. Jesus discerns that the devil is tempting Peter. The Lord loves Simon, and tells him what is happening in his heart at that very moment, but He says, "I have prayed for you." Think about it! The intimate care of Jesus is no more perfectly revealed than in this statement, "I have prayed for thee."

We will see in John 17 the high priestly prayer of our Lord Jesus Christ that includes us all, but He does pray for us. He does intercede for us. Paul says He is the mediator, the one mediator between us and God. He says to Peter, "I pray for you that you fail not, and when you are converted, then your work is to strengthen your brethren."

Luke 22:33-38

> And he said unto him, Lord, I am ready to go with thee, both into prison, and to death. And he said, I tell thee, Peter, the cock shall not crow this day, before that thou shalt thrice deny that thou knowest me. And he said unto them, When I sent you without purse, and scrip, and shoes, lacked ye any thing? And they said, Nothing.
>
> Then said he unto them, But now, he that hath a purse, let him take it, and likewise his scrip: and he that hath no sword, let him sell his garment, and buy one.
>
> For I say unto you, that this that is written must yet be accomplished in me, And he was reckoned among the transgressors: for the things concerning me have an end.
>
> And they said, Lord, behold, here are two swords. And he said unto them, It is enough.

"Enough" Meant Calvary

When Jesus said, "It is enough," He was not saying that they had enough swords. He was referring to the fact that everything that had been done so far toward Calvary was enough, and now the time was at hand. Jesus was referring to Isaiah 53:12. The whole of it reads like this: Therefore will I divide him a portion with the great, and he shall divide the spoil with the strong; because he hath poured out his soul unto death: and was numbered with the transgressors; and he bare the sin of many, and made intercession for the transgressors.

When they crucified Jesus, they did so at a time when others were crucified and they placed His cross between two other crosses on which two thieves were nailed. He was numbered among transgressors. These men crucified with Him were either thieves or murderers and He said that this must happen. He foresaw it. He knew in advance. He knew the scripture. He knew the whole of Isaiah 53. He knew it had to be accomplished and it would be.

Luke 22:39-44

And he came out, and went, as he was wont, to the mount of Olives; and his disciples also followed him. And when he was at the place, he said unto them, Pray that ye enter not into temptation.

And he was withdrawn from them about a stone's cast, and kneeled down, and prayed, saying, Father, if thou be willing, remove this cup from me: nevertheless not my will, but thine, be done.

And there appeared an angel unto him from heaven, strengthening him. And being in an agony he prayed more earnestly: and his sweat was as it were great drops of blood falling down to the ground.

Salvation in the Balance

If Satan succeeded in getting Jesus to refuse the cross, then he could have avoided his own doom and remained God of this world indefinitely. The battle was between God and the devil. The devil really did not want Jesus on that cross because he knew that would be the beginning of his own destruction. Jesus' agony was so severe as He prayed earnestly that His sweat was, as it were, great drops of blood falling down to the ground.

Talk about agony of choice! When it comes right down to the moment of truth, choice is often an agony because it is a choice between serving God and serving the devil. Jesus could have His own way, follow His own will, and go with the devil, or He could give up His own way and choose to follow His Father's will and go with God. When it came to that, the salvation of all of us was hanging in the balance and you can hear Him: "Father, if You be willing, remove this cup of death from Me. However, if it is not Your will to remove this cup of death, then I choose Your will."

If you ignore the fact that Jesus was a man, you will never understand Gethsemane, nor your own humanity when you have to make choices. Oral Roberts knows some of these choices. I had to choose. Many, many times my own will was to give up this healing ministry and go back to my home, to my wife and my children, and live a rather ordinary life. But, in order to do God's work, I had to give up rights to myself and take God's rights. Let His rights be exercised through me. I am not trying to lift myself up, but merely trying to illustrate the point so you can see in your own decision-making the choices you make are no different from those Jesus made in Gethsemane. We each have our Gethsemanes and we finally have the last one when all of our Gethsemanes reach their climax and we make the decision for time and eternity. It is no easy choice, but thank God, the Father is there and His angels always come to minister to you.

Luke 22:45-62

And when he rose up from prayer, and was come to his disciples, he found them sleeping for sorrow, and said unto them, Why sleep ye? rise and pray, lest ye enter into temptation. And while he yet spake, behold a multitude, and he that was called Judas, one of the twelve, went before them, and drew near unto Jesus to kiss him.

But Jesus said unto him, Judas, betrayest thou the Son of man with a kiss?

When they which were about him saw what would follow, they said unto him, Lord, shall we smite with the sword?

And one of them smote the servant of the high priest, and cut off his right ear. And Jesus answered and said, Suffer ye thus far. And he touched his ear, and healed him.

Then Jesus said unto the chief priests, and captains of the temple, and the elders, which were come to him, Be ye come out, as against a thief, with swords and staves? When I was daily with you in the temple, ye stretched forth no hands against me: but this is your hour, and the power of darkness.

Then took they him, and led him, and brought him into the high priest's house. And Peter followed afar off. And when they had kindled a fire in the midst of the hall, and were set down together, Peter sat down among them. But a certain maid beheld him as he sat by the fire, and earnestly looked upon him, and said, This man was also with him.

And he denied him, saying, Woman, I know him not. And after a little while another saw him, and said, Thou art also of them. And Peter said, Man, I am not. And about the space of one hour after another confidently affirmed, saying, Of a truth this fellow also was with him: for he is a Galilaean. And Peter said, Man, I know not what thou sayest. And immediately, while he yet spake, the cock crew.

And the Lord turned, and looked upon Peter. And Peter remembered the word of the Lord, how he had said unto him, Before the cock crow, thou shalt deny me thrice. And Peter went out and wept bitterly.

Dr. Luke is the only gospel writer who mentions that Jesus turned and looked upon Peter. This is a high point. It is a hinge upon which Peter's life turned. What would have happened after Peter had denied Christ three times if the Lord, in passing through the court on the way to the cross, had not turned and looked upon Peter? What would have happened to Peter? When Jesus looked at him and their eyes met, Peter remembered. The memories were stirred. He remembered the word of Jesus, how He had predicted Peter would deny Him.

Remembering that, his gaze lingering upon the face of Jesus, Peter turned and went out and burst into tears, the tears that broke him apart and caused him to know that he knew, that he knew, that he knew, that Jesus is the real Christ.

I have always believed that to win people to Christ you must in some way help them to see Jesus. People are just not going to turn away from the devil and turn completely to God with anything less than some kind of revelation of Jesus Christ to them. I assure you that while you may not see Him with your human eyes, or hear Him with your human ears, He is going to reveal himself to you. If you are sensitive, it will break you up and I believe you will let God have your life.

Luke 22:63-71

> And the men that held Jesus mocked him, and smote him. And when they had blindfolded him, they struck him on the face, and asked him, saying, Prophesy, who is it that smote thee? And many other things blasphemously spake they against him.
>
> And as soon as it was day, the elders of the people and the chief priests and the scribes came together, and led him into their council, saying, Art thou the Christ? tell us. And he said unto them, If I tell you, ye will not believe: and if I also ask you, ye will not answer me, nor let me go. Hereafter shall the Son of man sit on the right hand of the power of God. Then said they all, Art thou then the Son of God? And he said unto them, Ye say that I am. And they said, what need we any further witness? for we ourselves have heard of his own mouth.

Jesus' Three Replies

Jesus said three things to them in reply to their question, "Art thou the Christ?" He said, "If I show you again all the proofs that I am the Christ, you will not believe Me." Then He said, "If I ask you to show me one prophecy that I have not fulfilled, you will pretend ignorance." His third comment was, "The next proof I give you will be My exaltation at the right hand of My Father and at My second coming in glory."

Luke 23:1-8

> And the whole multitude of them arose, and led him unto Pilate. And they began to accuse him, saying, We found this fellow perverting the nation, and forbidding to give tribute to Caesar, saying that he himself is Christ a king.
>
> And Pilate asked him, saying, Art thou the king of the Jews? And

he answered him and said, Thou sayest it. Then said Pilate to the chief priests and to the people, I find no fault in this man. And they were the more fierce, saying, He stirreth up the people, teaching throughout all Jewry, beginning from Galilee to this place.

When Pilate heard of Galilee, he asked whether the man were a Galilaean. And as soon as he knew that he belonged unto Herod's jurisdiction, he sent him to Herod, who himself also was at Jerusalem at that time. And when Herod saw Jesus, he was exceeding glad: for he was desirous to see him of a long season, because he had heard many things of him; and he hoped to have seen some miracle done by him.

The Careless Curious

Herod represents those curious people who want to see a miracle but do not really care about the miracle worker, about Jesus of Nazareth being the Son of God.

Luke 23:9-12

Then he questioned with him in many words; but he answered him nothing. And the chief priests and scribes stood and vehemently accused him. And Herod with his men of war set him at nought, and mocked him, and arrayed him in a gorgeous robe, and sent him again to Pilate. And the same day Pilate and Herod were made friends together: for before they were at enmity between themselves.

Christ Reconciles

This is not the first time that enemies have been reconciled by the presence of Jesus Christ in their midst.

Luke 23:13-16

And Pilate, when he had called together the chief priests and the rulers and the people, said unto them, Ye have brought this man unto me, as one that perverteth the people: and, behold, I, having examined him before you, have found no fault in this man touching those things whereof ye accuse him: no, nor yet Herod: for I sent you to him; and, lo, nothing worthy of death is done unto him. I will therefore chastise him, and release him.

Healing Stripes

When he took the whip to beat His back, and to cut it, and lacerate it, and to lay it open, he little knew that Peter who had witnessed this scene would later say in I Peter 2:24, "By his stripes you were healed."

Luke 23:17-22

> (For of necessity he must release one unto them at the feast.) And they cried out all at once, saying, Away with this man, and release unto us Barabbas: (Who for a certain sedition made in the city, and for murder, was cast into prison.) Pilate therefore, willing to release Jesus, spake again to them. But they cried, saying, Crucify him, crucify him. And he said unto them the third time, Why, what evil hath he done? I have found no cause of death in him: I will therefore chastise him, and let him go.

This is the third time Pilate has made a positive statement about Jesus Christ. First, he said he found no fault in this man. Second, he found no fault in this man worthy of death. And third, he said he found no cause of death in Him, and so he decided to chastise Him and let Him go.

Luke 23:23

> And they were instant with loud voices, requiring that he might be crucified. And the voices of them and of the chief priests prevailed.

The Devil's Mob

That maddening crowd raised their voices until nothing else could be heard. The devil must really have to stir people up to get them into a frenzy of hate like that.

Luke 23:24,25

> And Pilate gave sentence that it should be as they required. And he released unto them him that for sedition and murder was cast into prison, whom they had desired; but he delivered Jesus to their will.

Freedom of Choice

Here is the shining example, in the midst of the greatest tragedy in history, that God honors the choice of will, that man is a free moral agent. If there had been any time in history that God would have removed man's will, He would have done it at the trial of Jesus, which was a mockery. But He risks everything to the will of us human beings. The will of man either lets God have His way, or the will of man repudiates the way of God and God allows the will of man to prevail.

Luke 23:26-31

> And as they led him away, they laid hold upon one Simon, a Cyrenian, coming out of the country, and on him they laid the cross, that he might bear it after Jesus. And there followed him a great company of people, and of women, which also bewailed and lamented him. But Jesus turning unto them said, Daughters of Jerusalem, weep not for me, but weep for yourselves, and for your children. For, behold, the days are coming, in the which they shall say, Blessed are the barren, and the wombs that never bare, and the paps which never gave suck. Then shall they begin to say to the mountains, Fall on us; and to the hills, Cover us. For if they do these things in a green tree, what shall be done in the dry?

The Abortion Issue

Jesus is referring to A.D. 70 when the Roman general Titus would destroy Jerusalem and kill hundreds of thousands of Jewish people. He is saying that if the Romans can be persuaded to put to death one who has done nothing but gone about doing good, healing the sick, teaching and preaching the kingdom of God, what will they do to rebels against them as a people, as a nation? They will be wiped out. They will beg for the hills to fall upon them.

Concerning the phrase "Daughters of Jerusalem, weep not for me but weep for yourselves and for your children," it was an honor to have children, but He was saying there was a time coming when they would wish they had no children. He was prophesying far beyond A.D. 70 into the centuries. Today it is deemed by some an honor to have children, as it was then. Today, we know that there have always been abortions, but about 10 years ago abortion was legalized in this country, and as a result we are told that more babies have been aborted, their lives have been destroyed, than have been killed in most of the wars in the last 100 years. Jesus foresaw all this because He saw how mankind would degenerate so rapidly. We see it all around us, that life really does not have much value. Certainly a newborn baby doesn't in tens of thousands of abortion cases. The degeneracy that Jesus talked about is right in front of us and we need to take a long look at it and realize that we are near the second coming of our Lord.

Luke 23:32-34a

And there were also two other, malefactors, led with him to be put to death. And when they were come to the place, which is called Calvary, there they crucified him, and the malefactors, one on the right hand, and the other on the left. Then said Jesus, Father, forgive them; for they know not what they do.

The Insanity of Sin

When He said, "Father, forgive them; for they know not what they do," He was showing us the nature of ourselves. He was saying that sin blinds us and virtually destroys our ability to understand spiritual things. In other words, sin is a form of insanity. People simply are not themselves in sin. When we recognize reality as God has given it to us, we instantly want to repent and turn away from sin because it is worse than the bite of a rattlesnake. It is death itself. We want to turn away from death and enter into life. This will help you when someone does something to you that is so utterly wrong. You, too, can pray for God to forgive and to remember that they do not know, they do not understand. Read Verse 34 again.

Luke 23:34,35

Then said Jesus, Father, forgive them; for they know not what they do. And they parted his raiment, and cast lots.

And the people stood beholding. And the rulers also with them derided him, saying, He saved others; let him save himself, if he be Christ, the chosen of God.

But, if He had saved himself, He could not have saved others.

Luke 23:36-42

And the soldiers also mocked him, coming to him, and offering him vinegar, and saying, If thou be the king of the Jews, save thyself. And a superscription also was written over him in letters of Greek, and Latin, and Hebrew, THIS IS THE KING OF THE JEWS.

And one of the malefactors which were hanged railed on him, saying, If thou be Christ, save thyself and us.

But the other answering, rebuked him, saying, Dost not thou fear God, seeing thou art in the same condemnation? And we indeed justly; for we receive the due reward of our deeds: but this man hath done nothing amiss. And he said unto Jesus, Lord, remember me when thou comest into thy kingdom.

Leap of Faith

When this thief rebuked the other and said, "We are justly condemned, but this man hath done nothing amiss," he was entering into a confession of repentance and faith, he was recognizing that Jesus as Lord had a kingdom, and he wanted Jesus to remember him when He came into His kingdom because he had faith. He could see beyond the nails driven into his body. He could hear something beyond the screams and yells of the audience, the onlookers. He could feel something over and beyond the hate and derision. Every sense of his being came alive because he was in the presence of the Lord. The important thing is, he recognized it. He saw his own sinfulness and his faith leaped, leaped upward and viewed the kingdom of Jesus. His heart's cry was, "Remember me."

Every one of us wants to be remembered. We want something higher than ourselves, more stable than our own ways and possessions. This is what the kingdom of God is all about. It provides something eternal that time cannot mar, or man stop, or sin destroy, timeless, eternal, the kingdom that rules forever.

Luke 23:43

And Jesus said unto him, Verily I say unto thee, Today shalt thou be with me in paradise.

Miracle of Repentance

One moment the man was a thief, the next a child of God. One moment he was dying, the next he was alive. One moment he was going to hell, the next he was on his way to paradise. One moment he was a forgotten thief, a man who did not deserve the memory of man, the next he was in the bosom of the Lord in paradise.

Luke 23:44-46

And it was about the sixth hour, and there was a darkness over all the earth until the ninth hour. And the sun was darkened, and the veil of the temple was rent in the midst. And when Jesus had cried with a loud voice, he said, Father, into thy hands I commend my spirit: and having said thus, he gave up the ghost.

Jesus was still in command of himself and of the situation. He always was, He is, and always will be in command. At high noon, while He hung on the cross, darkness flooded the earth. People could not see their hands before their eyes. At that moment the veil in the temple was rent and signified that the old had been fulfilled and the new covenant was going into effect.

At 3 p.m. in the midst of the darkness, Jesus cried in a loud voice, saying, "Father, into thy hands I commend my spirit." Then He gave up His spirit. That was a voluntary act of Jesus Christ. Jesus was always in control no matter what the suffering.

This is a perfect example of how you and I, despite circumstances, are in control because of our faith in Jesus Christ. He was the one who commended His spirit to God. Usually those who were crucified lingered half alive for 2 or 3 days, but in just a matter of hours He completed His mission and He, with the force of His will, commended His spirit to the heavenly Father. At that time they could do nothing to Him.

Luke 23:47-54

Now when the centurion saw what was done, he glorified God, saying, Certainly this was a righteous man. And all the people that came together to that sight, beholding the things which were done, smote their breasts, and returned. And all his acquaintance, and the women that followed him from Galilee, stood afar off, beholding these things.

And, behold, there was a man named Joseph, a counselor; and he was a good man, and a just: (The same had not consented to the counsel and deed of them;) he was of Arimathaea, a city of the Jews: who also himself waited for the kingdom of God.

This man went unto Pilate, and begged the body of Jesus. And he took it down, and wrapped it in linen, and laid it in a sepulchre that was hewn in stone, wherein never man before was laid. And that day was the preparation, and the sabbath drew on.

Joseph of Arimathea, a rich man, was a member of the Jewish Sanhedrin, the supreme court. It is stated here that Joseph did not cast his vote for the crucifixion of Jesus. It was not a unanimous decision. But having influence with Pilate and also being a man of faith, recognizing in Jesus who He was, Joseph asked Pilate to let him bury Jesus' dead body in a new tomb he had made for himself. It was approaching 6 p.m. Friday and soon would be the beginning of the Jewish sabbath on Saturday. They had to hurry in order not to violate the rules of the sabbath.

Luke 23:55-24:3

And the women also, which came with him from Galilee, followed after, and beheld the sepulchre, and how his body was laid. And they returned, and prepared spices and ointments; and rested the sabbath day according to the commandment.

Now upon the first day of the week, very early in the morning, they came unto the sepulchre, bringing the spices which they had prepared, and certain others with them. And they found the stone rolled away from the sepulchre. And they entered in, and found not the body of the Lord Jesus.

The Woman Witnesses

These women were there when Jesus was buried, watched it, marked where the tomb was, and watched carefully as they prepared His body. They also knew how Jesus' body had been wrapped from head to foot in linen cloths, and when they arrived they discovered the stone had been rolled away from the tomb. They went right in and found not the body of the Lord Jesus.

Luke 24:4

And it came to pass, as they were much perplexed thereabout, behold, two men stood by them in shining garments . . .

Angels Present

The two men doubtless are angels. The emphasis indicates that they were flashing like lightning.

Luke 24:5-9

And as they were afraid, and bowed down their faces to the earth, they said unto them, Why seek ye the living among the dead? He is not here, but is risen:

remember how he spake unto you when he was yet in Galilee, saying, The Son of man must be delivered into the hands of sinful men, and be crucified, and the third day rise again.

And they remembered his words, and returned from the sepulchre, and told all these things unto the eleven, and to all the rest.

A New Turning Point

From this point on, no one and nothing, not even the earth, would ever be the same again. The promise of restoration was now in full force like a mighty rushing river. The flow of the resurrection's power began its sweep through the earth and into time and eternity and there was a new turning point for all mankind.

Luke 24:10-12

> It was Mary Magdalene, and Joanna, and Mary the mother of James, and other women that were with them, which told these things unto the apostles. And their words seemed to them as idle tales, and they believed them not.
>
> Then arose Peter, and ran unto the sepulchre; and stooping down, he beheld the linen clothes laid by themselves, and departed, wondering in himself at that which was come to pass.

Doubt Prompts Faith

When the women gave their testimony that Jesus' body was no longer in the tomb, it seemed an idle tale and the disciples said, "We do not believe that." But Peter went inside and looked at the linen clothes laid by themselves. He wondered about those clothes being laid out as though Jesus' body had still been in them. How did He get out of them?

Now, let's not condemn these people, because the fact is that faith begins with doubt, with critical analysis or investigation. When I say doubt, I mean honest doubt. Faith is not so fragile that it cannot be investigated. Honest doubt prompts investigation and when investigation finds substance and evidence, doubt changes into faith. That is what this is all about. They were not going to believe anybody until they discovered for themselves the substance and the evidence.

As for myself, I don't believe everything I hear or everything I read or everything I feel. I investigate. I want to know the truth because it is the truth that will set me free, according to our Lord himself. I want to ask questions in order to be strong in faith. I want it because that is what God wants. In order to be a witness, your faith has to be the kind of faith that stands up to the test. God will meet the honest doubter with faith every time. The women at the tomb were the same women Dr. Luke refers to as having supported Jesus with their financial substance. They were the first group to step out in faith and plant their seeds of faith to support Jesus financially, and then they were the first to witness the evidence of His resurrection. When you and I regularly and faithfully plant our seeds of faith, give our best to God, God is going to give His best to us just like He did to these women when they were the first to witness the evidence of His resurrection.

Luke 24:13-27

And, behold, two of them went that same day to a village called Emmaus, which was from Jerusalem about threescore furlongs. And they talked together of all these things which had happened. And it came to pass, that, while they communed together and reasoned, Jesus himself drew near, and went with them. But their eyes were holden that they should not know him.

And he said unto them, What manner of communications are these that ye have one to another, as ye walk, and are sad?

And the one of them, whose name was Cleopas, answering said unto him, Art thou only a stranger in Jerusalem, and hast not known the things which are come to pass there in these days? And he said unto them, What things? And they said unto him, Concerning Jesus of Nazareth, which was a prophet mighty in deed and word before God and all the people: and how the chief priests and our rulers delivered him to be condemned to death, and have crucified him. But we trusted that it had been he which should have redeemed Israel: and beside all this, today is the third day since these things were done. Yea, and certain women also of our company made us astonished, which were early at the sepulchre; and when they found not his body, they came, saying, that they had also seen a vision of angels, which said that he was alive. And certain of them which were with us went to the sepulchre, and found it even so as the women had said: but him they saw not.

Then he said unto them, O fools, and slow of heart to believe all that the prophets have spoken: ought not Christ to have suffered these things, and to enter into his glory?

And beginning at Moses and all the prophets, he expounded unto them in all the scriptures the things concerning himself.

Old Testament Accuracy

Jesus was absolutely astounded at these men who had grown up reading the Old Testament, the scriptures that had prophesied the coming of the Messiah. So He began at Moses and all the prophets and explained to them where the scriptures were and what they meant concerning himself and His coming.

He could have referred to Deuteronomy 18:15 where Moses said there would arise a prophet "like unto me," and to Jeremiah 23:5,6 where the prophet had said that a branch of David would rise and this person would be the King of His people and over all the earth and would be called the Lord our righteousness.

Jesus could have referred to scores of scriptures in the Old

Testament concerning the coming of the Messiah and we should know these scriptures. We should read the Old Testament, looking closely at those scriptures concerning the coming of our Lord Jesus Christ because the unerring fact of the Old Testament was the accuracy with which the coming of Jesus was prophesied.

Luke 24:28-32

> And they drew nigh unto the village, whither they went: and he made as though he would have gone further. But they constrained him, saying, Abide with us: for it is toward evening, and the day is far spent. And he went in to tarry with them.
>
> And it came to pass, as he sat at meat with them, he took bread, and blessed it, and brake, and gave to them. And their eyes were opened, and they knew him; and he vanished out of their sight.
>
> And they said one to another, Did not our heart burn within us, while he talked with us by the way, and while he opened to us the scriptures?

That evening when they sat at table, Jesus gave them the Holy Communion and the most wonderful thing happened. Their minds opened, their eyes could see, and they knew Him. He looked exactly as He did when He was upon earth. That is a very important thing for us to remember — that He looks the same, He is the same yesterday, today, and forever. Then He vanished from sight.

Upon His absence, they said, "Did not our hearts burn within us while he talked with us and he opened the scriptures to us?" Ah, yes, there is a wonderful, mysterious, but very real, burning of the heart. I know the meaning of that, and you do, too. If you have really believed on the Lord Jesus Christ, your heart is strangely moved.

Luke 24:33,34

> And they rose up the same hour, and returned to Jerusalem, and found the eleven gathered together, and them that were with them, saying, The Lord is risen indeed, and hath appeared to Simon.

Remembrance In Communion

Simon, in I Peter 1:3, remembers this. He speaks of the resurrection of Jesus as the lively hope — not a dead hope — but a hope of life. In Verse 35, these two men in Emmaus began their witness and they told what things were done in the way and how He was known of them in breaking of bread.

This was a reference to the Holy Communion Jesus gave them

which caused the opening of their eyes, and which would be remembered by the other disciples, particularly the apostles who were the first to have had Communion with Jesus.

Luke 24:36

> And as they thus spake, Jesus himself stood in the midst of them, and saith unto them, Peace be unto you.

The Source of Peace

While the two men on the way to Emmaus were relating their personal experience, Jesus appeared in His resurrection body. He was just there. He said, "Peace be unto you." He knew this group did not have any peace. They were terrified by what they had heard, terrified it might not be true. They were perplexed. They really had no peace, just as people today who do not really know that Jesus Christ is risen from the dead have no peace, that He is the eternal Son of God and that He is in the now of their lives.

Luke 24:37-43

> But they were terrified and affrighted, and supposed that they had seen a spirit. And he said unto them, Why are ye troubled? and why do thoughts arise in your hearts? Behold my hands and my feet, that it is I myself: handle me, and see; for a spirit hath not flesh and bones, as ye see me have. And when he had thus spoken, he shewed them his hands and his feet. And while they yet believed not for joy, and wondered, he said unto them, Have ye here any meat? And they gave him a piece of a broiled fish, and of an honeycomb. And he took it, and did eat before them.

The body of Jesus is foreshadowing the kind of body you and I are going to have after our resurrection from the dead. Jesus was recognizable the same way that He was on the cross. He asked them to put their hands on Him and to examine Him, which they did. Jesus told them He could eat, and asked for something to eat. They gave Him a piece of broiled fish and some honeycomb and He ate it before them. There He was, the living Jesus.

By those nail prints and the sign of the spear in His side, we see Him as the living cross itself, living on, not just an event for that point in time, but the cross forever. Then we see Him as a human being glorified, as we will be when we are raised from the dead. I can tell you for certain that life will go on beyond the resurrection, and the joys we think we have here are virtually nothing compared with those unutterable and inexpressible joys we will have in eternity. If we think that eating and drinking have their places here, just wait until after the resurrection when we are in heaven and can eat and drink the way we will be capable of eating in our new bodies.

Luke 24:44

> And he said unto them, These are the words which I spake unto you, while I was yet with you, that all things must be fulfilled, which were written in the law of Moses, and in the prophets, and in the psalms, concerning me.

Canon Law and Christianity

These are the three sections of the Bible which are canon law in the Hebrew faith. Jesus said all of them spoke of Him and that He had referred to them within their hearing while He was still physically alive among them. He reminded them of that, that Christianity is not based upon supposition or upon the mere words of one man, but upon the Word of God that endures forever: the law of Moses, all the prophets, and the Psalms.

Luke 24:45

> Then opened he their understanding, that they might understand the scriptures . . .

The Holy Spirit entering your heart is the same one who inspired the men to write the Word of God, to put it in writing. The Holy Spirit, who revealed Jesus to us, testifying of him, will open our understanding. It is true that simply by the processes of our logical nature or reasoning, we will never understand the scriptures. Therefore, we must understand that only by the Spirit living in us, and our yielding ourselves to the Spirit, will we be able to understand the Word.

Luke 24:46

> And said unto them, Thus it is written, and thus it behooved Christ to suffer, and to rise from the dead the third day . . .

The Heart of Preaching

Later, after Christ had ascended to heaven and poured out the gift of the Holy Spirit on the day of Pentecost, and the apostles and disciples began to preach, the heart of their preaching was in these two statements of Jesus. They preached His suffering, that is, Calvary, and they preached the resurrection from the dead.

Luke 24:47-49

> And that repentance and remission of sins should be preached in his name among all nations, beginning at Jerusalem.
>
> And ye are witnesses of these things. And, behold, I send the promise of my Father upon you: but tarry ye in the city of Jerusalem, until ye be endued with power from on high.

The timbre of Jesus' voice changes, for He is now at that point in history when through His resurrection He is getting ready to ascend to the Father. And when He reaches the Father's right hand, He will pray the Father to send them another comforter, the Holy Spirit. The word "Power" is the Greek word "dunamus," the root of our words "dynamo" and "dynamite." You will be endued with power from on high, the power from above, the same power that endued Christ. Everything Jesus was able to do was by the Holy Spirit, and He said His disciples will receive the Holy Spirit. So everything we do for Christ will be by the enablement or the power of the Holy Spirit.

Luke 24:50-52

> And He led them out as far as to Bethany, and he lifted up his hands, and blessed them. And it came to pass, while he blessed them, he was parted from them, and carried up into heaven. And they worshipped him, and returned to Jerusalem with great joy . . .

Joy Unites Christians

There is that word joy again. The Old Testament told of the joy of the Lord being our strength, and throughout Matthew, Mark, and Luke, Jesus uses the word joy, joy, joy. Thank God for a Christian faith of joy!

When they worshipped him and returned to Jerusalem with great joy, it was very important, because had they scattered, the Christian movement would have been dissipated and there would have been no united impact by the Holy Spirit upon the world.

Luke 24:53

> And were continually in the temple, praising and blessing God. Amen.

The phrase "continually in the temple" means regularly and frequently. It means the thrust of their heart, the attitude of their spirit, the deepest desire of their being was to receive the promise of the Father, the Holy Spirit. They thought it was the most important thing in the world. He is telling us that the most important thing in our lives is to be endued with the power of the Holy Spirit, because it is through the Holy Spirit indwelling us that He will reveal Christ in His fullness, His glorified and resurrected being to us, and through that we will be the most effective and joyful witnesses of our Lord Jesus Christ.

The Gospel According to John

The Gospel According to John

John's gospel is vastly different from Matthew, Mark, and Luke's, the synoptic gospels, or the gospels that are so much alike. Most of the accounts given by these three writers cover Jesus' life in Galilee. John deals primarily with His life away from Galilee, with about the last 5 months of Jesus' life, and concentrates more on the last 7 days of Jesus' life, centering primarily on Judea and Jerusalem. Matthew traced Jesus' genealogy to Abraham. Mark opened his gospel with a revelation of Jesus as the miracle worker. Luke traced Jesus' genealogy to Adam. But John goes all the way back to God. As far as we know, John's gospel was written about A.D. 90 or after Jesus had ascended, after the gospel had begun its march across the earth. The world had seen the ministry of Peter, of Paul, and Luke, his traveling companion; several missionary journeys had been made. John not only was an eyewitness from the beginning, one of the original twelve apostles who went through Jesus' life with Him in His public ministry of about 3 years, but he was a man who lived through all of the spread of the gospel in most of the first century and was the one to look back upon it. Then, he saw the real need was to tell the deeper teachings and deeper sufferings of Jesus, talking more to the believer, although it is for the whole world.

John's Gospel is not so much about events but about truth. The other gospel writers, Matthew, Mark, and Luke, wrote mostly about Jesus the person, the places He went to, the things He did. John does that to some extent but mostly he is dealing with the eternal truths about the Son of God.

John 1:1

In the beginning was the Word, and the Word was with God, and the Word was God.

The Word

In the origin, or at the first, or in the dateless past, in the beginning, in the beginning was the word.

John 1:2

The same was in the beginning with God.

John is proving the preexistence of God. He was showing that the Son was eternal God just as the Father and the Holy Spirit are eternal God. John is showing the divine trinity.

John 1:3

All things were made by him; and without him was not any thing made that was made.

John states clearly that Jesus is the agent of creation.

John 1:4,5

In him was life; and the life was the light of men. And the light shineth in darkness; and the darkness comprehended it not.

The Cross Foils Satan

Satan represented the powers of darkness and he did not have the power to obliterate the light of Jesus Christ. Jesus is God's answer to the devil. "And the darkness comprehended it not" means that the Satanic presence of darkness could not destroy the light because God was sending His Son to go to the cross and there spoil the kingdoms of the devil.

John 1:6

There was a man sent from God, whose name was John.

This is a reference to John the Baptist.

John 1:7-9

The same came for a witness, to bear witness of the Light, that all men through him might believe. He was not that Light, but was sent to bear witness of that Light. That was the true Light, which lighteth every man that cometh into the world.

The Light Destroys Sin

The light that Jesus brought in himself and that was climaxed in Him was not a new light. The moment Adam and Eve fell in transgression and sin came into the world, God began to shine His light. John is the bridge and he is coming now as a witness of the light. Of the light that lighteth every man that comes into the world. In some mysterious way, God has built himself into man. Although man is in darkness, yet there is some light within man. He is saying that the presence of this man Jesus Christ, the logos, the incarnate Word of God, is near every human being. He is there so that in a moment's time, upon that person's belief in Him, the light enters his life and banishes the darkness, destroys sin, and opens up his life so he can walk in the light of God forever.

John 1:10,11

> He was in the world, and the world was made by him, and the world knew him not. He came unto his own, and his own received him not.

Rejected by Israel

When He came unto His own, He came unto the Jews, He came unto the children of Israel, and they received Him not.

John 1:12

> But as many as received him, to them gave he power to become the sons of God, even to them that believe on his name . . .

Power Given Believers

Instantly those who were receiving Christ were given something. They were given power, and power here is a Greek word for the legal right, for entitlement, to become what they were not, to become all that God intended, to become the sons of God.

John 1:13,14

> Which were born, not of blood, nor of the will of the flesh, nor of the will of man, but of God. And the Word was made flesh, and dwelt among us, (and we beheld his glory, the glory as of the only begotten of the Father,) full of grace and truth.

John was one of the three apostles who went with Jesus to the

Mount of Transfiguration where the glory of God shown through Him until His face was like light and God spoke about Him. John saw that glory and it was the glory of the only begotten of the Father. John says He was full of grace and truth. The grace of God had always been present in the world, as had truth, because God is truth. Jesus was full of the grace, the unmerited favor of God, the forgiving of us by God's love. He was walking truth.

John 1:15,16

> John bare witness of him, and cried, saying, This was he of whom I spake, He that cometh after me is preferred before me: for he was before me. And of his fulness have all we received, and grace for grace.

The Preferred One

John the Baptist had been given by the word of knowledge and the spirit of discernment that he was to be the forerunner of the Messiah. John knew that he was dealing with divinity, deity. He knew he was dealing with the Lamb of God. He is saying, This one who is coming, who was preferred before me and was before me, is grace after grace after grace, the continuing grace of God that moves in and among men forevermore.

John 1:17

> For the law was given by Moses, but grace and truth came by Jesus Christ.

The Limitation of Law

God chose Moses through whom to give the law which revealed to man his need of a Savior because of sin in his life. Until then, the mass of people had no sense of sin, but when the law with all of its rules and regulations by God was given and the people saw it, they compared themselves with it and saw that they fell short of the mark. They developed a sharp and acute sense of sin. But what could they do about it? They could go once a year to the high priest, who on the day of atonement would offer the blood of an animal sacrifice, but they could not be forgiven eternally. So they had this sense of sin which produced in them the need of a Redeemer. That was as far as the law could go. It was Jesus Christ who brought us grace and truth. He brought us the unmerited favor of God. He brought unto us an eternal salvation.

John 1:18-21

> No man hath seen God at any time; the only begotten Son, which is in the bosom of the Father, he hath declared him. And this is the record of John, when the Jews sent priests and Levites from Jerusalem to ask him, Who art thou? And he confessed, and denied not; but confessed, I am not the Christ. And they asked him, What then? Art thou Elias? And he saith, I am not. Art thou that prophet? And he answered, No.

Moses Prophesied Messiah

That is a reference to Deuteronomy 18:15,18 where Moses himself said, There will arise a prophet like unto me, and he described the characteristics of this prophet and all the Jewish people knew Moses was referring to the coming of the Messiah. So they asked, Are you that prophet? And John the Baptist again said, No.

John 1:22,23

> Then said they unto him, Who art thou? that we may give an answer to them that sent us. What sayest thou of thyself? He said, I am the voice of one crying in the wilderness, Make straight the way of the Lord, as said the prophet Esaias.

Introducing Jesus

He was not an echo, he was a voice. He was a man of firm convictions whom God had raised up to be the one who would introduce the Savior, and the one who would be crying out to the people to prepare for the Lord, make straight His way.

John 1:24-27

> And they which were sent were of the Pharisees. And they asked him, and said unto him, Why baptizest thou then, if thou be not that Christ, nor Elias, neither that prophet? John answered them, saying, I baptize with water: but there standeth one among you, whom ye know not; he it is, who coming after me is preferred before me, whose shoe's latchet I am not worthy to unloose.

Blind to Reality

The Pharisees had sent a delegation to question John the Baptist.

They were offended because he was baptizing with water. They laid claim to that themselves and they were jealous. John said, in effect, You are all upset because I am out here using water for baptism — something you Pharisees claim for yourselves. You better be thinking about reality, what all this concerns. I tell you that the Christ is already among us.

John 1:28,29

These things were done in Bethabara beyond Jordan, where John was baptizing. The next day John seeth Jesus coming unto him, and saith, Behold the Lamb of God, which taketh away the sin of the world.

The Real Sacrificial Lamb

The "Lamb of God" is a symbol of Christ used at least 32 times in the Bible. The important thing is that John told of the immediacy of it, that He would take the place of those animal sacrifices in the law of Moses. He would take away sin, not just roll it away for 1 year at a time, but He would leap over all national boundaries and racial cultures and take away the sin of the world, the sin of all people who would believe on Him, not just Jewish people. He would be the world's Savior.

John 1:30-34

This is he of whom I said, After me cometh a man which is preferred before me: for he was before me. And I knew him not: but that he should be made manifest to Israel, therefore am I come baptizing with water. And John bare record, saying, I saw the Spirit descending from heaven like a dove, and it abode upon him. And I knew him not: but he that sent me to baptize with water, the same said unto me, Upon whom thou shalt see the Spirit descending, and remaining on him, the same is he which baptizeth with the Holy Ghost. And I saw, and bare record that this is the Son of God.

John Used His Gifts

Here is the clear witness of the holy trinity. The Father sends the Spirit to manifest himself in the form of a dove upon the head of the Son, Jesus Christ of Nazareth — Father, Son, and Holy Ghost.

Let us not overlook John the Baptist. We are told that John did no miracle, not in the way that Jesus did. But it was a miracle in a way that his voice was so positive, his obedience so complete. He stood up without advance notice, with no one to introduce him, no one to vouch for him, no one to write favorable letters on his behalf. The Bible teaches that a man's gifts prepare him. John had accepted the gifts of God and was now making the best use of them by positive action, by faith that was fearless and by standing up at a time when no other voice was being raised.

John 1:35-37

Again the next day after John stood, and two of his disciples; and looking upon Jesus as he walked, he saith, Behold the Lamb of God! And the two disciples heard him speak, and they followed Jesus.

John Relinquishes Limelight

Here is the true test. John the Baptist had had the limelight, but when the Light of the world came, he said, There is the Light, and he said it in a way to direct attention from himself toward Jesus.

John 1:38-41

Then Jesus turned, and saw them following, and saith unto them, What seek ye? They said unto him, Rabbi, (which is to say, being interpreted, Master,) where dwellest thou? He saith unto them, Come and see. They came and saw where he dwelt, and abode with him that day: for it was about the tenth hour.

One of the two which heard John speak, and followed him, was Andrew, Simon Peter's brother. He first findeth his own brother Simon, and saith unto him, We have found the Messias, which is, being interpreted, the Christ.

Andrew Simply Convincing

The term Christ is a Greek word which means anointed. The Hebrew term was Messiah. Andrew, upon finding his brother Simon Peter, said, we found the Messiah. Andrew certainly was no outstanding public person; do not get the idea that he was some charismatic individual in gifts of oratory, or persuasion, or things of that nature. He just spoke from the inner self in such a convicting way that his own brother believed him. That should encourage us to just witness of Him, even to our own families.

John 1:42

And he brought him to Jesus. And when Jesus beheld him, he said,

> Thou art Simon the son of Jona: thou shalt be called Cephas, which is by interpretation, A stone.

Simon is a reference to a reed from the marshes, like a cane fishing pole that is turned every way by the wind. "You are Simon," and Jesus read him like a book. You are up and you are down, you are in and you are out. You are on fire one day and you are at the bottom the next day. This is what you are. But, I will not leave you as you are, I will make you into someone else. I will change that reed into a rock. And I am going to give you a name — Cephas, or Peter, which means rock, or stone. To change a person like Simon was a risk of God's faith, but God risks His faith all the time by believing you and me.

John 1:43-46

> The day following Jesus would go forth into Galilee, and findeth Philip, and saith unto him, Follow me. Now Philip was of Bethsaida, the city of Andrew and Peter. Philip findeth Nathanael, and saith unto him, We have found him, of whom Moses in the law, and the prophets, did write, Jesus of Nazareth, the son of Joseph. And Nathanael said unto him, Can there any good thing come out of Nazareth? Philip saith unto him, Come and see.

Nazareth was not a bad city, it was just one of the towns in Galilee where the mixed breed of people lived. In 722 B.C., the 10 northern tribes called Israel were taken into captivity by the Assyrians. The people began to intermarry. They were not a cultured or an educated people, they were just a mixed brood.

We cannot improve upon Philip's method. We cannot argue with people. We simply must say, find out for yourself. I tell you truly, you can find out for yourself. You can discover the facts.

John 1:47,48

> Jesus saw Nathanael coming to him, and saith of him, Behold an Israelite indeed, in whom is no guile! Nathanael saith unto him, Whence knowest thou me? Jesus Answered and said unto him, Before that Philip called thee, when thou wast under the fig tree, I saw thee.

Jesus was not necessarily speaking of physical sight here, but of seeing him through the gift of the word of knowledge by the Holy Spirit.

John 1:49-51

Nathanael answered and saith unto him, Rabbi, thou art the Son of God; thou art the King of Israel. Jesus answered and said unto him, Because I said unto thee, I saw thee under the fig tree, believest thou? thou shalt see greater things than these.

And he saith unto him, Verily, verily, I say unto you, Hereafter ye shall see heaven open, and the angels of God ascending and descending upon the Son of man.

Jesus Opens Himself!

This is a beautiful reference back to Jacob and his ladder, the ladder he saw that went to heaven with angels descending and ascending on it. This Israelite in whom there was no guile was a man who worshiped God with all the knowledge and sincerity he possessed. He had kept the law of Moses as God intended. He had known about the way God opened heaven and he certainly understood the term, "Ye shall see heaven open," because God had said to His people that when they brought in their tithes and offerings, they could test Him and the test would be that He would open the windows of heaven.

Jesus is saying this is going to be a continual experience with Him. One of the things Jesus did was to go up and down the main streets of Israel and into the marketplaces and private homes and synagogues, opening heaven to people. There was an excitement because wherever He went there were miracles. Jesus Christ brought a renewed vigor to the spirit of the people because He was opening heaven. Heaven was bending low. What He is saying to Nathanael, He is saying to every one of us who are sincere and believing with all our heart. God will open heaven to us and we will know the angels are ascending and descending on Jesus. Because we have Jesus, those angels are all around us. I praise God for that.

John 2:1-4

And the third day there was a marriage in Cana of Galilee: and the mother of Jesus was there: And both Jesus was called, and his disciples, to the marriage. And when they wanted wine, the mother of Jesus saith unto him, They have no wine. Jesus saith unto her, Woman, what have I to do with thee? mine hour is not yet come.

No Disrespect Intended

This did not mean disrespect by Jesus toward His mother. But now He had assumed the full role of His Sonship, of His divine nature and of the whole purpose of His coming into the world. Apparently He was not quite ready to release the full power of His ministry.

John 2:5

His mother saith unto the servants, Whatsoever he saith unto you, do it.

Whatever Jesus Says

These are the last recorded words of Mary, the mother of Jesus. She did not tell Him what to do. She just said, Whatever He says, you do it. Whatever He says. That is a powerful statement. Whatever Jesus says to you, do it.

John 2:6

And there were set there six waterpots of stone, after the manner of the purifying of the Jews, containing two or three firkins apiece.

These are the waterpots that were usually filled with water so the visitors could wash their feet and not track the dust of their feet into the house. It also was a manner of purifying themselves. As far as we know, each of these waterpots would contain about 20 gallons of water,so that 6 of them would have more than a hundred gallons of water.

John 2:7-11

Jesus saith unto them, Fill the waterpots with water. And they filled them up to the brim. And he saith unto them, Draw out now, and bear unto the governor of the feast. And they bare it. When the ruler of the feast had tasted the water that was made wine, and knew not whence it was: (but the servants which drew the water knew;) the governor of the feast called the bridegroom, and saith unto him, every man at the beginning doth set forth good wine; and when men have well drunk, then that which is worse: but thou has kept the good wine until now.

This beginning of miracles did Jesus in Cana of Galilee, and manifested forth his glory; and his disciples believed on him.

Miraculous New Wine

I think the writer is trying to tell us that Jesus can take the commonplace and change it into the miraculous, that when Jesus came He had to deal with us as we are, where we are, and at the point of our need. When we obey Him by our faith, then He takes control of the situation. I think we must remember in the world that is falling apart, that somebody is in control of His kingdom, and that is Jesus Christ of Nazareth.

Usually the bridegroom would serve the best wine first. As people kept on drinking it and getting drunk, they did not know the difference, so he would bring out a lesser quality of wine. But Jesus does not have any stages of quality. He is quality. So He brought out an unspoiled wine. He brought out a wine that had one class, super class. The kind of class that demonstrates how He can take the commonplace life of Oral Roberts, the commonplace life of yourself or any other person in the world, just flesh, and change us, miraculously transform us into a new creature — not by the world's methods as is demonstrated here where they took the juice of grapes and had it fermented into wine that would make people drunk, but by another method. It would be good when you first got it and good while you lived it, and good when you came to the last breath in your body and good in eternity. This is best wine. The real wine that lifts us up is the spirit of our Lord Jesus Christ taking over our lives.

The Word says, "This beginning of miracles did Jesus." It was not an ending but a beginning. The miracles of Jesus are not over. Do not let anybody kid you or convince you that there are no more miracles, that the miracles were only for that day. Jesus Christ is the same yesterday, today, and forever. I am a living example of miracles. I am a miracle because Jesus saved my soul, healed my body, delivered me from the power of darkness, turned my life around, and enabled me to do something of value in the world. Not only is that true of Oral Roberts and his ministry, but it is true of thousands upon thousands in the work of God. Even those quiet people out there who are serving God are seeing the new wine of the gospel. And this beginning of miracles is a very important statement because that is what it was, a beginning. The miracles continue.

Now I would like to pray with you because I know God is dealing with you. As you are reading and learning the New Testament, God is speaking in your heart and you need the courage to do those things. Let us pray.

Father, I thank you that you have spoken many things in my heart, things to do. I want to do them with all my heart. I pray now for my friend and partner as You deal with their hearts, that the doing of them will become the joy of their lives and that great things will happen, something good will happen to them through Jesus Christ our Lord. Amen and amen.

John 2:12

After this he went down to Capernaum, he, and his mother, and his brethren, and his disciples: and they continued there not many days.

Jesus' Headquarters

Jesus left Nazareth early in His ministry, got a house in Capernaum, and transferred His headquarters there. And it remained His headquarters for the rest of His ministry.

John 2:13-19

And the Jews' passover was at hand, and Jesus went up to Jerusalem, and found in the temple those that sold oxen and sheep and doves, and the changers of money sitting: and when he had made a scourge of small cords, he drove them all out of the temple, and the sheep, and the oxen; and poured out the changers' money, and overthrew the tables; and said unto them that sold doves, Take these things hence; make not my Father's house an house of merchandise. And his disciples remembered that it was written, The zeal of thine house hath eaten me up. Then answered the Jews and said unto him, What sign shewest thou unto us, seeing that thou doest these things? Jesus answered and said unto them, Destroy this temple, and in three days I will raise it up.

Doubtless, Jesus was pointing at His body when He said, "Destroy this temple and in three days I will raise it up," but certainly the Pharisees and others were not able to see what He was doing because their minds were more on the temple building.

John 2:20-22

Then said the Jews, Forty and six years was this temple in building, and wilt thou rear it up in three days? But he spake of the temple of his body. When therefore he was risen from the dead, his disciples remembered that he had said this unto them; and they believed the scripture, and the word which Jesus had said.

Resurrection the Cornerstone

We can talk all we want to about the resurrection, but until we believe the scriptures in the Old Testament and the words of our Lord in the New Testament, as well as His witnesses, we are not going to believe in the resurrection. The resurrection is the cornerstone of our Christian faith. Everything rises or falls upon the resurrection. If we trust in the resurrection, which means the living Christ who himself said, I am the resurrection, then we live and we live more abundantly.

John 2:23-3:12

> Now when he was in Jerusalem at the passover, in the feast day, many believed in his name, when they saw the miracles which he did. But Jesus did not commit himself unto them, because he knew all men, and needed not that any should testify of man: for he knew what was in man.
>
> There was a man of the Pharisees, named Nicodemus, a ruler of the Jews: the same came to Jesus by night, and said unto him, Rabbi, we know that thou art a teacher come from God: for no man can do these miracles that thou doest, except God be with him.
>
> Jesus answered and said unto him, Verily, verily, I say unto thee, Except a man be born again, he cannot see the kingdom of God.
>
> Nicodemus saith unto him, How can a man be born when he is old? can he enter the second time into his mother's womb, and be born?
>
> Jesus answered, Verily, verily, I say unto thee, Except a man be born of water and of the Spirit, he cannot enter into the kingdom of God. That which is born of the flesh is flesh; and that which is born of the Spirit is spirit. Marvel not that I said unto thee, Ye must be born again. The wind bloweth where it listeth, and thou hearest the sound thereof, but canst not tell whence it cometh, and whither it goeth: so is every one that is born of the Spirit.
>
> Nicodemus answered and said unto him, How can these things be? Jesus answered and said unto him, Art thou a master of Israel, and knowest not these things? Verily, verily, I say unto thee, We speak that we do know, and testify that we have seen; and ye receive not our witness. If I have told you earthly things, and ye believe not, how shall ye believe, if I tell you of heavenly things?

The Spiritual Rebirth

Nicodemus was a rabbi, a member of the Sanhedrin court which was composed of 70 leading men of the people of Israel. They acted more or less as the supreme court of the nation. Jesus' miracles had captured the attention of practically everyone in the land, and especially those in leadership. One of them, who had been deeply moved by these miracles and had thought long and hard about a man who could do such miracles, went to Jesus at night. He began his visit with Jesus by complimenting Him, but Jesus cut through everything, knowing what was in the man's heart, anticipating his questions, and said, I tell you, except a man be born again he cannot see the kingdom of God, and that the wind blows from where it was. Wind, here in the Greek, is "numa" which is also the word for spirit. Jesus says that you cannot see the wind but you can hear it, and you can observe the results of the blowing of the wind, but its source is hidden. So he that is born again receives life. He receives life that is much like the wind. It is observable in its results. Man's reasoning mind cannot comprehend it because it is spiritual, but it is even more real than the wind blowing, which you can hear. The spirit can also hear the voice of the Spirit. Jesus said, you must be born again — no ifs or maybes or perhapses, you must be born again or you have no life.

You are not born of that heavenly kingdom. There is a kingdom above the kingdom of this world. Jesus said He spoke of what He knew and He knew the Old Testament scriptures. He knew that He had come by the Holy Spirit and the Holy Spirit had been given to Him without measure. He is saying that the spiritual things transcend the physical. The fact is, you will have to get down into your spirit to understand your need of being born again.

John 3:13-15

> And no man hath ascended up to heaven, but he that came down from heaven, even the Son of man which is in heaven. And as Moses lifted up the serpent in the wilderness, even so must the Son of man be lifted up: that whosoever believeth in him should not perish, but have eternal life.

Jesus is referring to Numbers 21:9 where the Israelites in disobedience were bitten by snakes and were dying like flies. God had Moses make a brass serpent and put it upon a pole like a cross. Just as those who were bitten by serpents in Moses' time, and who by faith looked up at the brass serpent with faith in the coming Messiah were healed, so those who actually see by their faith the Son of God lifted up are saved. Jesus was referring to that to indicate that as He would go to the cross and be lifted up, whoever would look to Him and believe would not perish but have everlasting life.

John 3:16

> For God so loved the world, that he gave his only begotten Son, that

whosoever believeth in him should not perish, but have everlasting life.

Seed-Faith Principle

Jesus is visibly moved as He says this, and so am I at this time. He said, For God, the original cause of all things, For God so loved. He did not say, For God loved, which would have been true, but He said, For God so loved. He loved so much that He loved the world and He loved it with a love surpassing all understanding, the world that had gone from Him. Man, whom He had created in His own image and likeness, had chosen to repudiate his creator, follow the devil, and go to his death. God so loved the world of humanity that He gave. Everything begins with giving, with planting a seed. For God so loved the world that He gave, He put in that seed because He was looking for a harvest. God gave. Why did He give? Because He had a need. God gave out of His need the same way He tells us to give out of our need. That is the purpose of giving. There has to be a need for giving. What did God need? He needed man again. He needed His masterpiece restored to Him. Man is the crowning glory of God's creative purpose and act. The devil had stolen man away and God so loved him that He gave. And what did He give? His only begotten Son — not an angel, not a symbol, not anything or anyone else but one of a kind, unique, His only begotten Son. God had only one Son and He gave Him, that whosoever believeth — this is an absolutely new term as far as the Jews are concerned. Now Jesus opens the gate wide, flings out His arms, and tells how God loved the whole world,and then brings it down to an individual . . . "whosoever believeth in him should not perish but have everlasting life."

Here is the seed-faith principle lived out. God the source so loved that He gave His best. He gave His best seed and Jesus is called the seed of David, and the seed of the woman. He gave His best and He gave out of His need because He needed man back. He also gave for a desired result. Just as a farmer plants wheat in order to get wheat, so God planted the seed of His Son in order that men would believe on Him and have everlasting life and not die. First, seed-faith is making God the source of your life, the source of your total supply. Second, seed-faith is giving God your best, giving first, giving out of your need. And third, it is giving for a desired result, expecting a miracle harvest, expecting to receive it. This is why I continue to preach and teach seed-faith. It is the principle of the ages, it is the principle for us as individuals, as children of God. God is our source. We give our best. We expect to receive a miracle harvest.

John 3:17,18

For God sent not his Son into the world to condemn the world; but that the world through him might be saved. He that believeth on him is not condemned: but he that believeth not is condemned already, because he hath not believed in the name of the only begotten Son of God.

God Speaks Truth

Many people think this is a narrow view, that God is unjust when He says that if we do not believe upon Him, man is condemned and will be destroyed. But it is the truth, because God is our creator. We are His by creation. God is also our Redeemer. We are His by redemption and He is the only one who so loved us.

When you turn away from that and believe opposite from it, you have no agent of redemption. There is no way for you to be saved. That is why the condemnation is upon you. You have denied His redeeming power. You have denied His love. You have denied His care. And He is simply telling the truth. He is not trying to knock you. He is speaking to your heart and then to your mind.

John 3:19-21

And this is the condemnation, that light is come into the world, and men loved darkness rather than light, because their deeds were evil. For every one that doeth evil hateth the light, neither cometh to the light, lest his deeds should be reproved. But he that doeth truth cometh to the light, that his deeds may be made manifest, that they are wrought in God.

Fear of Exposure

After a person has given all the reasons why he does not come to God or believe, then what is the real reason? Jesus says the real reason is that he loves something other than God's way, that he is thinking in a sensual manner that the flesh can satisfy him rather than the Spirit of God redeeming his whole being including his soul. He does not come to the light because that light will reveal his sins, his true desires in this world. That is the reason. No matter what reason people give, that is the reason.

John 3:22-30

After these things came Jesus and his disciples into the land of Judaea;

and there he tarried with them, and baptized. And John also was baptizing in Aenon near to Salim, because there was much water there: and they came, and were baptized. For John was not yet cast into prison. Then there arose a question between some of John's disciples and the Jews about purifying. And they came unto John, and said unto him, Rabbi, he that was with thee beyond Jordan, to whom thou barest witness, behold, the same baptizeth, and all men come to him.

John answered and said, A man can receive nothing, except it be given him from heaven. Ye yourselves bear me witness, that I said, I am not the Christ, but that I am sent before him. He that hath the bride is the bridegroom: but the friend of the bridegroom, which standeth and heareth him, rejoiceth greatly because of the bridegroom's voice: this my joy therefore is fulfilled. He must increase, but I must decrease.

No Rivalry Existed

The Jews tried to start a rivalry between John the Baptist and Jesus. John was saying that he was the go-between for the girl and the boy who were going to get married. He had successfully introduced the bridegroom, Jesus Christ, as the Son of God so that others would hear Him and receive Him. When he had done that, his work was fulfilled and he must decrease while Christ must increase.

John 3:31-34

He that cometh from above is above all: he that is of the earth is earthly, and speaketh of the earth: he that cometh from heaven is above all. And what he hath seen and heard, that he testifieth; and no man receiveth his testimony. He that hath received his testimony hath set to his seal that God is true. For he whom God hath sent speaketh the words of God: for God giveth not the Spirit by measure unto him.

This is one of the great clear-cut patterns that John shows us about our Lord Jesus Christ. The Holy Spirit is so absolutely important to His function as the Son of God and the Son of Man that the Spirit is given to Him without measure and consequently we cannot live without some measure of the Holy Spirit in our lives. If we interpret the original correctly, it means that Jesus, who received the Spirit without measure, will also give us the Holy Spirit without measure.

I believe a limitless measure of the Holy Spirit will continually work through my life and other lives. This is the day of the Holy Spirit's work. This is the day when the charismatic power of the Spirit is being poured out. I praise God that I have had a part in the charismatic movement. We built a university upon the Holy Spirit and God's authority; the Oral Roberts University here in Tulsa was built upon the Holy Spirit.

We built the City of Faith Medical and Research Center and have staffed it with Spirit-filled doctors, nurses, health professionals, and prayer partners.

I have refused to compromise on this. From every side have come offers of compromise. They tried to get me not to emphasize the Holy Spirit so much, but without the Holy Spirit coming upon Jesus, He could not have become the Savior of the world. Unless the Spirit had been given to Him without measure, He could not have done His mighty deeds. He could not have endured what this world brought against Him. I know that I am not smart enough, and nobody else is smart enough, without the Holy Spirit's wisdom and knowledge to do God's work today. The pressures are too great. The devil is fighting too hard. But thank God we are winning. Victory is here through the power of the Holy Spirit indwelling us.

John 3:35

The Father loveth the son, and hath given all things into his hand.

Do you understand that when Christ lives in you, all things are in His hand?

John 3:36

He that believeth on the Son hath everlasting life: and he that believeth not the Son shall not see life; but the wrath of God abideth on him.

Hell Lurks on Earth

Hell begins on this earth. It begins when people reject the only source of life there is. God did not prepare hell for people. People go there because they are determined to follow the devil. Once they follow God they have life, they have it now, and at death they go to heaven.

John 4:1-6

When therefore the Lord knew how the Pharisees had heard that Jesus made and baptized more disciples than John, (Though Jesus himself baptized not, but his disciples,) he left Judaea, and departed again into Galilee. And he must needs go through Samaria. Then cometh he to a city of Samaria, which is called Sychar, near to the parcel of ground that Jacob gave to his son Joseph. Now Jacob's well was there. Jesus therefore, being wearied with his journey, sat thus on the well: and it was about the sixth hour.

Jesus, the Man, Tired

It was about noon. I want you to notice that Jesus as the Son of Man was weary in His body. He got tired. One of the surprising things that I have encountered in the healing ministry is that when I preach to the multitudes, preach long and under the anointing, winning sometimes three and four thousand souls in a single service, and follow that by praying for a hundred or more invalids and then have a public healing line, not getting through until late in the night — people are always surprised when I say I am tired. They seem to think that if a man is anointed by God he should never get tired. Jesus got tired. We are human beings. When Jesus got tired He sat down.

John 4:7-9

There cometh a woman of Samaria to draw water: Jesus saith unto her, Give me to drink. (For his disciples were gone away unto the city to buy meat.) Then saith the woman of Samaria unto him, How is it that thou, being a Jew, askest drink of me, which am a woman of Samaria? for the Jews have no dealings with the Samaritans.

Source of Astonishment

She was very astonished because she knew that because of the religious and racial animosity between her people and the Jews, the Jews had a feeling of superiority concerning Samaritans. Also, she was a woman. She knew that a Jewish rabbi would never speak to a woman in public, not even to his wife or his daughter. She also knew the Jewish prayer that the Jewish men prayed. Blessed art thou, oh God, who hast not made me a woman. And she was astonished.

John 4:10

Jesus answered and said unto her, If thou knewest the gift of God, and who it is that saith to thee, Give me to drink; thou wouldest have asked of him, and he would have given thee living water.

Women's Status Changed

He told her that her need was more spiritual than physical. Because Jesus always comes to people at the point of their need, He began with her in a spiritual way rather than a physical one because that happened to be her greatest need at that moment. Also, He was treating her as an equal. He did not have the Isamel or chauvinistic feeling toward women that the Jews had. This was never the way with God; God always gainfully employed women. There were many prophetesses in the Old Testament, and Jesus' mother was revered and highly favored of God. It was Jesus who made the greatest dent in the prejudice against women. He lifted up womanhood. He cared for them. He trusted them. He received financial help from a group of women. He does not discriminate against them.

John 4:11-18

> The woman saith unto him, Sir, thou hast nothing to draw with, and the well is deep: from whence then hast thou that living water? Art thou greater than our father Jacob, which gave us the well, and drank thereof himself, and his children, and his cattle?
>
> Jesus answered and said unto her, Whosoever drinketh of this water shall thirst again: but whosoever drinketh of the water that I shall give him shall never thirst; but the water that I shall give him shall be in him a well of water springing up into everlasting life.
>
> The woman saith unto him, Sir, give me this water, that I thirst not, neither come hither to draw. Jesus saith unto her, Go, call thy husband, and come hither. The woman answered and said, I have no husband. Jesus saith unto her, Thou hast well said, I have no husband: For thou hast had five husbands; and he whom thou now hast is not thy husband: in that saidst thou truly.

Extramarital Losers

He is telling her everything about her life and He is doing it by the spirit of discernment, by the power of the Holy Spirit within Him. She has had five husbands and recently had begun living with yet another man. Does that sound familiar? Today many people do not think marriage is sacred, that it is just a piece of paper and all they have to do is to live together without marriage. But such arrangements never have won. They are not winning and they never will. No one is ever going to win over the laws of God.

There is God's way. He said, A man shall leave his father and mother and cleave only unto his wife. We know that our God fixed it right. Those who live by it are going to prosper. Those who do not will be caught, maybe not by the law or the mores of society. People may pat them on the back and say how great it is, but those people know they are living in hell, and there is no other way but God's way.

John 4:19-24

> The woman saith unto him, Sir, I perceive that thou art a prophet. Our fathers worshipped in this mountain; and ye say, that in Jerusalem is the place where men ought to worship. Jesus saith unto her, Woman, believe me, the hour cometh, when ye shall neither in this mountain, nor yet at Jerusalem, worship the Father. Ye worship ye know not what: we know what we worship: for salvation is of the Jews. But the hour cometh, and now is, when the true worshippers shall worship the Father in spirit and in truth: for the Father seeketh such to worship him. God is a Spirit: and they that worship him must worship him in spirit and in truth.

The Key to Worship

Immediately the woman got into a theological discussion with Jesus and she met her match. She entered the arena of theology by saying, Our fathers for the past 700 years have worshipped in this mountain, but You and Your people have said Jerusalem is the only place for worship. Jesus replied, Listen to me, woman, the hour is here when it doesn't matter what mountain you are on or if you are not on a mountain. When it comes to worshipping God, you worship him in spirit and in truth. It is not a place, but an act of worship. Because God is spirit, worship must come from spirit and from sincerity, from the truth of God. People think of God in terms of a building. But Jesus, while He does not want us to forsake the assembling of ourselves together in private and public worship says that is not the key issue. The key issue is worshipping in spirit and in truth, whether it is in a tin barn or in a mighty, glorious cathedral. It is the praise and worship of the people of God that counts.

John 4:25

> The woman saith unto him, I know that Messias cometh, which is called Christ: when he is come, He will tell us all things.

Vital Observation

There are two observations here. One is that the woman said, I know that Messias, which is called Christ, is coming. The second is that she knew when He came He would tell them all things. This second thing was her image of the Messiah. From what she knew about the Bible teaching concerning the coming of Christ, she knew He would be able to tell the people all things.

John 4:26

> Jesus saith unto her, I that speak unto thee am he.

A Rare Revelation

Whereas on many occasions He refused to identify himself, to this seeking woman He very readily said, I am the Christ, I am the one that you're talking about.

John 4:27

> And upon this came his disciples, and marvelled that he talked with the woman: yet no man said, What seekest thou? or, Why talkest thou with her?

Equal Before God

They were taken aback by Jesus talking publicly with a woman. I am hoping we will see in Christ that in the kingdom of God, it is not male or female favoritism or this or that, but that we are all equal before God.

John 4:28-29

> The woman then left her waterpot, and went her way into the city, and saith to the men, Come, see a man, which told me all things that ever I did: is not this the Christ?

Marvelous Revelation

It is a marvelous thing God does when He reveals to us who we are, what we are, what we have done, and what He can make of us.

John 4:30-32

Then they went out of the city, and came unto him. In the mean while his disciples prayed him, saying, Master, eat. But he said unto them, I have meat to eat that ye know not of.

True Soul Food

He was leading a lost soul to the Lord, and that was refreshment of the soul. Nothing is so stimulating as doing the work of God.

John 4:33-37

Therefore said the disciples one to another, Hath any man brought him ought to eat? Jesus saith unto them, My meat is to do the will of him that sent me, and to finish his work. Say not ye, There are yet four months, and then cometh harvest? behold, I say unto you, Lift up your eyes, and look on the fields; for they are white already to harvest. And he that reapeth receiveth wages, and gathereth fruit unto life eternal: that both he that soweth and he that reapeth may rejoice together. And herein is that saying true, One soweth, and another reapeth.

Seed-Faith Excitement

Here is a beautiful illustration of seed-faith. Jesus has planted the seeds of faith in this woman's life. He has taken special time to treat her as an equal. He has come to her not racially or theologically prejudiced. He has talked with her openly without fear of what anyone would do or say. He has read her life like a book. He has sowed the seeds of faith. The woman was moved toward God. She was stirring up the men of the city to go see Him. The harvest was there. Disciples, He was saying, get ready. Get ready. We are going to reap a harvest for God here.

We ought to be the most excited after we give. It is after we give that God starts multiplying the seeds we sow. It may not come immediately. It may be weeks or months. It may be years. But you can trust God, your source, to grow the seeds you sow, and to reproduce those seeds into a harvest.

John 4:38-40

I sent you to reap that whereon ye bestowed no labour: other men laboured, and ye are entered into their labours.

And many of the Samaritans of that city believed on him for the saying of the woman, which testified, He told me all that ever I did.

So when the Samaritans were come unto him, they besought him that he would tarry with them; and he abode there two days.

Giving Our Best

That was unheard of in those days, that He would actually spend two full days with these despised Samaritans. But God always goes where the need is located. We need to refocus our thoughts, rearrange our priorities, and think of serving God by seeing people in their needs, by treating them in a way that their needs capture our attention. Then, at the point of those needs, we are going to begin our ministry, our witness — the giving of our best. That is what Jesus was doing.

John 4:41,42

And many more believed because of his own word; and said unto the woman, Now we believe, not because of thy saying: for we have heard him ourselves, and know that this is indeed the Christ, the Saviour of the world.

Reckoning With God

Although they said, We do not believe in him because of your saying, they were just talking. They did believe because of her saying. But they believed even more when they themselves dealt with Jesus. It is true that we can witness to others, and that witness will cause people to turn toward Christ. But in the final analysis, God has no grandchildren; He only has sons and daughters. Everyone must deal with God for himself, or herself.

John 4:43-50

Now after two days he departed thence, and went into Galilee. For Jesus himself testified, that a prophet hath no honour in his own country. Then when he was come into Galilee, the Galilaeans received him, having seen all the things that he did at Jerusalem at the feast: for they also went unto the feast. So Jesus came again into Cana of Galilee, where he made the water wine.

And there was a certain nobleman, whose son was sick at Capernaum. When he heard that Jesus was come out of Judaea into Galilee, he went unto him, and besought him that he would come down, and heal his son: for he was at the point of death.

Then said Jesus unto him, Except ye see signs and wonders, ye will not believe.

The nobleman saith unto him, Sir, come down ere my child die.

Jesus saith unto him, Go thy way; thy son liveth. And the man believed the word that Jesus had spoken unto him, and he went his way.

When God Speaks

Jesus had gone back to Cana where He did His first miracle. This time He responded to a father whose little boy was dying. The man really touched Jesus' heart when he said, Sir, please come down before my little son dies. Jesus saw his faith and said, Go, go your way, your son lives. Then we are told the man believed the word that Jesus had spoken unto him.

This is of great importance to you. You can read the Word, or you can hear the Word preached, but until you hear it spoken to you, it is not going to lodge in your heart. You must make an effort to hear, but you have to make a greater effort to hear something said to you. When you hear with faith, it is exactly like God is speaking to you individually, personally, calling you by name, knowing you just as you are.

So often I say that God spoke to me. When I hear the word of God, either through a sermon, through a song, through a word of prophecy, a word of knowledge, or reading the Word, or the Holy Spirit quickening a word of God that I have remembered, then I have to hear it. Oral Roberts has to hear it, or it is not spoken to me. It is not spoken to me from my standpoint until I take it personally. I would not dare attempt anything unless I knew God had spoken to me about it. I think every one of us can know that we know that God is dealing with us on a personal basis. He has a plan for our lives individually. And we can follow it if we will to do it.

John 4:51-54

And as he was now going down, his servants met him, and told him, saying, Thy son liveth. Then enquired he of them the hour when he began to amend. And they said unto him, Yesterday at the seventh hour the fever left him. So the father knew that it was at the same hour, in the which Jesus said unto him, Thy son liveth: and himself believed, and his whole house. This is again the second miracle that Jesus did, when he was come out of Judaea into Galilee.

Prayer Transcends Distance

Early in His ministry Jesus established the fact that there is no distance in prayer. People from all over America, Canada, and other parts of the world write me letters asking me to pray. And I pray. Why do I pray? Because I believe there is no distance in prayer. I believe that you are there and I am here, and that God is at both places, and we can bridge the distance by our faith in the living God.

John 5:1-18

After this there was a feast of the Jews; and Jesus went up to Jerusalem. Now there is at Jerusalem by the sheep market a pool, which is called in the Hebrew tongue Bethesda, having five porches. In these lay a great multitude of impotent folk, of blind, halt, withered, waiting for the moving of the water. For an angel went down at a certain season into the pool, and troubled the water: whosoever then first after the troubling of the water stepped in was made whole of whatsoever disease he had.

And a certain man was there, which had an infirmity thirty and eight years. When Jesus saw him lie, and knew that he had been now a long time in that case, he saith unto him, Wilt thou be made whole? The impotent man answered him, Sir, I have no man, when the water is troubled, to put me into the pool: but while I am coming, another steppeth down before me.

Jesus saith unto him, Rise, take up thy bed, and walk. And immediately the man was made whole, and took up his bed, and walked:

And on the same day was the sabbath. The Jews therefore said unto him that was cured, It is the sabbath day: it is not lawful for thee to carry thy bed. He answered them, He that made me whole, the same said unto me, Take up thy bed, and walk. Then asked they him, What man is that which said unto thee, Take up thy bed, and walk? And he that was healed wist not who it was: for Jesus had conveyed himself away, a multitude being in that place.

Afterward Jesus findeth him in the temple, and said unto him, Behold, thou art made whole: sin no more, lest a worse thing come unto thee. The man departed, and told the Jews that it was Jesus, which had made him whole. And therefore did the Jews persecute Jesus, and sought to slay him, because he had done these things on the sabbath day.

But Jesus answered them, My Father worketh hitherto, and I work.

Therefore the Jews sought the more to kill him, because he not only had broken the sabbath, but said also that God was his Father, making himself equal with God.

Ask for Wholeness

In Jerusalem there was a pool called Bethesda. There was a belief that at a certain season of the year an angel would come and stir the waters up. Whoever was fortunate enough to get into the waters while they were stirred up was healed of whatever disease he had. The place was just crowded with every kind of sick person you can imagine. Jesus walked through this group of very sick and afflicted people, and He selected one man who had been lying there, apparently carried there daily, for 38 long years. Then we are told when Jesus saw him lie (it does not say when he saw his body lie), Jesus looked inside that sick body and saw the inner man, and the inner man was lying down. Jesus knew that the inner man had been lying down a long time, and He said, Wilt thou be made whole? It seemed like a silly question. That is why the man was there. The man began to complain, Sir, I do not have anybody, when the water is troubled, to help me into the pool. He did not grasp that Jesus was talking about the whole man, not only the body. He knew that body within itself could not do much. The inner man was in control. That is the way God had made man. So Jesus asked him, Will you be made whole? He wanted the man to be made whole — whole-person healing, and that is the turning point of your life.

What is it you want God to do? To heal your finger? To heal your eye? To heal your heart? Or your blood pressure? Certainly you want those things. Do you want God to heal your spirit? Heal your emotions? Certainly you do. Do you want God to heal your financial problems? Certainly you do. But He asks you, Do you want to be made whole? He asks you to stand up on the inside. He reminds you that you are what you are inside. There's a man on the inside, there's a woman on the inside. The real person.

Christ said, Rise, take up your bed and walk. This man, from a physical standpoint, could not rise. Jesus therefore was speaking beyond his body to his inner man. He was telling that man on the inside, You get up. You get up and you tell your body to use its hands, its knees, and its feet to get up off that bed and walk. You know what? The man did it. He took up his bed and walked. He was made whole.

This is probably as perfect an example of what Jesus came to do as there is in the world. He came to make us whole. But you and I have to be made whole persons. We are not created one, we are not born one, so we have to be made one. We are made one by desiring to be made whole and by doing what the Master tells us to do.

The man got up and left and began to say, Jesus healed me, Jesus healed me. Then we are told that the Jews really began to persecute

Jesus because He had done this on the sabbath day. When they found Him and accosted Him, Jesus said, My Father worketh hitherto, and I work. They sought to kill Him not only because He had broken what they called their sabbath, but He said that He and His Father were one. He made himself equal with God. They really tried to kill Him.

John 5:19-23

> Then answered Jesus and said unto them, Verily, verily I say unto you, The Son can do nothing of himself, but what he seeth the Father do: for what things soever he doeth, these also doeth the Son likewise. For the Father loveth the Son, and sheweth him all things that himself doeth: and he will shew him greater works than these, that ye may marvel.
>
> For as the Father raiseth up the dead, and quickeneth them; even so the Son quickeneth whom he will. For the Father judgeth no man, but hath committed all judgment unto the Son: that all men should honour the Son, even as they honour the Father. He that honoureth not the Son honoureth not the Father which hath sent him.

Abraham, Moses Explained

Jesus was speaking to the Jewish religious leaders. They claimed to honor the Father. They made a great pretense of having the only religion, yet they have criticized God's Son. This is true today. One of the saddest facts of history is that those same dear people, whom we often call God's ancient people, do not honor the Son of God, Jesus Christ. They are not united in honoring the heavenly Father. I have never seen a group so split, so divided. It is a tragedy because the revelation of God is a continuing revelation.

It is never an end in itself.

Let me tell you why the law of Moses was given. It was not given as the main line. The main line was through the faith of Abraham, the faith in God. Whereas Abraham had known a sense of sin and knew he needed a Redeemer, for he had seen Jesus' day by faith and rejoiced in it, his descendants did not. In order for them to develop a sense of their sinfulness and to realize the need of a Redeemer, God established the law of Moses by which they could judge themselves. The heart of this was the Ten Commandments. When they saw their sinfulness they could make an offering to God. The high priest would make a sacrifice, a blood sacrifice, because it is through the shedding of blood that God forgives sin. Then they could have their sins rolled back for a year at a time and begin the new year with a clean slate. When Christ came to fulfill all that and at Calvary became the Lamb of God in person, in reality shedding His blood, He was answering the people's sense of sin by offering them perfect redemption once and for all. Jesus was telling these people who lived under the law of Moses that they once honored the Father, but they had stopped honoring Him. They were not honoring Him as they did back at Sinai. They were not feeling a sense of sin as their forefathers did. They were not looking for a Redeemer, a Messiah, as they once did. They do not honor the Father, and that is why they do not honor the Son.

All of us who love God, who truly honor and love the Jewish people, know in our hearts that if they love the Father, they will love the Son, and the split and the dispersion and all the things that they have gone through could have been prevented, if only they honored the Father through the Son. I do not say that with any degree of joy, but with the deepest regret. I care for Israel. I care for the leaders, I care for the people, I care for the Jewish people in my own country. Many of them are my friends. I receive letters from quite a number of rabbis across the country who are friendly toward my ministry, and sometimes even ask for my prayers.

Thank God for the Jewish race, but I would to God that they would remember Abraham and not stop at Moses, but go on back to Abraham. Study Abraham. Look at his faith. We who are Christians are descendants of Abraham because of our faith. Unless we have faith, we do not descend from him. The real Jews are not necessarily racial Jews, they are the ones who have the faith of Abraham. Every true Christian has the faith of Abraham. Every true Jew has the faith of Abraham. One of these days, God and His ancient people are going to have a very personal, serious dialogue. One of these days there is going to be a different confrontation than on the human level or the political level, or even the religious level. It is going to be between God and the people who represent His ancient people.

John 5:24-31

> Verily, verily, I say unto you, He that heareth my word, and believeth on him that sent me, hath everlasting life, and shall not come into condemnation; but is passed from death unto life. Verily, verily, I say unto you, The hour is coming, and now is, when the dead shall hear the voice of the Son of God: and they that hear shall live.
>
> For as the Father hath life in himself; so hath he given to the Son to have life in himself; And hath given him authority to execute judgment also, because he is the Son of man. Marvel not at this: for the hour is coming, in the which all that are in the graves shall hear

his voice, And shall come forth; they that have done good, unto the resurrection of life; and they that have done evil, unto the resurrection of damnation. I can of mine own self do nothing: as I hear, I judge: and my judgment is just; because I seek not mine own will, but the will of the Father which hath sent me. If I bear witness of myself, my witness is not true.

Jesus Has Authority

There is a dual resurrection. Even the wicked dead will be raised from the dead, not only those who believe in God. Those who have died in the faith shall be resurrected unto the good life eternally. Others shall be resurrected and they shall be judged, and be sent into eternity without God. Jesus makes it very clear that He is the one who is given authority and that is the key word — authority. Great faith is when you and I believe that Jesus has authority over all things.

John 5:32-39

There is another that beareth witness of me, and I know that the witness which he witnesseth of me is true. Ye sent unto John, and he bare witness unto the truth. But I receive not testimony from man: but these things I say, that ye might be saved. He was a burning and a shining light: and ye were willing for a season to rejoice in his light.

But I have greater witness than that of John: for the works which the Father hath given me to finish, the same works that I do, bear witness of me, that the Father hath sent me. And the Father himself, which hath sent me, hath borne witness of me. Ye have neither heard his voice at any time, nor seen his shape. And ye have not his word abiding in you: for whom he hath sent, him ye believe not. Search the scriptures; for in them ye think ye have eternal life: and they are they which testify of me.

Finding Jesus

Everything rises or falls on our Savior Jesus Christ. You do not have His Word abiding in you if you have not believed on the Lord Jesus Christ. He says, Search the Word of God because the scriptures testify of Me; and they do. As a hound goes by the scent, so by the deep senses of your inner being, search the scriptures — the scent is there. The way is plain before you. Seek Me through the Word of God.

John 5:40-43

> And ye will not come to me, that ye might have life. I receive not honour from men. But I know you, that ye have not the love of God in you. I am come in my Father's name, and ye receive me not: if another shall come in his own name, him ye will receive.

Acceptance of Antichrist

This is the first reference in John's gospel that Christ makes to the Antichrist. The Antichrist will come in his own name saying he is the true Christ, and the Jewish people will listen to him. I am not talking about every individual Jew, but he is saying, There is a people — those who have turned away from the faith of Abraham, who no longer recognize the heavenly Father, who have rejected Christ because of it, and who will receive one who comes in his own name.

John 5:44-46

> How can ye believe, which receive honour one of another, and seek not the honour that cometh from God only? Do not think that I will accuse you to the Father: there is one that accuseth you, even Moses in whom ye trust. For had ye believed Moses, ye would have believed me: for he wrote of me.

Moses' Accusation

Jesus is saying, I do not need to accuse you, but Moses, whom you believed in and whom you look on as a friend, he will accuse you when you come to the judgment, because Moses knew that Jesus would be Lord.

John 5:47-6:9

> But if ye believe not his writings, how shall ye believe my words?
>
> After these things Jesus went over the sea of Galilee, which is the sea of Tiberias. And a great multitude followed him, because they saw his miracles which he did on them that were diseased. And Jesus went up into a mountain, and there he sat with his disciples. And the passover, a feast of the Jews, was nigh. When Jesus then lifted up his eyes, and saw a great company come unto him, he saith unto Philip, Whence shall we buy bread, that these may eat? And this he said to prove him: for he himself knew what he would do. Philip answered him, Two hundred pennyworth of bread is not sufficient for them, that every one of them may take a little. One of his disciples, Andrew,

Simon Peter's brother, saith unto him, There is a lad here, which hath five barley loaves, and two small fishes: but what are they among so many?

The Great Salesman

Here is old silent Andrew again, who made two of the greatest sales in history: he sold his brother on Christ, and now he is about to make the sale of sales because to talk a little boy out of his lunch takes something. But Andrew sold him. And the little boy's imagination soared. He had been listening to Jesus, and he believed that Jesus could do anything. He said, Sure, Andrew, take these to Jesus. Tell Him to do His stuff. Can't you just hear a little boy say that? Tell Him to do His stuff.

John 6:10-12

And Jesus said, Make the men sit down. Now there was much grass in the place. So the men sat down, in number about five thousand. And Jesus took the loaves; and when he had given thanks he distributed to the disciples, and the disciples to them that were set down; and likewise of the fishes as much as they would. When they were filled, he said unto his disciples, Gather up the fragments that remain, that nothing be lost.

Jesus Makes Leftovers

There is no waste with Jesus. He changes the "not enough" to an "over supply." He is a glorious God who supplies all our needs. There were 12 baskets left over, and Jesus said, Do not waste a thing.

John 6:13

Therefore they gathered them together, and filled twelve baskets with the fragments of the five barley loaves, which remained over and above unto them that had eaten.

Jesus fed them over and above. These are the words that really characterize Christ as He truly is — over and above. Those 12 baskets may just have been a basket for each of the 12 apostles who first believed it could not be done. We remember Andrew because of the seed he planted, and the little boy because of the seed he planted.

Above all, we remember the harvest, the multiplication of what they gave.

You know, some people think when they give to God, they'll have less than what they gave, they will be diminished. That is not what the scriptures teach. He multiplies what we put in His hands. Remember above all things that God is greater, and I thank Him because you and I can will to obey, we can will to believe Him. Just start expecting God to do what He says so you can receive from the open windows of heaven and can receive His power to rebuke the devourer in your life for your sake.

John 6:14,15

> Then those men, when they had seen the miracle that Jesus did, said, This is of a truth that prophet that should come into the world. When Jesus therefore perceived that they would come and take him by force, to make him a king, he departed again into a mountain himself alone.

Pray for Humility

When Jesus saw that their main concept of the Messiah was to make Him king so He would restore their political glory, He left them and went off to himself in a mountain to pray. The thing to fear is the praise of men more than the opposition of men. If you are not careful when you have victory, you will make more mistakes than when it is tough and you are down on your knees seeking God. The more people praise us, the more we ought to get off alone and meditate before God and see to it that our hearts remain humble before Him.

John 6:16-33

> And when even was now come, his disciples went down unto the sea, and entered into a ship, and went over the sea toward Capernaum. And it was now dark, and Jesus was not come to them. And the sea arose by reason of a great wind that blew. So when they had rowed about five and twenty or thirty furlongs, they see Jesus walking on the sea, and drawing nigh unto the ship: and they were afraid. But he saith unto them, It is I; be not afraid. Then they willingly received him into the ship: and immediately the ship was at the land whither they went.
>
> The day following, when the people which stood on the other side of the sea saw that there was none other boat there, save that one whereinto his disciples were entered, and that Jesus went not with

his disciples into the boat, but that his disciples were gone away alone;(Howbeit there came other boats from Tiberias nigh unto the place where they did eat bread, after that the Lord had given thanks:) When the people therefore saw that Jesus was not there, neither his disciples, they also took shipping, and came to Capernaum, seeking for Jesus. And when they had found him on the other side of the sea, they said unto him, Rabbi, when camest thou hither?

Jesus answered them and said, Verily, verily, I say unto you, Ye seek me, not because ye saw the miracles, but because ye did eat of the loaves, and were filled.

Labour not for the meat which perisheth, but for that meat which endureth unto everlasting life, which the Son of man shall give unto you: for him hath God the Father sealed. Then said they unto him, What shall we do, that we might work the works of God?

Jesus answered and said unto them, This is the work of God, that ye believe on him whom he hath sent. They said therefore unto him, What sign shewest thou then, that we may see, and believe thee? what dost thou work? Our fathers did eat manna in the desert; as it is written, He gave them bread from heaven to eat.

Then Jesus said unto them, Verily, verily, I say unto you, Moses gave you not that bread from heaven; but my Father giveth you the true bread from heaven. For the bread of God is he which cometh down from heaven, and giveth life unto the world.

His Person Featured

From this point on in John's gospel, Jesus is going to build everything of God around a person. Very carefully He's going to lead them, and us, away from the outward observances of things from religiosity to inner salvation based upon a person — Jesus Christ.

John 6:34,35

Then said they unto him, Lord, evermore give us this bread. And Jesus said unto them, I am the bread of life: he that cometh to me shall never hunger; and he that believeth on me shall never thirst.

He is talking about the inner hungers and thirsts, the eternal things of God.

John 6:36,37

But I said unto you, That ye also have seen me, and believe not. All that the Father giveth me shall come to me; and him that cometh to me I will in no wise cast out.

Understand it. When you come to Him, He won't cast you away.

John 6:38-40

For I came down from heaven, not to do mine own will, but the will of him that sent me. And this is the Father's will which hath sent me, that of all which he hath given me I should lose nothing, but should raise it up again at the last day. And this is the will of him that sent me, that every one which seeth the Son, and believeth on him, may have everlasting life: and I will raise him up at the last day.

Road to Resurrection

He is talking about the resurrection, the cornerstone of our faith. As we read through John and into the book of Acts, the resurrection is going to meet us at every bend of the road. Get ready for the resurrection.

John 6:41-51

The Jews then murmured at him, because he said, I am the bread which came down from heaven. And they said, Is not this Jesus, the son of Joseph, whose father and mother we know? how is it then that he saith, I came down from heaven? Jesus therefore answered and said unto them, Murmur not among yourselves. No man can come to me, except the Father which hath sent me draw him: and I will raise him up at the last day. It is written in the prophets, and they shall be all taught of God. Every man therefore that hath heard, and hath learned of the Father, cometh unto me. Not that any man hath seen the Father, save he which is of God, he hath seen the Father.

Verily, verily, I say unto you, He that believeth on me hath everlasting life. I am that bread of life. Your fathers did eat manna in the wilderness, and are dead. This is the bread which cometh down from heaven: that a man may eat thereof, and not die. I am the living bread which came down from heaven, if any man eat of this bread, he shall live for ever: and the bread that I will give is my flesh, which I will give for the life of the world.

Jesus was reaching out to the Jewish people here on the promise of immortality, life after death, the resurrection. Part of them were Sadducees, that religious division which did not believe in the resurrection or angels or miracles. The Pharisees said they believed but did not. Jesus kept reminding them of the continuity of God, I am the God of Abraham, the God of Isaac, the God of Jacob.

Do you see what He was doing? He was God in continuity, God forever, life goes on. There is life after death. There is a resurrection. We will live after death. We do not just die and fade away into dust. Our bodies lie sleeping in the dust, but our souls remain conscious and await the resurrection when that soul reenters the dead body and the person is restored to life. If that person is a believer, he is restored to life eternal, but if he is not a believer, if he has cut himself off from God, and removed himself from the agent of salvation, he has afterlife, but it is a life of death and damnation and that is the way it is.

John 6:52-58

> The Jews therefore strove among themselves, saying, How can this man give us his flesh to eat? Then Jesus said unto them, Verily, verily, I say unto you, Except ye eat the flesh of the Son of man, and drink his blood, ye have no life in you. Whoso eateth my flesh, and drinketh my blood, hath eternal life; and I will raise him up at the last day. For my flesh is meat indeed, and my blood is drink indeed. He that eateth my flesh, and drinketh my blood, dwelleth in me, and I in him. As the living Father hath sent me, and I live by the Father: so he that eateth me, even he shall live by me. This is that bread which came down from heaven: not as your fathers did eat manna, and are dead: he that eateth of this bread shall live for ever.

Holy Communion Established

He is here establishing the Holy Communion, the bread and the cup symbolizing His death and resurrection.

John 6:59-7:5

> These things said he in the synagogue, as he taught in Capernaum. Many therefore of his disciples, when they had heard this, said, This is an hard saying; who can hear it? When Jesus knew in himself that his disciples murmured at it, he said unto them, Doth this offend you? What and if ye shall see the Son of man ascend up where he was before? It is the spirit that quickeneth; the flesh profiteth nothing: the words that I speak unto you, they are spirit, and they are life. But there are some of you that believe not.
>
> For Jesus knew from the beginning who they were that believed not, and who should betray him. And he said, Therefore said I unto

you, that no man can come unto me, except it were given unto him of my Father. From that time many of his disciples went back, and walked no more with him.

Then said Jesus unto the twelve, Will ye also go away? Then Simon Peter answered him, Lord, to whom shall we go? thou hast the words of eternal life. And we believe and are sure that thou art that Christ, the Son of the living God. Jesus answered them, Have not I chosen you twelve, and one of you is a devil? He spake of Judas Iscariot the son of Simon: for he it was that should betray him, being one of the twelve.

After these things Jesus walked in Galilee: for he would not walk in Jewry, because the Jews sought to kill him. Now the Jews' feast of tabernacles was at hand. His brethren therefore said unto him, Depart hence, and go into Judaea, that thy disciples also may see the works that thou doest. For there is no man that doeth any thing in secret, and he himself seeketh to be know openly. If thou do these things, shew thyself to the world. For neither did his brethren believe in him.

Let us go back over that and realize that these are Jesus' own brothers. They are saying to Him, in effect, Look, everything You have been doing down here miraculously, go up in Judaea and do it. Your disciples up there would like to see and know these things. Certainly You are not going to do them in secret, are you? Are You not going to proclaim yourself openly to the whole world? They said that skeptically, for neither did His brethren believe in Him.

John 7:6

Then Jesus said unto them, My time is not yet come: but your time is alway ready.

Jesus knew the plan and time of His life. His brothers did not. Their time to believe had already come. But they had not yet gone beyond their skepticism.

John 7:7,8

The world cannot hate you; but me it hateth, because I testify of it, that the works thereof are evil. Go ye up unto this feast: I go not up yet unto this feast: for my time is not yet full come.

God's Timetable

God has a timetable. He works by a plan. I personally know this to be true. How many times I have struggled with God's timetable, wanting to do it too early or standing by and waiting for it to happen of itself. More and more I have had to discover that God is operating on His timetable, and for me to do my work profitably for Him, I must get on His timetable — operate by His plan. And Jesus tells us we can know His plan. Thank God we can.

John 7:9-12

> When he had said these words unto them, he abode still in Galilee. But when his brethren were gone up, then went he also up unto the feast, not openly, but as it were in secret. Then the Jews sought him at the feast, and said, Where is he? And there was much murmuring among the people concerning him: for some said, He is a good man: others said, Nay: but he deceiveth the people.

Balance Essential

When somebody comes anointed of God and speaks in a decisive manner, proving the work by the miracles of God through his or her ministry, it divides people. They either overly praise them or overly blame them. We have to strike a balance. We need to hear some criticism, but we also need to have God's approval upon our lives and some good words from those who believe in us.

John 7:13-16

> Howbeit no man spake openly of him for fear of the Jews. Now about the midst of the feast Jesus went up into the temple, and taught. And the Jews marvelled, saying, How knoweth this man letters, having never learned? Jesus answered them, and said, My doctrine is not mine, but his that sent me.

Divine Knowledge

He is telling them there is something beyond book learning, something other than that which comes out of the mind of man. There is a divine knowledge, and God is a great teacher. Jesus, of course, had been reared in the synagogue schools. Jesus knew His letters. He knew the letters of this world, but He also knew those of God. And He knew that God had sent Him.

John 7:17

> If any man will do his will, he shall know of the doctrine, whether it

be of God, or whether I speak of myself.

Beyond Academics

They were trying to judge Him purely upon an academic level, while He was trying to enlarge their minds to go beyond the academic level and understand that there is a heavenly kingdom and a God of continuity through the ages who keeps His word and fulfills His promises. Jesus was the fulfillment of all prophesies concerning the Messiah.

John 7:18-24

He that speaketh of himself seeketh his own glory: but he that seeketh his glory that sent him, the same is true, and no unrighteousness is in him. Did not Moses give you the law, and yet none of you keepeth the law? Why go ye about to kill me? The people answered and said, Thou hast a devil: who goeth about to kill thee?

Jesus answered and said unto them, I have done one work, and ye all marvel. Moses therefore gave unto you circumcision; (not because it is of Moses, but of the fathers;) and ye on the sabbath day circumcise a man. If a man on the sabbath day receive circumcision, that the law of Moses should not be broken; are ye angry at me, because I

John 7:28-30

Then cried Jesus in the temple as he taught, saying, Ye both know me, and ye know whence I am: and I am not come of myself, but he that sent me is true, whom ye know not. But I know him: for I am from him, and he hath sent me. Then they sought to take him: but no man laid hands on him, because his hour was not yet come.

No Hurrying God

Notice that little phrase, "because his hour was not yet come." Nobody is going to rush God, nobody is going to hold God back. God sets His own pace, His own time. He is going to do it just as He said.

John 7:31-36

And many of the people believed on him, and said, When Christ cometh, will he do more miracles than these which this man hath done? The Pharisees heard that the people murmured such things concerning him; and the Pharisees and the chief priests sent officers to take him.

Then said Jesus unto them, Yet a little while am I with you, and then I go unto him that sent me. Ye shall seek me, and shall not find me: and where I am, thither ye cannot come. Then said the Jews among themselves, Whither will he go, that we shall not find him? will he go unto the dispersed among the Gentiles, and teach the Gentiles? What manner of saying is this that he said, Ye shall seek me, and shall not find me: and where I am, thither ye cannot come?

A Favorite Passage

I have now come to John 7:37-39, one of my favorite scriptures in the entire Bible and one of the most powerful ones as far as your life and the life of the body of Christ is concerned.

John 7:37-39

In the last day, that great day of the feast, Jesus stood and cried, saying, If any man thirst, let him come unto me, and drink. He that believeth on me, as the scripture hath said, out of his belly shall flow rivers of living water. (But this spake he of the spirit, which they that believe on him should receive: for the Holy Ghost was not yet given; because that Jesus was not yet glorified.)

The Joy of Belief

If your need is so great that you actually have a craving in you to be in complete union with the Lord and to have the fullness of the Holy Spirit in your life, Come unto me, Jesus said, and drink. For he that believes on Me — notice that — he that believes on Me. First, there is the thirst, or the need, and the recognition of the need, and second, it has to be made to happen. He that believeth on me . . . Believing is an act; you do something to believe, to release faith, to put it in God. He that believeth on Me — upon Me a person, not upon a thing, not upon a set of doctrines or rules and regulations, but upon a person. He is saying, out of our bellies will be a constant fullness of the Spirit that is always full and flowing. Out of our belly area — not the stomach cavity, but the belly, the solar plexus area where you feel joy or you feel fear, where you have the seat of your emotions there in your innermost being.

He is saying something glorious is going to happen and keep on happening. The Holy Spirit in this form could not be given while

Jesus was on the earth. That did not mean the Spirit did not come upon people or move people, but it did mean there was coming a new infilling of the Holy Spirit and it would come through our desire and through our believing on Jesus.

John 7:40-43

Many of the people therefore, when they heard this saying, said, Of a truth this is the Prophet. Others said, This is the Christ. But some said, Shall Christ come out of Galilee? Hath not the scripture said, That Christ cometh of the seed of David, and out of the town of Bethlehem where David was? So there was a division among the people because of him.

These people were so ignorant of where Jesus had been born, they did not know that He was of the seed of David and had been born in David's hometown of Bethlehem. They had not investigated. One of the most needful things for people today is to investigate what the Bible is teaching. We have got to know and God tells us we can know.

John 7:44-46

And some of them would have taken him; but no man laid hands on him. Then came the officers to the chief priests and Pharisees; and they said unto them, Why have ye not brought him? The officers answered, Never man spake like this man.

A Strong Appeal

In other words, those who were sent to arrest Him got caught up in what He was saying. Jesus is hard to resist.

John 7:47-8:8

Then answered them the Pharisees, Are ye also deceived? Have any of the rulers or of the Pharisees believed on him? But this people who knoweth not the law are cursed. Nicodemus saith unto them, (he that came to Jesus by night, being one of them,) Doth our law judge any man, before it hear him, and know what he doeth? They answered and said unto him, Art thou also of Galilee? Search, and look: for out of Galilee ariseth no prophet. And every man went unto his own house.

Jesus went unto the mount of Olives. And early in the morning he came again into the temple, and all the people came unto him; and he sat down, and taught them. And the scribes and Pharisees brought unto him a woman taken in adultery; and when they had set her in the midst, they say unto him, Master, this woman was taken in adultery, in the very act. Now Moses in the law commanded us, that such should be stoned: but what sayest thou? This they said, tempting him, that they might have to accuse him. But Jesus stooped down, and with his finger wrote on the ground, as though he heard them not.

So when they continued asking him, he lifted up himself, and said unto them, He that is without sin among you, let him first cast a stone at her. And again he stooped down, and wrote on the ground.

A Way of Deliverance

The scribes and Pharisees who caught this woman in the act of adultery knew that the Romans had taken away their power to enforce this law of Moses, which said that such a person should be stoned to death. So they brought Jesus in to trap Him and said, Master, here is the story, what do you say about it? They were trying to get Him to enforce the law so the Romans would put Him in jail, but He realized what they were up to. On the other hand, had He said, Let her go, they would have said that Jesus is a false prophet because He would been flying in the face of the law itself.

Now, it is very interesting that in the Greek the term "to write" is "graffin," but the word used here for Jesus' stooping down to write is "katalegein," or "a catalog," wherein He makes a catalog of sins. At least it suggests that when Jesus was writing on the ground, He was saying murder, greed, lust, lying, and other things as a record of the sins of these accusers. We do not know for certain, but the Greek word implies that it was more than just writing; He was making a catalog of the sins of these people.

I certainly know that something happened, because we read they were convicted in their own consciences, and one by one they got up and left Jesus and the woman alone. Jesus wanted to know where her accusers were and she said, Well, no man accuses me any further. He says, Neither do I condemn thee, go and sin no more.

The scene suggests that He never condoned sin, either in the woman or in the accusers of the woman or in anybody who ever lived, but He points out a way by which we can be delivered. This is a reference back to the law of Moses, which permitted accusers to throw the first stones and then the rest of the people could throw stones. Jesus simply stooped down and wrote on the ground, raised himself up, and said, You who are without sin, you cast the first stone at her.

John 8:9

And they which heard it, being convicted by their own conscience, went out one by one, beginning at the eldest, even unto the last: and Jesus was left alone, and the woman standing in the midst.

Double Standard Flawed

Jesus was appealing to their own consciences. How could the woman commit adultery without a man? They realized that, and one by one they walked away. This double standard was attacked by Jesus even then.

John 8:10,11

When Jesus had lifted up himself, and saw none but the woman, he said unto her, Woman, where are those thine accusers? hath no man condemned thee? She said, No man, Lord. And Jesus said unto her, Neither do I condemn thee: go, and sin no more.

A Second Chance

Some say Jesus is approving this woman. Oh, no. He is just giving her another chance. They were trying to tempt Jesus, to trick Him, to get Him to do or say something so they could further condemn Him. But there was one thing they could not do, and that was to scale the wall of the moral nature of Jesus. He would not compromise for man or woman, for religious or nonreligious people, nor would He refuse to give any human being another chance.

John 8:12-17

Then spake Jesus again unto them, saying, I am the light of the world: he that followeth me shall not walk in darkness, but shall have the light of life. The Pharisees therefore said unto him, Thou bearest record of thyself; thy record is not true. Jesus answered and said unto them, Though I bear record of myself, yet my record is true: for I know whence I came, and whither I go; but ye cannot tell whence I come, and whither I go. Ye judge after the flesh; I judge no man. And yet if I judge, my judgment is true: for I am not alone, but I and the Father that sent me. It is also written in your law, that the testimony of two men is true.

Religiosity Shrouds Faith

He is indicating that while He believes in the law of Moses originally as it was, He is not accepting it with all the traditions tacked onto it. The traditions had robbed it of its original purity and purpose. Understand that Jesus was not against the law of Moses. He and the Father and the Holy Spirit gave the law to Moses. But once the Christ had come as the Redeemer, there would be no further use for the law of Moses. They not only had clung to the law of Moses but they had shrouded it with their own personal traditions until you could scarcely see it! It was as though it was in a fog. That is what religiosity does. It adds so much to the Christian faith until a lot of poor old sinners out in the world cannot tell the real from the false.

John 8:18-24

I am one that bear witness of myself, and the Father that sent me beareth witness of me.

Then said they unto him, Where is thy Father?

Jesus answered, Ye neither know me nor my Father: if ye had known me, ye should have known my Father also. These words spake Jesus in the treasury, as he taught in the temple: and no man laid hands on him; for his hour was not yet come.

Then said Jesus again unto them, I go my way, and ye shall seek me, and shall die in your sins: whither I go, ye cannot come. Then said the Jews, Will he kill himself? because he saith, Whither I go, ye cannot come.

And he said unto them, Ye are from beneath; I am from above: ye are of this world; I am not of this world. I said therefore unto you, that ye shall die in your sins: for if ye believe not that I am he, ye shall die in your sins.

Hell Is Real

He is saying that the blood of bulls and goats of the sacrifices in the temple will no longer suffice. Now they are rejecting the true Messiah, the Lamb of God slain from the foundation of the world. They are removing from their faith the only one who can forgive their sins. By removing the agent of salvation, they are going to die in their sins.

More and more we hear people trying to eliminate hell, trying to say, God is not going to hold us accountable for our sins. Do not fool yourself. Just because people are changing their minds about

God, God does not change His mind about himself. People are going to die in their sins when they remove from their belief the only one who died for their sins.

He sent unto us a Messiah, a Redeemer, one to go to the cross and shed His blood for the eternal remission of our sins, to give us a new life so that we might live forever. If we do not believe in that divine sacrifice, we are not going to receive forgiveness of sins, we are going to die in our sins. This is a matter of life and death, of time and eternity. Believe me, this is the Word of God. The heavens and earth will pass away but God's Word will endure forever.

John 8:25-29

> Then said they unto him, Who art thou? And Jesus saith unto them, Even the same that I said unto you from the beginning. I have many things to say and to judge of you: but he that sent me is true; and I speak to the world those things which I have heard of him. They understood not that he spake to them of the Father.
>
> Then said Jesus unto them, When ye have lifted up the Son of man, then shall ye know that I am he, and that I do nothing of myself; but as my Father hath taught me, I speak these things. And he that sent me is with me: the Father hath not left me alone; for I do always those things that please him.

The Purpose of Life

Jesus said that everything He did was to please God. He had no other purpose in life. The purpose of coming into this world is to please God. In pleasing God, God is going to reward us. Jesus knew the rewards of God. He knew the greatest life was in pleasing the Father.

John 8:30-32

> As he spake these words, many believed on him. Then said Jesus to those Jews which believed on him, If ye continue in my word, then are ye my disciples indeed; and ye shall know the truth, and the truth shall make you free.

Christ Wants Students

Many of us believe in an instantaneous new birth. We are born again by the Spirit of God in a moment of time, and so we are. But Jesus says we are to continue in His words, and that is what makes us His disciples, or learners. Believing on the Lord with all your heart until you are instantly saved is the greatest point of beginning in your life. It can turn out in a wrong way unless you continue. Jesus is saying there is something greater. The truth is going to give you freedom as you follow in it. That freedom is not going to burst upon you fully grown at the instant you are born again. You must become a disciple, a learner, a student of Christ.

John 8:33-38

They answered him, We be Abraham's seed, and were never in bondage to any man: how sayest thou, Ye shall be made free? Jesus answered them, Verily, verily, I say unto you, Whosoever committeth sin is the servant of sin. And the servant abideth not in the house forever: but the Son abideth ever. If the Son therefore shall make you free, ye shall be free indeed. I know that ye are Abraham's seed; but ye seek to kill me, because my word hath no place in you. I speak that which I have seen with my Father: and ye do that which ye have seen with your father.

Follow Through in Faith

Jesus is again telling them that biologically descending from Abraham is something that He already knew about, but they were not following in the faith of Abraham. They were of the devil because they had left their faith, and without continuing faith they had no freedom. If they knew the Son, the Son would make them free.

John 8:39,40

They answered and said unto him, Abraham is our father. Jesus saith unto them, If ye were Abraham's children, ye would do the works of Abraham. But now ye seek to kill me, a man that hath told you the truth, which I have heard of God: this did not Abraham.

Abraham's Position

Abraham lined himself up with God and did the works of the Father, but Jesus is telling them, You are not acting like Abraham, you are trying to kill me. Abraham did not try to kill me.

John 8:41-59

Ye do the deeds of your father. Then said they to him, We be not born of fornication; we have one Father, even God.

Jesus said unto them, If God were your Father, ye would love me: for I proceeded forth and came from God; neither came I of myself, but he sent me. Why do ye not understand my speech? Even because ye cannot hear my word. Ye are of your father the devil, and the lusts of your father ye will do. He was a murderer from the beginning, and abode not in the truth, because there is no truth in him. When he speaketh a lie, he speaketh of his own: for he is a liar, and the father of it. And because I tell you the truth, ye believe me not. Which of you convinceth me of sin? And if I say the truth, why do ye not believe me? He that is of God heareth God's words: ye therefore hear them not, because ye are not of God. Then answered the Jews, and said unto him, Say we not well that thou art a Samaritan, and hast a devil? Jesus answered, I have not a devil; but I honour my Father, and ye do dishonour me. And I seek not mine own glory: there is one that seeketh and judgeth. Verily, verily, I say unto you, If a man keep my saying, he shall never see death.

Then said the Jews unto him, Now we know that thou hast a devil. Abraham is dead, and the prophets; and thou sayest, If a man keep my saying, he shall never taste of death. Art thou greater than our father Abraham, which is dead? and the prophets are dead: whom makest thou thyself?

Jesus answered, If I honour myself, my honour is nothing: it is my Father that honoureth me; of whom ye say, that he is your God: yet ye have not known him; but I know him: and if I should say, I know him not, I shall be a liar like unto you: but I know him, and keep his saying. Your father Abraham rejoiced to see my day: and he saw it, and was glad.

Then said the Jews unto him, Thou art not yet fifty years old, and hast thou seen Abraham? Jesus said unto them, Verily, verily, I say unto you, Before Abraham was, I am.

Then took they up stones to cast at him: but Jesus hid himself, and went out of the temple, going through the midst of them, and so passed by.

A Recapitulation

Let us recapitulate the important points of John, Chapter 8. When Jesus stood there in the temple on their great feast day and cried, "If any man thirst, let him come unto Me and drink," He was doing that on this tremendous feast day when the priests would go out to the pool of Siloam and get some water, bring it back into the temple, and put it on the altar, while the people outside were shouting for joy. At that moment, Jesus, while their joy was being shouted out to God, cried, If any man really wants joy, let him come unto Me and drink.

During this feast, the lights in the court of the women were kept lighted throughout all the feast, and when it was over they would snuff the lights out. Jesus took that occasion to say, I am the Light of the world.

When Jesus had this discussion with the Jews concerning Abraham, they were hanging onto the fact that they were biologically, or by blood, descended from Abraham. So therefore, he was their father. Jesus said, No, you are not the sons and daughters of Abraham, because you are trying to kill Me. And Abraham did not do that. Abraham was a man of faith and he saw My day and was glad and rejoiced in it. They said, You are not even 50 years old and Abraham has been dead all these years; also the prophets. Who do you think you are? He said, You may not know who you are but I know who I am and from whence I came. Before Abraham was, I am.

In the undated past, Jesus was the great "I Am." That was His name that He used with Moses — "I Am" hath sent thee. Tell the Israelites in the bondage of Egypt, when they ask who you are and why you came, that "I Am" hath sent you. Soon we will read in the 11th chapter of John where Jesus says, "I am" and really explains that statement "I am."

Jesus Christ was dealing with reality with those people and is with us today. He is talking about the eternity of God, that the God of the past is the God of the future and, therefore, the God of the present, the God of the now. Finally, because He was in such contrast with all their teachings and their practices, many of which were not in line with God, they got so mad that they wanted to kill Him, but they could not do that. He escaped from them — passed out of their midst and went on His way. As He was passing out of the hands of the Jews, He saw a man who had been born blind, and He demonstrated what He had been talking about.

John 9:1-3

> And as Jesus passed by, he saw a man which was blind from his birth. And his disciples asked him, saying, Master, who did sin, this man, or his parents, that he was born blind? Jesus answered, Neither hath this man sinned, nor his parents: but that the works of God should be made manifest in him.

Rabbi Confusion

The rabbis believed to some extent in reincarnation that when someone was afflicted, in some way it was connected with the spirit coming back to the body. And they were all mixed up in the way they looked at people's afflictions. They were always trying to fix blame for it. It has not changed much today.

John 9:4-6

> I must work the works of him that sent me, while it is day: the night cometh, when no man can work. As long as I am in the world, I am the light of the world. When he had thus spoken, he spat on the ground, and made clay of the spittle, and he anointed the eyes of the blind man with the clay . . .

Prayer, Medicine Combined

Jesus' ways are not our ways. Jesus had to get this man's faith into motion, into action, into being released. Jesus does not go by the conventional standards of this world, because He is more concerned about healing people than He is about pleasing the critics.

Here Jesus is taking something from His earth and also taking the supernatural power of God: He is using them both. We should be so open to all of God's healing resources and remember that He is the source of our healing. What a beautiful example this is of combining prayer and medicine.

John 9:7-11

> . . . and said unto him, Go, wash in the pool of Siloam, (which is by interpretation, Sent.) He went his way therefore, and washed, and came seeing. The neighbours therefore, and they which before had seen him that he was blind, said, Is not this he that sat and begged? Some said, This is he: others said, He is like him: but he said, I am he. Therefore said they unto him, How were thine eyes opened? He answered and said, A man that is called Jesus made clay, and anointed mine eyes, and said unto me, Go to the pool of Siloam, and wash: and I went and washed, and I received sight.

Do Your Part

Now, some people that I have prayed for have made a serious mistake in saying, Why doesn't God heal me? I usually say, God has already done what He is going to do. He has put His power in this world. He has sent His Son to the cross and through the resurrection has sent the Holy Spirit. God has already done it. He has finished

His work. It is up to us to connect with that work. The man said, I went and washed. If he had not gone and washed in obedience to Christ, nothing would have happened. Then he said, I received my sight. There is something for you to do. You have to get your inner man standing up and in motion and your faith released; you have got to cooperate with God, either through medical science or through those praying for you or as you read and study the Bible and hear the Word of God. You have to do your part.

John 9:12-23

Then said they unto him, Where is he? He said, I know not. They brought to the Pharisees him that aforetime was blind. And it was the sabbath day when Jesus made the clay, and opened his eyes. Then again the Pharisees also asked him how he had received his sight. He said unto them, He put clay upon mine eyes, and I washed, and do see. Therefore said some of the Pharisees, This man is not of God, because he keepeth not the sabbath day. Others said, How can a man that is a sinner do such miracles? And there was a division among them.

They say unto the blind man again, What sayest thou of him, that he hath opened thine eyes? He said, He is a prophet. But the Jews did not believe concerning him that he had been blind and received his sight, until they called the parents of him that had received his sight. And they asked them, saying, Is this your son, who ye say was born blind? how then doth he now see? His parents answered them and said, We know that this is our son, and that he was born blind: but by what means he now seeth, we know not; or who hath opened his eyes, we know not: He is of age; ask him: he shall speak for himself. These words spake his parents, because they feared the Jews: for the Jews had agreed already, that if any man did confess that he was Christ, he should be put out of the synagogue. Therefore said his parents, He is of age; ask him.

Uncomfortable Christians

One of the great burdens of my heart and visions of my soul is to see all of us in the Church become true Christians, that we confess that He is Christ, that we mean it. There are too many people in the Church who are true Christians who are being made to feel uncomfortable in such a way that many of them feel they are cast out.

John 9:24,25

Then again called they the man that was blind, and said unto him,

Give God the praise: we know that this man is a sinner. He answered and said, Whether he be a sinner or no, I know not: one thing I know, that, whereas I was blind, now I see.

A Way to Witness

You will never find a better way to give your witness. There was no argumentation by this man. When they accused him of being healed by a man who was a sinner, he said, I do not know about that, but there is one thing I do know. I was blind, and now I see. When you really have genuine salvation and people want to argue about it, you can just say, Well, I do not know about all the things you are saying, but there is one thing I know. I was a sinner and now I am a Christian. I was an unbeliever, and now I am a believer. I know that I know that I know I am a child of God. Then shut up, and let the Lord use it.

John 9:26-28

Then said they to him again, What did he to thee? how opened he thine eyes? He answered them, I have told you already, and ye did not hear: wherefore would ye hear it again? will ye also be his disciples? Then they reviled him, and said, Thou art his disciple; but we are Moses' disciples.

Moses Not Enough

Right here is that dividing line again. They were still on the other side — they had not crossed over into faith. Going back to Moses is not enough. We have got to go back to the faith of Abraham which is the faith of God.

John 9:29-38

We know that God spake unto Moses: as for this fellow, we know not from whence he is.

The man answered and said unto them, Why herein is a marvelous thing, that ye know not from whence he is, and yet he hath opened mine eyes. Now we know that God heareth not sinners: but if any man be a worshipper of God, and doeth his will, him he heareth. Since the world began was it not heard that any man opened the eyes of one that was born blind. If this man were not of God, he could do nothing.

They answered and said unto him, Thou wast altogether born in sins, and dost thou teach us? And they cast him out.

Jesus heard that they had cast him out; and when he had found him, he said unto him, Dost thou believe on the Son of God? He answered and said, Who is he, Lord, that I might believe on him? And Jesus said unto him, Thou hast both seen him, and it is he that talketh with thee. And he said, Lord, I believe. And he worshipped him.

Prayer For Witnessing

I want to pray with you that you will really be bold in your witness for Christ, just as this man was upon his healing of blindness. God has done things in your life of which you are very proud and which honor Him. And now, I am going to pray with you.

Father, I pray for each and every one of us to be bold as never before, to lift up the name of Jesus who has delivered us from the powers of this world. May my friends and partners feel a sense of boldness, a crying out within to speak of the goodness of God, to plant their seeds of faith through an active witness for Your name's sake. Father, I stand in agreement with my partners now that we do speak forth the wonderful things God has done for us. Amen and amen.

John 9:39-41

And Jesus said, For judgment I am come into this world, that they which see not might see; and that they which see might be made blind. And some of the Pharisees which were with him heard these words and said unto him, Are we blind also?

Jesus said unto them, If ye were blind, ye should have no sin: but now ye say, We see; therefore your sin remaineth.

Sin Explained

Jesus made a powerful theological explanation of sin here. He is saying, When you do wrong and you do not know it is wrong, it is a mistake, but when you do wrong and you know it is wrong it is sin.

John 10:1-8

Verily, verily, I say unto you, He that entereth not by the door into the sheepfold, but climbeth up some other way, the same is a thief and a robber. But he that entereth in by the door is the shepherd of the sheep. To him the porter openeth; and the sheep hear his voice:

and he calleth his own sheep by name, and leadeth them out. And when he putteth forth his own sheep, he goeth before them, and the sheep follow him: for they know his voice. And a stranger will they not follow, but will flee from him: for they know not the voice of strangers.

This parable spake Jesus unto them: but they understood not what things they were which he spake unto them. Then said Jesus unto them again, Verily, verily, I say unto you, I am the door of the sheep. All that ever came before me are thieves and robbers: but the sheep did not hear them.

Jesus As Shepherd

In those days, there were many sheep and many shepherds. At night, when they brought the sheep into the fold, the shepherd lay down in the door. An intruder had to get past the shepherd before he could get the sheep. Those who tried to get in the door of the sheepfold were those who would kill or steal the sheep. Jesus is telling the Jewish people that He is taking all the sins of the people, the sins of the world, upon himself, that He has voluntarily come to deal with the sheep who cannot protect themselves. He was the door and no one could get through to destroy them because He was there to save them.

John 10:9

I am the door: by me if any man enter in, he shall be saved, and shall go in and out, and find pasture.

A Final Plea

The sheep and the shepherd were so intertwined, 24 hours a day, that it was almost a human situation. The sheep had learned the shepherd's voice, and a stranger's voice they would not recognize, nor would they follow a stranger. Jesus is saying to the Jewish people, If you really were the sons and daughters of Abraham, if you really were the sheep of God's sheepfold, you would know My voice and hear it. You would not follow a stranger as you are doing today. I am the door. If you come in through Me, you will have protection and security. You can come in and go out, knowing that you are cared for and protected by God.

Jesus was within days of His crucifixion and the Jews were within days of having their house left desolate unto them. It would not be long until they were scattered to the ends of the earth. They would be straying and lost sheep, they would have no shepherd; this is one of Jesus' last pleas.

John 10:10,11

> The thief cometh not, but for to steal, and to kill, and to destroy: I am come that they might have life, and that they might have it more abundantly. I am the good shepherd: the good shepherd giveth his life for the sheep.

Abundant Life

Again, He is comparing himself with the shepherd or the door of the sheepfold. Those who came not in at the door were thieves, robbers, killers, destroyers. They did not care for the sheep, they wanted to devour them. But He said, I, the Good Shepherd, am come that you might have life and have it more abundantly.

In 1947, as I was down on my knees reading the four gospels and the book of Acts, and doing it consecutively three times in 30 days, this scripture leaped out at me and has remained with me since. Therefore, I saw on the one side that the devil is behind everything that destroys humanity. On the other side is the Lord Jesus Christ trying to save. This was immensely helpful to me because it was a dividing line. It drew a line right down the middle where on the devil's side was sin, disease, demons, poverty, fear, everything unlike God. And on the other side was the coming of Christ into our lives, bringing only life, healing, salvation, deliverance, and supply for our needs, and doing it abundantly. I heard myself saying, The devil is a bad devil and God is a good God. There is no goodness in the devil and no badness in God. The devil is totally bad and God is totally good. I began to shout it — God is a good God. Millions upon millions have heard me say it. They have read my writings about it. God is a good God. Why don't you say it out loud to yourself? God is a good God. Now say, The devil is a bad devil. That is really going to help you, and you will be able to know all bad is from the devil and all good is from God. That will cure you from thinking or saying God made me sick or God took away my money or God made me poor or God took my friends away from me, or God put this awful thing on me.

Believe me, your faith can operate better when you know that you are supposed to have all good and that Jesus came to give you that good — to give you life, and to give it to you more abundantly, not in scarcity, but in abundance. In other words, God came to take off of you what the devil put on you. To take out of you what the devil put in you, to put back on you what the devil took off, and back in you what the devil took out.

John 10:12-19

But he that is an hireling, and not the shepherd, whose own the sheep are not, seeth the wolf coming, and leaveth the sheep, and fleeth: and the wolf catcheth them, and scattereth the sheep. The hireling fleeth, because he is an hireling, and careth not for the sheep.

I am the good shepherd, and know my sheep, and am known of mine. As the Father knoweth me, even so know I the Father: and I lay down my life for the sheep. And other sheep I have, which are not of this fold: them also I must bring, and they shall hear my voice; and there shall be one fold, and one shepherd. Therefore doth my Father love me, because I lay down my life, that I might take it again. No man taketh it from me, but I lay it down of myself. I have power to lay it down, and I have power to take it again. This commandment have I received of my father.

There was a division therefore again among the Jews for these sayings.

Jesus Loves Us

You see, the people of God at that time were primarily the Jewish people who, for the most part, had been faithful to bring God's way down to that moment. The Gentile world had not heard the Word of God in Jesus' time and, therefore, they had no substance or evidence for their faith to act upon.

Jesus is looking forward to that time when there will be one fold, and we will not think of each other as Jews or Gentiles. We will just think of each other as children of God. Jesus knew who He was and knew He was going to win the victory. Nothing and nobody was going to stop Him forever. It is so terrific to be a Christian, a believer, to know you are on the winning side, to know that Christ is so real and that He's absolutely full of love. He cares for you and me beyond any care we have ever known. He is that way because it is in Him. When He went to the cross, He went there voluntarily. They went through all the motions to get Him there, but he could have stopped at any time. He did it because He loves us.

John 10:20-24

And many of them said, He hath a devil, and is mad; why hear ye him? Others said, These are not the words of him that hath a devil.

Can a devil open the eyes of the blind? And it was at Jerusalem the feast of the dedication, and it was winter. And Jesus walked in the temple in Solomon's porch. Then came the Jews round about him, and said unto him, How long dost thou make us to doubt? If thou be the Christ, tell us plainly.

New Scene, Old Dispute

John's gospel primarily covers the last 5 months of Jesus' life. In this scene, there is a new feast, what the Jews call Hanukkah, or the feast of dedication. It is about two or two and a half months later, and He is back in the temple. And the old argument of the Jews has begun again.

John 10:25-29

Jesus answered them, I told you, and ye believed not: the works that I do in my Father's name, they bear witness of me. But ye believe not, because ye are not of my sheep, as I said unto you. My sheep hear my voice, and I know them, and they follow me: and I give unto them eternal life; and they shall never perish, neither shall any man pluck them out of my hand. My Father, which gave them me, is greater than all; and no man is able to pluck them out of my Father's hand.

Jesus' Total Power

This is the incomparable, all-conquering power of our Savior — our Redeemer, Jesus Christ of Nazareth. The total source, the total power, the absolute security is in Jesus Christ our Lord, for truly greater is He that is in you than he that is in the world.

John 10:30-38

I and my Father are one. Then the Jews took up stones again to stone him. Jesus answered them, Many good works have I shewed you from my Father; for which of those works do ye stone me? The Jews answered him, saying, For a good work we stone thee not; but for blasphemy; and because that thou, being a man, makest thyself God.

Jesus answered them, Is it not written in your law, I said, Ye are gods? If he called them gods, unto whom the word of God came, and the scripture cannot be broken; say ye of him, whom the Father hath sanctified, and sent into the world, Thou blasphemest; because I said, I am the Son of God? If I do not the works of my Father, believe me not. But if I do, though ye believe not me, believe the works: that ye may know, and believe, that the Father is in me, and I in him.

Witness His Works

Jesus is saying, If there is something about Me that turns you off, look at My works, which are the works of the heavenly Father, the works of which Abraham spoke, Moses spoke, the prophets spoke, that all the Word of God spoke — look at those works and believe for the very works' sake. Do not just shut your eyes out of prejudice. Open your eyes to reality and believe.

John 10:39-42

Therefore they sought again to take him: but he escaped out of their hand, and went away again beyond Jordan into the place where John at first baptized; and there he abode. And many resorted unto him, and said, John did no miracle: but all things that John spake of this man were true. And many believed on him there.

Elijah Empowered John

They said that John did no miracle, but John could have because he came in the spirit and power of Elijah, the greatest prophet of Israel, and Elijah did many major miracles.

John 11:1-3

Now a certain man was sick, named Lazarus of Bethany, the town of Mary and her sister Martha. (It was that Mary which anointed the Lord with ointment, and wiped his feet with her hair, whose brother Lazarus was sick.) Therefore his sisters sent unto him, saying, Lord, behold, he whom thou lovest is sick.

Jesus As A Friend

Love and sickness. How they touch our Lord Jesus Christ. There is a closeness between Jesus and this family, this brother and his sisters, Mary and Martha. They opened their home to Him. They openly supported Him. They were His friends and He was their friend. Don't you see that Jesus wants to be our most intimate friend?

John 11:4-35

When Jesus heard that, he said, This sickness is not unto death, but for the glory of God, that the Son of God might be glorified thereby.

Now Jesus loved Martha, and her sister, and Lazarus. When he had heard therefore that he was sick, he abode two days still in the same place where he was. Then after that saith he to his disciples, Let us go into Judaea again. His disciples say unto him, Master, the Jews of late sought to stone thee; and goest thou thither again?

Jesus answered, Are there not twelve hours in the day? If any man walk in the day, he stumbleth not, because he seeth the light of this world. But if a man walk in the night, he stumbleth, because there is no light in him.

These things said he: and after that he saith unto them, Our friend Lazarus sleepeth; but I go, that I may awake him out of sleep. Then said his disciples, Lord, if he sleep, he shall do well. Howbeit Jesus spake of his death: but they thought that he had spoken of taking of rest in sleep. Then said Jesus unto them plainly, Lazarus is dead. And I am glad for your sakes that I was not there, to the intent ye may believe; nevertheless let us go unto him. Then said Thomas, which is called Didymus, unto his fellow disciples, let us also go, that we may die with him. Then when Jesus came, he found that he had lain in the grave four days already.

Now Bethany was nigh unto Jerusalem, about fifteen furlongs off: and many of the Jews came to Martha and Mary, to comfort them concerning their brother. Then Martha, as soon as she heard that Jesus was coming, went and met him: but Mary sat still in the house. Then said Martha unto Jesus, Lord, if thou hadst been here, my brother had not died. But I know, that even now, whatsoever thou wilt ask of God, God will give it thee.

Jesus saith unto her, Thy brother shall rise again.

Martha saith unto him, I know that he shall rise again in the resurrection at the last day.

Jesus said unto her, I am the resurrection, and the life: he that believeth in me, though he were dead, yet shall he live: and whosoever liveth and believeth in me shall never die. Believest thou this? She saith unto him, Yea, Lord: I believe that thou art the Christ, the Son of God, which should come into the world.

And when she had so said, she went her way, and called Mary her sister secretly, saying, The Master is come, and calleth for thee. As soon as she heard that, she arose quickly, and came unto him. Now Jesus was not yet come into the town, but was in that place where Martha met him. The Jews then which were with her in the house, and comforted her, when they saw Mary, that she rose up hastily and went out, followed her, saying, She goeth unto the grave to weep there. Then when Mary was come where Jesus was, and saw him, she fell down at his feet, saying unto him, Lord, if thou hadst been here, my brother had not died. When Jesus therefore saw her weeping, and the Jews also weeping which came with her, he groaned in the spirit, and was troubled, and said, Where have ye laid him? They said unto him, Lord, come and see. Jesus wept.

The Weepings of Jesus

Why did He wait the fourth day? Because there was a superstitious belief among the Jews that for 3 days after death the spirit that had departed the body remained near the place of death, wanting to reenter, and they believed it could actually be done. So He waited the fourth day when all their hope was gone. Martha said to him, Lord had you been here, my brother would not have died. He said, Martha, your brother shall rise again. She said, Yes, I know, at the resurrection, at the last day. He said Martha, I am . . . I am . . . I am the resurrection . . . I am the life. Martha, I never was, I never shall be because I am. I have always been I Am. I was I Am in eternity past. I will be I Am in eternity future. I am, I Am in the now. Jesus is always the resurrection. He is always the life.

Believest thou this, He said? Oh, she said, yes, I believe that you are the Son of God, that you have come into the world. Then Jesus asked for Mary. Martha said, the Master calleth thee, and Mary went to Him. She went through the same process that Martha did, and she began to cry. When Jesus saw and felt the grief, he groaned. He was deeply moved, and then he wept.

There are three times that we are told that Jesus wept. Here, over the death of this friend, over the power that death has, and then we are told that He wept during His lifetime. In the fifth chapter of Hebrews, the seventh verse, we are told that Jesus, in learning obedience to His Father's will, had strong crying, and wept often as He prayed in trying to bring His flesh around to obeying the Father. He wept. He cried. The Hebrew writer speaks of strong crying, strong tears, tears that burst from His eyes.

It is a struggle because we are going upstream. We are fighting against the devil. We are resisting the evil in the world which is trying to engulf us. Death remains as the last enemy and Jesus was weeping over that. He was weeping because they wept. The third time that we are told Jesus wept was just before His crucifixion when He stood on the Mount of Olives and looked down over Jerusalem and with tears rolling down His cheeks He said, Oh, Jerusalem, Jerusalem, how often would I have gathered thee as a hen would gather her little chicks, but ye would not. Your house is left desolate to you.

He saw the coming of the murderous armies of Rome that would destroy Jerusalem some 20 to 30 years after His death. He saw the dispersion of the people of God throughout the world. He saw the Holocaust coming. He saw all of it. He saw what disobedience will do to human beings, and He cried like a child.

In Hebrews we are told that we have a high priest who can be touched by the feelings of our infirmities. If you miss everything else that we are reading in the New Testament, do not miss this, that Jesus sits where you sit. He feels what you feel. He experiences what you do. He has been there. He was made sin, the Bible says, that we might be delivered from it. He was made sickness and bore it that we might be healed of it. He became poor for our sakes that we might be rich, that we might have plenty for our lives. Jesus wept.

John 11:36-40

> Then said the Jews, Behold how he loved him! And some of them said, Could not this man, which opened the eyes of the blind, have caused that even this man should not have died? Jesus therefore again groaning in himself cometh to the grave. It was a cave, and a stone lay upon it. Jesus said, Take ye away the stone. Martha, the sister of him that was dead, saith unto him, Lord, by this time he stinketh; for he hath been dead four days. Jesus saith unto her, Said I not unto thee, that, if thou wouldest believe, thou shouldest see the glory of God?

Origin of Belief

Believing is seeing. What does He mean? God has so constructed us as human beings that our seeing depends upon our believing, upon our faith. You can look at something with your eyes and you will see some part of it, or you can look at a person and you will observe certain features and characteristics, but you do not see the real person. Faith in God sees that which is possible. Faith can see that life overcomes death, that salvation overcomes sin, that victory overcomes defeat. Faith sees. So He says, If you believe, you will see. Somewhere, somehow, believing has to begin in us.

John 11:41-50

> Then they took away the stone from the place where the dead was laid. And Jesus lifted up his eyes, and said, Father, I thank thee that thou hast heard me. And I knew that thou hearest me always: but because of the people which stand by I said it, that they may believe that thou hast sent me.
>
> And when he thus had spoken, he cried with a loud voice, Lazarus,

come forth. And he that was dead came forth, bound hand and foot with graveclothes: and his face was bound about with a napkin. Jesus saith unto them, Loose him, and let him go.

Then many of the Jews which came to Mary, and had seen the things which Jesus did, believed on him. But some of them went their ways to the Pharisees, and told them what things Jesus had done. Then gathered the chief priests and the Pharisees a council, and said, What do we? for this man doeth many miracles. If we let him thus alone, all men will believe on him: and the Romans shall come and take away both our place and nation.

And one of them, named Caiaphas, being the high priest that same year, said unto them, Ye know nothing at all, nor consider that it is expedient for us, that one man should die for the people, and that the whole nation perish not.

Caiaphas' Saying

He was saying, It is to our interest for one man to die, rather than our entire nation.

John 11:51-57

And this spake he not of himself: but being high priest that year, he prophesied that Jesus should die for that nation; and not for that nation only, but that also he should gather together in one the children of God that were scattered abroad. Then from that day forth they took council together for to put him to death. Jesus therefore walked no more openly among the Jews; but went thence unto a country near to the wilderness, into a city called Ephraim, and there continued with his disciples.

And the Jews' passover was nigh at hand: and many went out of the country up to Jerusalem before the passover, to purify themselves. Then sought they for Jesus, and spake among themselves, as they stood in the temple, What think ye, that he will not come to the feast? Now both the chief priests and the Pharisees had given a commandment, that, if any man knew where he were, he should shew it, that they might take him.

"Contract" on Jesus

The excitement is growing, and the tension is rising. Already the chief priest had put the contract out on Jesus' life. Soon they would have everybody combing every place imaginable so they could lay hands on Jesus — the contract is out.

John 12:1

Then Jesus six days before the passover came to Bethany, where Lazarus was which had been dead, whom he raised from the dead.

Resuscitation, Not Resurrection

When He raised Lazarus from the dead it was not resurrection, it was resuscitation. Lazarus would die again and after death, in the final resurrection of the dead in Christ, would be resurrected. This was not a resurrection.

John 12:2-6

There they made him a supper; and Martha served: but Lazarus was one of them that sat at the table with him. Then took Mary a pound of ointment of spikenard, very costly, and anointed the feet of Jesus, and wiped his feet with her hair: and the house was filled with the odour of the ointment.

Then saith one of his disciples, Judas Iscariot, Simon's son, which should betray him, Why was not this ointment sold for three hundred pence, and given to the poor? This he said, not that he cared for the poor; but because he was a thief, and had the bag, and bare what was put therein.

Judas Submits to Weakness

The question arises, Was Judas Iscariot ever saved? I believe that Judas believed on the Lord Jesus Christ, but not necessarily for the same reason that some of the others did. I think his believing was based upon the belief that Jesus would restore the political kingdom to Israel, than it was upon the absolute Messiah. However, I think the weakness with which he came into the world was a weakness to steal, and the devil hit at that point all during Judas' life. Perhaps Judas conducted himself in such an efficient manner that it was natural for him to handle the money.

But John says something very significant about Judas. When Mary, the sister of Martha and of Lazarus, discerned in her spirit that her Savior and Master would soon be killed, and she wanted to anoint His body for the burial, she took the most expensive perfume she possessed and poured it upon the feet of our Lord and then wiped His feet with her hair. Judas Iscariot was upset with this. He said,

Why was not this perfume sold for a lot of money so we could give it to the poor? But John said, Not that Judas cared for the poor (he did not care whether they lived or died), but because he was a thief and had the money therein. He was already developing a thief's spirit. The devil was striking at him at the point of his weakness as he does everybody. Judas did not have to give in to that, even as we do not have to give in at the point of our weakness, because at the point of our weakness we can submit it to the Lord and the Lord will give us strength for our weakness. It is true that there was a man, Jesus said, who would be the son of perdition. However, Judas did not have to be that man. It could have been some other. He is now beginning to choose to be that man. At this point the Lord Jesus speaks directly to Judas.

John 12:7,8

> Then said Jesus, Let her alone: against the day of my burying hath she kept this. For the poor always ye have with you; but me ye have not always.

Appeal to Judas

Jesus was pointing up the magnificent spiritual significance of the deed of Mary, contrasting it with the thieving spirit of Judas who pretended to care for the poor. Our Lord said, You will always have an opportunity to help the poor, and they need help, but to have My presence with you is the most priceless thing of all, so get your priorities straight. Again He was saying to Judas, Judas, let Me help you. Judas, let Me deliver you. Judas, take this word of truth, look at this woman's deed of love and faith, and get in line with it.

John 12:9-11

> Much people of the Jews therefore knew that he was there: and they came not for Jesus' sake only, but that they might see Lazarus also, whom he had raised from the dead. But the chief priests consulted that they might put Lazarus also to death; because that by reason of him many of the Jews went away, and believed on Jesus.

Expect A Miracle

Many people were there at this Passover. It has been estimated at least three million had crowded in and around the city. Many of them were wanting to see Jesus, but not only for His sake. They had heard about Lazarus being raised from the dead.

The miracle of raising Lazarus from the dead had stirred the curiosity of the people just like a miracle today does. As I have traveled over this earth preaching, teaching, and healing in Jesus' name, I have seen one thing stand out — a miracle settles an issue. It gets the attention of the people and it happened with Lazarus being raised, to the point that the chief priests and other leaders wanted to put Lazarus to death again. They did not want a living witness as a walking miracle to stir the hearts of the people. They wanted to perpetuate their own aristocracy and their own arrogant way of ruling rather than receiving God's own Messiah, Jesus Christ. We see this today. There are many people who go in the guise of religion and will believe almost anything except a miracle. Well, that is for them to decide. As for me, and you, I hope, we believe in miracles. We know that God is alive and doing great things today. Let us turn our faith loose and expect a miracle.

John 12:12-13

> On the next day much people that were come to the feast, when they heard that Jesus was coming to Jerusalem, took branches of palm trees, and went forth to meet him, and cried, Hosanna: Blessed is the king of Israel that cometh in the name of the Lord.

"Hosanna! Hosanna!"

The very next day, this great crowd rushed out to meet Jesus, and the moment they saw Him they began to cry, "Hosanna! Hosanna!" which means "Save now, Lord." This is a reference to Psalms 1:18, 25, 26, which they all knew by memory from childhood up. Psalms 113 through 118 were memorized by those children when they went to the synagogue schools. They immediately applied these two verses:

"Save now, I beseech thee, O Lord. O Lord, I beseech thee, send now prosperity. Blessed be he that cometh in the name of the Lord; we have blessed you out of the house of the Lord."

Use Biblical Inspiration

It is a tremendous scene and they are seeing the nowness of God, seeing that their needs can be met now, and that is what God wants for us.

When you read the New Testament, go back to parts you want to read again until you learn it by memory. Then you can apply it to a situation, a need, a problem in your life. You can apply it to a moment of joy when you want to praise God. You can make the Bible come alive in the "nowness" of your life.

John 12:14-21

And Jesus, when he had found a young ass, sat thereon; as it is written, Fear not, daughter of Sion; behold, thy King cometh, sitting on an ass's colt. These things understood not his disciples at the first: but when Jesus was glorified, then remembered they that these things were written of him, and that they had done these things unto him.

The people therefore that was with him when he called Lazarus out of his grave, and raised him from the dead, bare record. For this cause the people also met him, for that they heard that he had done this miracle. The Pharisees therefore said among themselves, Perceive ye how ye prevail nothing? Behold, the world is gone after him. And there were certain Greeks among them that came up to worship at the feast: the same came therefore to Philip, which was of Bethsaida of Galilee, and desired him, saying, Sir, we would see Jesus.

Preview of the Future

The Greeks were representative of the world. It was so appropriate for Jesus to come face to face with this group of people who represented the Gentiles throughout all the world. This was a preview of what was to happen later in our Lord's risen life when the Gentiles would clamber to hear the Word of God and receive Jesus Christ as personal Savior. As they told Jesus about the Greeks wanting to see Him, He began to talk. This is Jesus' last public statement before the cross.

John 12:22-26

Philip cometh and telleth Andrew: and again Andrew and Philip tell Jesus. And Jesus answered them, saying, The hour is come, that the Son of man should be glorified. Verily, verily, I say unto you, Except a corn of wheat fall into the ground and die, it abideth alone: but if it die, it bringeth forth much fruit. He that loveth his life shall lose it; and he that hateth his life in this world shall keep it unto life eternal. If any man serve me, let him follow me; and where I am, there shall also my servant be: if any man serve me, him will my Father honour.

Mystery of Giving

He was speaking of a great mystery surrounding His own death and resurrection. In our seed-faith there is a mystery in our giving. We sow the seed, He grows it, and we reap it. But first, it must die, that is, something in us has to be given. Something must go out of us. The mystery of the Lord's power to transform what we give into a harvest is beyond our ability to understand, but believing it makes it possible and makes it glorious.

John 12:27

Now is my soul troubled; and what shall I say? Father, save me from this hour: but for this cause came I unto this hour.

Our Life's Cause

Every one of us should have a cause for our lives. A reason for our living, a purpose for our existence. Every morning millions of people wake up without a purpose for the day and lie down at night knowing that they have accomplished nothing, and they feel so useless. There is no reason for that. We have a Savior and our Savior's example is always before us. He gives us a cause. A reason for being.

John 12:28-33

Father, glorify thy name. Then came there a voice from heaven, saying, I have both glorified it, and will glorify it again. The people therefore, that stood by, and heard it, said that it thundered: others said, An angel spake to him. Jesus answered and said, This voice came not because of me, but for your sakes. Now is the judgment of this world: now shall the prince of this world be cast out. And I, if I be lifted up from the earth, will draw all men unto me. This he said, signifying what death he should die.

Jesus' Drawing Power

He is saying when they lift Him up on the cross there will be set in motion divine powers that will draw the hearts of men and women, convicting them of sin, drawing them unto God. Every one of us experiences the Lord's drawing of us to a cause higher than ourselves.

John 12:34-36

The people answered him, We have heard out of the law that Christ abideth forever: and how sayest thou, The Son of man must be lifted up? who is this Son of man?

Then Jesus said unto them, Yet a little while is the light with you. Walk while ye have the light, lest darkness come upon you: for he that walketh in darkness knoweth not whither he goeth. While ye have light, believe in the light, that ye may be the children of light.

These things spake Jesus, and departed, and did hide himself from them.

This is the end of Jesus' public ministry.

John 12:37-41

But though he had done so many miracles before them, yet they believed not on him: that the saying of Esaias the prophet might be fulfilled, which he spake, Lord, who hath believed our report? and to whom hath the arm of the Lord been revealed? Therefore they could not believe, because that Esaias said again, He hath blinded their eyes, and hardened their heart; that they should not see with their eyes, nor understand with their heart, and be converted, and I should heal them. These things said Esaias, when he saw his glory, and spake of him.

Satan Blinds

He is referring to Isaiah 53 which is the chapter that describes in intimate detail the sufferings and the death of our Lord Jesus Christ. Isaiah speaks of Him as a man who is despised and rejected of men. God never turns anybody away who has a heart open to Him, but when people close their hearts and their eyes to His reality, the darkness of sin coming from the devil blinds their eyes, hardens their hearts, and makes it impossible for them to understand that Jesus is the Son of God. But, when we open our hearts it is possible.

John 12:42-50

Nevertheless among the chief rulers also many believed on him; but because of the Pharisees they did not confess him, lest they should be put out of the synagogue: for they loved the praise of men more than the praise of God.

Jesus cried and said, He that believeth on me, believeth not on me, but on him that sent me. And he that seeth me seeth him that sent me. I am come a light into the world, that whosoever believeth on me should not abide in darkness. And if any man hear my words, and believe not, I judge him not: for I came not to judge the world, but to save the world. He that rejecteth me, and receiveth not my words, hath one that judgeth him: the word that I have spoken, the same shall judge him in the last day. For I have not spoken of myself; but the Father which sent me, he gave me a commandment, what I should say, and what I should speak. And I know that his commandment is life everlasting: whatsoever I speak therefore, even as the Father said unto me, so I speak.

Life or Death Matter

He is saying that the full authority of the heavenly Father is vested in Him. We cannot take Him lightly. It means life or death in the way we respond or react to Jesus Christ the Son of God.

John 13:1

Now before the feast of the passover, when Jesus knew that his hour was come that he should depart out of this world unto the Father, having loved his own which were in the world, he loved them unto the end.

The Great Contrast

Jesus' love is in stark contrast to the hatred of the devil who is now going to be shown up in Judas.

John 13:2

And supper being ended, the devil having now put into the heart of Judas Iscariot, Simon's son, to betray him . . .

Why Follow Christ

The devil finally found the opening he had been working on in Judas Iscariot. Instead of fighting this thing, Judas in effect encouraged it until he let the devil beat his way through his defenses, and now the devil was able to enter into Judas' heart so that he would betray Christ. The darkness could not enter Judas until he had put the light out in his own soul. Light is always stronger than darkness. Salvation is greater than sin. Life is above death. Eternity is more powerful than time. Only as we willingly extinguish the light of our souls can the devil's darkness enter in.

Understand that here is a great lesson for each of us. Judas' life had every opportunity. He was near Jesus, consulted with him often and had our Lord's trust, our Lord's believing. When he saw that Jesus' desire was not at that time to restore the kingdom to Israel, his faith began to fade. What are your reasons for following Christ? Every one of us should ask that question. If we are following Him because He is the Son of God and the ultimate winner over the devil, that is one thing, but if we are believing on Him for some private purpose, we are merely opening the door a little wider for the devil to hang his own will.

John 13:3-5

> Jesus knowing that the Father had given all things into his hands, and that he was come from God, and went to God; he riseth from supper, and laid aside his garments; and took a towel and girded himself. After that he poureth water into a basin, and began to wash the disciples' feet, and to wipe them with the towel wherewith he was girded.

Usually there was a servant present to wash the feet and to refresh them. But since this was a private meeting and apparently no disciple volunteered, Jesus himself volunteered to be the servant and started to wash His disciples' feet. It was not merely an act of hospitality, it was going to be a lesson in serving God, and through serving God, serving mankind. But Jesus was teaching a deeper lesson here. He was, in a sense, comparing the lives of His disciples and followers with sacrifices unto God. In the Old Testament, when the high priest offered the animal sacrifices, he first washed the legs. Our Lord was washing His disciples' feet to suggest to them that they were to be living sacrifices unto Him. And Peter had not yet quite come to that point where he wanted to give his life as a living sacrifice.

John 13:6-17

> Then cometh he to Simon Peter: and Peter saith unto him, Lord, dost thou wash my feet? Jesus answered and said unto him, What I do thou knowest not now; but thou shalt know hereafter. Peter saith unto him, thou shalt never wash my feet. Jesus answered him, If I wash thee not, thou hast no part with me. Simon Peter saith unto him, Lord, not my feet only, but also my hands and my head. Jesus saith to him, He that is washed needeth not save to wash his feet, but is clean every whit: and ye are clean, but not all.
>
> For he knew who should betray him; therefore said he, Ye are not all clean.

So after he had washed their feet, and had taken his garments, and was set down again, he said unto them, Know ye what I have done to you? Ye call me Master and Lord: and ye say well; for so I am. If I then, your Lord and Master, have washed your feet; ye also ought to wash one another's feet. For I have given you an example, that ye should do as I have done to you.

Verily, verily, I say unto you, The servant is not greater than his lord; neither he that is sent greater than he that sent him. If ye know these things, happy are ye if ye do them.

Foot Washing Incidental

He was speaking of something far larger than merely stooping down and washing the dust from somebody's feet. He was saying that our lives are not to be masters of men but to be servers, to be givers, to be doers. I know people can wash feet in a foot-washing service and yet not have the Spirit of God. It is not the act itself, it is the heart opening up through the spirit of Jesus to give our best. To give God our best and then to expect in return His best.

John 13:18-21

I speak not of you all: I know whom I have chosen: but that the scripture may be fulfilled, He that eateth bread with me hath lifted up his heel against me. Now I tell you before it come, that, when it is come to pass, ye may believe that I am he. Verily, verily, I say unto you, He that receiveth whomsoever I send receiveth me; and he that receiveth me receiveth him that sent me.

When Jesus had thus said, he was troubled in spirit, and testified, and said, Verily, verily, I say unto you, that one of you shall betray me.

Working in Sorrow

Judas and his betrayal had been on Jesus' mind. He had carried that all during the foot-washing service and His final teaching of His disciples. It shows that no matter what sorrowful thing we know, we can continue doing the work of God.

John 13:22-27

Then the disciples looked one on another, doubting of whom he spake. Now there was leaning on Jesus' bosom one of his disciples, whom Jesus loved. Simon Peter therefore beckoned to him, that he should ask who it should be of whom he spake. He then lying on Jesus' breast saith unto him, Lord, who is it? Jesus answered, He it is, to whom I shall give a sop, when I have dipped it. And when he had dipped the sop, he gave it to Judas Iscariot, the son of Simon. And after the sop Satan entered into him. Then said Jesus unto him, That thou doest, do quickly.

Detached from God

The devil and Judas have entered into their final agreement, and Jesus at that point detaches Judas from their midst. He has held onto him until the very last, unwilling that he should perish, loving him, even washing his feet. But there is a point when a person who knows Jesus and rejects Him has removed the agent of salvation from his life and therefore he is detached from God forevermore.

John 13:28-35

Now no man at the table knew for what intent he spake this unto him. For some of them thought, because Judas had the bag, that Jesus had said unto him, Buy those things that we have need of against the feast; or, that he should give something to the poor. He then having received the sop went immediately out: and it was night. Therefore, when he was gone out, Jesus said, Now is the Son of man glorified, and God is glorified in him. If God be glorified in him, God shall also glorify him in himself, and shall straightway glorify him.

Little children, yet a little while I am with you. Ye shall seek me: and as I said unto the Jews, Whither I go, ye cannot come; so now I say to you. A new commandment I give unto you, That ye love one another; as I have loved you, that ye also love one another. By this shall all men know that ye are my disciples, if ye have love one to another.

Love is so strong. It is the identifying sign that if we love one another, then people will know that we are Christ's disciples because His nature is love and there really is no other single identifying sign so powerful as that of love.

John 13:36-14:1

Simon Peter said unto him, Lord, whither goest thou? Jesus answered him, Whither I go, thou canst not follow me now; but thou shalt follow me afterwards. Peter said unto him, Lord, why cannot I follow thee now? I will lay down my life for thy sake.

Jesus answered him, Wilt thou lay down thy life for my sake? Verily, verily, I say unto thee, The cock shall not crow, till thou hast denied me thrice.

Let not your heart be troubled: ye believe in God, believe also in me.

Full Belief Asked

Trouble was on every hand and death was near. The props were about to be knocked out from under them. So He was saying, Let not your heart be troubled, ye believe in God, believe also in Me. He is reminding them that in this time of trouble they still have their belief in God, and to go on and fully believe in Him.

John 14:2,3

In my Father's house are many mansions: if it were not so, I would have told you. I go to prepare a place for you. And if I go and prepare a place for you, I will come again, and receive you unto myself; that where I am, there ye may be also.

Heaven: With Jesus

He said this in the outer court of the temple. There were many magnificent places in the temple, but mansions here could better be understood as places of abode or residence. Next He says, I will come again. Then He states, I will receive you unto myself. Receiving is an act. It takes action. Jesus would exert action to receive them and to receive us when we leave this world. Then He said, that where I am, you may be also. I think this is the best explanation of heaven that there is, that we may be where He is. That is really heaven.

John 14:4-6

And whither I go ye know, and the way ye know. Thomas saith unto him, Lord, we know not whither thou goest; and how can we know the way? Jesus saith unto him, I am the way, the truth, and the life: no man cometh unto the Father, but by me.

The Way

Jesus did not come to talk about the way; He *is* the way. He did not come to talk about truth; He *is* the truth. He did not come to talk about the life; He *is* the life. We must center our faith upon a person, Jesus Christ, because Jesus himself is the way, the truth, and the life.

John 14:7-9

> If ye had known me, ye should have known my Father also: and from henceforth ye know him, and have seen him. Philip saith unto him, Lord, shew us the Father, and it sufficeth us. Jesus saith unto him, Have I been so long time with you, and yet hast thou not known me, Philip? He that hath seen me hath seen the Father; and how sayest thou then, Shew us the Father?

God's Likeness Revealed

Do you want to know what God is like? Of course. Everyone wants to know what God is like. But that has been the problem. It was the problem for me from childhood. I did not know what the heavenly Father was like. I could not see Him with my eyes. My senses could not take Him in. I had no conscious experience of Him with my senses, so how am I going to know what God the Father is like? That is why Jesus came. He came not only to save us through the death on Calvary, but He came to let us see Him through the Bible, to see His deeds, the places He went, the things He said, the miracles He wrought, the life He lived, the death He died, the resurrection He had, His ascension, descent of the Holy Spirit, His living with us in His unlimited presence. Then we see the Father.

You see, because Jesus is good, we see that God is good. So many people do not think God is good. We talk about acts of God, referring to earthquakes, or buildings collapsing and things like that. Those are not acts of God. They are acts of nature which take the full effect of the fallen Adam. That is not God doing that. Jesus did not send earthquakes. Jesus did not make buildings collapse on people. Until we read Matthew, Mark, Luke, John, the book of Acts — particularly those five books — we are not going to see Jesus, and in not seeing Jesus, we will not know what the Father is like.

John 14:10

> Believest thou not that I am in the Father, and the Father in me? the words that I speak unto you I speak not of myself: but the Father that dwelleth in me, he doeth the works.

"Believe Me." Hear those words. Hear Him as He is now within hours of the cross. Believe Me. That is where it all starts. That is the entrance into the kingdom of God.

John 14:11,12

> Believe me that I am in the Father, and the Father in me: or else

> believe me for the very works' sake. Verily, verily, I say unto you, He that believeth on me, the works that I do shall he do also; and greater works than these shall he do; because I go unto my Father.

Jesus Empowers Us

Someone asks, How could we do greater works than Christ did? Because He said we could. I believe Him. Not in quality, certainly not, but in quantity we can. Also, He is saying this because He was still in His human form and He was about to go to His Father to send the Holy Spirit. The Holy Spirit would bring Him back in His unlimited invisible form, and indwell us. He would not be limited to time and space. Therefore, because of the unlimited power of this Christ in us, through the power of the Holy Spirit, we would be able to do greater works in quantity. I believe that.

When Christ spoke to my heart in 1947, saying, Do not be like other men, but be like Christ and heal the people as He did, I could see that Christ said what He meant and meant what He said and that I, that any and all of us as His followers who believe on Him, will do the works that He did and greater works because He went away to send the Holy Spirit to us. I hope you are encouraged by that and that you will take action on it.

John 14:13,14

> And whatsoever ye shall ask in my name, that will I do, that the Father may be glorified in the Son. If ye shall ask any thing in my name, I will do it.

"Power of Attorney"

We are now nearing the place in our Lord's life when for the first time He is giving us His name. He is giving us the power of attorney, only greater.

John 14:15-18

> If ye love me, keep my commandments. And I will pray the Father, and he shall give you another Comforter, that he may abide with you for ever; even the Spirit of truth; whom the world cannot receive, because it seeth him not, neither knoweth him: but ye know him; for he dwelleth with you, and shall be in you. I will not leave you comfortless: I will come to you.

Source of Christian Power

He says if we love Him we will do what He says and because we do what He says He will pray the Father in our behalf. Think of Jesus praying to the Father in your behalf and giving you another comforter, strengthener! He says, You have Me now in My flesh beside you, but I will pray the Father to give you another, one equal with Me in the Godhead, that He may abide with you forever. Then He said, You already know who He is because He dwells with you, but He shall be in you. With you, in you. There is a vast difference. It is different to have food on the table with you and to eat that food so you have it in you. Jesus was saying the Spirit, the Holy Spirit, is with you, but He is going to be in you. This is what makes the difference. This is how we can be Christians who can endure anything, withstand any temptation, overcome any evil, resist the devil any and all times and truly live for the Lord. Because we are indwelt by the unlimited invisible presence of Christ through the power of the Holy Spirit.

John 14:19

Yet a little while, and the world seeth me no more; but ye see me: because I live, ye shall live also.

The Blessed Promise

This is the most blessed promise of everlasting life, of the resurrection from the dead; because I live, ye shall live also.

John 14:20,21

At that day ye shall know that I am in my Father, and ye in me, and I in you. He that hath my commandments, and keepeth them, he it is that loveth me: and he that loveth me shall be loved of my Father, and I will love him, and will manifest myself to him.

Heart of Christianity

This 21st verse is the love feast. It is the heart of Christianity.

John 14:22-26

Judas saith unto him, not Iscariot, Lord, how is it that thou wilt manifest thyself unto us, and not unto the world? Jesus answered and said unto him, If a man love me, he will keep my words: and my Father will love him, and we will come unto him, and make our abode with him.

He that loveth me not keepeth not my sayings: and the word which ye hear is not mine, but the Father's which sent me. These things have I spoken unto you, being yet present with you.

But the Comforter, which is the Holy Ghost, whom the Father will send in my name, he shall teach you all things, and bring all things to your remembrance, whatsoever I have said unto you.

Depend on the Spirit

Number one, the Word of God is the foundation of all that Jesus said. But number two, it is the Holy Spirit who quickeneth the words of the Bible, the words that Jesus said. The Holy Spirit does a great work in our memory. We should depend on the Holy Spirit to remind us, to enable our memory to function better because the Spirit knows the meaning of every word, every statement that Jesus made.

John 14:27-30

Peace I leave with you, my peace I give unto you: not as the world giveth, give I unto you. Let not your heart be troubled, neither let it be afraid. Ye have heard how I said unto you, I go away, and come again unto you. If ye loved me, ye would rejoice, because I said, I go unto the Father: for my Father is greater than I. And now I have told you before it come to pass, that, when it is come to pass, ye might believe. Hereafter I will not talk much with you: for the prince of this world cometh, and hath nothing in me.

Satan Shut Out

As someone said, the devil does not have a nail to hang his hat on in Jesus' life.

John 14:31-15:1

But that the world may know that I love the Father; and as the Father gave me commandment, even so I do. Arise, let us go hence.

I am the true vine, and my Father is the husbandman.

Jesus Is Now

Remember the many times in the gospel that Jesus said, "I am." So often He began statements by saying, I am. That is because He always is. He is always in the now.

John 15:2

> Every branch in me that beareth not fruit he taketh away: and every branch that beareth fruit, he purgeth it, that it may bring forth more fruit.

In every grapevine there are suckers, the growths that suck away the life of the tree and the branch. So Jesus says those who are suckers, those who always take, they will not bear any fruit and they will be purged. But those who bear fruit will bear even more fruit.

John 15:3-5

> Now ye are clean through the word which I have spoken unto you. Abide in me, and I in you. As the branch cannot bear fruit of itself, except it abide in the vine; no more can ye, except ye abide in me. I am the vine, ye are the branches: He that abideth in me, and I in him, the same bringeth forth much fruit: for without me ye can do nothing.

Nothing Without Christ

There is nothing of value outside of Jesus Christ. The worldly can say and do what they want, but everything they do and say will come to naught unless it is tied in with Jesus Christ.

John 15:6-11

> If a man abide not in me, he is cast forth as a branch, and is withered; and men gather them, and cast them into the fire, and they are burned. If ye abide in me, and my words abide in you, ye shall ask what ye will, and it shall be done unto you. Herein is my Father glorified, that ye bear much fruit; so shall ye be my disciples. As the Father hath loved me, so have I loved you; continue ye in my love.
>
> If ye keep my commandments, ye shall abide in my love; even as I have kept my Father's commandments, and abide in his love. These things have I spoken unto you, that my joy might remain in you, and that your joy might be full.

The Joy of Jesus

Jesus Christ did not introduce into the world a religion of sadness, of a long face, but one of joy, joy bubbling up from inside, the joy that Jesus is alive. Jesus is real. Jesus is everything. We are abiding in Him and He is abiding in us; therefore, our joy is to be full, not half full but completely full.

John 15:12-14

> This is my commandment, That ye love one another, as I have loved you. Greater love hath no man than this, that a man lay down his life for his friends. Ye are my friends, if ye do whatsoever I command you.

There is no substitute for obedience.

John 15:15,16

> Henceforth I call you not servants; for the servant knoweth not what his lord doeth: but I have called you friends; for all things that I have heard of my Father I have made known unto you. Ye have not chosen me, but I have chosen you, and ordained you, that ye should go and bring forth fruit, and that your fruit should remain: that whatsoever ye shall ask of the Father in my name, he may give it you.

Power in Jesus' Name

Jesus is beginning now to say it over and over, that what we ask the Father in His name, the Father will give it to us. Jesus' name is our power of attorney. Let us pay special attention that as we ask of the Father in Christ's name, Christ is going to see we shall receive.

John 15:17-22

> These things I command you, that ye love one another. If the world hate you, ye know that it hated me before it hated you. If ye were of the world, the world would love his own: but because ye are not of the world, but I have chosen you out of the world, therefore the world hateth you. Remember the word that I said unto you, The servant is not greater than his lord. If they have persecuted me, they will also persecute you; if they have kept my saying, they will keep yours also. But all these things will they do unto you for my name's sake, because they know not him that sent me. If I had not come and spoken unto them, they had not had sin; but now they have no cloak for their sin.

Jesus' light condemned the darkness. Jesus' truth condemned the lie. Jesus' life came against death. Jesus' knowledge revealed to them their true state and what they could have. Therefore, they could no longer say, I have no sin. They knew from that point on that they were deliberately, maliciously doing what they did against the Lord.

That is how you know that you sin. It is based upon knowledge between good and evil. It is based upon what you know about the Lord's work. Therefore, it is incumbent upon us, the children of God, to spread the gospel so people's sin can be revealed to them and they can know that they must turn to God. What a responsibility upon those of us who are Christians.

John 15:23-25

> He that hateth me hateth my Father also. If I had not done among them the works which none other man did, they had not had sin: but now have they both seen and hated both me and my Father. But this cometh to pass, that the word might be fulfilled that is written in their law, They hated me without a cause.

The God Haters

He was saying they had added so many of their traditions to their law it had lost its original substance. Had they been following the true law of Moses, they would have believed in the "prophet like unto Moses" because they all talked about that prophet. In refusing to receive Jesus Christ as the true Messiah, they hated Him without a cause. But that does not make people hate God, just because they do not have a cause. They hate God because they love darkness rather than light. They love themselves more than they love God.

John 15:26

> But when the Comforter is come, whom I will send unto you from the Father, even the spirit of truth, which proceedeth from the Father, he shall testify of me . . .

Honoring Christ

The full purpose of the Holy Spirit is to testify of our Lord Jesus Christ. His work is built around Jesus. When we talk about the Holy Spirit, we are really giving testimony of Jesus Christ. The work of the Holy Spirit is to honor Christ in the world and in our lives.

John 15:27

> And ye also shall bear witness, because ye have been with me from the beginning.

Witnessing Is a Duty

Just as the Holy Spirit's purpose is to witness of Christ, so it is our purpose to witness of Him also.

John 16:1-3

> These things have I spoken unto you, that ye should not be offended. They shall put you out of the synagogues: yea, the time cometh, that whosoever killeth you will think that he doeth God service. And these things will they do unto you, because they have not known the Father, nor me.

Murder Is Out

Saul of Tarsus was later to do this. He thought he was doing the actual works of God in killing the new Christians. If we know the Father and the Lord Jesus Christ, there is no way we are going to kill anybody, that is, to murder them.

John 16:4-8

> But these things have I told you, that when the time shall come, ye may remember that I told you of them. And these things I said not unto you at the beginning, because I was with you. But now I go my way to him that sent me; and none of you asketh me, Whither goest thou? But because I have said these things unto you, sorrow hath filled your heart.
>
> Nevertheless I tell you the truth; It is expedient for you that I go away: for if I go not away, the comforter will not come unto you; but if I depart, I will send him unto you. And when he is come, he will reprove the world of sin, and of righteousness, and of judgment . . .

Comforter Is a Person

As long as Jesus was on earth He could not send the Comforter. He first had to return to the Father, to His original glory and position with Him, and at that time He would not leave us without the equivalent of His physical presence with us, but He would send us one who would take that place, but also indwell us. Having been with us, He will now be in us forever. Jesus calls the Holy Spirit a person. He says, "He." The Holy Spirit is not an it. The experience of the Holy Spirit is an it but the person himself is He.

John 16:9-12

. . . Of sin, because they believe not on me; of righteousness, because I go to my Father, and ye see me no more; of judgment, because the prince of this world is judged. I have yet many things to say unto you, but ye cannot bear them now.

Trust the Comforter

You see, Judas Iscariot has gone away to set in motion the betrayal. Things are coming to an end. The disciples are full of sorrow because of His imminent departure. Knowing that He is going away, He is trusting the Holy Spirit to do what He himself will no longer be able to do, and we can trust the Holy Spirit.

John 16:13-15

Howbeit when he, the Spirit of truth, is come, he will guide you into all truth: for he shall not speak of himself; but whatsoever he shall hear, that shall he speak: and he will shew you things to come. He shall glorify me: for he shall receive of mine, and shall shew it unto you. All things that the Father hath are mine: therefore said I, that he shall take of mine, and shall shew it unto you.

More of Jesus

We have not yet received all that the Holy Spirit can show us or give us. Jesus is telling us to open up our minds, our understanding, that there is more, more, more for us to receive of Him.

John 16:16-20

A little while, and ye shall not see me: and again, a little while, and ye shall see me, because I go to the Father.

Then said some of his disciples among themselves, What is this that he saith unto us, A little while, and ye shall not see me: and again, a little while, and ye shall see me: and, Because I go to the Father? They said therefore, What is this that he saith, A little while? we cannot tell what he saith.

Now Jesus knew that they were desirous to ask him, and said unto them, Do ye enquire among yourselves of that I said, A little while, and ye shall not see me: and again, a little while, and ye shall see me? Verily, verily, I say unto you, That ye shall weep and lament, but the world shall rejoice: and ye shall be sorrowful, but your sorrow shall be turned into joy.

Resurrection Reference

He is referring here to His death on the cross when the world will exalt and say, We have killed Him, and the disciples will be full of sorrow. Then He refers to His resurrection when their sorrow shall be turned into joy.

John 16:21-24

> A woman when she is in travail hath sorrow, because her hour is come: but as soon as she is delivered of the child, she remembereth no more the anguish, for joy that a man is born into the world.
>
> And ye now therefore have sorrow: but I will see you again, and your heart shall rejoice, and your joy no man taketh from you. And in that day ye shall ask me nothing. Verily, verily, I say unto you, Whatsoever ye shall ask the Father in my name, he will give it you.
>
> Hitherto have ye asked nothing in my name: ask, and ye shall receive, that your joy may be full.

The disciples, in all their preaching, had not gone over Israel in His name. But now, they are released and they can ask. Asking is an action. It is something you have to do. Things have to be made to happen.

John 16:25-32

> These things have I spoken unto you in proverbs: but the time cometh, when I shall no more speak unto you in Proverbs, but I shall shew you plainly of the Father. At that day ye shall ask in my name: and I say not unto you, that I will pray the Father for you: For the Father himself loveth you, because ye have loved me, and have believed that I came out from God. I came forth from the Father, and am come into the world: again, I leave the world, and go to the Father.
>
> His disciples said unto him, Lo, now speakest thou plainly, and speakest no proverb. Now are we sure that thou knowest all things, and needest not that any man should ask thee: by this we believe that thou camest forth from God.
>
> Jesus answered them, Do ye now believe? Behold, the hour cometh, yea, is now come, that ye shall be scattered, every man to his own, and shall leave me alone: and yet I am not alone, because the Father is with me.

Crucifixion Foreseen

He is speaking of His arrest, trial, and crucifixion, when the disciples will be scattered and He will be left alone with His Father.

John 16:33

> These things I have spoken unto you, that in me ye might have peace. In the world ye shall have tribulation: but be of good cheer; I have overcome the world.

We are on the winning side.

John 17:1-4

> These words spake Jesus, and lifted up his eyes to heaven, and said, Father, the hour is come; glorify thy Son, that thy Son also may glorify thee: as thou hast given him power over all flesh, that he should give eternal life to as many as thou hast given him.
>
> And this is life eternal, that they might know thee the only true God, and Jesus Christ, whom thou hast sent. I have glorified thee on the earth: I have finished the work which thou gavest me to do.

Unity of the Body

Jesus has accomplished all He set out to do during His lifetime. Now there remains for Him to plant the seed of His life upon Calvary, being the seed of David. His followers are going to be left in a hostile world. He begins to pray for them so they will be protected and come into the unity of the body, to have the love that He had and to experience the joy that He left them.

John 17:5-11

> And now, O Father, glorify thou me with thine own self with the glory which I had with thee before the world was. I have manifested thy name unto the men which thou gavest me out of the world: thine they were, and thou gavest them me; and they have kept thy word.
>
> Now they have known that all things whatsoever thou hast given me are of thee. For I have given unto them the words which thou gavest me; and they have received them, and have known surely that I came out from thee, and they have believed that thou didst send me.
>
> I pray for them: I pray not for the world, but for them which thou hast given me; for they are thine. And all mine are thine, and thine are mine; and I am glorified in them. And now I am no more in the world, but these are in the world, and I come to thee. Holy Father, keep through thine own name those whom thou hast given me, that they may be one, as we are.

Here is the first specific of Jesus' prayer, that the Father may make them one as He and the Father are one.

John 17:12,13

While I was with them in the world, I kept them in thy name: those that thou gavest me I have kept, and none of them is lost, but the son of perdition; that the scripture might be fulfilled. And now come I to thee; and these things I speak in the world, that they might have my joy fulfilled in themselves.

Joy Is Strength

There was an unearthly joy the Father held before our Savior that enabled Him to face the cross successfully. That joy was absolutely necessary or the human part of Jesus would have fallen apart. Jesus recognizes that His disciples, in taking up their cross and living in this hostile world, are going to have to have a joy greater than the hostilities that they will encounter. He wants them to have His kind of joy in the midst of the kind of world He lived in. That is a particularly encouraging thing for you and me today, that we can have this joy. Again and again we have run across the word joy as we have read the four gospels. The joy of the Lord is our strength.

John 17:14,15

I have given them thy word; and the world hath hated them, because they are not of the world, even as I am not of the world. I pray not that thou shouldest take them out of the world, but that thou shouldest keep them from the evil.

Or from the evil one, speaking of the devil.

John 17:16,17

They are not of the world, even as I am not of the world. Sanctify them through thy truth: thy word is truth.

Disciples Set Apart

Jesus is saying, Take Me and My words and so undergird these disciples that they will be sanctified, that they will be set apart for the service of God.

John 17:18

As thou hast sent me into the world, even so have I also sent them into the world.

Now, go back in your mind and try to recapture the way that Jesus entered the world; how He walked in the world; how He ministered to the world; how He lived, in spite of all sufferings and opposition, in the joy of His Father. He was determined to complete His mission. As we see the way Christ came into the world and lived in it, that is the way we believers are sent into the world, and that is the way we are to live.

John 17:19

And for their sakes I sanctify myself, that they also might be sanctified through the truth.

Calling Sanctified

Jesus had no sin from which to be sanctified. He is speaking here of being sanctified to His calling, not His own life or His own heart which was pure before God.

John 17:20,21

Neither pray I for these alone, but for them also which shall believe on me through their word; that they all may be one; as thou, Father, art in me, and I in thee, that they also may be one in us; that the world may believe that thou hast sent me.

Jesus included you and me and all future believers in His prayer. Why was He praying for us? So that we may have a unity together in Christ, that the world may believe that God has sent His Son into the world. Jesus is saying that His believers, though they may be small in number compared with the great numbers of unbelievers, will have in that small group unity and power — the power of the dynamo, power of dynamite — that it will literally, spiritually affect the rest of the unbelieving world. He has dumped the plans for the conquest of Satan's kingdom upon you and me. He has given to us the power to affect unbelievers, even those within our families.

John 17:22,23

And the glory which thou gavest me I have given them; that they may be one, even as we are one: I in them, and thou in me, that they may

> be made perfect in one; and that the world may know that thou hast sent me, and hast loved them, as thou hast loved me.

Communicating Jesus' Love

One of the greatest examples of what Jesus is saying was portrayed once in my presence when my father, in stoking a fire in the fireplace, took a poker to stir up the fire and left it in there until it got so hot, it turned red and golden like the fire all along its length. Papa said, "You notice, Oral, that the fire is in the poker and the poker is in the fire."

This is what Jesus was talking about — the Father in Me and I in the Father. I in My disciples and My disciples in me. So we have a unity. We have the red-hot unity of the Father's love in us, and we have our love in Him in the same degree of heat and dedication. Love is still the most powerful thing in the world. It is the thing that we are to work on.

Brotherly love is love because he is my brother. Agape love is the love that loves in spite of the worthlessness or the unlikableness of the other person. Jesus wants us to love the people in this world so much. Surely we cannot do that by ourselves, but just as surely, we can do it through Jesus loving through us.

John 17:24

> Father, I will that they also, whom thou hast given me, be with me where I am; that they may behold my glory, which thou hast given me: for thou lovedst me before the foundation of the world.

Beholding His Glory

That is a tremendous thing, that we might behold His glory. Moses was once heard to say, "God, show me Your glory." All believing people through the ages have wanted to see the glory of God.

John 17:25

> O righteous Father, the world hath not known thee: but I have known thee, and these have known that thou hast sent me.

The Great Demarcation

Jesus is telling the Father that He has excluded those who have gone their own way, but He wants those included that have loved Him. This is a great demarcation of the human family.

John 17:26-18:4

And I have declared unto them thy name, and will declare it; that the love wherewith thou hast loved me may be in them, and I in them.

When Jesus had spoken these words, he went forth with his disciples over the brook Cedron, where was a garden, into the which he entered, and his disciples. And Judas also, which betrayed him, knew the place: for Jesus ofttimes resorted thither with his disciples.

Judas then, having received a band of men and officers from the chief priests and Pharisees, cometh thither with lanterns and torches and weapons. Jesus therefore, knowing all things that should come upon him, went forth, and said unto them, Whom seek ye?

Christ's Marvelous Poise

See the poise and the control of Jesus Christ? In the presence of His disciples He has prayed the most deeply felt prayer that has ever been prayed in the history of the world. He had made love the capstone of everything. Judas now joins with his own following. He comes into the garden because he knows that is the place Jesus often went with his disciples. When Judas and his following came up to him, Jesus asked a question: Whom seek ye?

John 18:5,6

They answered him, Jesus of Nazareth. Jesus saith unto them, I am he. And Judas also, which betrayed him, stood with them. As soon then as he had said unto them, I am he, they went backward, and fell to the ground.

Unmatched Power!

The word from the lips of Jesus was so powerful because it represented the Godhead for all ages. It was the embodiment of everything He was. You talk about power that spins the universe, that scooped out the bed for the ocean, that sculpted the mountains, that hung the stars, moon, and sun in their place and even hung the earth on nothing. You talk about power! When He said, I am He, the force of His voice struck them with such a blow that they could not even stand on their feet! They hit the ground! So many people have looked at Jesus and His gentleness until they have tried to make

His followers be people without any power. But no one has had power like Jesus Christ.

John 18:7-12

Then asked he them again, Whom seek ye? And they said, Jesus of Nazareth. Jesus answered, I have told you that I am he: if therefore ye seek me, let these go their way: that the saying might be fulfilled, which he spake, Of them which thou gavest me have I lost none.

Then Simon Peter having a sword drew it, and smote the high priest's servant, and cut off his right ear. The servant's name was Malchus. Then said Jesus unto Peter, Put up thy sword into the sheath: the cup which my Father hath given me, shall I not drink it? Then the band and the captain and officers of the Jews took Jesus, and bound him . . .

Jesus' Peaceful Response

See the nonresistance of Jesus? Peter grabbed his sword, but Jesus did not.

John 18:13

And led him away to Annas first; for he was father in law to Caiaphas, which was the high priest that same year.

Priestly Power

Annas had been high priest, succeeded by his son-in-law, Caiaphas. Although Annas was not high priest at the moment, he still exerted tremendous power, so Christ was led to him first.

John 18:14,15

Now Caiaphas was he, which gave counsel to the Jews, that it was expedient that one man should die for the people. And Simon Peter followed Jesus, and so did another disciple: that disciple was known unto the high priest, and went in with Jesus into the palace of the high priest.

John's Privilege

Tradition says that John may have been related to the high priest through his mother. At any rate, he knew the high priest and was able to get into an area where others were forbidden.

John 18:16

But Peter stood at the door without. Then went out that other disciple, which was known unto the high priest, and spake unto her that kept the door, and brought in Peter.

Peter's Admission

This would have been John saying, This is my friend, Peter, let him in.

John 18:17-23

Then saith the damsel that kept the door unto Peter, Art not thou also one of this man's disciples? He saith, I am not. And the servants and officers stood there, who had made a fire of coals; for it was cold: and they warmed themselves: and Peter stood with them, and warmed himself.

The high priest then asked Jesus of his disciples, and of his doctrine. Jesus answered him, I spake openly to the world; I ever taught in the synagogue, and in the temple, whither the Jews always resort; and in secret have I said nothing. Why askest thou me? ask them which heard me, what I have said unto them: behold, they know what I said.

And when he had thus spoken, one of the officers which stood by struck Jesus with the palm of his hand, saying, Answerest thou the high priest so? Jesus answered him, If I have spoken evil, bear witness of the evil: but if well, why smitest thou me?

Jesus' Early Persecution

In the midst of this trial there was a hammer-like blow on the face of Jesus, and you could hear it clear across the courtyard. There is always that that comes against the people of God. You and I must not forget when we are struck either physically or by words or some other way that Jesus has been there before us.

John 18:24-28

Now Annas had sent him bound unto Caiaphas the high priest. And Simon Peter stood and warmed himself. They said therefore unto him, Art not thou also one of his disciples? He denied it, and said, I am not. One of the servants of the high priest, being his kinsman whose ear Peter cut off, saith, Did not I see thee in the garden with him?

Peter then denied again: and immediately the cock crew.
Then led they Jesus from Caiaphas unto the hall of judgment: and it was early; and they themselves went not into the judgment hall, lest they should be defiled; but that they might eat the passover.

Phony Purity

Jesus has been up all night, taken from one court to the other, slapped and struck and spit on and about everything you can imagine. Now they bring Him into the hall of judgment to Pilate himself. These religious leaders who were so angry with Jesus, and were determined to have Him killed, leaned back on their self-righteousness and would not go into the hall for fear they might defile themselves. I wonder if they had any purity to be defiled.

John 18:29-38

Pilate then went out unto them, and said, What accusation bring ye against this man? They answered and said unto him, If he were not a malefactor, we would not have delivered him up unto thee. Then said Pilate unto them, Take ye him, and judge him according to your law. The Jews therefore said unto him, It is not lawful for us to put any man to death: that the saying of Jesus might be fulfilled, which he spake, signifying what death he should die.

Then Pilate entered into the judgment hall again, and called Jesus, and said unto him, Art thou the King of the Jews?

Jesus answered him, Sayest thou this thing of thyself, or did others tell it thee of me?

Pilate answered, Am I a Jew? Thine own nation and the chief priests have delivered thee unto me: what hast thou done?

Jesus answered, My kingdom is not of this world: if my kingdom were of this world, then would my servants fight, that I should not be delivered to the Jews: but now is my kingdom not from hence.

Pilate therefore said unto him, Art thou a king then? Jesus answered, Thou sayest that I am a king. To this end was I born, and for this cause came I into the world, that I should bear witness unto the truth. Every one that is of the truth heareth my voice.

Pilate saith unto him, What is truth? And when he had said this, he went out again unto the Jews, and saith unto them, I find in him no fault at all.

Pilate Ignores Truth

Pilate came right down to the key issue of his life when he said,

What is truth? He did not recognize it when he saw it, for he did not wait for the answer. He simply went forth and said to the Jews, I do not find any fault in this man.

John 18:39-19:1

> But ye have a custom, that I should release unto you one at the passover: will ye therefore that I release unto you the King of the Jews? Then cried they all again, saying, Not this man, but Barabbas. Now Barabbas was a robber.
>
> Then Pilate therefore took Jesus, and scourged him.

What Pilate was trying to do was to take Him out and scourge Him and mutilate Him so that a crucifixion would not be required. Little did Pilate know that he was fulfilling the scripture in Isaiah 53 where the prophet said, By His stripes ye are healed.

John 19:2-5

> And the soldiers platted a crown of thorns, and put it on his head, and they put on him a purple robe, and said, Hail, King of the Jews! and they smote him with their hands. Pilate therefore went forth again, and saith unto them, Behold, I bring him forth to you, that ye may know that I find no fault in him. Then came Jesus forth, wearing the crown of thorns, and the purple robe. And Pilate saith unto them, Behold the man!

The Only King

I think Pilate was saying two things: First, "Look at what I have done to Him. Does not that satisfy you?" Second, he was saying, unwittingly, "Behold the man of the ages. Behold the only king that the world will ever have."

John 19:6-11

> When the chief priests therefore and officers saw him, they cried out, saying, Crucify him, crucify him. Pilate saith unto them, Take ye him, and crucify him: for I find no fault in him. The Jews answered him, We have a law, and by our law he ought to die, because he made himself the Son of God.
>
> When Pilate therefore heard that saying, he was the more afraid; and went again into the judgment hall, and saith unto Jesus, Whence art thou? But Jesus gave him no answer. Then saith Pilate unto him, Speakest thou not unto me? knowest thou not that I have power to crucify thee, and have power to release thee? Jesus answered, Thou

couldest have no power at all against me, except it were given thee from above: therefore he that delivered me unto thee hath the greater sin.

Pilate's Power Limited

The only thing that Jesus said to Pilate was to state his limitations. Pilate, you say you can do this or that . . . you cannot do anything that God does not permit you to do.

John 19:12-15

And from thenceforth Pilate sought to release him: but the Jews cried out, saying, If thou let this man go, thou art not Caesar's friend: whosoever maketh himself a king speaketh against Caesar. When Pilate therefore heard that saying, he brought Jesus forth, and sat down in the judgment seat in a place that is called the Pavement, but in the Hebrew, Gabbatha.

And it was the preparation of the passover, and about the sixth hour: and he saith unto the Jews, Behold your King! But they cried out, Away with him, away with him, crucify him.

Pilate saith unto them, Shall I crucify your King? The chief priests answered, We have no king but Caesar.

Destruction Chosen

They were choosing their own destruction. They little knew that Caesar would send his conquering armies into Jerusalem and wipe it out, killing at least a million Jews and dispersing the rest around the world.

John 19:16,17

Then delivered he him therefore unto them to be crucified. And they took Jesus, and led him away. And he bearing his cross went forth into a place called the place of a skull, which is called in the Hebrew Golgotha . . .

In the Latin it was Calvary. When we say Golgotha, that is the Hebrew.

John 19:18,19

Where they crucified him, and two other with him, on either side one, and Jesus in the midst. And Pilate wrote a title, and put it on the cross. And the writing was, JESUS OF NAZARETH THE KING OF THE JEWS.

Pilate let the world know who he had on the cross.

John 19:20-22

This title then read many of the Jews: for the place where Jesus was crucified was nigh to the city: and it was written in Hebrew, and Greek, and Latin. Then said the chief priests of the Jews to Pilate, Write not, The king of the Jews; but that he said, I am King of the Jews. Pilate answered, What I have written I have written.

It has endured through the ages.

John 19:23

Then the soldiers, when they had crucified Jesus, took his garments, and made four parts, to every soldier a part; and also his coat: now the coat was without seam, woven from the top throughout.

The Unifying Robe

The seamless robe of Jesus apparently was the symbol of unifying all people unto God. In Leviticus 16, we read that the high priest always wore a seamless robe. While Jesus' robe was not the same color, or made up in the same way, it was also a seamless robe, a very unique and costly garment.

John 19:24

They said therefore among themselves, Let us not rend it, but cast lots for it, whose it shall be: that the scripture might be fulfilled, which saith, They parted my raiment among them, and for my vesture they did cast lots. These things therefore the soldiers did.

The ones who were crucifying the person often got his personal effects and clothes.

John 19:25-27

Now there stood by the cross of Jesus his mother, and his mother's sister, Mary the wife of Cleophas, and Mary Magdalene. When Jesus therefore saw his mother, and the disciple standing by, whom he loved, he saith unto his mother, Woman, behold thy son! then saith he to the disciple, Behold thy mother! and from that hour that disciple took her unto his own home.

Jesus' Reasoning

Jesus' own brothers were not yet believers in Him. It is apparent that that disciple was John.

John 19:28

> After this, Jesus knowing that all things were now accomplished, that the scripture might be fulfilled, saith, I thirst.

Jesus stated this as a fact, not as an appeal. It was His physical being crying out.

John 19:29-34

> Now there was set a vessel full of vinegar: and they filled a sponge with vinegar, and put it upon hyssop, and put it to his mouth. When Jesus therefore had received the vinegar, he said, It is finished, and he bowed his head, and gave up the ghost.
>
> The Jews therefore, because it was the preparation, that the bodies should not remain upon the cross on the sabbath day, (for that sabbath day was an high day,) besought Pilate that their legs might be broken, and that they might be taken away. Then came the soldiers, and brake the legs of the first, and of the other which was crucified with him. But when they came to Jesus, and saw that he was dead already, they brake not his legs: but one of the soldiers with a spear pierced his side, and forthwith came there out blood and water.

Most people who were crucified died through suffocation; the weight of their body caused their lungs to collapse. As long as they could, they lifted themselves up, putting their legs against the front of the cross, so that they could breathe. But when their legs were broken, they could not do that. Jesus did not wait for that to happen. He voluntarily expelled the air from His lungs. He cried out with a great voice, It is finished, then consciously and with the power of His will, gave up His spirit and died.

Because the Jews had a law, and this was one of their high sabbaths, they wanted Pilate to have Jesus' legs broken. However, when they came to the cross, they found that He had already died, and there was no need to break His legs. The bloodthirsty Roman soldier, denied the privilege of breaking His legs, jabbed his sword into Jesus' side, and there poured out blood and water — blood for the sacrifice to forgive and cleanse our sins, and water symbolizing giving us a new life and a new start.

The Jews believed that a person's life consisted of spirit, blood, and water. This scene proves to them that Jesus gave up His entire life, holding nothing back.

John 19:35-38

> And he that saw it bare record, and his record is true: and he knoweth that he saith true, that ye might believe. For these things were done, that the scripture should be fulfilled, A bone of him shall not be broken. And again another scripture saith, They shall look on him whom they pierced.
>
> And after this Joseph of Arimathaea, being a disciple of Jesus, but secretly for fear of the Jews, besought Pilate that he might take away the body of Jesus: and Pilate gave him leave. He came therefore, and took the body of Jesus.

Importance of His Name

It is His name Jesus that is referred to here, not His name Christ. Christ referred more to His divinity, to His divine nature. They took the body — the human body of the man Jesus.

John 19:39

> And there came also Nicodemus, which at the first came to Jesus by night, and brought a mixture of myrrh and aloes, about an hundred pound weight.

Faithful Followers

These two secret disciples, Joseph of Arimathea and Nicodemus, both of whom were members of the Jewish Sanhedrin, the highest court in the land, were very busy in the death of Jesus Christ. Both had a major part: one in preparing for His burial, the other giving up his own newly made tomb that He might be placed in it. It had been to Nicodemus that Jesus said, when he came to Him at night, that God so loved the world that whosoever would believe in Him should not perish but have everlasting life. He also said to him, Except a man be born again he cannot see the kingdom of God.

John 19:40-20:10

> Then took they the body of Jesus, and wound it in linen clothes with the spices, as the manner of the Jews is to bury. Now in the place where he was crucified there was a garden; and in the garden a new sepulchre, wherein was never man yet laid. There laid they Jesus

therefore because of the Jews' preparation day; for the sepulchre was nigh at hand.

The first day of the week cometh Mary Magdalene early, when it was yet dark, unto the sepulchre, and seeth the stone taken away from the sepulchre. Then she runneth, and cometh to Simon Peter, and to the other disciple, whom Jesus loved, and saith unto them, They have taken away the Lord out of the sepulchre, and we know not where they have laid him. Peter therefore went forth, and that other disciple, and came to the sepulchre. So they ran both together: and the other disciple did outrun Peter, and came first to the sepulchre. And he stooping down, and looking in, saw the linen clothes lying; yet went he not in. Then cometh Simon Peter following him, and went into the sepulchre, and seeth the linen clothes lie, and the napkin, that was about his head, not lying with the linen clothes, but wrapped together in a place by itself. Then went in also that other disciple, which came first to the sepulchre, and he saw, and believed. For as yet they knew not the scripture, that he must rise again from the dead. Then the disciples went away again unto their own home.

Disciples' Actions

John outran Peter. But when Peter got there he went right into the tomb and saw all the burial clothes lying just as if Jesus were still in them. He came out and then John went in and saw the same thing, and he believed. It does not say that Peter did. It does say they did not yet understand that He must rise from the dead.

John 20:11-14

But Mary stood without at the sepulchre weeping: and as she wept, she stooped down, and looked into the sepulchre, and seeth two angels in white sitting, the one at the head, and the other at the feet, where the body of Jesus had lain. And they say unto her, Woman, why weepest thou? She saith unto them, Because they have taken away my Lord, and I know not where they have laid him. And when she had thus said, she turned herself back, and saw Jesus standing, and knew not that it was Jesus.

Apparently, Peter and John did not see the angels, but Mary did. Seeing the angels did not overwhelm Mary as commonly happened. She came out of the tomb and she saw Jesus but did not know it was Jesus.

John 20:15,16

Jesus saith unto her, Woman, why weepest thou? whom seekest thou? She, supposing him to be the gardener, saith unto him, Sir, if thou have borne him hence, tell me where thou hast laid him, and I will take him away. Jesus saith unto her, Mary. She turned herself, and saith unto him, Rabboni; which is to say, Master.

Mary's Confusion

Why did Mary not recognize the familiar form of Jesus Christ?

Well, possibly because her mind was on death, not upon life. Although she knew Him very well and would recognize Him anywhere, she found that her mind was not upon His living form; therefore, she could not see Him. The mind can blind the eyes. There is also another possible explanation. She came very early in the morning while it was still quite dark, and the figure might not have been so clearly discernible.

John 20:17

Jesus saith unto her, Touch me not; for I am not yet ascended to my Father: but go to my brethren, and say unto them, I ascend unto my Father, and your Father; and to my God, and your God.

She was trying to identify with Him on the old basis but Jesus was saying, No, I am not on the old basis, I am risen from the dead, I am ascending to My Father. Therefore, in the future, you will be touching Me by your faith.

John 20:18,19

Mary Magdalene came and told the disciples that she had seen the Lord, and that he had spoken these things unto her. Then the same day at evening, being the first day of the week, when the doors were shut where the disciples were assembled for fear of the Jews, came Jesus and stood in the midst, and saith unto them, Peace be unto you.

His Power Demonstrated

Jesus had the power to dematerialize His body. He simply came through the walls. The doors were shut and He appeared.

John 20:20-23

And when he had so said, he shewed unto them his hands and his side. Then were the disciples glad, when they saw the Lord. Then said Jesus to them again, Peace be unto you; as my Father hath sent me, even so send I you.

And when he had said this, he breathed on them, and saith unto them, Receive ye the Holy Ghost: whose soever sins ye remit, they are remitted unto them; and whose soever sins ye retain, they are retained.

Breathing Eternal Life

Nowhere in the New Testament do we see the disciples of the Lord or apostles or anybody forgiving sins. We see that He is speaking of the authority to proclaim there is forgiveness in that name and to proclaim it upon His conditions. Therefore, upon the conditions laid out in the Word of God for forgiveness, that forgiveness will unconditionally be granted. When God created man, creating his body from the dust of the earth, He breathed into him the breath of life and He placed him in a garden — the magnificent Garden of Eden where He walked and talked with him. Here now is Jesus, who has been killed, now risen from the dead, and again breathing the very breath of God, that they receive His Holy Spirit, so this time they would not fall, but live unto eternal life.

John 20:24

But Thomas, one of the twelve, called Didymus, was not with them when Jesus came.

He was the man who missed the meeting.

John 20:25

The other disciples therefore said unto him, We have seen the Lord. But he said unto them, Except I shall see in his hands the print of the nails, and put my finger into the print of the nails, and thrust my hand into his side, I will not believe.

Thomas' Honest Doubt

Here is the honest doubter. Here is the man that did not want another Jesus. Here is the man who wanted the same Jesus, yesterday, today, and forever. Here is a man who did not want to change the Lord in any way. He wanted Him to be the crucified Lord. How different from those who claim themselves as Christians but do not want to accept the fact of our Lord's sacrificial death.

John 20:26-28

And after eight days again his disciples were within, and Thomas with them: then came Jesus, the doors being shut, and stood in the midst, and said, Peace be unto you.

Then saith he to Thomas, Reach hither thy finger, and behold my hands; and reach hither thy hand, and thrust it into my side: and be not faithless, but believing. And Thomas answered and said unto him, My Lord and my God.

Gospel Climax

This is the climax of the whole gospel. John, in writing this, has shown him to have come to the place where the most honest doubter can find the proof.

Let me share with you that God will always give you the proof of an honest heart. Jesus could have said, Touch my head, or touch my back, or touch my feet . . . but that is not what Thomas asked. He wanted those nail-pierced hands, and the spear-riven side, and that is exactly what Jesus gave him.

By your faith you can overcome your honest doubts and you can prove to yourself that Christ is your Lord and Master. When Jesus gave him the proof he asked for, he told him not to be without faith. There is something to do in order to establish the proof in your own mind that Jesus is the Christ. Thomas even went ahead to say it out loud: My Lord and my God. None of this silent stuff, this secret doing, but an open confession before God and man that he is my Lord and my God. It is time we came out in the open and let the glory out.

John 20:29-31

Jesus saith unto him, Thomas, because thou hast seen me, thou hast believed: blessed are they that have not seen, and yet have believed.

And many other signs truly did Jesus in the presence of his disciples, which are not written in this book: but these are written, that ye might believe that Jesus is the Christ, the Son of God; and that believing ye might have life through his name.

This is especially precious and life-giving to you and me. Enough was written for us to believe that Jesus is the Christ and that He is the Son of God, and that believing Him we have life through His name. Do not let anybody talk you out of that. Do not let anybody tell you that Jesus is not the Christ. Or if they say that "there was an historical Christ; He is not the Son of God," do not believe that, and do not stop believing for the life that will come to you through believing in His name.

I feel led to emphasize the words, "but these are written that ye might believe that Jesus is the Christ, the Son of God, and that believing ye might have life through his name." He is talking to you. He is talking to me. All the things that you have been reaping in the New Testament are being said for the purpose that you, right where you are, will believe that Jesus is the Christ, the Son of the living God, and that in your believing — in turning your faith loose to God — you might have the more abundant life through His name.

This is so real. Our Lord is so real. Believe that with every ounce of faith you have in your being, and He will flood your life with His blessings from heaven, His abundance upon this earth, and He will really care for you. Let us pray.

Father, I thank You for the written Word of God. I thank You for the spoken word of God. I thank You that we have faith and we can believe now. I pray for my friends and partners to believe as never before and to take Christ into their heart and to know beyond all knowing that Christ lives in them. Amen and amen.

John 21:1

After these things Jesus shewed himself again to the disciples at the sea of Tiberias; and on this wise shewed he himself.

Change of Scene

The scene changes from Jerusalem to Galilee, the old familiar places.

John 21:2-12

There were together Simon Peter, and Thomas called Didymus, and Nathanael of Cana in Galilee, and the sons of Zebedee, and two other of his disciples.

Simon Peter saith unto them, I go a fishing. They say unto him, We also go with thee. They went forth, and entered into a ship immediately: and that night they caught nothing. But when the morning was now come, Jesus stood on the shore: but the disciples knew not that it was Jesus.

Then Jesus saith unto them, Children, have ye any meat? They answered him, No. And he said unto them, Cast the net on the right side of the ship, and ye shall find. They cast therefore, and now they were not able to draw it for the multitude of fishes.

Therefore that disciple whom Jesus loved saith unto Peter, It is the Lord. Now when Simon Peter heard that it was the Lord, he girt his fisher's coat unto him, (for he was naked,) and did cast himself into the sea. And the other disciples came in a little ship; (for they were not far from land, but as it were two hundred cubits,) dragging the net with fishes. As soon then as they were come to land, they saw a fire of coals there, and fish laid thereon, and bread.

Jesus saith unto them, Bring of the fish which ye have now caught.

Simon Peter went up, and drew the net to land full of great fishes, an hundred and fifty and three: and for all there were so many, yet was not the net broken.

Jesus saith unto them, Come and dine. And none of the disciples durst ask him, Who art thou? knowing that it was the Lord.

What precious memories came to these men. As we were told in Luke 5, when our Lord first came to them in a fishing experience, it was a net-breaking, boat-sinking load. That was a great experience, for He said to them, Follow Me and I will make you fishers of men.

Now they have another experience, after the resurrection, when they have not yet quite clearly understood the full import of the resurrection, in which they go fishing again. And again they have caught nothing. Early the next morning the Lord appeared. They did not recognize Him, but His voice did the job. They obeyed that voice. That voice had the ring of authority, and they caught 153 big fish.

The reference books tell us that there were 153 species of fish known at that time. This number, therefore, is very significant, for it specifically states there were 153 fish caught. Jesus had told the disciples that He would make them fishers of men, and that means us, too. He will make us fishers of men. So He was showing them that of all the known species of fish, this was an indication that He would make them fishers of all types of humanity. Still, as the net was not broken then for this mass catch, the kingdom of God would not be broken apart if we were to win every living human being to Christ. There would still be room.

I want to point out that Jesus demonstrated His concern for food, for prosperity, for meeting our needs. If we lose sight of Jesus entering into the needs of our daily lives with His all-consuming power to consume the forces of evil and to release the glory and the supply of God for us daily and personally, then Jesus Christ is never going to be truly real to us in any "now" period of our lives. The only unit of time that He really recognizes is the now, because that is the only moment that you and I live, moment by moment.

I thank God that He gave me a ministry of deliverance that demonstrates His power to bless us and prosper us spiritually, physically, emotionally, financially, in our families, and in making the kind of success in this world that honors God.

John 21:13-18

> Jesus then cometh, and taketh bread, and giveth them, and fish likewise. This is now the third time that Jesus shewed himself to his disciples, after that he was risen from the dead.
>
> So when they had dined, Jesus saith to Simon Peter, Simon, son of Jonas, lovest thou me more than these? He saith unto him, Yea, Lord; thou knowest that I love thee. He saith unto him, Feed my lambs. He saith to him again the second time, Simon, son of Jonas, lovest thou me? He saith unto him, Yea, Lord; thou knowest that I love thee. He saith unto him, Feed my sheep. He saith unto him the third time, Simon, son of Jonas, lovest thou me? Peter was grieved because he said unto him the third time, Lovest thou me? And he said unto him, Lord, thou knowest all things; thou knowest that I love thee. Jesus saith unto him, Feed my sheep.
>
> Verily, verily, I say unto thee, When thou wast young, thou girdedst thyself, and walkedst whither thou wouldest; but when thou shalt be old, thou shalt stretch forth thy hands, and another shall gird thee, and carry thee whither thou wouldest not.

Denial Cancelled

When Jesus asked Peter three times if he loved Him, He was giving Peter a chance to cancel out his threefold denial. Remember that Peter denied Jesus three times, and now three times Jesus is asking him, Do you love Me? To be able to entrust so much in Peter's hands for the future, He had to be absolutely sure of the undying love of this man, that never again would he deny his Lord.

Jesus also was talking about the kind of death that His disciple Peter would die when he was old. He saw him as he stretched forth his hands and they would nail them to a cross, for Peter would die as his Lord did. Peter's life actually began back there when his brother, Andrew, introduced him to Christ, and Jesus read him like a book and called him a reed like a fishing pole, so unstable was he. But Jesus saw the immense possibilities of His own transforming grace in Peter and said, You follow Me and I will make you, I will make you, I will change you. There have been those many ups and downs of this very human man,but there was also a gradual change. He has not made it yet at this point, but when we read the book of

Acts we are going to see Peter come into a spiritual experience that will forever change his life.

John 21:19-21

> This spake he, signifying by what death he should glorify God. And when he had spoken this, he saith unto him, Follow me. Then Peter, turning about, seeth the disciple whom Jesus loved following; which also leaned on his breast at supper, and said, Lord, which is he that betrayeth thee? Peter seeing him saith to Jesus, Lord, and what shall this man do? Jesus saith unto him, If I will that he tarry till I come, what is that to thee? follow thou me.

Obey Jesus

Jesus was saying, Peter, do not be distracted by something that is none of your business. Keep your mind on what I have called you to do. Follow Me.

John 21:23,24

> Then went this saying abroad among the brethren, that that disciple should not die: yet Jesus said not unto him, He shall not die; but, If I will that he tarry till I come, what is that to thee?
>
> This is the disciple which testifieth of these things, and wrote these things: and we know that his testimony is true.

Enduring Truth

As far as we know, John was between 90 and 100 years of age. It has been 60 or 70 years since this happened. John was now looking back. God's Holy Spirit was stirring his memory, recalling every detail to him, and he is saying, I was there, and now all these years afterward, it is still true.

John 21:25

> And there are also many other things which Jesus did, the which, if they should be written every one, I suppose that even the world itself could not contain the books that should be written. Amen.

Thus ends the book of John. As we prepare for the exciting book of Acts, which is really the Acts of the Holy Spirit, we are going to see transformations by the Holy Spirit that the world, before that time, had never seen. I cannot wait to get to the book of Acts with you.